Engaging and Transforming Global Communication through Cultural Discourse Analysis

The Fairleigh Dickinson University Press Series In Communication Studies

General Editor:
Gary Radford, Department of Communication Studies,
Fairleigh Dickinson University, Madison, New Jersey

The Fairleigh Dickinson University Press Series in Communication Studies publishes scholarly works in communication theory, practice, history, and culture.

On the Web at http://www.fdu.edu/fdupress

Recent Publications in Communication Studies

Michelle Scollo and Trudy Milburn (eds.), *Engaging and Transforming Global Communication through Cultural Discourse Analysis: A Tribute to Donal Carbaugh* (2018)

Isaac E. Catt, *Embodiment in the Semiotic Matrix: Communicology in Peirce, Dewey, Bateson, and Bourdieu* (2017)

Craig T. Maier, *Communicating Catholicism: Rhetoric, Ecclesial Leadership, and the Future of the American Roman Catholic Diocese* (2016)

Paul Matthew St. Pierre, *Cinematography in the Weimar Republic: Lola-Lola, Dirty Singles, and the Men Who Shot Them* (2016)

Anastacia Kurylo and Tatyana Dumov (eds.), *Social Networking: Redefining Communication in the Digital Age* (2016)

Phil Rose, *Radiohead and the Global Movement for Change: "Pragmatism Not Idealism"* (2015)

Brent C. Sleasman, *Creating Albert Camus: Foundations and Explorations in His Philosophy of Communication* (2015)

Michael Warren Tumolo, *Just Remembering, Rhetorics of Genocide Remembrance and Sociopolitical Judgment* (2015)

Phil Rose, *Roger Waters and Pink Floyd* (2015)

Ronald C. Arnett and Pat Arneson (eds.), *Philosophy of Communication Ethics: Alterity and the Other* (2014)

Pat Arneson, *Communicative Engagement and Social Liberation: Justice Will Be Made* (2014)

Erik A. Garrett, *Why Do We Go to the Zoo?: Communication, Animals, and the Cultural-Historical Experience of Zoos* (2013)

Philip Dalton and Eric Kramer, *Coarseness in U.S. Public Communication* (2012)

Catherine Creede, Beth Fisher-Yoshida, and Placida Gallegos (eds.), *The Reflective, Facilitative, and Interpretive Practices of the Coordinated Management of Meaning* (2012)

Jolanta Aritz and Robyn C. Walker, *Discourse Perspectives on Organizational Communication* (2011)

S. Alyssa Groom and J. M. H. Fritz, *Communication Ethics and Crisis: Negotiating Differences in Public and Private Spheres* (2011)

R. C. MacDougall, *Digination: Identity, Organization, and Public Life* (2011)

Deborah Eicher-Catt and Isaac E. Catt (eds.), *Communicology: The New Science of Embodied Discourse* (2010)

Dan Cassino and Yesamin Besen-Cassino, *Consuming Politics: Jon Stewart, Branding, and the Youth Vote in America* (2009)

Engaging and Transforming Global Communication through Cultural Discourse Analysis

A Tribute to Donal Carbaugh

Edited by
Michelle Scollo
Trudy Milburn

FAIRLEIGH DICKINSON UNIVERSITY PRESS
Vancouver • Madison • Teaneck • Wroxton

Published by Fairleigh Dickinson University Press
Copublished by The Rowman & Littlefield Publishing Group, Inc.
4501 Forbes Boulevard, Suite 200, Lanham, Maryland 20706
www.rowman.com

6 Tinworth Street, London SE11 5AL

Fairleigh Dickinson University Press gratefully acknowledges the support received for scholarly publishing from the Friends of FDU Press.

British Library Cataloguing in Publication Information Available

Library of Congress Control Number: 2018951181
ISBN 9781683930389 (cloth : alk. paper)
ISBN 9781683930396 (electronic)

∞ ™ The paper used in this publication meets the minimum requirements of American National Standard for Information Sciences Permanence of Paper for Printed Library Materials, ANSI/NISO Z39.48-1992.

Printed in the United States of America

To Donal Carbaugh

Teacher, Scholar, Mentor, Colleague, Friend

Contents

Preface

Gerry Philipsen

I met Donal Carbaugh at the University of Washington shortly after he arrived there to pursue a doctorate in communication. I got to know him well there and have followed his career ever since. In this I am not unique among contributors to this volume: Chuck Braithwaite (chapter 13) and Tamar Katriel (chapter 4) were also there, working toward their doctorates. They shared many classes, seminars, and other experiences. They, a few others, and I were a small community of scholars within the larger department and university. We worked on the study and practice of the ethnography of communication and on cultural communication: the study of how individuals and societies come to terms with the communicative demands of their culturally distinctive life-worlds.

In those years, the early to mid-1980s, I watched and listened to Donal find, develop, and enact a scholarly program, identity, and modus operandi. The man I saw then is strikingly like the man I see today—not a man stuck in the past but a man with what we now know as enduring dispositions and qualities. I think what I saw and heard then helps me both understand and appreciate the man he has become.

The first of these qualities and dispositions is *a sharp and disciplined focus* on developing the capacity for uncovering a particular type of knowledge, what we might refer to as ethnographic insight or knowledge of a distinctive culture in a distinctive life situation. We can narrow this further by saying that he was, and is, fundamentally and irreducibly interested in knowledge that permits effective communication between and among people who are, in some nontrivial way, different from each other.

When Donal entered the doctoral program he was already an able quantitative researcher, the bearer of a strong undergraduate education, and conversant with the dominant approaches to intercultural communication then regnant in the communication discipline. Soon it became apparent to me, to others, and, I think, to him that he wanted to pursue a deeper understanding of intercultural encounters and intercultural communication than he had previously encountered, and to this end he set a course of study for himself that included (1) active practice of cultural fieldwork and (2) course work in, among other subjects, linguistic anthropology, interpretive anthropology, philosophy of communication, classical rhetoric, contemporary rhetoric (in which he was introduced to the work of Kenneth Burke and through him to the idea of radiants of meaning), sociolinguistics, and the ethnography of communication. This was a rich and broad curriculum.

After a year of this practical and theoretical study, Donal submitted a paper to a national conference, a paper that set forth a rigorous conceptual and philosophical foundation for the study of intercultural communication. In this conceptual work he tried to pull together much of what he had learned from philosophy, rhetoric, ethnography of communication, and a kind of Schneiderian interpretive anthropology, and to make of it a coherent approach to the class of phenomena he sought to encounter, interpret, and explain. When the paper was not accepted for presentation, Donal was discouraged. But he knew that he was laying the groundwork for serious work on the subject. He was in it, it seemed then, for the duration. He knew there were easier paths to take toward short-term success, but he kept his head down and pressed on. He also knew that he was pressing toward a way of working that was not recognized as within the mainstream of contemporaneous scholarship in communication and that much of what he was doing was not (yet) intelligible to many readers and reviewers. As I listened to his concerns, and noted his commitment, I thought not only was he focused and hard-working, but he had a quality that would stand him in good stead in the coming months and years: *grit*.

With such doctoral student colleagues as Chuck Braithwaite and Tamar Katriel, Donal had a priceless intellectual, scholarly, and personal resource—*collegiality and collegial conversation*—that not only supplemented the practical learning of individual fieldwork and the book learning of graduate seminars but constituted a curriculum of its own, albeit one intricately interwoven with the more obvious curricular threads. The three of them, and a few others, read each other's papers, listened to each other in seminars, collaborated in group projects of scholarly inquiry, and provided to each other a running dialogue and critique of their work. Each of them *drew from* each other and each *contributed to* each other. It was through these individual efforts that a real community of scholars was constituted.

The fact that both Tamar and Chuck contributed to the present volume, published thirty-four years after Donal finished the Ph.D. degree, suggests that these three might have, in the early 1980s, established early a practice that they have continued to this day—working with each other as part of a common enterprise to which each contributes something that is his or her own and from which each benefits. It can be noted that Tamar is a coauthor of an empirical chapter in the recent volume edited by Donal on communication in cross-cultural perspective (Carbaugh, editor, 2017) and she served as an international associate editor of the volume. Chuck served as an editorial advisory board member for that same volume. These are but the most recent manifestations of a decades-long pattern of collaboration and friendship that they have enjoyed and that has fueled their individual work. Each of them—Donal, Tamar, and Chuck—has separately authored award-winning scholarly books, and they each celebrate and nurture a common enterprise.

After three years of intense doctoral study, Donal proposed a dissertation that was to be based on ethnographic fieldwork in a television station in Seattle. All the necessary permissions from field site and doctoral committee were in good order, several months of intensive exploratory fieldwork had been completed, and Donal was ready to begin, officially, to do the projected fieldwork for the data collection phase of the study. The day before he was scheduled to begin on this project that had been months in preparation, he learned that the television station had withdrawn permission for him to do the on-site fieldwork. It was inescapable: the dissertation project had to be canceled. The next day Donal and I met over some type of beverage in the Parnassus coffee shop at UW, and after an hour of discussion, Donal had decided on a totally new dissertation project; thus, within twenty-four hours of hearing that his permission for the long-planned study had been withdrawn, he was hard at work on the new topic, the code of communication spoken on the U.S. television show *Donahue. Grit*, again.

Thirteen years after Donal's remarkable recovery from a bitter setback, Lisa Coutu, who had been a student in Donal's undergraduate course on cultural communication at the University of Massachusetts, sat in that same Parnassus coffee shop. Her dissertation site had, eerily, withdrawn permission for her to do her fieldwork, and like her former teacher, she was stuck with no dissertation project that could be implemented. Within twenty-four hours she was hard at work on a new project, the codes of justification and explanation to be found in Robert S. McNamara's book, *In Retrospect*. Perhaps her former teacher's grit had rubbed off on her. Perhaps, thinking about her former teacher, she had a great example in how to rebound from a difficult setback.

While Donal was in the final months of data analysis for, and writing of, his dissertation, he and I sat one day in the middle of a large lecture room in the University of Washington's Kane Hall. Spread throughout the building, and in the immediate lecture hall, were the 240 students in my introduction to communication course, divided into 24 discussion groups of 10 students each. Each of these groups was facilitated by an upper-division student who was taught the art of facilitation by Donal. As we sat there overseeing the activity, Donal turned to me and declared that the analytic and interpretive work he was doing in trying to figure out the communication codes he heard spoken on *Donahue* was very hard, because sometimes he thought he was "getting it right," that is, that he was able to hear in the *Donahue* discourse evidence of subtle cultural expressions, and then, just as he thought he was getting it, all of a sudden he wasn't so sure. I answered, "me too."

It's not hard to find scholars in the halls of academia who seem supremely confident of their methods and capabilities to claim that they have found the true interpretation of a text or a body of material. This might be especially true in the contemporary study of culturally shaped expressions, where it seems so easy to diagnose the presence of some condition in the speaker of an utterance whom one might classify as racist, republican, reluctant, or something else. What I heard in Donal's statement in Kane Hall that day in 1983 is something different, a statement that acknowledges the profound difficulty in hearing, and fairly interpreting, what someone else is saying. For a shorthand phrase, I'll call this *interpretive humility*, one of the many humilities that seem to me to be crucial to the honest practice of research and the making of knowledge claims.

It is tempting to call interpretive humility a virtue, and I am reasonably comfortable in doing so, but I think of it as more like a disposition, a disposition that is necessary for good work in interpretive study and research. Over many years now, I have read and heard Donal make interpretive claims, claims as to what someone is doing, or thinks they are doing, in their communicative activity. He has a long and distinguished record of making such claims, always making them only after a long period of intensive and extensive research into the lives and activities of some people whose communicative actions he has been painstakingly noticing, recording, puzzling over, and eventually, tentatively interpreting. These efforts have, at various places and times, involved discourses on the *Donahue* show, at basketball games at a U.S. university, talk at a television station, teaching public speaking to Native American students, Finnish everyday and public talk, Russian discourse, Blackfeet expressions, talk in a car, and more.

In each of the many separate studies he has conducted, there has been a long period of exploratory fieldwork, then more focused and highly detailed collection and preparation of a corpus of utterances and other actions, then systematic combing of the materials in search of tentative interpretations, and finally carefully crafted and judiciously argued interpretive claims. Here, in the following statement, is a hint as to his enduring method of interpretive humility in approaching the possibility of claiming that he has discovered what might appear to be "a cultural discourse," presented in two parts:

In my experience, the interpretive account is successful if participants say something like (2007, p. 174)

"That's right, that's how we do things, but I hadn't thought of it quite like that before." (1988, p. xiv)

Let us examine these two statements. First, he radically positions himself *in conversation* with the people whose discourses he presumes to notice and examine. He, the interpreter, has said something to the participant, and he, the interpreter, *listens for* the participant's responsive act of speech, *the participant's act of saying something*. Second, he is concerned with the *participant's sense of membership*, expressed in "that's how *we*" (emphasis added). Third, he is concerned with the *participant's sense* of *communication as action*, in "that's how we *do things*" (emphasis added).

So the interpreter radically positions himself in conversation with people, conversation about, radically, the participant's sense of membership and, radically, the participant's sense of communication as action.

Although there are other aspects of these two statements, here I focus on what makes them a practice that can be characterized as interpretive humility, a practice whose "success" depends upon *what the participants themselves "say."* There is, in such a practice, no mention of exposing the false consciousness of the participants!

I think it is fair to say that Donal's work as a doctoral student, and ever since, has had one principal focus: how to find, in the communication of some person or some people, participants' sense of how they do things, communicatively, and the meaning to them of what they do. This is not to say that Donal has not done very important things in addition to zeroing in on this principal focus. He has also examined other approaches to intercultural understanding and compared and contrasted them with his own preferred approach; these comparisons and contrasts have been enlightening to many and liberating and clarifying to those who have followed him in taking up his approach. He has done important comparative analysis, analysis across multiple studies of culturally distinctive ways of communicating that has provided useful syntheses of large bodies of cross-cultural evidence. He has done important historical treatments of important bodies of scholarship. Recently, he has completed the conception, design, execution, and publication of an impressive collection of original empirical studies of how, across thirteen language varieties, seventeen countries, and six continents communication is distinctively conceptualized and enacted (Carbaugh, 2017). But standing above all these other efforts is the persistent production of new and vital interpretive, ethnographic studies of ways of communicating across multiple languages, societies, and social contexts.

As a final comment on the Donal Carbaugh I first met at the University of Washington circa 1980, I mention something that was in the air in the discipline of communication at that time: theory. Specifically, there was a discipline-wide push toward theoretical accounts of human communication, and

Donal participated in the fervor. Many of us felt, and pronounced, and taught, that the study of communication could only reach its highest potential if we generated general accounts of communication, that is, if we produced, tested, and developed theories of communication.

A theoretical account of communication is something that was of distinctive importance to those of us doing ethnography of communication in a department of communication. The rough catechism was that to do good ethnography required that one have a theory of how to do it. Each ethnography was concerned with a culturally particular way of communicating, and so to discover such ways was always a very particularized act and experience, but nonetheless it was possible to honor and use a system of inquiry that was purpose-built to enable one to systematically discover the particularity that is an ethnographic reality. The theory underlying such inquiry was a general theory of how to discover the particularities of a given case. And each such ethnography was potentially capable of helping to assess, or evaluate, or extend, or limit, the extant model(s) used to guide such ethnographic inquiry.

And here we have another enduring disposition of Donal Carbaugh: to advance ethnography of communication, or the study of cultural discourses, by advancing the art of the discovery of the particularities of ways of communicating in any given speech community, culture, or discourse. His answer is cultural discourse analysis, and it is, in my opinion, a theoretical answer. It is, of course, a theoretical answer to the general question asked of any ethnography of communication: how to proceed to discover the particularities of the case. It provides a set of concepts, of places to go to and in which to find evidence of a cultural discourse in a given case, and it says, in effect, these are the necessary and sufficient places to go to in search of such evidence. If, according to the logic of such a theory, we can discover, through a particular ethnographic endeavor, something that seems to be missing, that should be added to the scheme, to account for what we find in the case under examination, then we have the basis for a theoretical advance. Likewise, when we apply the discovery scheme and it seems to work, for a particular instance, we have some basis for affirming the utility and adequacy of the scheme. Donal came into the program at Washington already oriented to theory, particularly the type of theory that is usually associated with quantitative methods and measures. But he was able to remain a theorist, and indeed to advance theory, as someone who is primarily an ethnographer per se. And by establishing his own data- and experience-based "approach" to the discovery and analysis of a cultural discourse, he enjoys (and perhaps suffers) the designation *theorist*.

Now we can turn to the volume at hand, and I seek to explain how this remarkable volume was made possible. Central to such an explanation must be a consideration of the person to whom it is dedicated, but the nature of the volume also requires a consideration of some very particular aspects of the volume and the person.

I have mentioned and bolded several of what I believe to be enduring dispositions and qualities of the person who is the object of appreciation here, and I restate them below.

I approach these as ways to answer the question, how do we explain the volume? One sense of that question is, how do we explain that so many people have taken the time and effort to produce, and herein have published, an original piece of work that traces its inspiration and its method to the approach to discourse analysis that originates with the honoree? A second question is, how do we explain more broadly the remarkable success of the man this volume honors?

To set forth a few facts: forty-four people contributed to the published work of the volume. Forty-two of those people contributed as coauthors of an original chapter, and these were distributed among sixteen separate original chapters that use cultural discourse analysis (CuDA) as their principal approach. None of the chapters is solely authored, which means that everyone contributing did so in cooperation with one or more other scholars.

A SHARP AND DISCIPLINED FOCUS

Simplicity and clarity are not necessarily easily achieved in a program of scholarship, especially one that deals with cultural productions in many countries and across several different languages. But in each case presented here, CuDA offers a simple and inviting opportunity: find and report a cultural discourse that has not been reported before, and use the heuristic approach provided by CuDA. This is not easy work by any stretch of the imagination. But the charge is clear to those who take the time to study the call and the method. In this sense there is an openness to the enterprise, and this makes it extremely inviting, if extremely difficult to do.

INTERPRETIVE HUMILITY

This is also an exacting condition. As the late great Mikhail Bakhtin once wrote, people speak about discourse all the time (this is a paraphrase). I would add, they interpret it "all the time" and much of that interpretation is negative, or critical. Any idiot can write or speak a criticism of the discourse of someone else, and many idiots do so quite frequently. But if one is willing to accept the conditions of CuDA, that is, to follow its procedures, they will find that it has a wonderful openness that comes with, and in part because of, the humility expectation. The easy version: you just have to listen to other people. You aren't required to find something wrong with the way they talk.

The instructions are clear: listen, ask the other person if you understand them right, listen to their response to your question. We know that many people will not sign up for the program because they want to find fault with someone else's way of speaking, and they know what's wrong with it right away. But you don't have to buy into a daft political or ideological scheme to do this work. You can act humbly and still do it. Interpretive humility is thus a difficult burden to bear but a liberating one. And it helps you not make some stupid mistakes.

THEORY

A way to do the work is provided. Three key questions are provided. Several categories for observation and analysis are provided. None of this is easy. But it is exceptionally clear. And the author of the approach has demonstrated through many books and articles just how he used the particular parts of the approach to help generate his findings. They are not just things he thought up as an idle hypothetical exercise. Each part of the framework of the approach has, through his extensive labor, been generated, tested, and demonstrated through original ethnographic fieldwork reports. And if you are smart, and perhaps a little lucky, you might be able to argue for a revision of the discovery scheme; that is, you might be able to make a theoretical argument about how the approach could be modified. Don't count on it, but it's worth a try. Warning: this might take you several years.

GRIT

The man who created the CuDA approach has grit. He has worked very hard, very consistently, over almost four decades to produce the set of empirical studies that underlie the approach he refers to as CuDA, and he has worked very hard to teach the art he offers to many people, some of whom contributed to one of the sixteen original studies presented here. Some stories of grit have been provided, that is, of how he not only worked hard, but how he persevered when things were tough. Furthermore, he has promoted his ideas in many difficult forums and academic arenas where there were sharks hungry for the kill. He got a few bites along the way, but he recovered, and rather well, don't you think?

COLLEGIALITY AND COLLEGIAL CONVERSATION

The man who is honored through this volume has received the highest honors that can be bestowed by his discipline (the academic discipline of communication), by his employing university (the University of Massachusetts) and by the department that conferred his doctorate (the Department of Communication at the University of Washington). And now there appears this volume that includes tributes to him by former doctoral students, fellow alums of the department that awarded his doctorate, and by others who just wanted to join in. In part these honors flow from the quality of the work that he has produced individually. But in part these honors flow from, and reveal, the persistence and generosity of his reaching out to others to include them in the scholarly enterprise he serves and enriches. His is an intensive, and intentional, and a career-long disposition toward engagement with, and support of, other scholars.

A FINAL COMMENT

The original research in this volume consists of the sixteen different ethnographic applications of CuDA. Each of the chapters presents a substantial piece of original work. Fourteen of the chapters are focused entirely on the details of a particular case, a case constructed, built, and interpreted in the terms of the extant version of CuDA. When these fourteen chapters are taken as a whole, as a set of studies, the set provides dramatic evidence of the *range* of CuDA, that is, of its capacity to bear fruit when it is used in studies situated in discourses in several different countries and in several distinctive contexts or arenas of communicative practice. The set of studies suggests, in a powerful way, the robustness of the approach.

Two of the sixteen chapters also do something a little different. Although they are grounded in, and indebted to, CuDA, they also make a contribution that suggests a modification of the approach or a theoretical claim that goes beyond the task of discovery and interpretation of a situated discourse. The first of these cases, the chapter by Tamar Katriel and Oren Livio, proposes an addition to the CuDA framework as presently constituted. Specifically, they argue that the data they present and examine interpretively can most fully be appreciated and accommodated by adding to the CuDA framework a sixth discursive hub, the hub of temporality. If their suggestion is taken, that would expand the framework from five to six discursive hubs. This is an example of what I mean when I say that a particular ethnographic study or a collection of one or more such studies can, when examined in a persuasive way, yield a new category, or place of inquiry, to an extant discovery scheme. I think a temporality hub can usefully expand CuDA, as I understand it, and more broadly could contribute to an expansion of other descriptive and interpretive schemes, including that of the ethnography of communication itself. This is a remarkable and considerable gift to our theorist.

The second of the two studies that seem to move beyond an application of the CuDA framework is in the chapter by Patricia Covarrubias, Dani Kvam, and Max Saito. Their chapter focuses on "symbolic agonistics." They consider three different agonistic events or episodes, drawn from their ethnographic fieldwork, and on the basis of these cases or instances they generate six general propositions about agonistic encounters. Where Katriel and Livio reported participant propositions about communication, that is, localized meanings expressed in propositional form, Covarrubias, Kvam, and Saito formulate universal propositions about the functioning of agonistic discourse in social interaction, propositions suggested by their readings of their cases. This is a form of theorizing that takes these authors outside the scope of CuDA, which, as I understand it, is devoted to the development of an approach to how to capture local meanings, as opposed to the search for universal propositions about the process of discursive action. The six propositions they generate are a useful contribution to a theory of communicative encounters, and there are theories that could be further developed by the formulation this trio of authors has proposed. Their move does not, however, expand CuDA.

In both of these two studies, the authors show how studies inspired by CuDA can either elaborate or expand the CuDA framework or, incidentally, contribute to other theoretical enterprises. In singling out these two studies, I intend no comparative evaluation between the fourteen studies that report new applications of the extant framework and the two that seem to push the framework or extend into other theoretical explorations. Rather I am simply pointing descriptively to some differences across types of studies, and I note that the CuDA framework is capable of inspiring multiple types of theoretic work in human communication.

REFERENCES

Carbaugh, D. (1988). *Talking American: Cultural discourses on DONAHUE*. Norwood, NJ: Ablex.

Carbaugh, D. (2007). Cultural discourse analysis: The investigation of communication practices with special attention to intercultural encounters. *Journal of Intercultural Communication Research , 36,* 167–182.

Carbaugh, D. (Ed.). (2017). *The handbook of communication in cross-cultural perspective*. New York: Routledge.

Acknowledgments

As most great endeavors take a village, this book has been no different. I want to first thank the incredible Gary Radford, professor and chair of communication studies at Fairleigh Dickinson University (FDU) and editor of the Communication Studies Series at FDU Press, for his unfailing, enthusiastic support of this book from the moment we approached him. His early ideas—along with former director of FDU Press, Harry Keyishian—were formative in shaping this book to be more than a festschrift. I cannot thank both of them enough for their steadfast support and guidance. Harry, I wish you well in your much-deserved retirement!

I would also like to thank the new director of FDU Press, James Gifford, for his support and advisement of our book, and the amazing Zachary Nycum, assistant editor at Rowman & Littlefield, for his guidance, attention to detail, quick response to our many questions, and help with numerous aspects of the book. I could not be more grateful!

While this book pays honor to Donal Carbaugh—his work, career, and major theoretical and methodological framework, cultural discourse analysis—the true stars of this book are the forty-two contributors who worked in teams to produce sixteen chapters of data-based cultural discourse analysis studies of communication around the world. Their work is astonishing and brilliant. There is perhaps no greater honor to Donal than to use this framework—along with the ethnography of communication and speech codes theory—to continue to do great work that has a constructive impact on our world. It has been my great pleasure—along with coeditor Trudy Milburn—to work with all the contributors. Each one enthusiastically responded to our call and was eager to work in chapter teams (due to the high number of interested contributors), often with people they had not collaborated with before. Everyone contributed phenomenal work, made all revisions requested, and responded to our many queries regarding the book. I cannot thank you enough. Somehow all of us were able to keep this a secret from Donal for a year, until surprising him with the book-in-process at the New Horizons in the Ethnography of Communication Conference at the College of Mount Saint Vincent in June 2017, so I thank you also for your discretion. It has been an absolute joy to work with each of you and we look forward to many future collaborations.

I would also like to acknowledge several scholars who wished to contribute to the book but could not due to time constraints. We are all very busy, but your spirit and work has guided us in the book and our overall endeavors. In addition, I would like to thank all our Language and Social Interaction colleagues, whose work inspires us every day and can be seen throughout the book.

I would also like to thank Gerry Philipsen, professor emeritus of communication at the University of Washington, for generously writing the preface of the book. He came out of retirement to do so, and his preface is an enormous tribute to Donal and a significant piece of academic history on one of the communication field's most important scholars and the development of his research program. Gerry, I also want to thank you for bringing the ethnography of communication to the communication field and your work on developing this important research program. Without you, none of this work would be possible.

I would also like to acknowledge my coauthor on chapter 8 of the book, Saila Poutiainen. It has been an absolute pleasure to work with you on a project we started long ago that seems now more relevant than ever. Our Skype calls as we worked on the chapter were always fascinating and compelling, and I appreciate your fine attention to detail and "interpretive humility," following Gerry and Donal, when making claims about communication culture. I look forward to future collaborations and appreciate your collegiality and friendship over the years.

I would like to thank my colleagues at the College of Mount Saint Vincent, New York, who have been gracious and supportive as I worked on this endeavor, particularly my department chair, Ted Kafala, and department colleagues, Brad Crownover, Vince Fitzgerald, and Cynthia Meyers.

I cannot thank Trudy Milburn, my coeditor on the book, enough for joining me on this project, as well as for her collegiality and friendship over the years. I still remember the first time we met at a Starbucks in Manhattan, after I had moved to New York City and Donal had suggested we meet up. I was most nervous about finding my way on the train, but we had a thrilling and inspiring scholarly conversation, and they have continued ever since. It has been a long friendship and collaboration, and I thank her for all her collegiality as we have worked on co-organizing the New Horizons in the Ethnography of Communication Conference, at which much of the work for this book was presented and collaborated on, and coediting this book together. There have been many phone calls and numerous emails, but what has been constant is the exhilarating intellectual conversations regarding work on this book and the ethnography of communication overall. Like any great partnership, where I lacked she had strengths and vice versa, so we made a great team. I would like to thank and acknowledge Trudy for all her hard work over the years in the ethnography of communication and language and social interaction scholarship, her excellent research, collaborations with and support of EC and LSI colleagues. She truly embodies the spirit of an academic and a generous, erudite, engaged colleague.

To Donal Carbaugh, my mentor for master's and doctoral degrees at the University of Massachusetts Amherst, I owe a great debt. I went to graduate school searching for a systematic way to study ordinary language, based on my studies in social constructionism as an undergraduate at the University of New Hampshire. I found it in the ethnography of communication and Donal graciously took me on as an advisee. I want to thank him for standing by me as I have walked through my academic career and life. Everyone should be so lucky as to have such an incredible mentor. As is evidenced in this book, we have all benefited from his tremendous scholarship, teaching, mentorship, collegiality, and friendship. I want to thank him for that and for helping to develop a research program and community that has helped us all to do great work in the communication field and that is increasingly making important impacts on the world. I would also like to thank Donal's wife, LuAnne Carbaugh, for all her support of Donal's advisees over the years, and for his time spent mentoring us. Theirs is a wonderful partnership that we have all been enriched by in our endeavors. Lastly, we would like to thank Donal for his wonderful epilogue for and enthusiastic support of the book. We are grateful to hear from him in his own words at the end of the book on cultural discourse analysis and the incredible contributions in this book.

Finally, I would like to thank my husband, Scott Jacobson, for all his patience, love, and support as I worked on this book. It has been a lot of work, but a great joy, and he has encouraged me all along the way. I would also like to thank him for all the wonderful meals he cooked, nourishing my heart and soul, as I toiled away and wrote by his side.

—Michelle Scollo

I want to extend my appreciation to Michelle Scollo for approaching me to collaborate on this amazing project. It was fortuitous that Donal suggested we meet when she moved to NYC so many years ago. My own scholarship has been enriched by our talks over the years, as has my understanding of cultural discourse analysis. It has truly been a pleasure working with you. I appreciate your meticulousness and quest to faithfully represent our field and deep commitment to this work that is truly inspiring and uplifting.

I'm also very grateful to Tabitha Hart for generously including me on a research endeavor she began long before I arrived. It was a pleasure to work with you over the past couple years, presenting at conferences and culminating in this chapter.

I feel fortunate to have been Donal's second doctoral graduate behind Sally Hastings. Working with him during the formative years of theory building was not something I fully appreciated until now. Over the years, he has introduced me to all his subsequent students and kept me connected to him, the field, and the evolving theory in ways I also could not have anticipated. Donal has created an academic family that transcends institution, place, and time. It is my great pleasure to call him a friend.

The authors in this volume have been such a pleasure to work with; thank you to everyone for meeting deadlines, sending materials, and making revisions as requested. I also want to acknowledge additional scholars in our field who are not authors of chapters in this volume. Their work is felt, appreciated, and cited throughout. We all face multiple commitments that at times preclude us from being able to contribute in ways we would wish and we want to acknowledge that this work continues and, we trust, will become more inclusive of new voices over the next years.

Finally, I want to thank my husband, Chris Christian, for his ability to enjoy spending weekends working on our respective scholarly endeavors. It has been a partnership that flourishes when we author side-by-side, especially dwelling in our cottage in Clinton, Connecticut.

—Trudy Milburn

Mike Alvarez: Donal is a fantastic teacher and mentor who has encouraged me to take my research in new and surprising directions; I will always appreciate his advice to not put labels on our work, for his advice allowed me to see connections I might not have otherwise seen.

David Boromisza-Habashi, Leah Sprain, Natasha Shrikant, Lydia Reinig, and Katherine R. Peters: We would like to express our gratitude to Donal for his unwavering support and mentorship, and to Karen Tracy and Jessica Robles for their insightful comments on earlier versions of our chapter.

Charles Braithwaite, Eean Grimshaw, and Jay Leighter: We would like to thank and acknowledge all the tribal partners and representatives for their support and advice on this project; we would also like to thank Trudy Milburn and Michelle Scollo for their tireless effort curating this excellent book; and Donal Carbaugh, without whose friendship and scholarship we would not be able to engage in such rewarding collaborative work.

Tovar Cerulli: I am grateful to the hunters, two- and four-footed, among whom I have learned so much, and to my advisor and friend Donal Carbaugh, whose keen insight, deep knowledge, and generous heart bless us all.

Patricia Covarrubias: Con gratitud y cariño muy estimados Gerry Philipsen y Donal Carbaugh por su dedicación a la etnografía de la comunicación la cual cambió nuestras vidas para siempre.

Tabitha Hart: I want to express how much I appreciated working with Trudy on the chapter for the book. I am grateful for Donal's scholarship, and for all the new research that his work continues to generate.

Sally Hastings: A favorite graduate school memory: venting frustration to Donal about not getting the responses I expected when doing fieldwork. His calm response involved instructing me to stop worrying and to remember that, whatever happens, "it's all data." I am forever grateful to Donal for sharing so much wisdom.

Evelyn Ho: Our team would like to thank research assistants Tan Yue Qian (Clarissa) and Zhi Qi Yeo, who helped conduct, translate, and transcribe many of our interviews and give special thanks to Donal Carbaugh for all his work over the years to advance EC research and CuDA, and to Trudy and Michelle for bringing us all together in New York and in this volume.

Tamar Katriel: I have greatly cherished Donal's gift of friendship and collegiality since our days together as graduate students sharing an office at UW, and am truly grateful for them.

Sunny Lie: Thank you, Donal, for creating such a supportive, loving, and inspiring intellectual community!

Lauren Benotti Mackenzie: I would like to thank Donal for believing in this insecure grad student back in 1998 and being a model of intellectual curiosity and cultural humility for her ever since.

Tema Milstein: Thanks to Donal for his friendship and for his gift of CuDA and other generative frameworks to help us better understand discourse as both culturally and ecologically meaningful.

Saila Poutiainen: Thank you, Donal, for teaching that Culture in Conversation class in Finland in the early '90s, and for your kind and ever-supporting mentorship. I would also like thank Trudy and Michelle for all their hard work, and especially for the original idea of this book.

Lisa Rudnick: Ruth and I would like to acknowledge the community members who worked with us in Ranjitpur and beyond, for their generosity of time and tutelage; our Nepali colleagues; our UNIDIR teammates; and our colleagues in the EC community who contributed in different ways to the SNAP project at different points in time. And I would like to thank Donal for his generous mentorship, his enthusiastic support, and his insightful scholarship, which provides us all with generative ways and means to engage the world deeply, and with humility.

Max Saito: I am grateful for Donal's lesson that before objecting to certain communication practices, I should try my very best to understand the practices from within. This in turn increases my awareness about my own beliefs, values, and norms that I did not notice before, and can be a liberating experience.

Nadezhda Sotirova: Thank you, Donal, from the bottom of my heart for introducing and welcoming me so warmly to our fantastic EC and CuDA family!

Richard Wilkins: No one individual continues to have a formative impact on the discipline of cultural discourse analysis in the way that Donal does. My eternal thanks to him for helping to shape both my own scholarship and how best to teach our discipline to the scholars of the future.

Saskia Witteborn: Thank you, Donal, for having been such a good mentor over the years and a key link between EC and CuDA researchers.

Karen Wolf: Thank you, Donal, for your continuous and insightful mentorship along with your enthusiastic support throughout my academic career.

Introduction

Cultural Discourse Analysis — Yesterday, Today, and Tomorrow

Michelle Scollo and Trudy Milburn

In its earliest usage, "communication" invoked meanings of making "common to many," sharing, and participation, linking people into communities of shared meaning (Barnhart, 1988, p. 195; Carey, 1975). As Carey explained, this "ritual view of communication is not directed toward the extension of messages in space but the maintenance of society in time; not the act of imparting information but the representation of shared beliefs" (p. 6).

This dual capacity of communication to both reflect and constitute community has long captured ethnographers of communication's attention, from Hymes's (1962) initial concept of "speech community" to Philipsen's (1989) "communal function of communication" and (1997) speech codes theory to Carbaugh's (2005) cultural discourse analysis.

Initially conceived by Dell Hymes in the 1960s and brought to the communication field in the 1970s by Gerry Philipsen, "the ethnography of communication (EC) is an approach to human communication with its own philosophy, theory, and methodology" (Carbaugh, 1995, p. 269).[1] Philipsen's pioneering studies of communication in "Teamsterville" in the United States in the 1970s ushered in a new approach to, and the import of, the cultural study of communication. In the decades that followed, he further developed this approach, conducting research, developing important theoretical and methodological frameworks, and mentoring a number of graduate students in the approach, notably Tamar Katriel, Donal Carbaugh, Charles A. Braithwaite, and Kristine Fitch Muñoz. They have all gone on to conduct their own ethnography of communication research, develop its theory and methodology, and educate undergraduate and graduate students in its use.

The ethnography of communication today is a thriving worldwide community of students, scholars, and practitioners. We are using a written form of communication—this book—to honor one of its most devoted, distinguished, and cherished practitioners, Donal Carbaugh: teacher, scholar, mentor, colleague, and friend to all the contributors in this volume and to countless others in the communication field and related disciplines. [2]

The book focuses on cultural discourse analysis, a theoretical and methodological framework that Carbaugh has been developing over the past three decades as part of the ethnography of communication tradition. The book likewise not only honors Carbaugh for his work, but also extends his contributions by using cultural discourse analysis to both conduct and teach others how to use the framework for communication research from a cultural perspective. Such is the power of communication, to both honor and extend, reflect and constitute, and engage and transform—as we will see in the chapters that follow.

In this introduction, we explain the historical development of cultural discourse analysis, its current theory and methodology, the plan of the book, and the roots of the ethnography of communication research community and this book.

CULTURAL DISCOURSE ANALYSIS[3]

Cultural discourse analysis (CuDA) is indebted to both the ethnography of communication (Hymes, 1962, 1972; Philipsen & Carbaugh, 1986) and interactional sociolinguistics traditions (Gumperz, 1982; Carbaugh & Cerulli, 2017, 2013; Carbaugh, 2007). Carbaugh has spent his entire career developing this framework, beginning with his 1984 doctoral dissertation under the direction of Philipsen at the University of Washington, and continues to refine it today. It is important to note that CuDA developed in tandem with Philipsen's cultural communication and speech codes theory (1987, 1997, 2002; Philipsen, Coutu, & Covarrubias, 2005) and both are mutually inspired by each other (Scollo, 2011; Carbaugh, 2017b). While Hymes's initial conception of the ethnography of speaking—later the ethnography of communication[4] —offered heuristic tools for the comparative description and interpretation of the means and meanings of communication in diverse speech communities, speech codes theory and CuDA have created additional tools for deepening this, particularly interpretive analysis.

In Carbaugh's first book, *Talking American: Cultural Discourses on Donahue* (1988), we find his first use of the term *cultural discourse* in the interrelated cultural discourses of "personhood" and "speaking" on the television talk show *Donahue*, among other U.S. American scenes.[5] We also find his beginning definition of cultural discourse, composed of interrelated thematic codes that are "subsystems of symbols, symbolic forms and their meanings," the meanings formulated into cultural premises—which are combinations of belief and value (Carbaugh, 1988, p. 8). Here Carbaugh also begins an explanation of how to analyze and theorize communication with the construct (Scollo, 2011).

Several publications followed that further developed the budding theory, including integral components and theoretical frameworks such as agonistic discourse (Carbaugh, 1988/1989), cultural terms for talk (Carbaugh, 1989, 2017b), and social identity (Carbaugh, 1996; Scollo, 2011).[6] In 1997, Carbaugh published a landmark piece with Timothy A. Gibson and Trudy Milburn that contained the most robust explanation of the theory and method to that date. In it, the authors explicated an evolving approach to the study of social interaction and culture, with a trio of concepts including communicative scene, communication practice, and cultural discourse. The basic idea was to describe and interpret the deep cultural meanings of communication practices by examining them situated in scenes with an eye to the cultural discourses imminent in, radiating through, and composed of them (pp. 6–7). They defined communication practice as a "*pattern of situated, message endowed action*," noting a part-whole relationship (emphasis original, p. 6). That is, communication practices are part of larger cultural discourses and expressive systems, while those systems are inherent in communication practices. It is in this sense that communication practices are "message endowed," "symbolic," and "systemic" as they richly radiate and implicate cultural discourses (p. 7; Carbaugh & Cerulli, 2013, p. 5).

Turning to cultural discourse, they defined them as "systems of symbols, symbolic acts, sequential forms, rules, and their meanings" (p. 22). Further, that "the meanings of cultural discourses—of the symbols, acts, forms, rules—consist in basic premises about being (identity), doing (action), relating (social relations), feeling (emoting), and dwelling (living in place)" (p. 22).

The (1997) article outlined a comprehensive theory and method for CuDA, from how to collect data, what counts as a datum, to how to interpret their meaningfulness in situated scenes with the concept of cultural discourse. Importantly, we see the full complement of cultural premises in the article—of being, acting, relating, feeling, and dwelling—that have become a cornerstone of CuDA today.[7]

During the next decade, Carbaugh further applied CuDA with a number of data-based studies, largely on communication practices in Blackfeet, Finnish, and U.S. American cultures, as well as extensions of CuDA to particular fields such as environmental communication (Carbaugh, 1996; Carbaugh &

Cerulli, 2013), rhetoric (Carbaugh & Wolf, 1999), and health communication (Suopis & Carbaugh, 2005; Scollo, 2011, p. 15).[8]

Much of this culminates in his (2005) award-winning book,[9] *Cultures in Conversation*, which focuses on a CuDA approach to the study of intercultural and social interaction, including Blackfeet, British, Finnish, Russian, and U.S. American cases. His thesis in the book extends his earlier work, that *"communication, conversation and social interaction involves a complex metacultural commentary, explicitly and/or implicitly, about identities, actions, feelings, relations, and living in place"* (emphasis original, p. 129). That is, as we communicate, we are saying something, implicitly or explicitly, about who we are and should be, how we can and should act, feel, relate, and live in place. These deep cultural premises shape communicative conduct and reveal its meaningfulness, which analysts can interpret with systems of cultural premises concerning each dimension, some more relevant than others at times (p. 129). The book also offers the most in-depth and fully developed explanation of the theory and methodology of CuDA up to that point that readers can follow to conduct their own cultural discourse analyses.

Since and prior to the (2005) book, Carbaugh and others have used the CuDA framework to productively guide studies on various foci of communication including, but not limited to, being, acting, relating, feeling, and dwelling.[10] Recent work has continued to explore questions of identity and personhood. Carbaugh (1988, 1996, 2007, 2009) has addressed this question numerous times over the years. More recently, Rudnick (2001), LaGrande and Milburn (2003), Boromisza-Habashi (2007), Witteborn (2007), Coutu (2008), and Saito (2009) have written work on this topic.

Recent work has also examined metapragmatic terms for communicative action and the acts and events they label, including Wolf (1998), Carbaugh (1999, 2002), Suopis and Carbaugh (2005), Covarrubias (2008), Milstein (2008, 2011), Wolf, Milburn, and Wilkins (2008), Leighter and Castor (2009), Molina-Markham (2012), and Boromisza-Habashi (2013).

Interpersonal and intercultural relations have also been addressed in recent research, including Carbaugh, (1990, 1993, 2005, 2007, 2012), Covarrubias (2002), Poutiainen (2005), Poutiainen and Gerlander (2009), Carbaugh, Nuciforo, Saito, and Dong-Shin (2011), and Carbaugh and van Over (2013).

Feeling or emotion expression has been examined in a number of studies, including Boromisza-Habashi (2007, 2011, 2012, 2013), Saito (2009), and Molina-Markham (2012). Lastly, for dwelling or living in place, recent research has included Carbaugh (1999), Carbaugh and Rudnick (2006), Townsend (2006), Morgan (2007), Gilbertz and Milburn (2011), and Carbaugh and Cerulli (2013).

Based on the above and additional work, Carbaugh has continued to further refine and explain the theory and methodology of CuDA in depth, with examples of how to conduct such analysis, in multiple works (e.g., Carbaugh & Cerulli, 2017, 2013; Carbaugh, 2017b, 2007). Much of this refinement focuses on evolving identification and explanation of key constructs in CuDA, such as "discursive hubs" and "radiants of meaning," as well as the modes of inquiry involved. These constructs and modes guide all the chapters in this book and represent the latest theory and methodology in CuDA work today.

The most recent definitions of cultural discourse remain quite similar, for example, "a set of communication practices—acts, events, and styles—which is treated as a historically transmitted expressive system of symbols, symbolic forms, norms, and their meanings" (Carbaugh & Cerulli, 2013, p. 7). What is a more recent development is the construct of "discursive hubs," which ground analysis in situated communication practice (Carbaugh, 2007, 2017b; Carbaugh & Cerulli, 2013, 2017). Based on prior ethnographic and CuDA research, there are five main hubs of communication practice: being, acting, relating, feeling, and dwelling. A cultural analyst may focus on any hub in a particular study, keying in on participants' discursive devices, such as cultural terms or a "phrase, form, gesture," that identify significant practices in that area (Carbaugh, 2017b, p. 19). For example, in Chapter 1 of this book, Ho, Lie, Luk, and Dutta focus on the identity hub, examining being "heaty" in Singapore, while in Chapter 8 Scollo and Poutiainen focus on the relating hub, examining the relationship stages of "talking" in the United States and *tapailla* ("seeing someone") in Finland. Cultural discourses may be topical, for example, discourses of health or romantic relating, and each discourse is comprised of multiple, interrelated hubs, associated practices, norms, and their meanings (Carbaugh, 2017b).

While hubs and the discursive devices that activate them convey explicit, literal messages—for example in the above, about being healthy or romantic relating—communication practices also implicitly radiate a web of interrelated, taken-for-granted, cultural meanings, concerning being, acting, relating, feeling, and dwelling (Carbaugh, 2007, p. 174). These are the deep cultural meanings of communication practices, presumed for and activated in their enactment, "part of an unspoken coherence participants take-for-granted in order to understand their communication" (e.g., "this is what we are doing and why we do it this way"), called "semantic radiants" or "radiants of meaning" (Carbaugh, 2017b, p. 19; Carbaugh & Cerulli, 2013). For example, while the cultural term "heaty" explicitly addresses a state of being, it may also implicitly (or explicitly) convey messages about proper ways of feeling, acting, relating, and/or dwelling in Singapore. In the United States, while the cultural term "talking" explicitly addresses a romantic relationship stage, it may also implicitly (or explicitly) convey messages about proper ways of acting, being, feeling, and/or dwelling. As Carbaugh and Cerulli (2013) explain:

> When practiced, communication makes explicit some meanings more than others. . . . Any one hub about identity, or action, or emotion, or relations, or dwelling may be made explicit in discourse; as any one is made an explicit discursive hub of concern, the others may tag along as part of its implicit meanings. Part of the importance in understanding cultural discourses through discursive hubs is interpreting the more taken-for-granted, implicit meanings brought along in participants' discourses. . . . We call this complex of explicit meanings about a discursive hub plus the implicit meanings attached to it, a *meta-cultural commentary*. . . . Being able to understand and interpret the meta-cultural commentary in communication practice helps cultural analysts penetrate the surface of meanings, to the deeper significance and importance of the matters at hand. This interpretive work is a key objective of cultural discourse analyses. (emphasis original, pp. 6–7)

Likewise, to understand the full range of cultural meaning active in communication practice, one must interpret the explicit and implicit meanings in this metacultural commentary. This is most often done by formulating cultural propositions (statements of participants' beliefs and values in their own terms) and deeper, broader premises of being, acting, relating, feeling, and dwelling active in the practice at hand (Carbaugh & Cerulli, 2017, p. 5).[11]

Lastly, CuDA today involves four important modes of analysis: descriptive, interpretive, comparative, and critical (Carbaugh & Cerulli, 2017, 2013; Carbaugh, 2017b, 2007). Descriptive and interpretive analysis are part of all CuDA studies, while comparative and critical analysis may be employed. In each of the chapters in this book, you will see descriptive and interpretive analysis of communication practices as they are described in rich detail and interpreted for their deep cultural meanings from participants' perspective. Unique to this book, several chapters include multiple cultural cases enabling cross-cultural comparative analysis of what is similar and different in a common communication practice or set of related practices, fostering generation of local and general communication theory, a key feature of the EC research program (see, e.g., Carbaugh & Hastings, 1995).[12] The cultural cases in the book also offer a fund of studies for future cross-cultural comparative analysis of communication practices.

Several chapters also include critical analysis. Some include "natural criticism" from cultural members concerning their own communication practices (e.g., Chapter 5, Flanigan & Alvarez; Chapter 8, Scollo & Poutiainen) (Carbaugh, 1989/1990). Others include "academic criticism" by the authors, some on the basis of local communication theories developed in their work compared to "dominant" practice today (e.g., Chapter 5, Flanigan & Alvarez; Chapter 9, Cerulli & Milstein; Chapter 13, Leighter, Grimshaw, & Braithwaite; Chapter 14, Rudnick, Witteborn, & Edmonds), and others on the basis of cross-cultural comparative analysis in their work suggesting cultural bias in general communication theory (e.g., Chapter 8, Scollo & Poutiainen) (Carbaugh, 1989/1990). While critical analysis may be part of CuDA, it is always on the basis of thorough description and interpretation of communication practices from participants' perspective first, and the "ethical juncture" from which practices are critically evaluated must be explicitly noted (Carbaugh & Cerulli, 2013, p. 7, 2017; Carbaugh, 2007). Thus, taken together in the book, all four modes of CuDA inquiry are productively engaged, descriptive, interpretive, comparative, and critical.

PLAN OF THE BOOK

Turning to the plan of the book, when we reached out to interested contributors and the number was high—forty-two[13] —we recognized the potential for unique collaborations and cross-cultural comparisons, among those who, for the most part, had not worked together in the past. We formed sixteen chapter teams of ethnography of communication (EC) scholars, many from different generations and teachers of EC, which produced some very interesting results as explained below.

A unique contribution of this book is multiple chapters in which a common communication practice or set of related practices are examined across cultures with CuDA. Several chapters, conversely, analyze one case in depth, with all the cultural cases of communication in the book offering a fruitful avenue for future cross-cultural inquiry.

Resulting from this, several cultures and communities are represented in the book. Returning to the roots of EC, Hymes (1972) directed ethnographers to begin with what he termed as the primary unit of analysis, a "speech community." Following this, he suggested examining practices within a secondary unit, speech situation, or a tertiary unit, speech event. Hymes (1974) then broadened his instructions about where to begin by explaining, "the starting point is the ethnographic analysis of the communication conduct of a community" (p. 9). Over the years, the starting place, "community" versus "conduct," as well as the parameters or boundaries of communities has been debated (see Milburn, 2004). This book remains agnostic and includes both types.

For instance, some chapters describe communities defined by or within national boundaries, such as Bulgaria, China, Finland, Israel, Japan, Latvia, Mexico, Nepal, Singapore, and the United States. We also include chapters that focus community based on ethnic ties, including multiple Native American peoples such as Blackfeet, Ojibwe and Winnebago, Mexican@ immigrants, and African Americans. Still other researchers focus on the primary unit, speech community, as a group who shares at least "one way of speaking" (Hymes, 1972). These communities may be composed of people designated as "asylum seekers," or users of online platforms or websites such as LinkedIn or SuicideForum.com. The range of groupings extends to auto-mobile drivers and those who participate in activities such as museum tour-ing, whale watching, or hunting. Participation in similar community groups, such as the U.S. military, the Texas Chamber of Commerce, and residents of an "intentional community" round out the range of communities that are addressed within this volume.

Following Carbaugh (2005), as we draw attention to different cultures and communities represented in the book, we would like to note that in each case in the book the

> objective is to identify a practice or a feature of a practice that is prominent within, and distinctive of, some scenes of each society. Each of the identifying terms [such as "Finnish" or "Mexican"], then, draws attention to qualities of some interactive practices in a society; the claim thus applies to a class of practice, not to a population of people. (p. xxvii)

Turning to communication practice, the book addresses a broad array of types of communication and research areas in the communication field, in-cluding environmental communication (Chapter 9, Cerulli & Milstein), health communication (Chapter 1, Ho, Lie, Luk, & Dutta; Chapter 5, Flani-gan & Alvarez), intercultural and international communication (Chapter 10, Covarrubias, Kvam, & Saito), interpersonal communication (Chapter 8, Scollo & Poutiainen), mass communication (Chapter 11, van Over, Dori-Hacohen, & Winchatz), organizational communication (Chapter 2, Hart & Milburn; Chapter 6, Mackenzie & Tenzek), political communication (Chap-ter 4, Katriel & Livio; Chapter 16, Boromisza-Habashi, Sprain, Shrikant, Reinig, & Peters), religious communication (Chapter 12, Graham & Has-tings), and rhetoric (Chapter 7, Wilkins, Gulinello, & Wolf). Some chapters extend our knowledge in the areas of educational communication (Chapter 13, Leighter, Grimshaw, & Braithwaite), immigration and public policy (Chapter 14, Rudnick, Witteborn, & Edmonds; Chapter 15, Locmele & Soti-rova), and technology (Chapter 3, Rosenbaun, Winter, & van Over). Another new theme in communication studies is to foster work in social justice. Certainly, one could reasonably argue that many scholars in this volume would see their work as pursuing this laudable goal. Taken together, the broad array of research areas covered in the book shows the utility of the CuDA approach for examining a range of significant issues in the communi-cation field and today's global world.

Turning to the organization of the book, the five primary hubs and radi-ants of CuDA—being, acting, relating, feeling, and dwelling—serve as its organizational structure. We grouped chapters into sets where we thought interesting juxtapositions of similar hubs and/or radiants could be examined in close proximity. By creating discrete sections for being, acting, relating, feeling, and dwelling, readers may miss the similar issues that chapters in other sections touch on. Note that several chapters could fit in other sections, including multiple hubs or radiants in their analysis or multiple cases that foreground different ones. The particular chapters included in each section are meant to throw into sharper relief the various ways that people in distinct places conduct themselves. By examining cultural practices through a primary hub, researchers foreground local interpretations. Certainly, we welcome and hope this volume contributes to scholarship that juxtaposes chapters—or scenes from chapters—across sections to bring into relief very different comparisons.

When reading the book, readers will also see that contributors in each chapter use CuDA in distinct ways. Some of this is due to learning CuDA at different points in its evolution, others due to the data being examined drawing researchers into different uses of the theory and methodology, others to their own unique interpretations of the framework. Note that because of this, you will see subtle differences in the use and application of CuDA in each chapter. We believe these differences strengthen the volume as a whole because readers can find nuanced examples and interpretations that may spark their interest. We also consider this a prosperous sign of a theoretical and methodological framework in use, with each chapter likely contributing to its further understanding, application, and refinement.

Turning to the five sections of the book, Part I on "Being" includes three chapters that focus primarily on identity. In the first chapter, Ho, Lie, Luk, and Dutta focus on a key term for being in their chapter, "Speaking of Health in Singapore Using the Singlish Term *Heaty*." In the chapter, the four authors work together on data gathered in Singapore on a native approach to health and well-being. In the second chapter, Hart and Milburn focus on a set of data gathered across a variety of different people, all of whom describe the way they display their professional identities in "Applying Cultural Discourse Analysis to an Online Community: LinkedIn's Cultural Discourse of Professionalism." Finally, Rosenbaun, Winter, and van Over work together in the third chapter to provide an interesting way that in-car voice technology begins to take on an identity as drivers express strong preferences for interaction. "Voice Persona Perceptions: Apologies in In-Car Speech Technology" widens our scope of the ways we consider being and identity in practice.

In Part II, we bring together four chapters that primarily address "Acting." In the first, Katriel and Livio make the bold move of considering the way time impacts action in "When Discourse Matters: Temporality in Discursive Action." Following that in Chapter 5, Flanigan and Alvarez present data from both an intentional community and an online suicide discussion forum. "Cultural Discourse Analysis as Critical Analysis: A View from Twin Oaks and SuicideForum.com" includes a critical component to consider each case from alternate normative perspectives. The next chapter, "Cultural Variation in End-of-Life Conversations: Using Cultural Discourse Analysis to Inform Case Studies Designed for Professional Military Education" is about discussions concerning proper actions to be taken and conversations to engage in when loved ones are dying. In the chapter, Mackenzie and Tenzek seek to use real examples to provide cross-cultural teaching and learning moments for U.S. military who may be unfamiliar with the variety of actions that appropriately and preferably accompany the end of life. The final chapter in this section, Chapter 7, explores talk during museum tours. Wilkins, Gulinello, and Wolf consider the change of communicative acts that are deemed appropriate today within "Museum Tour Talk: Communicative Acts, Associated Identities, and their Idealizations."

Although several chapters include the theme of "Relating," Part III focuses on two chapters that foreground different types of relationships. In the first, Chapter 8, Scollo and Poutiainen explore the way romantic relationships communicatively develop in two different cultural contexts. "'Talking' and *Tapailla* ('Seeing Someone'): Cultural Terms and Ways of Communicating in the Development of Romantic Relationships in the United States and Finland" illuminates an evolution of communicatively engaging in romantic relationships in the United States and Finland. The next chapter by Cerulli and Milstein focuses on human-animal relationships and the ways that humans draw analogies and often anthropomorphize animals in those relationships. However, "'Fellow Hunters' and 'Humans of the Ocean': Identity and Relations across Species" does not valorize a single way of relating with wolves or whales; rather, the chapter demonstrates that these relationships can be quite complex and include a variety of levels and cultural norms.

Part IV on "Feeling" includes three chapters with authors who had not worked together in this way before. The willingness of Covarrubias, Kvam, and Saito to consider the comparisons between Mexican, Mexican@, and Japanese discourses makes for a truly remarkable chapter. In "Symbolic Agonistics: Stressing Emotion and Relation in Mexican, Mexican@, and Japanese Discourses," readers are treated to three unique scenes where emotion work is carried out. All three scenes work to illustrate a new way of thinking about agonistic discourse. In the next chapter, we find another novel approach to collaboration. Van Over, Dori-Hacohen, and Winchatz create a window into controversial public discourse. By blending three scenes in "Policing the Boundaries of the Sayable: The Public Negotiation of Profane, Prohibited, and Proscribed Speech," readers can learn more about how audiences and speakers set or reach limits about what can be said. In the last chapter in this section, Chapter 12, Graham and Hastings provide a detailed glimpse into African American funeral practices. The chapter confronts stereotypes and interprets cultural meanings underlying particular emotional displays. "'We Know How to Cry Out': Emotion Expression at an African

American Funeral" illustrates the way emotion work is integral to expressions of identity and relationships.

The final section, Part V, on "Dwelling" includes four chapters that illustrate the range of ways we can conceptualize communicative practices within and about places and spaces. The first chapter brings together three authors' work in Native American scenes. Leighter, Grimshaw, and Braithwaite provide insights into the ways educational spaces and scenes can impact learning. Reading "Cultural Discourses in Native American Educational Contexts" can set the stage for reimagining alternate ways of educating and learning. Taking a more direct policy approach in Chapter 14, Rudnick, Witteborn, and Edmonds tackle the difficult challenges of what it means to be a child or a refugee within different cultural scenes. In "Engaging Change: Exploring the Adaptive and Generative Potential of Cultural Discourse Analysis Findings for Policies and Social Programs," readers will value the authors' explication of locally situated practices whose understanding should be part and parcel of decision-making within quite difficult contexts. The third chapter in this section brought together two researchers, Locmele and Sotirova, who combined and compared two cases in "'The Things I Leave Behind': Negotiating Bulgarian and Latvian Identities in Relation to Dwelling and 'Proper Action' in Public Discourses on Remigration." In this chapter, the identities displayed within the two countries demonstrate different ways to address migration. Finally, concluding this section is a broader comparison by five contributors from the University of Colorado Boulder: Boromisza-Habashi, Sprain, Shrikant, Reinig, and Peters. Although dwelling can focus on place-bound comparisons, the chapter "Cultural Discourse Analysis within an Ecosystem of Discourse Analytic Approaches: Connections and Boundaries" uses one case in Texas to illustrate three distinct ways to address the same data.

Rounding out the book, Gerry Philipsen, professor emeritus of communication at the University of Washington and National Communication Association Distinguished Scholar, generously introduces the book with his preface. The preface offers a unique glimpse into Carbaugh's development as a scholar, and of the CuDA framework, as a doctoral student under his direction and later during his career. The book closes with an epilogue by Carbaugh, another generous contribution, in which he ties together the chapters in the book and offers a nuanced explanation of CuDA that builds on the introduction and completes the book.

Taken together, the preface and introduction of the book cover important historical context for the development of the ethnography of communication, speech codes theory, and CuDA, all significant research programs and frameworks within the communication field, as well as one of its major scholars, Donal Carbaugh. In addition, the introduction and epilogue offer detailed explanations of CuDA, such that readers can learn the framework, understand how it grounds analysis in each chapter, and guide them in their own future CuDA studies. Lastly, the sixteen data-based chapters in the book offer outstanding, diverse examples of cultural discourse analyses of communication practices across the world. The chapters are all exemplars of CuDA research, instructive in their own right to those interested in EC and CuDA, and also representative of the wide array of significant work and issues being addressed with the framework. As such, the book is more a "handbook" of cultural discourse analysis than festschrift for Carbaugh, which we believe is exactly the way he would most appreciate being honored.[14]

HONORING OUR ROOTS

Lastly, the title of our book and cover image have special meaning. The ethnography of communication is a global academic community. The contributors in this volume work and study in Bulgaria, Finland, Israel, Japan, Latvia, Mexico, Norway, Singapore, the United Kingdom, and the United States. Many hail from different countries around the world. We examine, along with other fellow ethnographers of communication, communication practices in a range of cultures and communities across the globe, many of which are represented in this book.

In each case in the book, we are *engaging* cultural and intercultural communication in a deep way through cultural discourse analysis. We hope that this work can help people understand how and why people communicate in the ways they do, fostering deeper understanding, respect, collaboration, and productive ways of living together in our global world. This has been a guiding principle of Carbaugh's work and many others in the ethnography of communication. In our cover image, this is represented by the "hands" of people collaborating together across the globe.

Some of the chapters in the book also seek to *transform* communication through cultural discourse analysis. Whether using the framework to train U.S. military in intercultural end-of-life conversations (Chapter 6, Mackenzie & Tenzek), to design in-car speech technology in culturally meaningful ways (Chapter 3, Rosenbaun, Winter, & van Over), to reshape mental health treatment toward patients' lived experience (Chapter 5, Flanigan & Alvarez), to rethink humans' ways of relating to nature (Chapter 9, Cerulli & Milstein), to reexamine ways of teaching when dominant and local cultures interplay (Chapter 13, Leighter, Grimshaw, & Braithwaite), or to reform international policy and programming based on local participants' everyday lives (Chapter 14, Rudnick, Witteborn, & Edmonds), each such case goes beyond engaging to work toward *transforming* communication. Thus, in the book, we are "Engaging and Transforming Global Communication through Cultural Discourse Analysis" in honor of Carbaugh and the research program he has helped to develop over the years.

Our cover image also features a small tree branch, representing the academic tree of the ethnography of communication, growing and thriving today through our global research community. The book embodies four intertwined generations of ethnography of communication students, scholars, and practitioners. Gerry Philipsen, the "father" of the ethnography of communication (EC) in the communication field in the United States, mentored three of the contributors in this book early on in his career and the EC research program—Tamar Katriel, Donal Carbaugh, and Charles A. Braithwaite. Philipsen also mentored later generations of graduate students in this book, including Patricia Covarrubias, Michaela R. Winchatz, Saskia Witteborn, Tema Milstein, James L. Leighter, Leah Sprain, and Tabitha Hart. Katriel has mentored several students, including Gonen Dori-Hacohen and Oren Livio, both contributors in this volume. Carbaugh has also mentored several generations of students, numerous in this book, including Sally O. Hastings, Trudy Milburn, Karen Wolf, Richard Wilkins, Saila Poutiainen, Lisa Rudnick, Michelle Scollo, Lauren Mackenzie, Max Saito, David Boromisza-Habashi, Jolane Flanigan, Brion van Over, Sunny Lie, Nadezhda Sotirova, Tovar Cerulli, Natasha Shrikant, Liene Locmele, Mike Alvarez, and Eean Grimshaw. Kristine Fitch Muñoz, another early student of Philipsen, mentored Evelyn Y. Ho, a contributor in this book.

Many of these EC scholars have gone on to mentor their own students, some of whom are included in their chapters in the book. Richard Wilkins mentored Fran Gulinello, Patricia Covarrubias mentored Dani S. Kvam, Sally O. Hastings mentored Danielle Graham, and David Boromisza-Habashi mentored Katherine R. Peters. Leah Sprain is currently mentoring Lydia Reinig, while Jay L. Leighter mentored her in her undergraduate work.

Finally, the academic tree extends to practitioners in their respective fields. For instance, Carbaugh mentored several people at General Motors, and we can see evidence of this in Rosenbaum and Winter's chapter in the book. In addition, Philipsen and Carbaugh worked with Rudnick and a host of people that now include Edmonds on research and programming with the United Nations.

Unique to this book—and as Philipsen points out in his preface, on the foundation of Carbaugh, Katriel, and Braithwaite's friendship and collegiality—students of different generations and teachers are working together in compelling ways on chapter teams in the book. We consider this a sign of a thriving, synergistic research community, and commitment to the academic and professional development of our students. Certainly these are commitments of Carbaugh that he has instilled in his students and EC through his scholarship, teaching, mentorship, and collegiality. Moreover, Carbaugh and many in this volume share a deep commitment to developing *communication theory* first and foremost, and the communication field. That this is done through the EC research program, cultural discourse analysis, and speech codes theory is secondary to this aim and overall goal. That it is done so from a cultural perspective is a deep and abiding commitment to the belief that communication is cultural, varies by culture, and should be studied and theorized as such.

And so we come together, to celebrate and honor through research and written communication, a beloved, respected, and distinguished scholar. As Carbaugh once said of his undergraduate studies at Manchester University, coming of age in the Vietnam War, "To be in a place where people were engaged in thinking globally, and how different people can get along together better, and the means for achieving that sort of world—that was part of my enduring learning and life's quest" (Weber, 2011).

NOTES

1. See Philipsen (1990), Carbaugh (1995), and Carbaugh & Hastings (1995) for more on the ethnography of communication research program and its methodology.
2. Donal Carbaugh is professor of communication at the University of Massachusetts Amherst, National Communication Association Distinguished Scholar, and award-winning author of numerous books, edited volumes, and journal articles, among numerous other accomplishments. See https://www.umass.edu/communication/people/profile/donal-carbaugh for more information.
3. Parts of this section occur earlier in a (2011) article by Scollo. Carbaugh's publications of data-based cultural discourse analysis studies and theoretical and methodological expositions are vast; see Scollo (2011) for more information.
4. See Leeds-Hurwitz (1984) on the relationship of the "Ethnography of Speaking" to the "Ethnography of Communication."
5. Following Carbaugh (2005), we locate culture in communication practice; likewise, contributors to the book make claims about discourse concerning practices prominent in some scenes of social life in their respective field sites. Our claims are thus about cultural discursive practices, not populations of people. We, and some contributors to the book, use the term *U.S. American* to mean, following Carbaugh (2005), "practices prominent and potent in some scenes of the United States," though he uses the term *USAmerican* (p. xxiv). Note that contributors to the book use participant terms and conceptions to identify cultures and their meanings and thus vary. This is part of the work of cultural discourse analysis.
6. Note that these were developed in tandem with speech codes theory. For example, terms for speech events were suggested by Hymes as important entry points into cultural systems of communication, which were examined early on in ethnography of communication (EC) research (e.g., Katriel & Philipsen, 1981; Carbaugh, 1988) and became integral components of important EC theories, e.g., speech codes theory (Philipsen, 1992, 1997; Philipsen, Coutu, & Covarrubias, 2005), the terms for talk framework (Carbaugh, 1989), and CuDA (Carbaugh, 1988, 2005). To bring a CuDA approach, e.g., to examining cultural terms for communicative action there is a tripartite focus: the metapragmatic term, the act or event so labeled, and the potential messages of being, acting, relating, feeling, and dwelling they may radiate (Carbaugh, 2017b).
7. Note that Carbaugh identified the premises of being, acting, and relating as part of cultural discourses since his doctoral dissertation (1984) and first book, *Talking American* (1988). See also Carbaugh (1996) for elaborations of hubs of being and Carbaugh (1989, 2017b) on acting. He added premises of emotion in a (1990) article and elaborated this in 2017a. He introduced premises of dwelling in his (1996) book *Situating Selves*; see also

Carbaugh and Cerulli (2013) for an important extension. These were combined in his (1997) article with Gibson and Milburn, with the full system of premises used in CuDA to this day including being, acting, relating, feeling, and dwelling (see Scollo, 2011, for more information).

8. See Scollo (2011) for more information.

9. Carbaugh's (2005) book, *Cultures in Conversation*, received the National Communication Association International and Intercultural Communication Division Outstanding Book of the Year award in 2006 and the National Communication Association Language and Social Interaction Division Outstanding Scholarly "Old Chestnut" Publication award in 2015.

10. Our list of recent CuDA work is certainly not meant to be exhaustive, but representative.

11. See Carbaugh and Cerulli (2013, 2017) for more explanation of how to formulate cultural propositions and premises, and data-based examples of how to do so.

12. Note that cross-cultural comparative analysis has been a foundational feature of the ethnography of communication since its inception by Dell Hymes, particularly regarding his descriptive theory (1962, 1972), which enables such analysis. It has also featured strongly in the EC research program, speech codes theory, and CuDA, using cross-cultural analysis of communication practices to critique not only potential cultural bias in general or "universal" communication theories, but also on the basis of such analysis to create general communication theories that work across cultures. Terms for talk or metapragmatic action (Carbaugh, 1989, 2017) is one such example. Chapter 10 in this book by Covarrubias, Kvam, & Saito is another example. In it they use three cultural cases of agonistic discourse to develop a general theory of symbolic agonistics. Thus, at times, we may be reinforcing extant CuDA theory and methods and, at other times, we may be branching off to forge new paths.

13. Note that additional scholars wished to participate, but due to time constraints, had to withdraw.

14. Please note that in the remainder of this book all research participant names other than public figures have been changed for purposes of anonymity.

REFERENCES

Barnhart, R. K. (Ed.) (1988). *Chambers dictionary of etymology.* New York, NY: Chambers.

Boromisza-Habashi, D. (2007). Freedom of expression, hate speech, and models of personhood in Hungarian political discourse. *Communication Law Review, 7,* 54–74.

Boromisza-Habashi, D. (2011). Dismantling the antiracist "hate speech" agenda in Hungary: An ethno-rhetorical analysis. *Text & Talk, 31,* 1–19.

Boromisza-Habashi, D. (2012). The cultural foundations of denials of hate speech in Hungarian broadcast talk. *Discourse & Communication, 6,* 3–20.

Boromisza-Habashi, D. (2013). *Speaking hatefully: Culture, communication, and political action in Hungary.* University Park, PA: Pennsylvania State University Press.

Carbaugh, D. (1984). *On persons, speech, and culture: American codes of "self," "society" and "communication" on DONAHUE* (Unpublished doctoral dissertation). Seattle, WA: University of Washington.

Carbaugh, D. (1988). *Talking American: Cultural discourses on* Donahue. Norwood, NJ: Ablex.

Carbaugh, D. (1988/1989). Deep agony: "Self" vs. "society" in *Donahue* discourse. *Research on Language and Social Interaction, 22,* 179–212.

Carbaugh, D. (1989). Fifty terms for talk: A cross-cultural study. *International and Intercultural Communication Annual, 13,* 93–120.

Carbaugh, D. (1989/1990). The critical voice in ethnography of communication research. *Research on Language and Social Interaction, 23,* 261–282.

Carbaugh, D. (1990). Toward a perspective on cultural communication and intercultural contact. *Semiotica, 80,* 15–35.

Carbaugh, D. (1993). "Soul" and "self": Soviet and American cultures in conversation. *Quarterly Journal of Speech, 79,* 182–200.

Carbaugh, D. (1995). The ethnographic approach of Gerry Philipsen and associates. In D. Cushman & B. Kovacic (Eds.), *Watershed research traditions in human communication theory* (pp. 269–297). Albany, NY: State University of New York Press.

Carbaugh, D. (1996). *Situating selves: The communication of social identities in American scenes.* Albany, NY: State University of New York Press.

Carbaugh, D. (1999). "Just listen": "Listening" and landscape among the Blackfeet. *Western Journal of Communication, 63*(3), 250–270.

Carbaugh, D. (2002). "I speak the language of the universe": A universally particularizing form of native American discourse. In D. C. S. Li (Ed.), *Discourse in search of members: A festschrift in honor of Ron Scollon* (pp. 319–334). Lanham, MD: University Press of America.

Carbaugh, D. (2005). *Cultures in conversation.* New York, NY: Routledge.

Carbaugh, D. (2007). Cultural discourse analysis: Communication practices and intercultural encounters. *Journal of Intercultural Communication Research, 36*(3), 167–182.

Carbaugh, D. (2009). Coding personhood through cultural terms and practices: Silence and quietude as a Finnish natural way of being. In R. Wilkins & P. Isotalus (Eds.), *Speech culture in Finland* (pp. 43–61). Lanham, MD: University Press of America.

Carbaugh, D. (2012). Cultures in conversation: Cultural discourses of dialogue in global, cross-cultural perspective. In X. Dai & S. Kulich (Eds.), *Intercultural adaptation (I): Theoretical explorations and empirical studies* (pp. 115–133). Shanghai, China: Shanghai Foreign Language Education Press.

Carbaugh, D. (2017a). Cultural discourse and emotion: The death of bin Laden. Keynote address, New Horizons in the Ethnography of Communication Conference, New York, NY.

Carbaugh, D. (2017b). Terms for talk, take 2: Theorizing communication through its cultural terms and practices. In D. Carbaugh (Ed.), *The handbook of communication in cross-cultural perspective* (pp. 15–28). New York, NY: Routledge.

Carbaugh, D., & Cerulli, T. (2013). Cultural discourses of dwelling: Investigating environmental communication as a place-based practice. *Environmental Communication: The Journal of Nature and Culture, 7*(1), 4–23.

Carbaugh, D., & Cerulli, T. (2017). Cultural discourse analysis. In Y. Y. Kim (Gen. Ed.) & K. L. McKay-Semmler (Assoc. Ed.), *The international encyclopedia of intercultural communication* (pp. 1–9). Hoboken, NJ: John Wiley & Sons. doi: 10.1002/9781118783665.ieicc0117

Carbaugh, D., Gibson, T., & Milburn, T. A. (1997). A view of communication and culture: Scenes in an ethnic cultural center and private college. In B. Kovacic (Ed.), *Emerging theories of human communication* (pp. 1–24). Albany, NY: State University of New York Press.

Carbaugh, D., & Hastings, S. O. (1995). A role for communication theory in ethnographic studies of communication. In W. Leeds-Hurwitz (Ed.), *Social approaches to communication* (pp. 171–187). New York, NY: Guilford Press.

Carbaugh, D., Nuciforo, E. V., Saito, M., & Dong-Shin, S. (2011). Cultural discourses of "dialogue": The cases of Japanese, Korean and Russian. *Journal of International and Intercultural Communication, 4*(2), 87–108. doi: 10.1080/17513057.2011.557500

Carbaugh, D., & Rudnick, L. (2006). Which place, what story? Cultural discourses at the border of the Blackfeet Reservation and Glacier National Park. *Great Plains Quarterly, 26,* 167–184.

Carbaugh, D., & van Over, B. (2013). Interpersonal pragmatics and cultural discourse. *Journal of Pragmatics, 58,* 138–151. doi:10.1016/j.pragma.2013.09.013

Carbaugh, D., & Wolf, K. (1999). Situating rhetoric in cultural discourses. *International and Intercultural Communication Annual, 22,* 19–30.

Carey, J. (1975). *Communication and culture.* Thousand Oaks, CA: Sage.

Coutu, L. M. (2008). Contested social identity and communication in text and talk about the Vietnam War. *Research on Language and Social Interaction, 41*(4), 387–407.

Covarrubias, P. (2002). *Culture, communication, and cooperation: Interpersonal relations and pronominal address in a Mexican organization.* Lanham, MD: Rowman & Littlefield.

Covarrubias, P. O. (2008). Masked silence sequences: Hearing discrimination in the college classroom. *Communication, Culture & Critique, 1*(3), 227–252.

Gilbertz, S., & Milburn, T. (2011). *Citizen discourse on contaminated water, Superfund cleanups, and landscape restoration: (Re)making Milltown, Montana.* Amherst, NY: Cambria Press.

Gumperz, J. J. (1982). *Discourse strategies.* Cambridge, UK: Cambridge University Press.

Hymes, D. (1962). The ethnography of speaking. In T. Gladwin & W. Sturtevant (Eds.), *Anthropology and human behavior* (pp. 13–53). Washington, D.C.: Anthropological Society of Washington.

Hymes, D. (1972). Models of the interaction of language and social life. In J. J. Gumperz & D. Hymes (Eds.), *Directions in sociolinguistics: The ethnography of communication* (pp. 35–71). New York, NY: Holt, Rinehart & Winston.

Hymes, D. (1974). *Foundations in sociolinguistics: An ethnographic approach.* Philadelphia, PA: University of Pennsylvania Press.

Katriel, T., & Philipsen, G. (1981). "What we need is communication": "Communication" as a cultural category in some American speech. *Communication Monographs, 48*, 301–317.

LaGrande, S., & Milburn, T. (2003). "Keeping it real": Identity management strategies used by teens in conversation. *Communication Studies, 54*(2), 230–247.

Leeds-Hurwitz, W. (1984). On the relationship of the "ethnography of speaking" to the "ethnography of communication." *Research on Language and Social Interaction 17*(1), 7–32.

Leighter, J., & Castor, T. (2009). What are we going to "talk about" in this public "meeting"?: An examination of talk about communication in the North Omaha Development Project. *International Journal of Public Participation, 3*, 57–75.

Milburn, T. (2004). Speech community: Reflections upon communication. In P. J. Kalbfleisch (Ed.). *Communication Yearbook, 28*, (pp. 410–440). Washington, D.C.: International Communication Association.

Milstein, T. (2008). When whales "speak for themselves": Communication as a mediating force in wildlife tourism. *Environmental Communication, 2*(2), 173–192.

Milstein, T. (2011). Nature identification: The power of pointing and naming. *Environmental Communication, 5*(1), 3–24.

Molina-Markham, E. (2012). Lives that preach: The cultural dimensions of telling one's "spiritual journey" among Quakers. *Narrative Inquiry, 22*(1), 3–23.

Morgan, E. (2007). Regional communication and sense of place surrounding the Waste Isolation Pilot Plant. In B. C. Taylor, W. J. Kinsella, S. P. Depoe, & M. S. Metzler (Eds.), *Nuclear Legacies: Communication, Controversy, and the U.S. Nuclear Weapons Complex.* Lanham, MD: Lexington Books.

Philipsen, G. (1975). Speaking "like a man" in Teamsterville: Culture patterns of role enactment in an urban neighborhood. *Quarterly Journal of Speech, 61*, 13–22.

Philipsen, G. (1976). Places for speaking in Teamsterville. *Quarterly Journal of Speech, 62*, 15–25.

Philipsen, G. (1986). Mayor Daley's council speech: A cultural analysis. *Quarterly Journal of Speech, 72*, 247–260.

Philipsen, G. (1987). The prospect for cultural communication. In L. Kincaid (Ed.), *Communication theory: Eastern and Western perspectives* (pp. 245–254). New York: Academic Press.

Philipsen, G. (1989). Speech and the communal function in four cultures. *International and Intercultural Communication Annual, 13*, 79–92.

Philipsen, G. (1990). An ethnographic approach to communication studies. In B. Dervin, L. Grossberg, B. O'Keefe, & E. Wartella (Eds.), *Rethinking Communication (Vol. 2), Paradigm exemplars* (pp. 258–268). Newbury Park, CA: Sage.

Philipsen, G. (1992). *Speaking culturally.* Albany, NY: State University of New York Press.

Philipsen, G. (1997). A theory of speech codes. In G. Philipsen & T. Albrecht (Eds.), *Developing communication theories* (pp. 119–156). Albany, NY: State University of New York Press.

Philipsen, G. (2002). Cultural communication. In W. Gudykunst & B. Mody (Eds.), *Handbook of international and intercultural communication* (pp. 51–67). Newbury Park, CA: Sage.

Philipsen, G., & Carbaugh, D. (1986). A bibliography of fieldwork in the ethnography of communication. *Language in Society, 15*, 387–398.

Philipsen, G., Coutu, L., & Covarrubias, P. (2005). Speech codes theory: Revision, restatement, and response to criticisms. In W. Gudykunst (Ed.), *Theorizing about communication and culture* (pp. 55–68). Newbury Park, CA: Sage.

Poutiainen, S. (2005). Kulttuurista puhetta deittaamisesta. [Cultural talk about dating.] *Puhe ja kieli, 25*(3), 123–136.

Poutiainen, S., & Gerlander, M. (2009). Cultural dialectics in Finnish advising relationships. In R. Wilkins & P. Isotalus (Eds.), *Speech culture in Finland* (pp. 85–116). Lanham, MD: University Press of America.

Rudnick, L. (2001). "Hygge" and "jantevlon": An ethnographic study of two symbolic terms in the communication of Danish cultural identity and a Danish model of personhood (Unpublished master's thesis). Amherst, MA: University of Massachusetts Amherst.

Saito, M. (2009). Silencing identity through communication: Situated enactments of sexual identity and emotion in Japan (Doctoral dissertation). Saarbrücken, Germany: VDM Publisher.

Scollo, M. (2011). Cultural approaches to discourse analysis: A theoretical and methodological conversation with special focus on Donal Carbaugh's cultural discourse theory. *Journal of Multicultural Discourses, 6*(1), 1–32.

Suopis, C., & Carbaugh, D. (2005). Speaking about menopause: Possibilities for a cultural discourse analysis. In J. Duchan & D. Kovarsky (Eds.), *Diagnosis as a cultural practice* (Series in Language, Power, and Social Process) (pp. 263–276). Berlin, Germany: Mouton de Gruyter.

Townsend, R. M. (2006). Widening the circumference of scene: Local politics, local metaphysics. *KBJournal*. Retrieved from www.kbjournal.org/townsend

Weber, A. (June 8, 2011). Carbaugh named 2011 distinguished alumnus. University of Washington. Retrieved from http://www.com.washington.edu/2011/06/carbaugh-named-2011-distinguished-alumnus/

Wilkins, R. (2005). The optimal form: Inadequacies and excessiveness within the "asiallinen" [matter-of-fact] nonverbal style in public and civic settings in Finland. *Journal of Communication, 55*, 383–401.

Wilkins, R. J. (1999). "Assia" (matter-of-fact) communication: A Finish cultural term for talk in educational scenes (Unpublished doctoral dissertation). Amherst, MA: University of Massachusetts Amherst.

Wilkins, R., & Isotalus, P. (Eds.). (2009). *Speech culture in Finland.* Lanham, MD: University Press of America.

Witteborn, S. (2007). The expression of Palestinian identity in narratives about personal experiences: Implications for the study of narrative, identity, and social interaction. *Research on Language and Social Interaction, 40*(2–3), 145–170.

Witteborn, S. (2010). The role of transnational NGOs in promoting global citizenship and globalizing communication practices. *Language and Intercultural Communication, 10*(4), 358–372.

Witteborn, S. (2011). Discursive grouping in a virtual forum: Dialogue, difference, and the "intercultural." *Journal of International and Intercultural Communication, 4*, 109–126.

Wolf, K. (1998). Communicating culture: Public discourse and ritualized action in a Jewish community (Unpublished doctoral dissertation). Amherst, MA: University of Massachusetts Amherst.

Wolf, K., Milburn, T., & Wilkins, R. (2008). Expressive practices: The local enactment of culture in the communication classroom. *Business Communication Quarterly, 71*(2), 171–183.

Part I

Being

Chapter One

Speaking of Health in Singapore Using the Singlish Term *Heaty*

Evelyn Y. Ho, Sunny Lie, Pauline Luk,
and Mohan J. Dutta

Lee Kuan Yew, the first prime minister and founding father of Singapore, passed away on March 23, 2015. In the days immediately afterward, thousands of mourners lined up outside for 8 to 12 hours to walk by his body lying in state. Government officials and hundreds of volunteers directed the tens of thousands of mourners through orderly lines winding for miles around the Parliament area. When (authors) Luk and Ho joined the queue at around 2:30 p.m. in the blazing sun (5 days after his passing), the estimated wait was only 5 hours. As we snaked through the empty barricades that had been set up for earlier queuers, we were handed water bottles, orange juice, rain ponchos, umbrellas, candies, and snack bars. At one point, a group of teenagers were cutting apart corrugated cardboard into small rectangles and handing them to people to use as fans. It was typical Singaporean weather, sunny, then cloudy, then raining, then sunny again, all the while never dipping below 90 degrees Fahrenheit and at least the same in humidity.

At one point, when officials stopped our section of people to wait under the covering of the The Float@Marina Bay Grandstand, we took stock of our freebies. We had three bottles of water, a can of orange juice, two cardboard fans, two rain ponchos, four Mentos candies, and two cans of something with Chinese characters Ho could not read and a picture of a root/herb. Ho actually had not taken that can because she did not recognize it and it looked too medicinal to taste good. She asked Luk, "What is that?" "Oh, *liang cha*, do you want one? I grabbed two." "I don't know what that is?" "You know, it's for when you're too heaty, you drink this to cool off." Literally translated as "cooling tea," once Luk explained, Ho began to notice different forms of

3

"cooling" drinks all over the place. After having lived in Singapore for the last two months, Ho knew exactly what heaty was—the sore throat and pimple forming the morning after eating too much fried, spicy food—but it was not until we experienced the hours of sweat-drenching baking in the sun that Ho understood the need for all the different forms of *liang cha* that were sold in markets and vending machines throughout Singapore.

Our chapter analyzes the Singaporean key health term "heaty." Heaty is a Singaporean Singlish[1] term used to describe the following: (1) innate physical quality of a person, where one's body could be more "hot" or "cool," depending on one's inherent constitution or current health situation; (2) innate quality in certain foods; and (3) a state of being that results from consuming/not consuming certain foods. As one discusses being "heaty" or consuming "heaty" products, one is expressing concern over one's overall health and well-being, i.e., how to preserve it by responding to ever-changing conditions of "heatiness" and "coolness" found in one's body and the environment. In the next section, we will discuss the history of Chinese medicine and then present the methods used in this study.

CHINESE MEDICINE

Chinese medicine is a 2,000-plus-year-old health system that originated in China (Kaptchuk, 2000) but has evolved and changed over time as its practice has migrated throughout the world (Ward, 2012). Often called "traditional Chinese medicine" (TCM), historians of Chinese medicine recognize that TCM is actually the name of the codified system of medicine that was sanctioned by Mao Zedong after 1949 (Hsu, 2008). At that time, because of a shortage of biomedically trained practitioners in China and in a show of nation-building, the Communist government (the Chinese Communist Party) institutionalized texts, curriculum, and the practices of Chinese medicine (Hsu, 2008). However, the unifying name of TCM often obscures the varied history and spread of Chinese medicine theories, practices, and adaptations throughout the world and especially in Asia (Scheid, 2002). Therefore, in this chapter we will refer to the more broad practice as "Chinese medicine" or CM and use the term TCM when it refers to terminology that participants themselves used regardless of if they were referencing TCM or CM.

Singapore is a multicultural city-state in which ethnic Chinese make up 74.3% of the population (Department of Statistics Singapore, 2016) with nearly 99% of the Chinese in Singapore using some form of CM (Lim, Sadarangani, Chan, & Heng, 2005). Linguistically and perhaps culturally, the Chinese in Singapore have historically been divided into those who have been English-educated and those who are Chinese-educated. English-educated, mostly Straits Chinese, are more Western-oriented elites, with higher education and income, while Chinese-educated Chinese are mostly migrants who are often more traditional and more aligned with Chinese culture (Chang, 2015). While this dichotomy does hold true to some extent, since the 1990s, the rise of China has coupled with an increased (state) recognition of the cultural and economic value of "Chineseness" in Singapore (Chang, 2015). Regarding healthcare, this can be seen in Singaporeans' different ethnic groups' mix of biomedical ("modern") healthcare with various traditional Asian healing practices (Chang & Basnyat, 2015; Rittersmith, 2009). In fact, studies find that Chinese medicine is the most widely used traditional medicine being used regularly among Indians and Malays as well as Chinese (Lim et al., 2005).

In many Westernized countries, what is licensed and practiced as Chinese medicine comes from the standardized TCM practice. In Singapore, licensed TCM providers are educated and tested on this form of CM including Chinese herbal medicine and acupuncture. However, there also exists a robust practice of unlicensed forms of therapies and healthcare that in this chapter we name "folk or lay Chinese medicine." These practices include things like postpartum and other dietary therapies (including medicinal soups/drinks), body practices (such as cupping, massage, and foot reflexology), and movement/energy/spiritual practices (such as Qigong and TaiQi). What binds these practices together is their basis in a Chinese medical theory of health and the body. CM views the body holistically, drawing from a shared Asian philosophy of balance of opposing forces (e.g., yin versus yang or cold versus hot) (Kaptchuk, 2000). Within the body are vital energies (qi) and essences that flow through meridians (nonphysical) and are regulated by major and minor organs (most of which are also physical organs such as the heart, spleen, or kidney) (Kaptchuk, 2000). Because excess heat (heatiness) is widely recognized as a health imbalance, there are many foods and drinks commercially marketed for cooling and reducing heatiness. They are as ubiquitously found in stores as Gatorade in the United States. As much as people living in America know that when one sweats, one needs water, Singaporeans know that when one is feeling heaty, one needs to drink something cooling (e.g., barley tea, chrysanthemum drink, or *luo han guo*).

THEORY AND METHODOLOGY

Data Collection

Data were collected by the first and third authors (EYH and LPL) and two trained research assistants who conducted 6 months total of ethnographic fieldwork in Singapore in 2015 (5 months) and 2016 (1 month). These data come from a larger study called *Asian Pathways of Healing* conducted at the Center for Culture-Centered Approach to Research and Evaluation (CARE) under the leadership of the fourth author. The larger project uses a culture-centered approach (Dutta, 2007, 2008) to examine traditional health practices used throughout Singapore. The goal of the larger study is understanding health and healthcare in Singapore as a basis for forming community-based actions for addressing health disparities. Data for this paper were drawn from a portion of the study that examined informal, unlicensed, or lay forms of Chinese medicine and Chinese medicine–based self-care. A separate phase of the study examined licensed TCM usage such as seeing a TCM practitioner who dispenses herbs and/or acupuncture.

As part of the fieldwork, we collected 34 semistructured interviews with practitioners and users of TaiQi and Qigong, foot reflexology, tuina/massage, over-the-counter herbal medicine, herbal medicine tonics/soups, medicinal foods, and postpartum rituals. Questions focused on understandings and theories of health and illness and the meanings and importance of these therapies in relationship to any other health therapies. In early interviews, we asked participants (yes or no) if they considered the idea of heaty/cold foods part of CM. In later interviews, we iteratively developed questions to explicitly ask about the meaning and usage of heaty.

Almost all our interview participants (31/34) were ethnically Chinese and spoke and understood at least some Chinese. The other three participants were Indian, Malay, and Sikh. Ages of participants ranged from 20 to over 65 with about half (15) over age 56; there were 27 female and 7 male participants. Interviews were conducted in the participants' language of choice, which resulted in 16 Mandarin Chinese, 12 English, 5 mixed English-Mandarin, and 1 Cantonese interview. Interviews averaged 56 minutes with the shortest just under 10 minutes and the longest lasting 1 hour and 44 minutes. Audio files were transcribed and translated into English by trained research assistants.

Data Analysis

Cultural discourse analysis (Carbaugh, 2007), the main theoretical framework guiding this analysis, follows the intellectual tradition of the Hymesian program of work (Hymes, 1972; Philipsen & Carbaugh, 1986) and stands at the juncture of the theories of cultural communication (Philipsen, 1987, 2002) and communication codes (Philipsen, 1997; Philipsen & Coutu, 2005). The framework addresses questions relating to functional accomplishment, structure, and specific sequences pertaining to a particular practice.

In order to properly address these questions, Carbaugh (2007) suggests applying five modes of inquiry, which include descriptive and interpretive modes: the two modes we applied in our analysis for this chapter. As an elaboration on the interpretive mode, Carbaugh introduced the concept of *discursive hub* and *radiants of meaning* (Carbaugh & Cerulli, 2017). A discursive hub, or an explicit cultural term, contains within it radiants of meaning active to members of a speech community (Milburn, 2009). These radiants include meanings of identity, action, relations, emotion, and dwelling. Both the hub and radiants are conceptualized based on the premise that as we communicate, so do we engage in a metacultural commentary about (1) who we are, (2) how we are related to one another, (3) what we are doing, (4) how we feel, and (5) how we are placed in certain locations.

For descriptive analysis in this study, we extracted main themes from participants' discussion of the term "heaty" during interviews conducted on common CM practices in Singaporean daily life. All data were initially analyzed in English, but we went back and listened to those excerpts that were originally in Chinese in an effort to delineate whether participants were discussing "heaty" or an equivalent/similar Chinese term. Unless noted, all excerpts presented in this paper were originally discussed in English.

For interpretive analysis, we started by identifying the key term "heaty" as a hub of being in daily Singaporean communicative practice. We then explored other meanings radiating from it, namely acting, feeling, and dwelling (Carbaugh, 2007). Next, we combined key cultural terms to formulate *cultural propositions*, in which statements are created using participants' own words when describing and interpreting their own communicative behavior (Carbaugh, 2007). Lastly, we formulated *cultural premises*, in which we highlighted participants' beliefs about what exists, and/or what is proper or valued.

FINDINGS: DESCRIPTIVE ANALYSIS

Heaty as a Singaporean Singlish Cultural Term for Health

We begin our descriptive analysis with a comment from Genevieve, whom we believe adequately summarized multiple meanings of the term "heaty":

> Heaty and cold is the "make up" of the body system. But it's also influenced by the environment you live in (and) the food that you take. So I think if your body constitution has a certain base, and you are influenced by the outer environmental (factors) which is where you live in, the intake of food, then that will create a certain reaction because you really have a certain constitution of health.

As the abovementioned participant explained, heatiness is influenced by (1) the constitution of one's body, whether one is inherently "hot" or "cool"; (2) environmental factors including one's location and its climate (whether it is a "hot" or "cold" location); and last but not least, (3) one's food intake, whether one is consuming an imbalanced amount of "heaty" or "cooling" foods, as "heaty" is also used to describe inherent qualities of certain foods and the ways certain foods are prepared (e.g., frying increases heatiness). The term, especially as it is used in English, allows the speaker to quickly distinguish between speaking about health from a Western biomedical perspective where the temperature of the environment or nature of foods is not really relevant to health and instead index a CM perspective of health where heat-cool imbalance is an important measure of potential health/illness.

The daily usage of heatiness is based on a taken-for-granted, basic knowledge of CM, specifically assigned by participants to the notion of "yin" and "yang." Simplified to the idea of cool and warm respectively,[2] balancing yin and yang is necessary for the sake of one's health and general well-being. As Divya, who is Sikh, explained, "Chinese believe in yin and yang—it's the mixture of the hot and cold and it had to be in balance for your body to function. If one is over, say too much heaty stuff in your system, the yang is higher, you will develop problems." In other words, being heaty is an indication of large amounts of "yang" elements in one's body, which causes one to be in a state of imbalance. Like the more common concepts of yin and yang, "heaty" is an everyday term used to speak about health from this CM perspective.

Symptoms of someone suffering from heatiness range from pimples and rashes to sore throat and bodily fatigue. They manifest differently for different people. As Genevieve described, "the general symptoms, generic across could be like flared up, a lot of pimples or rashes . . . break[ing] out." Divya described "little cuts from inside (his/her mouth) (and) sores in the mouth" as indicators of an overheated body.

Feelings as an Internal Alarm for Heatiness

For the most part, detecting the state of heatiness is an act of self-diagnosis. Very rarely does one visit a TCM doctor to receive a prognosis of being "heaty."[3] Instead, one notices whether the abovementioned symptoms manifest in one's body. One also relies on one's feelings to alert oneself of this state of imbalance. As Lisa shared, "heaty and cool has got nothing to do with the weather, nor the temperature. It is what the internal body feels (like)." When one feels heaty, one does not feel well and has low energy: "When I say I'm heaty, I feel like . . . heaty, or sometimes you know when you don't want to talk too much so it's like, just feel very heaty" (Lisa). One needs to be attuned to one's feelings as one navigates the constantly changing balance in one's body.

Consuming Heaty Foods

A state of balance or imbalance is greatly influenced by what one consumes. As previously mentioned, the term "heaty" also refers to innate qualities of certain foods as well as how foods are cooked. If one consumes too much heaty food, one risks becoming too heaty and experiencing a variety of the abovementioned unpleasant symptoms. In their interviews, participants designated certain foods as heaty, such as

> rojak (mixed tropical fruit salad with spicy peanut and shrimp sauce), *cha kway teow* (stir-fried rice noodles), (and) durian (a type of tropical fruit). These are the norm heaty food that after we eat, our parents will tell us "很热啊, 不要吃那么多" [*hěn rè a, bùyào chī nàme duō*][very heaty ah, do not eat so much]. Like fried chicken, all these stuff. (Evan)

Fried food was often given as an example of food with heaty properties. As Christine explains, "heatiness is the food you eat. If you eat a lot of fried food, you will get heatiness." The way food is processed influences the food's degree of heatiness. When mentioning chestnut, a food that is commonly thought of as heaty, Chloe mentioned how instead of frying it she steamed it, therefore making it less heaty. Other heaty foods mentioned during the interviews include fruits such as lychee, meat dishes such as mutton soup, spices like ginger, and chocolate. Notably, these are also foods that most people find most tasty. In the excerpt above in which Evan code-switches from English to Mandarin and back to English, the switch occurs when Evan voices what "our parents" will say to us when we eat too much heaty (good) food. Relationally, it is the parent's role to remind children how to eat healthier and it is the children's (even adult children's) role to listen. In this way, heaty, especially as it relates to good eating practices, can be seen as a cultural persuadable (Fitch, 2003).

Not all heaty foods are bad for one's health. Since being healthy is about achieving balance, there are times when heaty foods need to be consumed, namely when one's body is too "cool" due to weather influences, having given birth (which will both be explained in later sections), or if someone has eaten too many foods with cooling properties. In these cases, when one's body is too cool, Mrs. Ho explains that one needs to "intake heaty foods to go back to normal." Heaty or cool foods can be ingested to *treat* imbalance. As an herbal medicine shop manager (Ma) described, it can also be used to *diagnose* an imbalance. Ma explained in Mandarin:

> A good doctor will cure an illness before it becomes an illness. For example, I see that you enjoy eating watermelon and drinking cold drinks, I will know that your body is too "cool" and you will be more susceptible to getting lung

related illnesses. So I will suggest that you consume some kind of food to balance that out even before you get the lung-related illnesses.

Watermelon is known in CM to be a food item with highly cooling properties. This excerpt is important in the level of specificity used. Stated in Mandarin, and by a practitioner (CM shop manager), coolness is specifically linked not just to "imbalance" broadly but specifically to lung imbalance. Before one suffers from a lung-related illness, thought to be suffered by people whose bodies are too "cool," one should consume heaty foods to regain one's "internal temperature balance." In this way, CM is *holistic* and can be preventative, taking into account imbalances in the whole person as opposed to focusing only on a particular biomedical illness in isolation (Kaptchuk, 2000). A person interested in maintaining his/her health and well-being needs to feed his/her body with what is needed at the moment, whether it is heaty or cooling foods.

It is important to note, however, that a person's awareness of heatiness does not automatically mean that the person believes in or uses more formal TCM practices. As a rudimentary practice, one can balance "heaty" and "cool" without much knowledge or acknowledgment of CM. As Shyan, a 20-something-year-old student, explained about the typical Singaporean, "Yeah, like I don't feel that my peers will actually go to TCM, ok the only extent that they go to is, 'Oh I feel very heaty today, I will drink 凉茶 (liang cha: cooling tea/herbal tea),' then they will go and buy the bottled ones they sell in school [canteen]." Unlike the hypothetical peer that Shyan is describing in this quote, she had a long history of using CM herself and in her family and heatiness was just one aspect of the larger system of CM.

Lack of Rest or Sleep

In addition to food consumption, heatiness can be caused by lack of sleep or rest in general. As one participant describes, "To me, heaty comes from either lack of sleep, lack of rest, and taking certain foods" (Theresa, English). When one has either "been taking on too many things or hasn't been sleeping well" (Lisa), one is prone to develop a state of heatiness. Lack of sleep or rest was described by participants as a possible secondary cause to heatiness, with consuming too much "heaty" food being the primary reason for one to find oneself in a state of imbalance.

Postpartum Dietary Practices

Postpartum dietary practices have a long tradition from the variety of cultures present in Singapore, especially among Chinese, Malay, and Indian women, with nearly 95% of Chinese mothers adhering to at least some traditional confinement dietary practices (Chen et al., 2013). Simply stated, after a woman gives birth, she is considered very cold, and warm or hot foods and food preparation as well as avoiding cold or "wind"[4] (in food, drink, and exposure such as air-conditioning and hair washing or showers) are essential for the health and recovery of the mother (Sandel, 2014). In the following quote from Esther, she describes the difference in body constitution postpartum using heaty as a descriptor:

> Esther (E): Yes, I kind of comfort myself that I'm doing this, because it's really like a punishment. The same type of food every day. Once or twice is nice, but every day for a month is not. And it's really heaty food, so actually like, say my husband. When my mum cooks pork knuckles and all that, all these food are really heaty, and the other people in my family will eat a bit, because I cannot finish a lot. So they do get sore throat and all that, but the mummy amazingly doesn't.
>
> Interviewer (I): You don't? So you don't get any signs of being too heaty?
>
> E: I don't. And I eat it for the whole month? So it's actually a sign to say that the body is actually quite cooling. And this heaty food actually helps to balance. So that to me, is a sign that my body is not so well. Whereas my husband, mum, and grandma will be like "okay, I will eat that," and they will get heaty and sick.

In this excerpt, Esther uses heaty as a measurement of her own imbalance that she experienced due to giving birth as well as a description of the foods needed to bring her back into balance. Although Esther refers to the pork knuckles "and all that" as being "really heaty," from an actual Chinese medicine perspective, it is typically the "all that"—cooking with large amounts of ginger and Chinese vinegar (both hot foods)—that is actually considered hot. As Esther explained later, "The ginger is to rid of the wind inside." However, pork knuckles on their own are fairly neutral (Pitchford, 2002), but are also known to help mothers produce breast milk and perhaps increase calcium intake. It is important to recognize that this fine distinction between the property of the food and the cooking process is not as relevant here to the conversation as the overall imbalance.

In the same interview, Esther also shared a story of drinking coconut water after she was six months pregnant because it was known to "help the body to cool down, and when you give birth, the baby will be pretty." Esther's first baby was born without any of the "fluffy white stuff" that some babies are born with, and she attributed this to her drinking coconut water at the right time. However, with her second baby, she waited to have the coconut drink because of some other complications. As she described it, "I had a coconut drink. Then the next moment, I had blood flow, and I had to be admitted. Although the gynae says that there was no correlation between the coconut water and the blood flow, it could be that my body is too cooling and all of a sudden it triggered this childbirth." In this case the knowledge of pregnancy practices related to heaty and cool foods helped Esther to make sense of a difficult and unexplainable health incident. In this case even though her gynecologist does not believe there is a connection, Esther uses this vocabulary to offer her own explanation of the cause of her sudden bleeding.

How the Weather Influences Heatiness

Aside from one's actions, heatiness is also influenced by one's environment and surroundings, mainly weather conditions. As Hong explains:

> So, in Singapore the weather is very very hot. It's very warm. I don't know how it is with western medicine. They don't really see the cold relation between eating um stuff like chocolates and fried stuff. Because in a hot day, I will get a sore throat very quickly. Yeah because these are like heaty stuff and I don't know how to explain these things to western people because these are very different concept and way of understanding.

The connection between hot weather and heaty foods leading to sore throats is very much a factor of Singaporean understanding of health. Singapore's tropical climate exposes one to a greater risk of heatiness than living in a country with four seasons, such as countries located in Europe. Hong continues by contrasting her experience in Europe:

1	Hong:	I remembered that many years ago, I spent winter in
2		Germany and is very cold
3	Interviewer:	Right, it was so cold.
4	H:	Yes and I remembered that I was eating chocolates every day
5		and nothing happen to me.
6	I:	Oh.
7	H:	Yes, if I did that in Singapore, confirm I will be sick within
8		two days.

Chocolate, as Hong described in the first extract, is considered a food item with high heaty properties, which most Singaporeans understand but which may be difficult to explain to Westerners because it is not part of Western medicine. According to Hong, when she ate chocolate every day during winter in Germany, she did not experience heatiness. In fact, it makes sense that Germans may not recognize heatiness not just because their (Western) medicine does not recognize it, but also because it just does not happen as often because of the cool weather. Yet as Hong describes, she firmly believes that if she were to eat this way in Singapore, she would fall sick—perhaps get a sore throat—in two days. In Singapore's tropical weather "heatiness is more frequent" (Christine). And in Singapore's CM-oriented view of every-day health, people are more attuned to the effects of heatiness. According to participants, colds are more frequent in the "West" (as in "Western" countries) due to seasonal weather. It is not easy to catch a cold in Singapore unless one is exposed to the cold air from air-conditioning for many hours.

INTERPRETIVE ANALYSIS

Next we move on to interpretive analysis where, following the CuDA frame-work, we extract cultural propositions (formed using participants' own words) and then formulate cultural premises (analytic statements about what exists and what is valued) to unveil deeply seated Singaporean cultural be-liefs surrounding health and well-being. The following is a list of cultural propositions (key terms in the participants' own words):

- Everyone has a "certain" "constitution" of "health"
- This "constitution" has a "base" of either "heaty" or "cool"
- "Heaty" and "cool" is what the "internal body" "feels" like
- "Heaty" and "cold" is the "make-up" of the "body" "system"
- This "system" is also "influenced" by "outer" "environmental" "factors"
- "Outer" "environmental" "factors" include "where you live" and "food intake"
- "Heatiness" is the "food" you "eat"
- If one "eats" a lot of "fried food," one will get "heatiness"
- "Heaty" comes from "lack of sleep," "lack of rest," and "taking certain foods"
- When one has been "taking on too many things" or "hasn't been sleeping well," one is more "prone" to becoming "heaty"
- If one has "too much" "heaty stuff" in one's "system," the "Yang element" will be higher
- When one is "cool," one "eats" something "heaty." When one is "heaty," one eats something "cool."
- Symptoms of "heatiness" include "pimples," "ulcers," "sore throat," "little cuts" and "sores" inside the "mouth"
- When the day is "so hot" and one "exposes" oneself to the "sun," one is more prone to becoming "heaty"
- When the day is "hot," one cooks something "cool"
- "Heaty" is a way of determining "healthy" and "unhealthy"

And these are the premises (based on *heaty* = discursive hub of being):

What Exists

- the body's constitution or a person's original state of heatiness or coolness, or balance (being)
- awareness of body's heatiness (feeling)
- outer environmental factors, such as weather and food consumption, which influence the body's state of heatiness and coolness (dwelling)
- internal factors, such as giving birth, which influence the body's state of heatiness and coolness or windiness (being and feeling)
- unexplained "illnesses" such as delivering a baby too early, which heaty and cool are used to explain (being)

What Is Valued

- the ability to regain balance when the body is either too hot or too cold/windy (acting)
- cooking and/or consuming certain foods for health (acting)
- the CM-derived knowledge of food properties: whether they are heat-inducing or cooling (being and acting)
- the ability to recognize when one is in a state of imbalance (feeling)
- the ability to measure or understand health and illness either currently experienced or in retrospect (being and feeling)
- the ability to adapt to outer environmental factors such as weather, exposure to sun, and food consumption (acting and dwelling)
- the ability to talk about health and illness as experienced in Singapore's hot, humid, tropical climate (acting and dwelling)

Figure 1.1 is a visual representation of the delineation of heaty as a discursive hub of *being*, with the radiants of *acting, feeling, dwelling*, and combinations of these meanings, radiating from the main hub as they are manifested in each premise.

DISCUSSION

Interviewees who participated in this project on CM displayed lay understandings of health as *balance.* This balance comes from CM ideas of yin and yang; however, as previous studies have also found, not all participants used this more technical vocabulary (Rittersmith, 2009) especially as they talked about heatiness in Singlish. While everyday Singaporeans may not always state the Chinese medicine explanation behind heatiness, they do use the

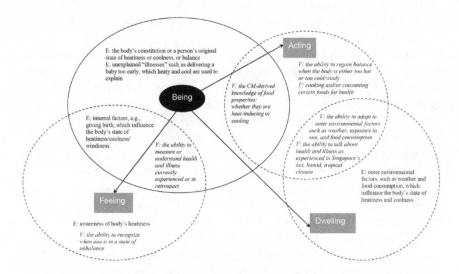

Figure 1.1. Hub (being) and radiants (feeling, acting, dwelling): E = what exists; V = *what is valued*.

terminology of heatiness as a taken-for-granted way to describe their everyday experiences of imbalance. This was most apparent when we recruited interviewees. When we approached prospective participants, there were times when people would state, "I don't use Chinese medicine." When we followed up, asking whether they consumed Chinese herbal and medicinal foods and drinks, then some would then say, "Oh, yes, of course I eat those." This knowledge of food properties, while based on CM, is knowledge passed down by way of family and/or society-at-large. The connection of heatiness to Chinese medicine is perhaps less important than the tie behind the term heatiness and being in Singapore. What is important to recognize here from a cultural and discursive perspective is how heatiness allows Singaporeans to talk about a state of being that would otherwise be unremarkable using a biomedical understanding of health and without needing to speak in Chinese.[5] Similar to what Flanigan and Alvarez present in their chapter (this volume) examining suicide forums, there are potentially important therapeutic implications to examining (in their case suicide or) heatiness as a cultural and communicative category that allows people agency in their health-related actions. While neither mainstream biomedicine nor English allows people a way to speak about the hot/cold balance in their bodies, for Singaporeans, it is worth noting that participants could have used the English terms *fire*, *hot*, or *heat*, all more direct translations of the various Chinese terms used (上火 *shang huo*, rising fire; 燥熱 *zhao re/zao re*, heat from heat and dryness; 熱 *re*, hot) to describe heatiness. However, by using a term that is not found in

English, the Singlish term heaty allows participants to quickly mark a difference—that they are talking about heatiness and not just the temperature words hot or fire.

Singaporeans' use of the term heaty confirms and reifies the existence of an alternative bodily constitution from that which is expected in Western biomedicine; a body that can be innately more hot, more cool, or in a state of balance. This "inner body" is greatly influenced by external factors, namely the weather and one's food consumption patterns, which can all be categorized along a spectrum of hot to cold. It is within this system of thinking about balance of opposing forces that the concept of heatiness resides. People are constitutionally born, some more warm/hot, others more cool/cold, and some in balance. In Singapore, because the weather is so hot, most people experience some form of heatiness regardless of their body's constitution. Valued acts of health maintenance include the ability to correctly detect a state of imbalance and take the necessary steps to regain balance in one's internal temperature. These steps include consuming (or avoiding) certain foods and beverages, combining opposing foods to avoid problems, cooking foods in particular ways, avoiding too much sun or air-conditioning, or getting enough rest. In fact, when illness does occur, participants can also use heatiness retrospectively to explain why illness occurred. All actions are taken in an effort to strike a balance between opposing forces of hot and cool in one's body and environment.

As a term for describing this everyday imbalance, heaty also functions as a communicative tool for laypeople to engage with CM without requiring the technical knowledge and vocabulary that comes with fully understanding Chinese medicine. In this way, it recognizes the everyday ways that people engage in their own healthcare, often outside of formal medical contexts. For example, as we have demonstrated in this chapter, heatiness can be caused by the outside weather, foods, food preparation, and having a baby. However, based on a CM understanding of health, a completely balanced person should be able to eat heaty foods and not end up with mouth ulcers or headaches. If and when patients go to see a TCM practitioner, they are not diagnosed with heatiness per se, but rather with something more technically complex such as liver fire that may have been exacerbated if there is underlying dampness. These more technical distinctions are not necessary if one uses the simple term heaty.

Because of the everydayness of the concept of heaty, in Singapore, a large amount of food and health-related products are sold to everyday consumers. Besides the *liang cha* described in the opening and by participants, not only are there chain herbal medicine shops across Singapore that prepackage and prebrew herbal remedies for heatiness, but the grocery stores and convenience stores also carry a wide range of supposed cooling drinks, which some participants dismissed as just sugar water. In addition, there is a whole market for professional "confinement ladies," often from Malaysia, who will come to live with a family for 30 days to cook, tend to, massage (a Malay postpartum practice), and make sure new moms boost their strength and rebuild their constitutions following childbirth.

However, this large and well-developed market for treating heatiness may actually detract from its legitimacy as a "medical" treatment. In Singapore, people are required to obtain MCs (medical certificates) for missing work or school. However, the only place to get an MC is from a biomedical provider. As Xu, a CM provider said, "This is very strange. TCM can cure you but we can't give them MCs." In a place with all the available remedies and every-day knowledge to treat heatiness, it is not legitimized fully as an illness such that one could avoid work obligations because of it. Thus, its ubiquity may actually be part of why it is not understood as specialty or professional treatment. Future research should examine this potential connection between the availability of Chinese medicinal products and its decrease in profession-al status.

This project was limited in the fact that our interviewees were all people who already used some form of "lay Chinese medicine." Future research should examine the use of heaty among the mainstream population of Sin-gaporeans, paying special attention to its use intergenerationally. Research has shown that young Singaporeans are losing heritage language skills in favor of English (Ng, 2014). While heaty is a useful Singlish term for lay CM users, future research should examine to what extent it may also be a result of a variety of factors including the loss of Chinese language skills in younger Singaporeans, moving away from CM, both, or something else more com-plex. In addition, because we did not collect naturally occurring talk, we do not have many examples of how heaty is actually used in relationships and among family members maybe to support or to critique others' behaviors. At least for the time being, we understand heaty to be a positive linguistic resource for Singaporeans to actively engage in their own health participa-tion.

NOTES

We would like to thank all our research participants for being willing to share their experiences with Chinese medicine with us. Thank you also to two research assistants, Clarissa Tan Yue Qian and ZhiQi Yeo, for helping collect data. This project was made possible because of a sabbatical leave and faculty development funds (for EYH) from the University of San Francis-co. The project was funded by the Office of the Provost, National University of Singapore.

1. Singlish refers to the colloquial/creole form of English used in Singapore that includes Hokkien words and Malay grammar, which some argue is most useful for expressing practical everyday experiences such as bodily functions or states (see Goh, 2016).

2. Yin and yang refer to much more than just cool and warm. Yin is the night, passive, restful dialectical half while yang is the day, active, and movement side. See Kaptchuk (2000) for a more extensive explanation.

3. However, a Chinese medicine practitioner would certainly diagnose heatiness if it were there. In everyday experience, heatiness is not serious enough to go especially to a practitioner to be treated (see Rittersmith, 2009).

4. Wind is the English translation of 风(feng) and is one of the causes of illness and imbalance related to too much movement or a lack of stillness. To read more about wind, see Kaptchuk (2000).

5. As a Chinese American, I (Ho) know about *heaty*, but I have never used the English term to describe the concept. Instead, in my family, we use the Chinese term 火气 (*huo qi* or literally fire energy), and if I described this in English, I would say "huo qi" (Ho, 2004).

REFERENCES

Carbaugh, D. (2007). Cultural discourse analysis: Communication practices and intercultural encounters. *Journal of Intercultural Communication Research, 36*(3), 167–182.

Carbaugh, D., & Cerulli, T. (2017). Cultural discourse analysis. In Y. Kim (Ed.) & K. L. McKay-Semmler (Assoc. Ed.), *The international encyclopedia of intercultural communication* (pp. 1–9). Hoboken: NJ: John Wiley & Sons. doi: 10.1002/9781118783665.ieicc0117

Chang, L., & Basnyat, I. (2015). Negotiating biomedical and traditional Chinese medicine treatments among elderly Chinese Singaporean women. *Qualitative Health Research, 25*(2), 241–252. doi:10.1177/1049732314551991

Chang, P.-C. (2015). Rewriting Singapore and rewriting Chineseness: Lee Guan Kin's diasporic stance. *Asian Ethnicity, 16*(1), 28–42. doi:10.1080/14631369.2014.1001148

Chen, L. W., Low, Y. L., Fok, D., Han, W. M., Chong, Y. S., Gluckman, P., . . . van Dam, R. M. (2013). Dietary changes during pregnancy and the postpartum period in Singaporean Chinese, Malay and Indian women: The GUSTO birth cohort study. *Public Health Nutrition*, 1–9. doi:10.1017/s1368980013001730

Department of Statistics Singapore. (2016). *Singapore in figures 2017*. Singapore. Retrieved from http://www.singstat.gov.sg/docs/default-source/default-document-library/publications/publications_and_papers/reference/sif2017.pdf

Dutta, M. J. (2007). Communicating about culture and health: Theorizing culture-centered and cultural sensitivity approaches. *Communication Theory, 17*(3), 304–328. doi:10.1111/j.1468-2885.2007.00297

Dutta, M. J. (2008). *Communicating health*. Cambridge, England: Polity Press.

Fitch, K. L. (2003). Cultural persuadables. *Communication Theory, 13*(1), 100–123.

Goh, R. B. H. (2016). The anatomy of Singlish: Globalisation, multiculturalism and the construction of the "local" in Singapore. *Journal of Multilingual and Multicultural Development, 37*(8), 748–758. doi:10.1080/01434632.2015.1133628

Ho, E. Y. (2004). *"French fries have too much huo qi": An ethnographic study of the discourse of traditional Chinese medicine* (Doctoral dissertation). Retrieved from ProQuest Dissertations & Theses Global. (Order No. 3129302).

Hsu, E. (2008). The history of Chinese medicine in the People's Republic of China and its globalization. *East Asian Science, Technology and Society, 2*(4), 465–484.

Hymes, D. (1972). Models of interaction of language and social life. In J. Gumperz & D. Hymes (Eds.), *Directions in sociolinguistics: The ethnography of communication* (pp. 35–71). New York, NY: Holt, Rinehart and Winston.

Kaptchuk, T. J. (2000). *The web that has no weaver* (2nd ed.). New York, NY: Congdon & Weed.

Lim, M. K., Sadarangani, P., Chan, H. L., & Heng, J. Y. (2005). Complementary and alternative medicine use in multiracial Singapore. *Complementary Therapies in Medicine, 13*(1), 16–24.

Milburn, T. (2009). *Nonprofit organizations: Creating membership through communication*. Cresskill, NJ: Hampton Press.

Ng, C. L. P. (2014). Mother tongue education in Singapore: concerns, issues and controversies. *Current Issues in Language Planning, 15*(4), 361–375. doi:10.1080/14664208.2014.927093

Philipsen, G. (1987). The prospect for cultural communication. In D. Kincaid (Ed.), *Communication theory from the Eastern and Western perspectives* (pp. 245–254). San Diego, CA: Academic Press.

Philipsen, G. (1997). A theory of speech codes. In G. Philipsen & T. L. Albrecht (Eds.), *Developing communication theories* (pp. 119–156). Albany, NY: SUNY Press.

Philipsen, G. (2002). Cultural communication. In W. Gudykunst & B. Mody (Eds.), *Handbook of international and intercultural communication* (pp. 51–67). London and New Delhi: Sage.

Philipsen, G., & Carbaugh, D. (1986). A bibliography of fieldwork in the ethnography of communication. *Language in Society, 15*, 387–397.

Philipsen, G., & Coutu, L. M. (2005). The ethnography of speaking. In K. L. Fitch & R. E. Sanders (Eds.), *Handbook of language and social interaction* (pp. 355–381). Mahwah, NJ: Erlbaum.

Pitchford, P. (2002). *Healing with whole foods: Asian traditions and modern nutrition.* Berkeley, CA: North Atlantic Books.

Rittersmith, A. (2009). Contextualising Chinese medicine in Singapore: Microcosm and macrocosm. *Journal of the Anthropological Society of Oxford: Online, 1*, 1–24.

Sandel, T. (2014). Enacted social support and cultural practices among women and families observing a postpartum rest in Taiwan. *China Media Research, 10*, 48–59.

Scheid, V. (2002). *Chinese medicine in contemporary China.* Durham, NC: Duke University.

Ward, T. (2012). Multiple enactments of Chinese medicine. In V. Scheid & H. MacPherson (Eds.), *Integrating East Asian medicine into contemporary healthcare* (pp. 55–74). Edinburgh, Scotland: Churchill Livingstone Elsevier.

Chapter Two

Applying Cultural Discourse Analysis to an Online Community

LinkedIn's Cultural Discourse of Professionalism

Tabitha Hart and Trudy Milburn

LinkedIn has a strong presence in the online lives of adults around the world; according to the Pew Research Center, 25% of all Americans use it (Greenwood, Perrin, & Duggan, 2016). However, with its nearly 500,000,000 members worldwide at the time of this writing (LinkedIn, 2017a), over 70% of which are located outside the United States (LinkedIn, 2017a), LinkedIn is arguably the most popular social media site for work-related purposes. According to the company itself, the primary purpose of LinkedIn "is to connect the world's professionals to make them more productive and successful" (LinkedIn, 2016a). As ethnographers of communication, we were intrigued by LinkedIn's emphasis on the concept of *professionalism,* not only as applied to the nature and purpose of its network, but also in relation to the identities of its users and the ideal communicative behaviors to be performed in its virtual community. Having done work in the area of usability research and design (Milburn, 2015), we were also interested in how the LinkedIn platform was implicated in ideas about—as well as the performance of—professionalism. Using the theoretical and methodological tools of the ethnography of communication (EC) and cultural discourse analysis (CuDA), we studied what it meant to be professional and to perform professionalism on LinkedIn. In so doing, we discovered that a particular *cultural discourse—a discourse of professional communication—*was expressed and promoted via the LinkedIn platform. In this chapter, after reviewing literature on professional talk and its settings, we will present our analysis of this discourse and the way it was encoded into the LinkedIn platform. Specifically, we will show how an ideal LinkedIn user performs a professional self, engages in professional communicative behaviors, and connects with other professionals via LinkedIn.

PROFESSIONAL TALK AND ITS SETTINGS

Among discursive research about institutional talk, we find descriptions about how individual employees' identities are shaped and displayed (Drew & Heritage, 1993; Dyer & Keller-Cohen, 2000; Holmes, 2006; Holmes, Stubbe, & Vine, 1999). The two main ways professionalism is characterized are within an expressive system of work (see Carbaugh, 1996) or as a display or performance of speaker competence (see Blazkova, 2011). Mada and Saftoiu (2012) summarize the way "professional communication" can be accomplished through either individual speech acts or joint, pragmatic actions. However, still missing are descriptions of professionalism in general, i.e., how professional selves are displayed outside of the organizations in which they work. Is professionalism an identity category that transcends a specific organization? Can one's professional identity be shaped by an organization for which an employee does not work?

Creating a professional self is not done in isolation. It presumes at least a community of like-minded professionals or what has been theoretically described as a community of practice (Lave & Wenger, 1991) who will understand one's display of personhood. LinkedIn is such a community, albeit an online one, providing a *setting* where participants can display their membership and their professional identities in a specific, locally comprehensible way. Approaching a technological platform as a setting is a useful way to make sense of it as a scene for social activity, one replete with roles, rules, premises, and norms. By setting we refer to Hymes's SPEAKING heuristic (1964, 1972), which helps ethnographers of communication categorize different *facets* or aspects of communication situations. Each letter of the mnemonic (S-P-E-A-K-I-N-G) represents different communication-related variables or categories, with the "S" referring to "setting" or "scene," i.e., the "place of a speech act and, in general [its] physical circumstances" (Hymes, 1972, p. 60). While in Hymes's time the setting and scene denoted the physical location in which communication activity took place, the concept is valid in describing online spaces as well (Beneito-Montagut, 2011; Herring, 2007; Pfister & Soliz, 2011), whether immersive multidimensional virtual worlds or significantly "flatter" online spaces (Boellstorff, 2008; Hart, 2015; Paolillo, 1999; Tosca, 2002).

Approaching LinkedIn's technological platform as a setting makes sense from an EC perspective, because it foregrounds the assumption that such spaces have their own particular rules, norms, premises, and meanings pertaining to communicative conduct. Hymes's concept of a setting was a "psychological" space linked with "cultural definition[s] of an occasion" (Hymes, 1972, p. 60). Settings are cognitive as well as spatial (or physical) places, and they are intricately linked with scripts and rules of communicative conduct. Settings are mental constructs that we associate with guidelines for communicative behavior. In other words, the people present in a given setting generally have ideas in mind about their roles there, as well as the norms, rules, and premises governing communicative conduct in that place. What's more, in an online environment, the norms, premises, and rules guiding communicative conduct may actually be encoded into the platform itself (Hart, 2016). This is because interfaces are a means not only of presenting information, options, and activities to the user, but also of organizing information, options, and activities. The very design of an online platform serves to enable and/or constrain communicative action, allowing some activities and restricting others; in this way interfaces are implicated in users' interpretational and sense-making processes (Beer, 2008; Gane & Beer, 2008; Manovich, 2001, 2003). Whether explicitly or not, the technological platform supporting user interactions is implicated in local understandings of sanctioned communicative behavior.

METHODS

Data Collection

When people make use of an interactive online platform such as LinkedIn, they must navigate what is possible, what is permissible, and what is not. This is especially true within an unfamiliar online community where a user might be a new and/or novice member, and/or when the protocols for engaging in that community are frequently changing. For users and researchers alike there is a learning curve to determine how interactions are supposed to proceed and what they are supposed to signify. In our case, applying CuDA to LinkedIn's community required carefully investigating users' experiences as well as the online setting on and through which those experiences occur (here, an interactive, technology-mediated platform). Drawing on Hart's (2015) methods for analyzing the ways in which digital interfaces enable and constrain users' experiences, we therefore engaged in a two-pronged approach to data collection.

First, we collected users' stories of and perspectives on their experiences of professionalism on LinkedIn. To do this we circulated a call for interviewees among our own social and professional networks, using Facebook, LinkedIn, and other networking tools that we had access to, such as intraorganizational Listservs. Once we began interviewing those who responded to our initial calls, we used snowball sampling to identify other likely interview candidates. In total we interviewed 20 LinkedIn users who, when geographical location as well as linguistic/cultural backgrounds were taken into account, represented a variety of different countries, including Australia, Britain, Canada, China, Estonia, Germany, Japan, and the United States.

In conducting the interviews, we learned that our interviewees ranged from experts who used LinkedIn frequently for complex communication tasks, to novices who used the platform infrequently and were not familiar with many of its functionalities. Because our purpose in conducting the interviews was to elicit all types of user experiences with the platform, as well as a range of perceptions on it, we utilized open-ended interview questions that allowed users to discuss actions and/or emotions. To this end, we asked questions that began with their origins of use, addressed specific goals and purposes, and concluded with thoughts on future expectations.

All the interviews were conducted in English and were done either in person or remotely using Skype. When participants granted us permission, we recorded the interviews using either Apple's Voice Memos app (in person) or Audio Hijack Pro (remote). All recordings were transcribed; in those cases where no recording was made, we transcribed our notes. All recordings, notes, and transcriptions were added to our data set.

In the second phase of data collection, we focused on the LinkedIn platform itself. Drawing on our training in the ethnography of communication, we engaged in participant observation by spending time on LinkedIn using our own accounts, from which vantage point we studied the platform. We collected screenshots and jotted down notes, paying attention to the various communication options and protocols for what LinkedIn terms a basic account. We also pored over the public LinkedIn help pages at https://www.linkedin.com/help/linkedin, which provided detailed descriptions of the platform's functionalities, as well as protocols for its use. Finally, we collected other materials pertaining to the platform and its use, including LinkedIn's terms of service, the account-related emails that we (as LinkedIn users) received, and how-to materials for LinkedIn account holders from other professional development sites. All these materials were added to our data set.

Data Analysis

Our data analysis process was multistep. The initial data analytic tool that we used in our examination of *professionalism* is what Carbaugh (1989) described as *terms for talk* or "communication codes for talk and pragmatic action" (Carbaugh, 2017; Carbaugh, Nuciforo, Saito, & Shin, 2011). We used this conceptual frame to determine what counted as *professional* talk on the LinkedIn platform. Accordingly, we asked, "are there cultural terms for communication" in use and if so, what kinds of communication-based practices do those cultural terms point to (Carbaugh, 2017; Carbaugh et al., 2011,

p. 88)? To discover cultural terms and their concomitant cultural practices, we began by scrutinizing the data set for particular terms suggesting a way to communicate properly and *professionally* on LinkedIn, such as "networking," "connecting," etc. Specifically, we examined terms related to professional talk as they occurred in the interview data, including how such terms figured into our participants' accounts and experiences. Additionally, we examined the LinkedIn platform to identify which forms of professional talk existed there, which practices they involved, and how they were enabled or discouraged by the platform's build. In essence, we analyzed how local ideas and practices of professionalism were encoded into the LinkedIn platform itself.

Next, we applied the conceptual suite of *meanings, premises, and rules pertaining to communicative conduct*, drawn from both speech codes theory (Philipsen, 1992, 1997; Philipsen, Coutu, & Covarrubias, 2005) and CuDA (Carbaugh, 2017). In speech codes theory (SCT), a speech code is defined as "a system of socially constructed symbols and meanings, premises, and rules, pertaining to communicative conduct" (Philipsen, 1997, p. 126). EC researchers use SCT and the concept of *speech codes* to examine situated communication within particular communities, and to understand the ways that its strategic use enables community members to develop shared understandings and coordinate their activity (Fitch, 1998; Philipsen, 1997; Schwartzman, 1989). Similarly, in CuDA all communication practices involve underlying (cultural) meanings and premises, the discovery and the description of which is a foundational step in the research venture (Carbaugh, 2017). For our study, we examined patterns in the meanings (i.e., significance) of professional talk on LinkedIn, the premises underlying professional talk (i.e., the assumptions about its value, operation, etc.), and the rules governing its execution.

Finally, we used CuDA to direct our attention to three particular discursive hubs—being/identity, doing/action, and relating (Carbaugh & Cerulli, 2018; Carbaugh, 2017)—as they emerged from the data. Discursive hubs refer to previously identified sites of cultural meaning. To address questions about identity we focused on the being hub, analyzing what it meant to be professional on LinkedIn, including how a professional self ought to be displayed. To address questions about action we focused on the doing hub, asking what "professional" behavior entailed, including what specific acts a professional ought (or ought not) to engage in on LinkedIn. Finally, to address questions about how people interact we focused on the relating hub, studying how users were expected to engage "professionally" with one another. From there, evidence of a cultural discourse emerged, conveyed both explicitly and implicitly by the company, applied by our interviewees, and encoded into the LinkedIn platform itself.

FINDINGS

The purported utility of having a LinkedIn account is to become "more productive and successful" in one's professional persona (LinkedIn, 2016a). Here, *professional* is equated with labor and employment. Of course, LinkedIn users need not be employed to use the site; however, LinkedIn is explicitly designed to showcase those facets of a user's life that relate to their careers, whether past, present, or future. The three CuDA hubs that directly pertained to professionalism on LinkedIn as reflected in our data were strategically displaying one's professional self (identity); connecting with other users (action); and engaging with other users in professional ways (relating). Here we will describe our findings on each hub, including how each hub was encoded into the platform.

Displaying the Professional Self (Identity)

Creating a profile is the first step to using LinkedIn; without one only a limited amount of information on the platform can be searched for or viewed. To create and modify one's profile, LinkedIn offers a worksheet-style interactive web page with which a LinkedIn user can add, edit, or remove information simply by clicking on the relevant section of the page. The key information shared via a LinkedIn profile is featured at the top of each profile page, i.e., what LinkedIn terms the "Intro" section. The Intro section highlights information that is foundational to a LinkedIn profile: a profile photo, first and last name, current position, geographical region, and professional industry. Beneath the Intro is the "Experience" section, where users can list their past and present positions; for each one, users can enter the job title, the company, start and end dates, and a brief description of the position. Following the Experience section is "Education," where users can list any degrees earned. Progressing down the profile page, other possible sections to include in a user's profile are "Featured Skills and Endorsements," "Recommendations" (received and/or given), Accomplishments, Interests, and so on. Additional sections in a user profile can include things like Publications, Certifications, Courses, Projects, Honors & Awards, Test Scores, Languages, etc.

The more information users include in their profiles, the greater their "Profile Strength": a built-in "Profile Strength meter" measures "how robust [one's] profile is" and provides "recommendations on which profile sections to add to improve the discoverability of [one's] profile in search results and increase profile search appearances" (LinkedIn, 2017e). When a user's profile is deemed complete, LinkedIn rates it as "All-Star." Taken as a whole, the profile sections available to LinkedIn users affirm what facets of a person's life are relevant to their professional identity. Simultaneously, the categories that are omitted from a LinkedIn profile—such as marital and/or family status, hobbies, interests outside of work, etc.—make an explicit statement about what is considered to be irrelevant to one's professional self in this environment. As one interviewee reported (all names have been changed):

> If somebody sets up a LinkedIn profile in the way that it was probably de-signed to be done—it's an online resume—so you are seeing everybody's skills and everybody's work they have done throughout their career. You are basically seeing what somebody's skills or somebody's interests, or some-body's talents are. . . . You are not seeing whether Joanie has three kids, how much Ginny loves to bake bread, how much Joanie loves watching *Dancing with the Stars*. It's all about their professional—all their career based skills and talents. (Trisha)

In this way, the LinkedIn user interface is encoded with expectations for what comprises a professional identity, and it explicitly directs users to dis-play the appropriate facets of that identity, and to suppress (omit) those facets that are irrelevant.

As users build out their profiles, a key rule in operation is that they must portray their professional self *truthfully*. This is explicitly communicated in LinkedIn's User Agreement, where under section 8.2 (Don'ts) it states that each user agrees not to "create a false identity on LinkedIn"; "misrepresent [their] identity (e.g., by using a pseudonym), [their] current or previous posi-tions, qualifications or affiliations with a person or identity"; or "create a member profile for anyone other than [themselves] (a real person)" (Linke-dIn, 2017h). This rule was not lost on our interviewees, all of whom ex-pressed the assumption that LinkedIn should only be used to display one's real professional self. As another interviewee explained:

> Everything that I want expose[d] professionally in my real life, in my real professional life, would go onto my [LinkedIn] profile So anything I would reveal in a professional encounter I would also consider putting it on my LinkedIn profile. My photos, what skills I have, what my goals are, what my education is, my professional background, my previous jobs, maybe even my stance on certain technologies. . . . I would stress that [people] should use LinkedIn in such a way that it reflects their professional life and not something else, and that they don't use it as—that they don't lie on their profile or that they don't exaggerate and that they try to have it reflect their true business and their true professional person-personality. (Matthew)

In fact, in the event that a user detects "inaccurate" or false information on another user's profile, they may "file a formal complaint" using LinkedIn's Notice of Inaccurate Profile Information form, on which they must assert how they "know [the] account or other information to be inaccurate or false" (LinkedIn, 2017c). All such forms are said to be reviewed by the company's "Trust and Safety" team (LinkedIn, 2017g).

Although the platform is not equipped to automatically verify the truth-fulness of a user's LinkedIn profile, it does include built-in mechanisms that could encourage honesty in the portrayal of one's professional self. There is, for example, LinkedIn's Skill Endorsements feature, which allows users to list their own proficiencies, which can then be "endorsed" by any 1st-degree connections. Users can also use the Recommendations feature either to elicit recommendations from and/or give them to 1st-degree connections (a feature that we will return to shortly). Here again, the expectation of our interview-ees was that users be honest in their evaluations of one another, such that these profile features would represent their "true" or "actual" skills and qual-ities. Some interviewees took this so seriously that they refused to endorse their connections unless they were absolutely certain of the genuineness of their purported qualities. Without this honesty, one interviewee said, she would "just [be] adding mush" to someone's profile. (Trisha)

Connecting with Others (Action)

As a social networking site, LinkedIn's explicit purpose is to connect its users with one another. On the LinkedIn platform, to *connect* means to estab-lish a symbolic link with another user, thereby demonstrating an association or a relationship. LinkedIn displays only three types of connections: 1st-degree (users are directly connected to one another); 2nd-degree (users are not directly connected to one another, but they share a 1st-degree connec-tion); and 3rd-degree (users have a 2nd-degree connection in common). If two users are not connected in any of these ways, then the default status of their relationship is "Out of Network," which means that the two users have no recognized connection on LinkedIn. The number of connections that a user has is prominently noted at the top of the profile page, up to 500 (be-yond that the number is displayed simply as 500+).

Knowing the local rules for how and when to connect with other LinkedIn users is fundamental to being a competent member of this community. On the one hand, as our interviewees reported, it can be tempting to make con-nections less discriminately with the simple aim of enlarging one's network. However, from the administrative viewpoint, it is not appropriate to connect with just anyone. On the contrary, LinkedIn explicitly instructs users to con-nect only with "contact[s] you know personally and who you trust on a professional level" (LinkedIn, 2017b). LinkedIn's User Agreement goes so far as to forbid connecting with unknown users, also prohibiting "solicit[ing] email addresses or other personal information" from unknown LinkedIn us-ers, as well as "us[ing] LinkedIn invitations to send messages to people who don't know you or who are unlikely to recognize you as a known contact" (LinkedIn, 2017h). According to LinkedIn, this rule is in place because only known and trusted contacts can be considered "quality connections," and only they can be "trust[ed] to be part of [one's] network" (LinkedIn, 2017d). This underlying rule of knowing and trusting one's connections was also communicated by our interviewees:

- I choose not to allow connections of anyone that I have not personally done business with, or have shared information, or provided resources to in some form or shape. (Dustin)
- My own policy [on having LinkedIn connections] is people I have actually worked with are the only people I have [in my network]. (Adam)
- [In my network] it would probably be past colleagues that I actually worked with, within the same company [and] customers that I worked with. . . . I don't know if I would use it initially to contact an unknown person. I probably would contact people that I've had, you know, a previous relationship with somehow. (Molly)
- I tend not to connect with people who I don't know, even if I know them through somebody else. I tend not to have too many connections with people who I vaguely know. When I get connection requests, unless I know them or they are familiar to me I tend not to accept, unless they are people who I've heard about. For example, I might have heard about somebody mentioning a chap who is the HR director or the L&D director at HP or Nokio, or something, and they've mentioned this guy's got really interesting ideas, and then if I come across them, or they have asked to connect to me, then I'll accept. But if it's just some guy I've never heard of before then I tend to ignore them. (Charles)
- Do I know them and have I worked with them for over, let's say, a year? In other words I might have to write a reference for them—do I have the capability to do that? People that I've worked with for a week or whatever, or maybe someone [from a] company [that] once sold me something—I just ignore those people. But people that I have worked with for more than a year, I accept their LinkedIn requests. (Richard)

As the excerpts above illustrate, our interviewees recognized and followed LinkedIn's suggested strategies for making network connections.

The expectation that LinkedIn networks must be comprised only of known and trusted others is encoded into the platform in explicit ways. For example, when users click on the "My Network" tab, LinkedIn displays a "people you may know" field, listing other people who might be "known" to that user. Beneath each person's name and information is a direct invitation to either "Connect" with them or "Invite" them to join LinkedIn. Users are also asked to consider importing their email address books from their devices into LinkedIn via the "Grow Your Network" page, a feature described by LinkedIn as "the fastest way to grow your network," with known (and presumably) trusted people. Using these data, LinkedIn also makes suggestions

for additional known contacts by inferring relationships from "shared connections or shared managers, employers, educational institutions and other
such factors." While users can make connection requests to anyone, asking
unknown people to connect on LinkedIn does have a potential penalty. Specifically, if the person receiving the request chooses to click "Ignore" in
response to the request, they then have the chance to report that rejected
invitation as, "I don't know this person." If enough invitees make this report
about the user issuing invitations, then the offending user's account may be
suspended. These features, encoded into the platform, impose norms for
connecting on LinkedIn, the most prominent of which is that users should
connect only with those people who are known to them, ideally in a professional context.

Engaging with Others Professionally (Relating)

The third hub of communicative activity that we explored was relating with
other LinkedIn users; specifically, with one's connections, i.e., the people
within one's LinkedIn network. A key rule operating on the platform is to be
positive and constructive in one's communication. This rule is strongly expressed in LinkedIn's user guidelines, which exhort members to be "nice,"
"courteous," "professional," and "respectful." Users are told not to "promote
negativity" or "be rude"; this would, in fact, be grounds for removal from the
platform. Users must also "keep comments, postings, and interactions constructive." This entails "shar[ing] ideas and opinions openly," "answer[ing
questions] with thoughtful and friendly contributions," and "shar[ing] best
practices, ideas, and knowledge with other users." By offering up "constructive feedback," the LinkedIn community can purportedly become a better
and more professional space (LinkedIn, 2013, 2015, 2016b).

The expectation to be positive and constructive was also visible in LinkedIn's user interface (UI). For example, the Endorsements feature allows users
to list their skills directly on their own profiles. 1st-degree connections can
offer endorsement by clicking on a skill; thereafter the skill displays the text,
"Endorsed by [1st-degree connection name]." Users cannot endorse themselves—they can only be endorsed. Furthermore, negative endorsements, i.e.,
those representing opposition or censure, are not supported by the platform.
Similarly, the Recommendation feature gives users the chance to "recognize
or commend" a 1st-degree connection (LinkedIn, 2017f); here too, the emphasis is on positivity, with users encouraged to "be as specific as possible
about [the recommended person's] strengths and skills . . . and the positive
effects [of what they did]." Conversely, the UI does not afford any means of
directly critiquing one's connections. The only possible way to complain or
critique a fellow connection is through omission, i.e., not offering any
endorsement or recommendation.

DISCUSSION

In this chapter we described three main hubs of communicative activity pertaining to professionalism on LinkedIn: strategically displaying one's professional self (identity); connecting with other professionals (action); and engaging with other users in professional ways (relating). Taken as a whole, these three hubs indicate that a cultural discourse is in play, which we will refer to as LinkedIn's cultural discourse of professionalism. The cultural discourse of professionalism is localized within LinkedIn's particular online setting, and points to associated practices for enacting professionalism (locally defined) within this setting, including how to relate to or connect with other users, and how to communicate appropriately while doing so.

Interestingly, the cultural discourse of professionalism relies upon, but also transcends, specific organizational affiliations that LinkedIn users reference in their profiles. Nevertheless, the discourse of professionalism as it is enacted through and on the LinkedIn platform affords limited—even restricted—possibilities for being, acting, and relating. When users compose and display their online professional selves, contextualized only within the limited setting of the LinkedIn platform, a fragmentary picture emerges. A LinkedIn profile cannot encompass a professional identity, even when it is of "All Star" quality. Similarly, by limiting what users can display about themselves on the platform (i.e., who users can "be" in this setting), LinkedIn effectively limits how users can relate with one another. For example, by omitting any additional information included in a user's profile, 1st-, 2nd- or 3rd-degree connections may feel prevented from knowing a more "authentic self" with facets beyond job skills and experiences. Furthermore, by prescribing a limited type of interactions, the site does not encourage what we might have deemed as important relationship-building activities in other interpersonal settings, such as greeting sequences, going through stages of relational development, and sustaining interaction in ongoing ways (also see Scollo and Poutiainen's chapter, this volume).

Although we didn't apply the CuDA hub of dwelling per se, by examining a Hymesian *setting* we approach a dwelling-like hub. People do not live on LinkedIn, as the term *dwelling* might suggest, but the UI is constructed as a place within which shadow-selves—users' profiles—reside, and a particular type of being and relating by these professional selves makes sense. What is more, our investigation of the cultural discourse of professionalism on LinkedIn included analysis of how the discourse itself is encoded into (and promoted by) the setting itself, here the LinkedIn platform or UI. We illustrated how the LinkedIn UI plays a significant role in cuing users to engage in professional conduct in a manner deemed appropriate to this online setting. Put differently, the LinkedIn UI "encodes" (cf. Katriel, 2015) a particular notion of professional communication, and is intended to guide users through the actions determined to be correct and legitimate for this setting. By providing users with limited (and limiting) functionalities, the UI also blocks users from engaging in activities that would be considered unprofessional or inappropriate in this space. Users learn about legitimized and non-legitimized ways of being and communicating as they become more expert members of this community. The LinkedIn platform encodes ideas about the professional self and how that self should be expressed; it also serves to regulate professional communication in this space.

Finally, we want to address the notion of cross-cultural comparisons. In our findings we noticed that what is conceived of as professional communication on LinkedIn resonates with the way expertise typical of North American culture is enacted (Dyer & Keller-Cohen, 2000). These practices also resonate with some features of what Carbaugh (1988) referred to as "Talking American." In particular, the preference for "honest" communication on LinkedIn is similar to the American practice of "being honest" designated by "truthful and open talk where individual rights are exercised and self is displayed" (Carbaugh, 1988, p. 110). The difference might be that on LinkedIn, individual rights are limited; we did not find users describing their communication on LinkedIn as "open" (although some interviewees described "sharing" on the platform). Further, what we observed was akin to Carbaugh's (1996) discussion of working selves articulated through and implicating communication practices. We conceived of LinkedIn as a rich, cultural site where professional selves (who may be working in a particular organization at the moment) connect with known others via invitations and acceptances to form a network. It was through these cultural practices that the relationship between communication and professional identity became noticeable.

In sum, our study illustrates the utility of using CuDA to examine how LinkedIn users present themselves, connect with others, and establish (and maintain) professional relationships in this online environment. How people further interact with others on LinkedIn, and the possibility of what they do there transcending and/or blending into other settings certainly warrants further exploration.

REFERENCES

Beer, D. (2008). The iconic interface and the veneer of simplicity: MP3 players and the reconfiguration of music collecting and reproduction practices in the digital age. *Information, Communication & Society, 11*(1), 71–88.

Beneito-Montagut, R. (2011). Ethnography goes online: Towards a user-centered methodology to research interpersonal communication on the internet. *Qualitative Research, 11*(6), 716–735.

Blazkova, H. (2011). Telling tales of professional competence: Narrative in 60-second business networking speeches. *Journal of Business Communication, 48*(4), 446–463.

Boellstorff, T. (2008). *Coming of age in Second Life: An anthropologist explores the virtually human*. Princeton, NJ: Princeton University Press.

Carbaugh, D. (1988). *Talking American: Cultural discourses on Donahue*. Norwood, NJ: Ablex.

Carbaugh, D. (1989). Fifty terms for talk: A cross-cultural study. In S. Ting-Toomey & F. Korzenny (Eds.), *Language, communication, and culture: Current directions* (pp. 93–120). Newbury Park, CA: Sage.

Carbaugh, D. (1996). *Situating selves: The communication of social identities in American scenes*. Albany, NY: State University of New York Press.

Carbaugh, D. (2017). Terms for talk, take 2: Theorizing communication through its cultural terms and practices. In D. Carbaugh (Ed.), *The Handbook of communication in cross-cultural perspective* (pp. 15–28). London: Routledge.

Carbaugh, D., & Cerulli, T. (2018). Cultural discourse analysis. In Y. Kim (Ed.), *The international encyclopedia of intercultural communication* (pp. 1–9). John Wiley & Sons.

Carbaugh, D., Nuciforo, E. V., Saito, M., & Shin, D. (2011). "Dialogue" in cross-cultural perspectives: Japanese, Korean, and Russian discourses. *Journal of International and Intercultural Communication, 42*(2), 87–108.

Drew, P., & Heritage, J. (1993). *Talk at work: Interactions in institutional settings*. Cambridge, England: Cambridge University Press.

Dyer, J., & Keller-Cohen, D. (2000). The discursive construction of professional self through narratives of personal experience. *Discursive Studies, 2*, 283–304.

Fitch, K. L. (1998). *Speaking relationally: Culture, communication, and interpersonal connection*. New York, NY: Guilford Press.

Gane, N., & Beer, D. (2008). *New media: The key concepts*. Oxford, UK: Berg.

Greenwood, S., Perrin, A., & Duggan, M. (November 11, 2016). Social media update 2016. Retrieved from http://www.pewinternet.org/2016/11/11/social-media-update-2016/

Hart, T. (2015). Analyzing procedure to make sense of users' (inter)actions: A case study on applying the ethnography of communication for interaction design purposes. In T. Milburn (Ed.), *Communicating user experience: Applying local strategies research to digital media design*. Lanham, MD: Lexington Books.

Hart, T. (2016). Learning how to speak like a "native": Speech and culture in an online communication training program. *Journal of Business and Technical Communication, 30*(3), 285–321.

Herring, S. C. (2007). A faceted classification scheme for computer-mediated discourse. *language@internet, 4*(1).

Holmes, J. (2006). Workplace narratives, professional identity and relational practice. In A. D. Fina, D. Schiffrin, & M. Bamberg (Eds.), *Discourse and identity. Studies in interactional sociolinguistics* (Vol. 23, pp. 166–187). Cambridge, England: Cambridge University Press.

Holmes, J., Stubbe, M., & Vine, B. (1999). Constructing professional identity: "Doing power" in policy units. In S. Sarangi & C. Roberts (Eds.), *Talk, work and institutional order discourse in medical, mediation and management settings*. Berlin, Germany: Mouton de Gruyter.

Hymes, D. (1964). Toward ethnographies of communication. *American Anthropologist, 66*(6), 1–34.

Hymes, D. (1972). Models of the interaction of language and social life. In J. J. Gumperz & D. Hymes (Eds.), *Directions in sociolinguistics: The ethnography of communication* (pp. 35–71). New York, NY: Holt, Rinehart and Winston.

Katriel, T. (2015). Expanding ethnography of communication research: Toward ethnographies of encoding. *Communication Theory, 25*(4), 454–459.

Lave, J., & Wenger, E. (1991). *Situated learning: Legitimate peripheral participation*. Cambridge, England: Cambridge University Press.

LinkedIn. (2013). Help forum guidelines. Retrieved from https://www.linkedin.com/help/linkedin/answer/28410?query=be constructive

LinkedIn. (2015). Acceptable behavior for teens on LinkedIn. Retrieved from https://www.linkedin.com/help/linkedin/answer/62939?query=be constructive

LinkedIn. (2016a). How LinkedIn can help you. Retrieved from https://www.linkedin.com/help/linkedin/answer/45/how-linkedin-can-help-you?lang=en

LinkedIn. (2016b). LinkedIn professional community guidelines. Retrieved from https://www.linkedin.com/help/linkedin/answer/34593

LinkedIn. (2017a). About LinkedIn. Retrieved from https://press.linkedin.com/about-linkedin

LinkedIn. (2017b). Connections—overview. Retrieved from https://www.linkedin.com/help/linkedin/answer/15495/connections-overview?lang=en

LinkedIn. (2017c). Contact us: Let us know about inaccurate information listed on another person's profile. Retrieved from https://www.linkedin.com/help/linkedin/ask/TS-NFPI

LinkedIn. (2017d). Invitation limitations. Retrieved from https://www.linkedin.com/help/linkedin/answer/4800

LinkedIn. (2017e). Profile strength. Retrieved from https://www.linkedin.com/help/linkedin/answer/391/profile-strength?lang=en

LinkedIn. (2017f). Recommendations—overview. Retrieved from https://www.linkedin.com/help/linkedin/answer/90/recommendations-overview?lang=en

LinkedIn. (2017g). Reporting inaccurate information on another member's profile. Retrieved from https://www.linkedin.com/help/linkedin/answer/30200/reporting-inaccurate-information-on-another-member-s-profile?lang=en

LinkedIn. (2017h). User agreement. Retrieved from https://www.linkedin.com/legal/user-agreement

Mada, S., & Saftoiu, R. (2012). *Professional communication across languages and cultures.* Amsterdam, Netherlands: John Benjamins Publishing Company.

Manovich, L. (2001). *The language of new media.* Cambridge, MA: MIT Press.

Manovich, L. (2003). New media from Borges to HTML. In N. Wardrip-Fruin & N. Montfort (Eds.), *The new media reader.* Cambridge, MA: MIT Press.

Milburn, T. (2015) (Ed.), *Communicating user experience: Applying local strategies research to digital media design.* Lanham, MD: Lexington Books.

Paolillo, J. (1999). The virtual speech community: Social network and language variation on IRC. *Journal of Computer Mediated Communication, 4*(4).

Pfister, D. S., & Soliz, J. (2011). (Re)conceptualizing intercultural communication in a networked society. *Journal of International and Intercultural Communication, 4*(4), 246–251.

Philipsen, G. (1992). *Speaking culturally: Explorations in social communication.* Albany, NY: State University of New York Press.

Philipsen, G. (1997). A theory of speech codes. In G. Philipsen & T. L. Albrecht (Eds.), *Developing communication theories* (pp. 119–156). New York, NY: State University of New York Press.

Philipsen, G., Coutu, L. M., & Covarrubias, P. (2005). Speech codes theory: Restatement, revisions, and response to criticisms. In W. Gudykunst (Ed.), *Theorizing about intercultural communication* (pp. 55–68). Thousand Oaks, CA: Sage.

Schwartzman, H. B. (1989). *The meeting: Gatherings in organizations and communities.* New York, NY: Plenum.

Tosca, S. (2002). *The Everquest speech community.* Paper presented at the Digital Games and Computer Cultures, Tampere, Finland.

Chapter Three

Voice Persona Perceptions

Apologies in In-Car Speech Technology

Laura Rosenbaun, Ute Winter, and Brion van Over

Speech systems, also described as "conversational agents" or "artificial entities that communicate conversationally" (Jurafsky & Martin, 2014, p. 9), are becoming increasingly ubiquitous in domestic and public environments, from vehicles to mobile devices and smart homes. As this technology becomes more ingrained in our daily lives, the focus will not only be on the system's ability to interpret the meaning of user utterances, but rather the quality and design of entire communication events in a given context, such as the driver's communicative situation and the voice persona of the speech interface (the personal digital assistant). Research has shown how the cultural nature of communication influences the user's perception of interaction (Carbaugh, 1990, 2005; Hymes, 1972; Philipsen, 2002; Tsimhoni et al. 2009; Nass & Brave, 2005). By employing cultural discourse analysis (Carbaugh, 2007; Scollo, 2011) and in synergy with user-centered human-machine interaction (HMI) design principles, Carbaugh et al. (2016) have developed a framework to formally study the cultural dimensions of communication and the design implications for speech-enabled human-machine interfaces in the automotive environment. Various field studies have been conducted based on this framework (the first one in 2012 as described in Carbaugh et al., 2016), on which we now draw to analyze users' orientations toward the apologies produced by the speech system.

Human-like behavior and social cues in in-car speech systems constitute a rich design area, as these elements evoke perceptions of personality traits that may over time lead to increased likability and trust. Such human-like speech responses accomplish various self-presentational goals and touch upon different expectations in terms of the relationship users build with their in-car systems. In general terms, within an in-car communication event, practices that orient toward relational aspects rather than purely task-oriented turns become salient, as they may come across as unexpected and outside the canonical strategies so far used by speech-enabled technologies, thus adding a surprising and delightful layer to the user experience. In this chapter, we delve into strategies to convey apologies as key relational elements that may increase phatic communication during the user-vehicle interaction. Drawing on user-car interactions and interviews from two user studies, we analyze participants' orientations toward the system's apologies. In particular, we discuss expectations of compliance to communication norms when the system is perceived either as a mere tool, or rather as a social tool.

THEORETICAL FRAMEWORK AND RELATED LITERATURE

Culture and Communication Practices

We view the car and the interactions with the in-car speech system as a specific "communication situation," following the tradition of the ethnography of communication (e.g., Hymes, 1972) and cultural discourse analysis (CuDA) (Carbaugh, 2007; Scollo, 2011). From this key concept, we derive that the car is a discursive space where people communicate with each other and with the car in cultural discursive ways. Cultural discourse, in this use, refers to "a historically transmitted expressive system of communication practices, of acts, events, and styles, which are composed of specific symbols, symbolic forms, norms, and their meanings" (Carbaugh, 2007, p. 169). As a result, culture is understood as both constituted by, and constitutive of, discursive practice. Therefore, it is illuminated by analyses of social interaction as interlocutors express their understanding of the premises and norms that inform that interaction both in the culturally distinctive ways it is performed, and also in the taken-for-granted shared knowledge that renders this expression mutually intelligible.

This formulation of culture does not, then, rely on geography as fundamentally bounding shared communicative practice, but rather conceives of cultural communities as bound by the symbols, premises, norms, and meanings that are shared and employed by members in varied communication situations and events. This conceptualization informs our approach to studying cultural communication in the car, as focus on interaction between human participants and speech-enabled in-car systems can help to uncover preferred norms and ways of speaking, which help to inform the design of human-machine interfaces (Cohen, Giangola, & Balogh, 2004; Nass & Brave, 2005; Pearl, 2016). Similar to the points discussed by Leighter, Grimshaw, and Braithwaite in this volume, an underlying concern in this chapter relates to the expectations of how interactions with nonhuman entities should be handled.

Within the in-car communication situation, there are smaller sequences of acts that can be understood as "communication events" with each such event composed of "communication acts" (Hymes, 1972). Typical communication acts in our field data are openings, directives, confirmations, and closings. Together with communication act sequences, the applied framework explores important extralinguistic, multimodal cues active in these communication practices, as well as the cultural premises that inform the production and interpretation of the meaningfulness of the practice, and the norms that regulate the moral dimension of their use. Cultural premises, in their conceptualization under CuDA, are analytical formulations that direct our attention to various semantic "hubs," rich with cultural meanings about personhood, relations, emotion, place, and communication itself, that are both presumed and enacted in discourse. Relatedly, as seen from the lens of interpersonal ideology, formulations of actions toward others and interpretations of others' actions are guided by expectations of personhood, relations, and communication that take place during social interaction (Poutiainen, 2015).

Another key concept we rely on is "conversational inference" (see Gumperz, 1982, 1992; Carbaugh, 2005), which uncovers how participants assign meaning to nonverbal cues within the ongoing sequence of communication events using shared cultural means. In a multimodal conversational interface, multimodal means, such as visual cues on displays, play a significant role, and so their design—and the ways participants use and interpret them—partly determines the success of a communication event (Levinson, 1997; Pearl, 2016).

Human-Interface Relationship

Apart from the key communication concepts described above, we draw on the notion of social presence to understand the social dimensions that come to play when humans interact with interfaces through speech. Social presence can be defined as the sense of "being with another" including primitive responses to social cues, simulations of "other minds," and automatically generated models of the intentionality of others. Similar to the notion of "being with others" (Goffman, 1959, 1963) or "phatic communion" (Malinowski, 1923), social presence is activated as soon as a user believes that an entity in the environment displays some minimal intelligence in its responses (Nowak & Biocca, 2003). In interactions with speech systems, social presence can be said to take place at intermittent moments in which users overlook the artificial nature of the experience and can immerse themselves in a natural conversation, relying on their instinctive use of communication patterns (see Rosenbaun et al., 2016, for a review).

Because of its implications for interaction, social presence has been identified as a key variable in building the relationship between a given technology and its users (Hassanein & Head, 2007; Kumar & Benbasat, 2006), affecting perceptions of user trust (Gefen & Straub, 2004; Hassanein & Head,
2007) and serving as an enabler for trust-building cues (Gefen & Straub,
2003). Research has shown that perceptions of social presence influence
perceptions of system usefulness (Karahanna & Straub, 1999), enjoyment
(Hassanein & Head, 2007), involvement (Fortin & Dholakia, 2005), and trust
(Gefen & Straub, 2003; Gefen & Straub, 2004). We understand social presence to include the feeling of warmth and sociability conveyed through interaction with a human-like voice assistant, which may be affected by and
accomplished through levels of relational talk produced by the system. In this
study, we focus on apologies as a key type of relational talk.

Apologies in HMI

Extensive research has been done on apologies in human-human interaction
and on how they are accomplished. Broadly speaking, these speech acts are
realized through routinized patterns used to "save face" with various degrees
of effectiveness (Scher & Darley, 1997). Apologies serve as remedial work,
designed to smooth over or recover from any social disruption caused by a
normative violation (Blum-Kulka, 1984). For an apology to be legitimate,
transgressors must recognize their wrongdoings and explicitly show regret
(Fraser & Coulmas, 1981). Five strategies for apologizing have been suggested: (1) an illocutionary force-indicating device (IFID) such as "I'm sorry"; (2) an explanation of the violation; (3) a display of responsibility for the
fault; (4) an offer of compensation; and (5) a promise of avoidance of wrong-
doing in the future (Olshtain & Cohen, 1983; Blum-Kulka & Olshtain, 1984).
Apology studies have shown that an apology draws favorable responses only
when the genuineness of the apology is convincing (Skarlicki, Folger, &
Gee, 2004). Furthermore, it has been argued that the use of just one apology
strategy is more effective than the use of multiple strategies (Scher & Huff,
1991).

Within the HMI community, research has shown that when an interface
has high autonomy, users are more likely to treat it as human and thus, the
interface needs to live up to users' expectations in order not to be negatively
assessed (e.g., Serenko, 2007). For example, an interface's modesty, in blaming itself and calling it an error in "the system," makes users feel better and
more comfortable with the system (Nass & Brave, 2005). However, when the
interface engages in self-criticism, users perceive the interface as generally
less competent (Park et al., 2015). These findings point to the delicate balance required when designing a modest yet competent voice assistant. Similarly, certain preferences of some apology strategies over others have been

reported in computerized environments, indicating a strong correlation with preferences in social contexts, further supporting the notion that social dynamics that guide human-human interaction also apply to HMI (Akgun, Cagiltay, & Zeyrek, 2010).

DATA AND METHODOLOGY

The field data analyzed in this chapter have been referenced and discussed in previous publications (e.g., Carbaugh et al., 2016; Molina-Markham et al., 2016) and consist of interactions and interviews from two studies conducted in 2012 in the area of Amherst, Massachusetts, and in 2014 in the area of Columbus, Ohio.

The first study followed a naturalistic approach with participants driving their own car and choosing their destinations. We equipped the participants' cars with an external multimodal interface for an infotainment system supporting three typical in-car domains: phone calling, radio tuning, and music selection. This system was Wizard of Oz enabled, allowing for complete natural language understanding of the user utterances as well as supporting touch interaction at any turn in the dialog, except while driving on public roads due to field study regulations.

Once in the car, the participant was invited to explore the interface for a variety of tasks while remaining in an off-road area. Afterward, the participant performed a sixty- to seventy-five-minute drive of their choosing. Throughout the driving session and after its completion, the experimenter asked the driver a series of open questions relating to observations during the drive and to many dimensions of the communication experience. Twenty-six participants were selected so as to represent a wide variety of characteristics. The number of participants was balanced across gender, tech savviness, early and old technology adopters, age, use of smartphones, and driving experience.

The second study presented a Wizard of Oz–type speech-enabled system based on the design concept derived from the findings of the first study. Unlike the naturalistic inquiry followed in the first study, here we prompted twenty-four participants to perform a series of predesigned communication events with the system while driving a rental car in a predetermined driving course. Otherwise, the field study methodology was preserved as closely as possible to the first study. Despite being a more controlled study, participants' responses to the system were naturally occurring and indicative of their communicative expectations. We label these two data sets "Study 1" and "Study 2."

Our analysis methodology stems from the eight basic components of the Setting, Participants, Ends, Acts, Key, Instrumentalities, Norms, Genre

(SPEAKING) mnemonic proposed by Hymes (1972) that helps to describe, organize, and interpret human behavior in cultural scenes (see Hymes, 1972; Carbaugh, 2012). We use the set as a conceptual foundation for an initial descriptive analysis, in which the components function as a series of questions that help to unveil how communication is done within and about the car. As a next step, these eight basic components are used for interpretive inquiry (Carbaugh et al., 2016).

In an additional step, design questions highlight HMI-relevant insights from the data. The design of an in-vehicle multimodal interface traditionally follows the paradigm of user-centered design (Norman & Draper, 1986; Nielsen, 1993; Vredenburg & Butler, 1996). As such, design dimensions identified and further explained in Carbaugh et al. (2016) are user satisfaction, user trust, ease of use, turn taking, grounding, cooperation, interaction style, multimodal use, conflict resolution, and information distribution across a communication act sequence, level of formality, among others.

Finally, interview data were analyzed by comparing the major themes that emerged as participants verbalized their experiences with the system and their various expectations toward voice assistants. This analysis framework was applied iteratively, as a series of frequent observations led to patterns and expectations that emerged from the data. In short, in the tradition of CuDA, we analyzed not only interaction data from communication occurring with the in-car system but also communication about the system, for evidence of cultural premises about personhood, relations, emotion, place, and communication itself, where relevant. We included our observations from HMI analysis as a complementary perspective to enrich and confirm the conclusions.

Data from both studies are included here to provide a sense of the range of orientations to communication in and with the car, and the potential cultural variation in the means and meanings employed in these interactions. We do not claim here to be presenting discrete cultural practices constitutive of a particular cultural community, but rather seek to explore the range of these practices, recognizing that all cultural discourses are "multidimensional, polysemic, deeply situated, and complex functional accomplishments" (Carbaugh, 2007, p. 169).

ANALYSIS

We would like to first frame our analysis by illustrating how some expectations from human-human interactions are transferred to in-car interactions with speech technologies. The following example shows how certain norms of politeness and ways to handle communication violations are displayed by participants' apologies to the system. Such apologies are non-task turns that indicate users' adherence to a broader sense of cultural norms, and premises informing expectations of personhood, rights, and obligations.

Example 1: Context General, Participant 13—34:15 Minutes into the Session

1	P:	(participant touches speech button) Call [H-
2	S:	(audible ding)]
3	*P:*	*Oh, I'm sorry.*
4		(6.1)
5	S:	Please confirm calling H- S-.
6	P:	Yes, call H- S-
7		(2.3)
8	S:	Calling H- S- on mobile.

The participant initiates a new speech session by pressing the speech button and immediately phrasing his directive as a single turn ("Call H-", Line 1). However, in the sequential organization of the interaction, pressing the speech button constitutes a turn-at-talk in itself, and so the speech system responds with an audible ding while the participant is saying the contact name "H-". Although it is the system that overlaps with the participant's intended turn, the participant orients to this overlap as being her responsibility, since the participant has already gone through various cycles in which the speech system responds with a ding when activated by the touch button, explicitly yielding the floor. The acknowledgment of responsibility by expressing mild surprise ("oh") is then followed by the apology "I'm sorry," immediately yielding the floor back to the system for further instructions on how to proceed.

As this example illustrates, and as has been demonstrated in related work (see van Over et al., 2016), human-machine communication is partly regulated by expectations derived from human-human communication, and deviations from such expectations are interpreted as having social meaning. In what follows, we explore the design tensions between apology strategies to convey a polite yet self-confident voice assistant.

Study 1

In the design for Study 1, the speech system apologized in two different types of situations. First, when users asked for a task the system could not accomplish, for example a request for route guidance that was not supported. Second, when the system repeatedly did not understand the user request. In both cases, the apology was short, either "sorry" or "I'm sorry," immediately followed by a brief explanation or account of the problem, an optional expression of the system's responsibility for the fault, and if possible, a follow-up request offered as a means to continue with the task. The instance below shows the first type of apology, produced when the participant asked for a music item not contained in the system music collection.

Instance 1: Context General, Participant 14—31:46 Minutes into the Session

1	P:	(participant touches speech button)
2	S:	(audible ding)
3		(3.1)
4	P:	Play John Lee Hooker.
5	S:	Pardon?
6	P:	Play John Lee Hooker.
7		(11.9)
8	S:	Processing.
9		(11.3)
10	S:	I am sorry. I am unable to find the music item that you are looking for.
11	P:	(shrugs shoulders)

The participant presses the speech button, which starts a new speech session while the system is in the home screen with no specific task at hand. The system responds with an audible ding, after which there is a 3.1-second pause (Line 3), interpreted by the participant as his signal to take the conversational floor and utter a directive ("Play John Lee Hooker," Line 4). The system immediately indicates a communication problem by asking the user to utter the directive again ("Pardon?" in line 5). Although this system response does not state the kind of problem at hand, it clearly signals that the request was not understood. The participant interprets the system's response as a misrecognition and repeats his directive verbatim (Line 6). While the participant waits for the system response (Lines 7–9), he glances multiple times at the display to understand whether the system is still engaged in the interaction. Since prolonged pauses in conversation are usually interpreted as indicators of an upcoming dispreferred response (e.g., McLaughlin & Cody, 1982; Pomerantz, 1984), the user may, borrowing from human-human interactional norms, interpret the system as having difficulties answering appropriately. The subsequent apology in line 10 ("I'm sorry") with the explanation "I am unable to find the music item that you are looking for" unsurprisingly confirms this communication breakdown, to which the participant simply shrugs his shoulders. About ten seconds later, the participant initiates a new speech session and asks for a different artist (section not transcribed).

The second type of apology trigger is illustrated in the example below. Here, the system apology is a result of multiple subsequent instances of mishearing or misrecognition.

Instance 2: Context XM Talk Radio, Participant 9 — 27:58 Minutes into the Session

1	P:	(participant touches microphone button)
2	S:	(audible ding)
3		(2.2)
4	S:	What talk channel do you want to hear?
5	P:	Let's listen to something conservative.
6		(4.5)
7	S:	Pardon?
8	P:	Something conservative, right wing.
9		(4.3)
10	S:	Could you repeat that please?
11	P:	You know, fire and brimstone, that kind of stuff.
12		(4.8)
13	S:	Sorry. I did not understand your request. [Please] repeat it again
14	P:	[Fox-] F- Fox news
15		(7.2)
16	S:	Please confirm 98 XM The Fox xhole
17		(3.2)
18	P:	What's that? Fox hole? Ok
19		(5.8)
20	S:	Tuning radio to 98 XM The Fox xhole

At the time the participant initiates a speech session by touching the microphone button, the speech system's context is the XM Talk Radio context, and as per design the system triggers an XM Talk Radio–related question ("What talk channel do you want to hear?", Line 4). The participant does not request a specific channel number or name, but rather his directive is descriptive of the type of talk station he wants to hear (Line 5, "Let's listen to something conservative"). What follows is a series of turns in which the speech system asks to repeat the directive after a four- to five-second pause (Lines 7, 10, and 13), and the participant rephrases his directive, but continues to describe the preferred type of channel (Lines 5, 8, and 11). In line 13, the third request for the command repetition, the system starts the response with a short apology to account for the multiple misunderstandings and takes responsibility for them. It explicitly states the reason behind the communication breakdown ("I did not understand your request") and follows up with an offer to continue ("Please repeat it again"). The participant changes his directive and asks for a specific XM channel, "Fox news" (Line 14). While the speech system still does not accurately recognize the command, it offers a similar-sounding alternative, which the user accepts (Line 18).

As these examples illustrate, the voice assistant was designed to take responsibility for the problem, whether the issue is triggered by the system's limited scope of tasks or by the system's misunderstanding of a user utterance. As such, the apology serves the main purposes of grounding and hinting toward a task completion issue, letting the users know that their way of interacting with the system is not necessarily wrong. In this sense, the apology removes any potential user's uncertainty regarding how to interact with the speech system. Such short and concise apologies did not contain any markers of regret, and consequently, no emotion was evoked or alluded to by participants during the subsequent interviews.

"Does It Apologize?"

As evidenced in the interviews, participants indicated feeling well informed of how the interaction unfolded and appeared to orient toward the apology in an unmarked manner, just as intended. In the various instances of apologies present in the data set, the most common reaction was to simply continue with the task as seen in instance 2, or to initiate a new task as at the end of instance 1. Occasionally, participants would add a verbal backchannel, indicating their understanding or agreement, such as "ok" or "I know," or a gesture such as head nodding. In short, participants oriented to these apologies as discourse markers acting as indicators of issues within a task completion cycle. Because of this, the example below is the only mention across all participants regarding the system apologies.

Participant 7: Final Interview—1:42:10 into the Session

P: [I mean] *does it say "I'm sorry"?* I didn't understand, does it say "I'm-" . . . *does it apologize?*

E: Sometimes it does yeah. Did you hear that? ((Both laugh)) did you like that it [apologized]?

P: Well . . . "I'm sorry" . . . well, yeah, . . . I don't know

This participant vaguely recalled the apologies when the system's level of politeness was discussed during the interview. This general absence of focus on system apologies seems to indicate that the apologies were perceived as natural and unmarked within the sequential organization of the interaction. The absence of any marker of regret, which can be part of canonical apologies, was not mentioned in the data, neither negatively or positively. As observed in instances 1 and 2, all participants continued with the interaction after the system apology, strongly pointing toward the use of apologies for grounding purposes. Still unclear is whether apologies are heard and understood as sincere sayings, where the connotative meaning of apology is active versus the more instrumental use of apology to mark problematic interactional moments for structural correction. The latter indicates a potential premise of personhood that does not grant the system the status of a full interactant and, as a result, without the same social responsibility of their human interactional partner. In Study 2 below, on the other hand, more elaborate apologies conveying regret were employed.

Study 2

For the design in this study, the speech system was prepared to apologize essentially in the same two situations as discussed above, but in a more elaborated manner to add regret as illocutionary force, conveying hints of emotion. The following two instances show this system behavior.

Instance 3: Context General, Participant 20 — 17:44:38

1	P:	Wake up
2	S:	(audible beep)
3	P:	Call Charles Wilson at home
4	S:	No home number for Charles Wilson. Mobile or work?
5		(~3)
6	P:	Neither
7	S:	Pardon?
8	P:	No
9	S:	Sorry, I didn't understand. Please try again
10		(2.5)
11	P:	End call
12	S:	I'm so sorry, I still didn't understand. Clearly I'm limited. Please try one more
13		time.
14	P:	Call mobile
15	S:	Calling mobile

The participant enables the speech system by addressing it with a name chosen in advance, in this case the expression "wake up" (Line 1), to which the system responds with an audible sound to signal it is listening (Line 2). Similar to instance 2, what follows is a sequence of turns in which the speech system asks the participant to select an alternative phone type to the one initially requested (Lines 4, 7, and 9). However, the participant rejects the two phone types proposed by the system (Line 6, "Neither"), triggering a series of misrecognitions as the system is expecting a phone type selection from the proposed options instead of a rejection (Lines 8, 10, and 11). For the first misunderstanding, the system requests a directive repetition ("Pardon?", in line 7). The second time around, it adds a short apology marker "sorry" in frontal position, followed by an explanation of the problem and another request for repetition (Line 9, "Sorry, I didn't understand. Please try again"). So far, although more elaborate, this system behavior is similar to the one designed for Study 1. That is, the system relies on short apologies to assure participants they are not to blame for the misunderstanding, and to encourage them to try again.

However, in line 12, the apology introduces the illocutionary act of regret to account for the multiple failures and further elaborates on the notion of being at fault for the communication breakdown (Line 12, "I'm so sorry, I still didn't understand. Clearly I'm limited"), inviting the user to repeat the selection ("Please try one more time."). The apology starts with a slightly more upgraded expression of regret ("So sorry"), followed by an account for the ongoing inability to proceed with the task ("I still didn't understand") and an explicit account of the system's responsibility for the fault ("Clearly I'm limited"). This last apologetic turn includes multiple strategic elements, to which participants orient as a marked system response. As such, several participants refer to this turn in the subsequent interviews, as we later discuss.

Instance 4 below shows a similar progression. Here, the apology is triggered after the system mistakenly tries to confirm a song title (Line 4, "Colder Weather. Correct?"). As a result, the participant corrects the speech system with the rejection "no" followed by the repetition of the desired song title (Line 5, "No. Come Together"). However, due to technical limitations, the system can only understand the rejection "no," but misses the desired song title.

Instance 4: Context General, Participant 7—1:04:15 Minutes into the Session

1	P:	Garbanzo
2	S:	(audible beep)
3	P:	Play Beatles song called Come Together.
4	S:	Colder Weather. Correct?

5	P:	No. Come Together.
6	S:	Oh! I'm sorry. So embarrass[sing].
7	P:	[aww.]
8	S:	[What would you like?]
9	P:	The Beatles singing Come Together.
10	S:	Great! I found more than one copy for Come Together. I'll play them all.

In line 6, the system responds with an elaborate apology containing an expression of negative surprise and change-of-state token "oh!" in initial position (Heritage, 1984), indicating the user rejection was unexpected. This is then followed by the apology "I'm sorry." The strong sense of regret is emphasized by an emotional disclosure "so embarrassing," which causes the participant to mumble "aww" (Line 7). The participant clearly orients to this phrase as an expression of human emotion, which is later verbalized during the interview as evoking an undefined negative feeling on the part of the participant, broadly characterized as an inappropriate reaction when coming from a machine.

The highly elaborate and recursive apologetic sequences suggest that the system seeks not only some absolution for the communication issue, but also the user's affiliation. By overemphasizing responsibility and alluding to human emotions, apologizers also portray a negative judgmental stance toward themselves and the action undertaken. This, in turn, would promote a recipient's response similar to the one triggered by self-critiques and expressions of self-contempt in human-human communication. That is, the recipient of the elaborate apology disagrees with the apologizer and thus, supports the speaker, reassuring that their "morality" is preserved and publicly acknowledged instead (Pomerantz, 1984), which here would break the suspension of disbelief required for human-machine interaction.

The quality of such mixed emotional reactions toward the elaborated apologies becomes more evident in the interview data. In what follows, we incorporate some excerpts from interviews to further illustrate this evaluation.

"I Do Like Polite, But I Don't Need Apologetic"

These excerpts indicate that participants valued brief apologies along the lines of a politeness discourse marker rather than an attempt at an apology per se. As this study evidences, an overapologetic tone breaks the suspension of disbelief, creating a push back in terms of a negative threatening face act. As the system imposes a regretful tone on the interaction and makes the user feel either guilty for triggering an apology or awkward for interacting with a system that evokes this type of human emotion.

1. "Hmm the thing where it said, The first thing was 'I'll try not to mess this up' couple of calls ago, or 'I'm so embarrassed,' to me *it sounded a little neurotic*"
2. "Cut off the apologies . . . I mean . . . *it's a computer, why does it have to apologize?*"
3. "I'd get rid of the sorry word . . . *I do like polite, but I don't need apologetic*"

Interestingly, although participants in general judged elaborate apologies as a negative trait, for participants who prefer a more interactive conversational style with the system, this evaluation was slightly different from those who preferred a more efficient interaction. The conceptual distinction between predominantly efficient versus predominantly interactive users in spoken human-machine communication was introduced in Winter, Shmueli, and Grost (2013) and Carbaugh et al. (2016). While the predominantly interactive users tended to feel guilty or awkward for having triggered such system responses, the efficiency-biased users mainly assessed the overapologetic tone as unnecessary coming from a computer and thus, simply a waste of time. Note that in each case, the semantic structure of the apology, its conversational position, or its verbiage are not problematized; rather, the fundamental idea that the system purports to have human emotion is rendered unacceptable.

Such apologetic expressions also made the prompts lengthier than desired, adding time toward the goal completion as apologies got gradually more elaborate with each system turn. While for some participants acknowledging impact and limitations of one's actions may be perceived as polite behavior, efficient participants perceived it as adding to their frustration exactly because they were continuously attempting a given command or task. Lengthy apologies backfired for these users in particular, rendering the system not only as incompetent but also as inefficient. The progression, however, was positively perceived in terms of acknowledging the severity of the issue.

This suggests that the status of personhood granted to the system is variable on grounds of cultural premises held by users that informs whether users are willing to suspend their disbelief and enter into a human-like interaction with the system, versus those who do not grant the system this kind of personhood and prefer it behave as an efficiently functional machine. As suggested by Carbaugh (2007), cultural premises often implicate other radiants of implicit meaning and so the granting of a temporary or contingent personhood to a machine may be tied to the consequences of giving such personhood, i.e., implications of relationship development, concern for the feelings and wants of others, etc., that may be connected to that attribution.

As evidenced by users' resistance to responding to the system's emotional apologies with supportive affirmations, no user appears to grant the system full human interactional status. However, it is clear that some variation exists between those who dislike the more elaborate emotional apologies on the grounds that there is something fundamentally wrong with a machine trying to be *that* human, versus those who dislike it because machines are *a priori* always already not human, making the elaborate apologies a waste of time. Some explanation for this may lie in user premises of emotion, where users who prefer a predominantly elaborate interactional style are willing to grant enough personhood to the system to accept some mimicry of human dimensions of interaction, but where the system's purported experience of emotion is too far. In the case of some predominantly efficient users, very little personhood is granted to the machine and most attempts at human interactional mimicry beyond the minimum necessary for task completion are evaluated negatively. The question then is where and in what domain of human interaction do users draw the line? In this case, a premise of personhood and emotion might be articulated that *machines are not granted human personhood*, with an accompanying normative rule that *machines, even when interactionally capable of doing so, ought not purport to have human emotions.* For predominantly interactive users, however, *machines ought to some degree play at being human,* while for predominantly efficient users *machines ought not play at being human beyond the minimum interactional capacity to accomplish the task.*

DISCUSSION AND DESIGN CONSIDERATIONS

Analyzing different user orientations toward apologies, we argue that not all relational acts are created equal, in part because users' interpretations of the goodness of a particular speech act from the system relies on cultural premises for personhood, social relations, emotion, and communication where some acts may be presumed as appropriate relationally generative interactions performed with a proper interactional partner (a humanistic car), or as inappropriate intimations misusing particular communicative acts with the wrong kind of interactional partner.

In general, our observations indicate that elaborated apologies were negatively evaluated by most participants, and that the reasons behind this evaluation can be attributed to two different rationales. For some participants, the issue stemmed from feeling guilty because of their unintended contribution to the system's failure or violation of rules, or from perceiving the system as awkward and "too neurotic." However, for others, the in-car system was characterized as a mere tool and as such, displays of human-like emotions in length or intensity were seen as an unnecessary waste of time. A key observation is that participants' displayed interactional style seems to play a central role in terms of how they evaluated elaborated apologies: evoking a sense of awkwardness on the one hand, or an irritating waste of time on the other. This observation correlates with previous findings stating that there are competing cultural norms in participants' communication about the appropriate relationship between machines and humans (Molina-Markham et al., 2016). Furthermore, the authors explain that participants' interaction with the system indicate a lack of crystallization of what constitutes proper interaction with machines and appropriate system responses.

Generally speaking, apologies seem to be related to self-presentational goals and the judgments people make about the transgressor. In our study, we observed that the use of apologies has an effect on the judgments related to the identity of the system. Similar to previous research, we found that the desired user evaluation was triggered by one apology strategy, rather than by the use of multiple strategies. It has been stated that speaker responsibility tends to be implied by each of the apology strategies (Scher, 1989). If explicit, these elements may evoke a sense of recipients' relational obligation, which was evidenced during interviews as participants shared their perceptions of the system as having a "neurotic" persona, or evaluate the exchange as a "waste of time" or perceiving "insincerity" in the system responses. Given the implicational nature of apology strategies, some of these strategies may remain implied and still have effect on the judgment of the transgressor (Blum-Kulka, 1997). Heritage and Raymond (2016) propose that different formats of apologizing (e.g., bare versus expanded) may appear proportionally to certain dimensions of the violation, such as whether it is minimal and proximate to the participants, or distal offenses that require more elaboration from the transgressor. Our findings seem to orient to these prior observations, as participants' reactions to concise versus elaborate apologies further strengthen the notion of a degree of appropriateness for apology elaborations: brief apologies are valuable for grounding during communication breakdowns, as politeness markers, as well as to indicate source of error. However, "genuine" elaborate apologies that evoke emotion are negatively evaluated, as the type of issues encountered during exchanges with the speech system are generally not perceived as requiring such extensive interactional work.

This can in part be explained using Brown and Levinson's politeness theory, which suggests that certain acts, such as apologies, are inherently threatening to the face wants of both speaker and hearer. As a result, interlocutors may choose to "pay face" as a way of advertising an upcoming threat to face, as in the prefatory work done to assure you have conveyed that you understand and appreciate the importance of someone's time before asking for a ride to the airport. In this way, instances of upgraded apology, as in the case of the system's use of "so sorry" rather than "sorry" may work to advertise, or seek to compensate for, a face-threatening act that is not evaluated by the user as proportionally appropriate to the advertisement of it.

Needless to say, as speech technologies continue to mature and spread across everyday environments such as the vehicle, design decisions to build a well-rounded voice assistant become even more salient. Users' expectations are invariably related to the social aspect of interacting with technology through speech. As such, appropriate levels of sociability in the voice assistant, which align well with cultural premises about personhood, relations, emotion, and communication, seem to influence perceptions of trust, usefulness, and overall enjoyment. As the user–voice assistant relationship evolves, a key design consideration—and an ongoing challenge—is the degree to which speech systems adapt to users' changing expectations for cultural and communicative appropriateness.

REFERENCES

Akgun, M., Cagiltay, K., & Zeyrek, D. (2010). The effect of apologetic error messages and mood states on computer users' self-appraisal of performance. *Journal of Pragmatics, 42*(9), 2430–2448.

Blum-Kulka, S., & Olshtain, E. (1984). Requests and apologies: A cross-cultural study of speech act realization patterns CCSARP. *Applied Linguistics, 5,* 196.

Carbaugh, D. (1990). Toward a perspective in cultural communication and intercultural contact. *Semiotica, 80*(1–2), 15–36.

Carbaugh, D. (2005). *Cultures in conversation.* Mahwah, NJ: Erlbaum.

Carbaugh, D. (2007). Cultural discourse analysis: Communication practices and intercultural encounters. *Journal of Intercultural Communication Research, 36*(3), 167–182.

Carbaugh, D. (2012). A communication theory of culture. In A. Kurylo (Ed.), *Inter/cultural communication: Representation and construction of culture* (pp. 69–87). Thousand Oaks, CA: Sage.

Carbaugh, D., Winter, U., Molina-Markham, E., van Over, B., Lie, S., & Grost, T. (2016). A model for investigating cultural dimensions of communication in the car. In *Theoretical Issues in Ergonomics Science, 17*(3), 304–323.

Cohen, M. H., Giangola, J. P., & Balogh, J. (2004). *Voice user interface design.* Boston, MA: Addison-Wesley.

Fortin, D., & Dholakia, R. (2005). Interactivity and vividness effects on social presence and involvement with a web-based advertisement. *Journal of Business Research, 58,* 387–396.

Fraser, B., & Coulmas, F. (1981). Conversational routine. *On apologizing,* 259–272.

Gefen, D., & Straub, D. (2003). Consumer trust in B2C e-Commerce and the importance of social presence: Experiments in e-Products and e-Services. *Omega, 32*(6), 407–424.

Gefen, D., & Straub, D. (2004). Managing user trust in B2C e-services. *E-Service Journal.* Bloomington, IN: Indiana University Press.

Goffman, E. (1959). *The presentation of self in everyday life.* Garden City, NY: Doubleday.

Goffman, E. (1963). *Behavior in public places: Notes on the social organization of gatherings.* New York, NY: Free Press of Glencoe.

Goffman, E. (1978). Response cries. *Language, 54*(4), 787–815.

Goffman, E. (1981). *Forms of talk.* Philadelphia, PA: University of Pennsylvania Press.

Gumperz, J. J. (1982). *Discourse strategies.* Cambridge, UK: Cambridge University Press.

Gumperz, J. J. (1992). Contextualization and understanding. In A. Duranti & C. Goodwin (Eds.), *Rethinking context: Language as an interactive phenomenon* (pp. 229–252). Cambridge and New York: Cambridge University Press.

Hassanein, K., & Head, M. (2007). Manipulating perceived social presence through the web interface and its impact on attitude toward online shopping. *International Journal of Human-Computer Studies, 65,* 689–708.

Heritage, J. (1984). A change-of-state token and aspects of its sequential placement. Structures of social action. In J. M. Atkinson & J. Heritage (Eds.), *Structures of Social Action* , (pp. 299–345). Cambridge, UK: Cambridge University Press.

Heritage, J., & Raymond, C. (2016). Are explicit apologies proportional to the offenses they address? *Discourse Processes, 53*(1–2), 5–25.

Hymes, D. (1972). Models for the interaction of language and social life. In J. J. Gumperz & D. Hymes (Eds.), *Directions in sociolinguistics: The ethnography of communication* (pp. 35–71). New York, NY: Basil Blackwell.

Hymes, D. (1974). *Foundations in sociolinguistics: An ethnographic approach.* Philadelphia, PA: University of Pennsylvania Press.

Jurafsky, D., & Martin, J. H. (2014). *Speech and language processing* (Vol. 3). London: Pearson.

Karahanna, E., & Straub, D. (1999). The psychological origins of perceived usefulness and ease-of-use. *Information and Management, 35,* 237–250.

Kumar, N., & Benbasat, I. (2006). The influence of recommendations and consumer reviews on evaluations of websites. *Information System Research, 17*(4), 425–439.

Levinson, S. (1997). Contextualising contextualisation cues. In S. Eerdmans, C. Prevignano, & P. Thibault (Eds.), *Discussing communication analysis 1: John Gumperz* (pp. 24–30). Lausanne: Beta Press.

Malinowski, B. (1923). The problem of meaning in primitive languages. In C. K. Ogden, *The meaning of meaning.* Orlando, FL: HBJ.

McLaughlin, M. L., & Cody, M. J. (1982). Awkward silences: Behavioral antecedents and consequences of the conversational lapse. *Human Communication Research, 8*(4), 299–316.

Molina-Markham, E., van Over, B., Lie, S., & Carbaugh, D. (2015). "OK, talk to you later": Practices of ending and switching tasks in interactions with an in-car voice enabled interface. In T. Milburn (Ed.), *Communicating user experience: Applying local strategies research to digital media design* (pp. 7–25). London: Lexington Books.

Molina-Markham, E., van Over, B., Lie, S., & Carbaugh, D. (2016). "You can do it baby": Non-task talk with an in-car speech enabled system. *Communication Quarterly, 64*(3), 324–347.

Nass, C., & Brave, S. (2005). *Wired for speech. How voice activates and advances the human-computer relationship.* Cambridge, MA: MIT Press.

Nielsen, J. (1993). *Usability engineering.* San Francisco, CA: Morgan Kaufmann Publishers.

Norman, D. (2004). *Emotional design: Why we love (or hate) everyday things.* New York, NY: Basic Civitas Books.

Norman, D., & Draper, S. (1986). *User centered system design; New perspectives on human computer interaction.* Mahwah, NJ: Erlbaum.

Nowak, K. L., & Biocca, F. (2003). The effect of the agency and anthropomorphism on users' sense of telepresence, copresence, and social presence in virtual environments. *Presence: Teleoperators and Virtual Environments, 12*(5), 481–494.

Olshtain, E., & Cohen, A. (1983). Apology: A speech act set. In N. Wolfson and E. Judd (Eds.), *Sociolinguistics and language acquisition* (pp. 18–35). Rowley, MA: Newbury House.

Park, E. K., Lee, K. M., & Shin, D. H. (2015). Social responses to conversational TV VUI: Apology and voice. *International Journal of Technology and Human Interaction (IJTHI), 11*(1), 17–32.

Pearl, C. (2016). *Designing voice user interfaces: Principles of conversational experiences.* Newton, MA: O'Reilly Media.

Philipsen, G. (2002). Cultural communication. In W. Gudykunst & B. Mody (Eds.), *Handbook of international and intercultural communication* (pp. 51–67). London and New Delhi: Sage.

Pomerantz, A. (1984). Agreeing and disagreeing with assessments: Some features of preferred/ dispreferred turn shapes. In J. M. Atkinson & J. Heritage (Eds.), *Structures of social action* (pp. 57–101). Cambridge, UK: Cambridge University Press.

Poutiainen, S. (2015). Interpersonal ideology. In Y. Y. Kim (Gen. Ed.) & K. L. McKay-Semmler (Assoc. Ed.), *The international encyclopedia of language and social interaction* (pp. 1–6). Hoboken, NJ: John Wiley & Sons

Robinson, J. D. (2004). The sequential organization of "explicit" apologies in naturally occurring English. *Research on Language and Social Interaction, 37*(3), 291–330.

Rosenbaun, L., Rafaeli, S., & Kurzon, D. (2016). Blurring the boundaries between domestic and digital spheres: Competing engagements in Public Google Hangouts. *Pragmatics 26*(2), 291–314.

Scher, S. J. (1989). *The effects of apologies and apology structure on social perception and social action* (Unpublished doctoral dissertation). Princeton University, Princeton, NJ.

Scher, S. J., & Darley, J. M. (1997). How effective are the things people say to apologize? Effects of the realization of the apology speech act. *Journal of Psycholinguistic Research, 26*(1), 127–140.

Scher, S. J., & Huff, C. W. (1991). Apologies and causes of transgressions: Further examination of the role of identity in the remedial process. In *Meetings of the Midwestern Psychological Association*, Chicago.

Scollo, M. (2011). Cultural approaches to discourse analysis: A theoretical and methodological conversation with special focus on Donal Carbaugh's cultural discourse theory. *Journal of Multicultural Discourses, 6*(1), 1–32.

Serenko, A. (2007). Are interface agents scapegoats? Attributions of responsibility in human–agent interaction. *Interacting with computers, 19*(2), 293–303.

Short, J., Williams, E., & Christie, B. (1976). *The social psychology of telecommunications.* London: John Wiley & Sons Ltd.

Skarlicki, D. P., Folger, R., & Gee, J. (2004). When social accounts backfire: The exacerbating effects of a polite message or an apology on reactions to an unfair outcome. *Journal of Applied Social Psychology, 34*(2), 322–341.

Tsimhoni, O., Winter, U., & Grost, T. (2009). Cultural considerations for the design of automotive speech applications. In *Proceedings of the 17th World Congress on Ergonomics IEA 2009,* Beijing, China.

van Over, B., Molina-Markham, E., Lie, S., & Carbaugh, D. (2016). Managing interaction with an in-car infotainment system. In N. Shaked & U. Winter (Eds.), *Design of multimodal mobile interfaces* (pp. 145–168). Berlin: De Gruyter.

Vredenburg, K., & Butler, M. (1996). Current practice and future directions in user-centered design. In *Proceedings of Usability Professionals' Association Fifth Annual Conference,* Copper Mountain, CO.

Winter, U., Shmueli, Y., & Grost, T. (2013). Interaction styles in use of automotive interfaces. In *Proceedings of the Afeka AVIOS 2013 Speech Processing Conference,* Tel Aviv, Israel.

Part II

Acting

Chapter Four

When Discourse Matters

Temporality in Discursive Action

Tamar Katriel and Oren Livio

In proposing the research program of cultural discourse analysis (CuDA), Donal Carbaugh has formulated a systematic approach for the study of the interplay of communication and culture. In a recent articulation of this approach, Carbaugh states that "communication presumes and creates a *rich metacultural commentary* through socially situated, culturally named practices" (Carbaugh, 2017, p. 19, emphasis in the original). Tracing this metacultural commentary is a central goal and method of the study of communication as a cultural practice. Carbaugh's CuDA program provides a systematic way to do so by, inter alia, organizing the interpretive process associated with the cultural analysis of communication practices in terms of "discursive hubs," i.e., an open set of (etic) semantic nodes around which communicative practices can be analytically organized, including themes related to participants' identity, relationship, action, feeling, and dwelling (and potentially others). In any situated communicative action, these hubs are structured through "radiants of meaning" (Carbaugh, 2007) that are mostly implicit in interlocutors' utterances. Analysts' interpretive moves are designed to make these implicit and taken-for-granted meanings visible by giving articulation to the cultural premises that ground them. Studies conducted within this framework typically analyze communicative exchanges in terms of the main discursive hubs operative in them (see Carbaugh & Cerulli, 2013, on discourses of dwelling), while also pointing out the different ways in which they relate to other discursive hubs (e.g., dwelling and identity).

Considered within the CuDA framework sketched above, this chapter addresses two recent case studies of political speaking in Israeli speech culture in which the nature of communicative action was intensively discussed

57

and debated, both of which foreground the discursive hub of action. These case studies involved high-profile political moments, marking the potential for political change. In thematizing the discursive hub of action, both foregrounded a cultural tension central to Israeli speech culture—the categorical distinction between words and deeds as a binary opposition (Katriel, 1986).

We have chosen these two cases for both their shared and distinctive features: (1) They each represent a historical moment in which the discursive hub of communicative action was thematized through metadiscursive references in the Israeli political arena; (2) They complement each other, as enactments of grassroots politics of people power (in the first case), and as a top-down, highly institutionalized speech occasion in which state power was put on display (in the second case); (3) Both cases, each in its own way, involve an affirmation that public discourse matters, yet also destabilize entrenched cultural arrangements concerning communicative action. In both cases, too, this affirmation is contested; (4) Both cases provide an empirical anchor for an expansion of the CuDA framework so as to include what we believe is an undertheorized additional discursive hub in it—the temporality of communicative action. We consider the temporality hub to be a necessary counterpart to dwelling-in-place in the theorization of context. Studies of communicative action in struggles for political change provide a productive site for explorations of the interplay between the discursive hubs of action and temporality (Katriel, 2017), and are a good place to start a concerted discussion of the hub of temporality as an additional component of the CuDA framework.

The first case study takes us back to the Israeli social protest of summer 2011. The embodied nature of street protests as a form of bottom-up political action suggests a general feeling that ordinary channels of public communication have run their course, and out-of-the-ordinary forms of discursive action are required to give presence to individuals and groups whose voices are marginalized by political institutions and public media. In a sense, then, it was people's frustration with available means of public communication that gave rise to the protest in the first place, but this widespread discontent was coupled with the belief that public discourse matters and that the populace should reclaim control of it through a creative combination of embodied and discursive means. Thus, although the vibrant communal conversation that arose during and in the aftermath of the 2011 Israeli protest involved a focus on the protest's material goals, its overarching goal was stated in discursive terms as "changing the discourse," or creating "a new discourse" (Livio and Katriel, 2015). As we will show, many of the protesters' practices directly responded to this discursively based transformative vision, which will be explored here in terms of the discursive hubs of action and temporality.

The second case study takes us to the realm of high politics, to the high-profile occasion of Israeli Prime Minister Benjamin Netanyahu's controversial delivery of a speech before the U.S. Congress in March 2015 and the resulting public debate, in which the legitimacy, appropriateness, and potential effects of the speech were discussed. In this context of high-level diplomacy, public discourse in the form of ceremonial speech clearly mattered as Netanyahu's attempt to persuade the United States to change its policy toward Iran's nuclear program put great store on the power of words in the halls of power. In this case, too, the discursive hubs of action and temporality are key to understanding the meanings attending this communicative occasion.

In concluding, we will reflect on what these two very different cases of political discourse can teach us about communicative action and temporality as discursive hubs that give shape to the sphere of political action, which is comprised of various configurations of bottom-up and top-down communication.

ON "CHANGING THE DISCOURSE"

Israel's "tent protest," which began in Tel Aviv in July 2011 and swept across the country during the summer months of that year, involved a vocal demand for social change, resonating with the Occupy movement in countries around the world, which involved, inter alia, a highly visible spatial dimension as street protests do (see Enders & Senda-Cook, 2011). Protesters voiced their discontent with the government's neoliberal economic policies and its relentless move toward the privatization of public services, a policy that led to a rise in housing and living costs and dramatically increased the gap between rich and poor.

Since the grievances that triggered the protest involved issues of distributive justice as they relate to basic goods such as housing, food, employment, health, and education, many of the changes proposed focused on policies that regulate or affect citizens' access to these social goods (e.g., Ram & Filk, 2013; Schechter, 2012). To the ethnographer of communication's ear, however, one strand of discourse stood out in this wide-ranging cultural conversation about change—multiple metadiscursive references by protesters and commentators concerning the need to "change the discourse" [*leshanot et hasi'ax*] or observations concerning the emergence of "a new discourse" [*si'ax xadash*] (e.g., Bing & Wolfson, 2012; Landau, 2011). This focus on discourse as the target of change is grounded in a number of cultural premises concerning communicative action and temporality:

• *There is a dominant public discourse, controlled by the socially and economically powerful, and changing it is a path to social and political change.* [action]

- *Street protest and the discourse produced therein are designed to change public discourse to suit the goals of ordinary citizens.* [action]
- *Street protest is warranted when citizens are disaffected with their current social and political circumstances.* [action, temporality]
- *Street protest is an effective way for citizens to demand change that will affect their future.* [action, temporality]

In framing their demands in terms of new discursive possibilities, participants in the protest thus affirmed their belief in the consequentiality of speech (see also van Over, Dori-Hacohen, & Winchatz, this volume). "Changing the discourse" implied first of all a move away from the usual, highly divisive political Israeli focus on matters of national security, and a direct engagement with social and economic concerns shared by citizens of all political persuasions. This resetting of the public agenda was grounded in (and simultaneously reinforced) the demarcation between the "economic" and the "political," which characterizes Israeli political discourse, and thereby helped to suppress any discussion of the Israeli/Palestinian conflict, the occupation, and the controversial West Bank settlement project (see Gordon, 2012), leading to the claim that the protest was "apolitical." In this context, the invocation of security issues was considered to be a governmental ploy to extinguish the protest. As one activist wrote (Matar, 2011, para. 4):

> In return for our social demands the government offers war. It reinstates the old discourse of security, in which the citizens are required to stand aside, not interfere with the discourse of army generals and experts, and report when they are called up to the flag.

The call to shift the public agenda by focusing attention on socioeconomic issues was grounded in the following cultural premises:

- *The term "political" is restricted to national security issues; therefore, socioeconomic concerns are not political.* [action]
- *While the political establishment (supported by mainstream media) seeks to maintain its dominance by focusing attention on security matters, it is up to the citizenry to contest this power by resetting the public agenda.* [action]

The move away from divisive political issues was attended by the discursive construction of "the people" as a cultural-political category, as expressed by the protest's main slogan, "The people demand social justice." This slogan blurred the fact that not all sectors of Israeli society were in fact represented in the protest scene, and those that were did not have equal weight (Ram & Filk, 2013). By promoting the category of "the people" as a central imaginary figure, protesters attempted to create a sense of unity and common purpose (Laclau, 2006). The common economic issues that stood at the heart of the protest were felt to transcend traditional social divisions, positioning "the people" as a whole as victims of the current exploitative neoliberal economic system.

The call for social inclusiveness and egalitarianism was reflected both in the content of discourse and in the distribution of discursive rights. Thus, both protesters' everyday communicative engagements and the movement's written campaigns emphasized the search for common ground, positioning the people's quest for solidarity as an alternative to the government's "divide and rule" policies. As Stav Shaffir, one of the protest's leaders, claimed:

> I think that something like eighty percent of the Israeli public agree on some-thing like seventy or eighty percent of things. . . . When we sit together, we succeed in reaching agreement. . . . The protest has proven this first and foremost in the tent encampments. People sat in community circles and started reaching agreements. (Oren et al., 2012, p. 340)

In this, as in many other descriptions of the protest scene, newly devised patterns of interaction and forms of communication came to stand for the goal of "changing the discourse." Indeed, we were struck by protesters' heavy reliance on a range of prefigurative strategies in which their vision of a new expressive order was enacted in the form of alternative discursive and interactional patterns, speech occasions, and ways of speaking, as well as a great deal of metadiscursive commentary about them. In what follows, we address these strategies in order to tease out the discursive hubs that organize their enactment and the main radiants of meaning implicit in them.

Our observations indicate that participants in the 2011 protest gravitated to the tent dwellings for the opportunities they provided for direct, face-to-face communicative engagements, relishing in the immediacy of interpersonal yet public-based exchanges. This is notable in the age of social media. Tent compounds were filled with people talking one-on-one, in small groups, and in loosely organized "dialogue circles." Protesters' preference for direct, unmediated exchanges was associated with a quest to promote open and authentic discussion. Encounters were open to all, and participants were encouraged to share both opinions and personal experiences as these related to socioeconomic issues. The adoption of a nonverbal interactional code of gestured feedback borrowed from the Indignados movement in Spain protected turn-taking procedures, enhanced listening, and contributed to a mutually respectful communicative environment, while at the same time delineating borders between protest "insiders" and "outsiders."

Prefiguring an envisioned social and communicative possibility, these exchanges momentarily replaced the usual Israeli media-dominated cacophony of heated public debates, characterized by competition for the floor, impatient overlaps, and interrupted utterances.

Thus, a prominent placard in Tel Aviv's main protest site on Rothschild Boulevard attributed the protest's success to embodied presence and the efficacy of face-to-face interaction, declaring, "The revolution will not be Facebooked!"—intertextually referencing Gil Scott-Heron's protest anthem, "The Revolution Will Not Be Televised."

Clearly, in claiming the streets as urban sites for civic action, and in making the cost of housing the protest's central theme, protesters foregrounded the discursive hub of dwelling (Livio & Katriel, 2014). However, other discursive hubs and radiants of meaning were also operative in the protest's communicative landscape, as indicated by the following set of cultural premises:

- *The street protest scene should prefigure the desired patterns of sociality and communication envisioned by protesters.* [action, relations]
- *Various configurations of unmediated, nonhierarchical, and affirmative face-to-face communication enacted in protest sites, ranging from more formalized "dialogue circles" to ad hoc interactional encounters, prefigure the spirit of solidarity promoted by the protest.* [action, relations, temporality]

These prefigurations of the future were enacted through language creativity and play. Traditional lexical sign systems were resemanticized. For example, the term "security" [*bitaxon*], which is customarily linked in Israeli speech to national security–related threats, was reinterpreted in civic terms. As Matar (2011, para. 5) explained:

> In the new civic dictionary security is no longer war. . . . This summer we said that security is also the knowledge that a person will have a roof over his head for the night, food and water, proper and equal access to education, strong and functioning healthcare and welfare systems, social rights and stability at work.

Furthermore, protesters playfully manipulated linguistic symbols as a means of challenging the ideological constraints embedded in traditional language structures. Signs scattered across protest sites suggested a "new alphabet" in which letters stood for words signaling the protest's targets for change, such as "education," "welfare," and "rights." The headline of one of these signs proclaimed, "We have resuscitated language, we will resuscitate education as well." Protesters also played with grammatical gender rules, creating hybrid masculine and feminine neologisms that they claimed would lead to "an upgrading of the Hebrew language, a release from the chains of gender" (cited in Oren et al., 2012, p. 276).

A demand for transparency and an aversion to behind-the-scenes politicking also marked the cultivation of democratic participation within the protest scene. Deliberations and decision-making took place in public meetings open to all (Schechter, 2012). One of the main protest websites was the wiki "Transparent in the Tent" (*shakuf baohel*), on which members were encouraged to upload protocols of local meetings. Failures of transparency on the part of the protest's recognized "leaders" were criticized as undemocratic practices. And while the protesters' demand that their planned meeting with the prime minister be broadcast live in the service of transparency was dropped after being harshly criticized in the press, transparent communication as both a tool and an emblem of democratic inclusivity was generally upheld.

These creative practices were grounded in cultural premises that linked linguistic action and form, including:

- *Verbal and nonverbal modes of expression, such as displays of attentiveness, displays of considerateness, and nonintrusive regulation of turns-at-talk prefigure the distinctive mode of sociality envisioned by the protesters.* [action, relations, temporality]
- *Extending the forms and meanings of the culture's lexicon and its interactional possibilities symbolizes the protest's spirit of promise in the present moment.* [action, temporality]

The novelty of the speech forms and practices cultivated in the "tent republic" was a source of fascination, as expressed by a blogger-visitor who wrote, "I have never seen so many people listening to one another with such politeness and respect" (Free in Israel, 2011, para. 14).

In sum, throughout much of the 2011 Israeli summer protest and in its aftermath, protesters and commentators often constructed and evaluated the desired social change in metadiscursive rather than in institutional, regulatory, or material terms. The protest's call for "changing the discourse" was prefigured in various levels of linguistic enactment, including the facilitation of face-to-face encounters in the public sphere through new rules of interpersonal engagement, the resemanticization of core language symbols, and the reflexive and playful attention to language form and usage in constructing a distinctive and localized protest-related, homogenizing lexicon. In some commentaries, "changing the discourse" was described as the protest's primary goal (e.g., Bing & Wolfson, 2012); in others it was seen as a necessary prelude to changing material reality (e.g., Feuer, 2011); in yet others, changes in discourse and changes in the real world were presented as dialectically constitutive (e.g., Misgav, 2012).

Notably, however, the protest movement was also criticized for its over-emphasis on discourse, which was considered by some critics as a frivolous and illusory distraction in a world where real change requires structurally oriented political action (e.g., Landau, 2011; Nosatzky, 2013). These critics contested basic cultural premises upheld by calls for a new discourse, offering alternative ones:

- *Discursive activity does not amount to political action.* [action]
- *Social and political change involves structural changes, policy changes, and a redistribution of wealth.* [action, relations]

Can we then say that the protest's intervention in the discursive and power arrangements was consequential? Does the eruption of a bottom-up public discourse matter? These questions are still asked in postmortem analyses of the 2011 summer protest. The answers to these questions, as we have attempted to show, at least partly depend on the cultural premises concerning the working of discourse.

Our second case, which involves the public debate surrounding Prime Minister Netanyahu's U.S. Congress speech in March 2015, similarly addresses a communicative occasion in which the question of the consequentiality of discourse came to the fore. The heated controversy that arose on this occasion of speechmaking can, we believe, also be productively addressed with reference to the discursive hubs of action and temporality, among others.

BENJAMIN NETANYAHU'S 2015 U.S. CONGRESS SPEECH

On March 3, 2015, at the invitation of Republican leaders, Israeli Prime Minister Benjamin Netanyahu delivered a speech in the American Congress. As one Israeli journalist wrote, it "was one of the most widely covered speeches in the modern era" (Shalev, 2015, para. 9). In this speech Netanyahu reiterated his well-publicized opposition to then U.S. President Barack Obama's plan to sign a nuclear weapons agreement with Iran.

In a political culture where public speaking matters, as it does in contemporary democratic societies, high-profile political speeches tend to draw extensive media commentary that gives rise to divergent political assessments and articulates implicit cultural premises about public communication. Notably, all commentators—whatever their position about the speech—shared a basic premise concerning its importance as a public gesture, affirming the following premises:

- *The U.S. Congress is a cultural arena designated for consequential speech occasions and speeches delivered in it do and should matter.* [action, dwelling]

- *Official speeches in the U.S. Congress are regulated and restricted to ratified speakers.* [action, dwelling, identity]

Despite these shared assumptions about the import of congressional speeches, the particular oratorical event we address triggered an unusually heated public debate. Initially, the debate was anticipatory, as commentators disputed whether Netanyahu should accept the invitation to the U.S. Congress. Following the event, the speech's content, delivery, and potential outcomes were variously evaluated, with multiple metadiscursive references to elements of the speech itself, to its situational anchoring, and to the rules of appropriateness that grounded its enactment. In what follows, we explore the major strands of controversy that surrounded this speech, bringing out the discursive hubs around which these positions were organized and the radiants of meaning implicit in them.

The main controversy surrounding Netanyahu's appearance before Congress was related to its timing since the speech was scheduled for just two weeks before the 2015 Israeli elections. In the past, care had been taken not to schedule such speeches during election campaigns, as the White House sought to avoid the appearance of intervention in foreign elections. In addition, the White House appeared to be displeased with Netanyahu's publicized plans to accept the invitation, which had been issued by the Republican wing in Congress only, rather than being a bipartisan initiative that might have justified this diplomatic *faux-pas* (and as originally reported in Israeli media).

Opponents and supporters of Netanyahu's Congress appearance held conflicting assumptions about this discursive performance. The opponents' underlying premise was, *Invitations to guest speakers before Congress, which mark high-profile ceremonial moments, should be issued by overwhelming consent and avoid controversial issues, especially the appearance of intervention in foreign countries' political processes* [identity, dwelling, relation].

In contradistinction, Netanyahu's supporters in this matter held that *The urgency of the moment—the impending nuclearization of Iran—justifies the violation of diplomatic protocol* [action, temporality].

This speech occasion thus emerged as a peak moment in the ongoing clash of political wills between Netanyahu and Obama over questions of foreign policy. Shortly before the event, the White House spokesperson issued an unprecedentedly sharp warning to Netanyahu, urging him not to include confidential information in his speech (Dyer & Reed, 2015). At the same time, while the Israeli press was filled with articles warning of a total breakdown of relations between Israel and the United States, President Obama drew a line between the anticipated speech and long-term Israel-U.S. diplomatic relations. As one journalist wrote before the speechmaking event:

"Netanyahu's speech in Congress will not be permanently destructive to the relations between Israel and the US, but it will be a distraction from what should be our focus," said Obama in an interview to Reuters. . . . "It is a mistake for the Prime Minister of any country to come to speak before Congress a few weeks before they are about to have an election. It makes it look like we are taking sides." (Eichner, 2015, p. 4)

It appears that in addition to defending the integrity of the Israeli political process, the White House sought to maintain the status of Congress as a distinctly American political arena. Netanyahu's recruitment by the Republicans was perceived by the White House and many Democrats as an inappropriate intervention in the ongoing foreign policy debate between Democrats and Republicans. In the case of Netanyahu, this resonated with his blatant support of Republicans in the U.S. elections two years earlier. Thus, the U.S. president's explicit reluctance to intervene in the Israeli elections was implicitly contrasted with the Israeli prime minister's repeated willingness to play his cards in the American political arena. This willingness, in turn, was interpreted in radically different ways—by his supporters as marking Netanyahu's political stature and personal courage, and by his opponents as signaling his provocative and meddlesome stance, to the point of speculating that it would encourage the anti-Semitic view of Jews as bent on manipulating world leaders into war (e.g., Shalev, 2015).

Much of the anticipatory metadiscursive discussion, then, focused on the contextual elements of the speech as a public event, including the conditions of domestic political rivalry in the United States, the diplomatic conflict in which it became embroiled, and the situational parameters associated with the particular arena in which it was delivered, rather than with its content. "The speech" thus became a metonymic replacement for the political and diplomatic relations of power that its delivery simultaneously reflected and constituted. In accepting the invitation to Congress, Netanyahu placed language and oratory at the center of the political process and positioned himself as his people's messenger:

I must fulfill my obligation to speak up on a matter that affects the very survival of my country. . . . And I intend to speak in the US Congress because Congress might have an important role [*sic*] on a nuclear deal with Iran. (Netanyahu, 2015, para. 12–13)

In accounting for his decision to hold the speech, Netanyahu employed the language of duty, appealing to the following cultural premise: *As Israel's leader, Netanyahu has a duty to represent his people's interests and speak his mind under any circumstances (even at the risk of violating diplomatic protocol)* [action, dwelling, temporality, identity].

Since Netanyahu objected to the U.S. negotiations with Iran over the latter's nuclear program, considering this diplomatic move as a danger to Israel's security, he saw it as his duty to seize any opportunity he was given to have his say, brushing aside any suggestion that it had anything to do with electioneering, i.e., with timing. This self-presentation, however, was met with considerable mistrust. As explained by *Haaretz* political analyst Yossi Verter (2015, para. 1), "Netanyahu hopes to win the 2015 elections with what he does best: an onslaught of words," explicitly comparing Netanyahu's speech with Israeli Prime Minister Menachem Begin's decision to order the destruction of an Iraqi nuclear reactor during the 1981 election campaign.

American commentators stressed that the speech's content did not justify the violation of diplomatic protocol it entailed. For example, immediately following the speech President Obama declared that "there was nothing new" in it (Calamur, 2015), and CNN correspondent Jake Tapper quoted an anonymous White House official who claimed that the speech contained "literally, not one new idea; not one single concrete alternative; all rhetoric, no action" (Taub, 2015, para. 1). The cultural premise underlying this critique was that *The violation of discursive rules of appropriateness is warranted only when it facilitates the presentation of important new ideas.*

In mainstream Israel the speech was proclaimed a resounding success, with its character framed in terms of a variety of action-infused verbs such as "demanded," "presented an alternative," "offered a new strategy," "forewarned," "walked like a rhetorical artist," and so forth. Israeli public opinion appeared to side with this latter view: whereas polls carried out before the speech found only 36 percent of Jewish Israelis supporting Netanyahu's decision to speak, with 52 percent opposed and the rest undecided (Nrg News, 2015), polls carried out after the speech demonstrated an increase in positive evaluations of the speech's efficacy and in support for Netanyahu and his Likud Party. In the one poll directly asking about the effect of the speech (Channel 2 News, 2015), 44 percent said that it had positively influenced their support of Netanyahu, 43 percent said it had had no effect, and only 12 percent said it had weakened their support. Thus, the Israeli public accepted the cultural premise that *International diplomacy is an extension of warfare via other (discursive) means, and the American Congress is an important arena where Israel's struggle over its security must be waged, as Netanyahu has appropriately done* [action, dwelling, relations].

It appears, then, that the controversy surrounding Netanyahu's Congress speech was less about the consequentiality of speech than about its conditions of appropriateness. The U.S. Congress, as a culturally ratified "house of speaking," gives resonance to public speaking, at times generating clashing waves of commentary grounded in conflicting cultural premises, as in the case at hand.

CONCLUDING REMARKS

The two case studies we have discussed both relate to historical junctures in which Israeli cultural conversation became momentarily dominated by attention to speech action and by extensive metadiscursive discussion that affirmed the basic cultural assumption that discourse matters, even though the extent to which and the ways in which it mattered were open to contestation. The two cases were deliberately chosen for the very different positions they represent as forms of political discourse. While the city streets that housed the 2011 summer protest were turned into an ad hoc site for political expression, the House of Congress is an established location for the discursive enactment of the democratic process; and while protesters mobilized "people power" to make their voices heard in "conquering" urban spaces, Congress is an institutional yet discursively anchored political arena in which speech is formal, and even becomes ceremonial when nonmember guests are invited to speak.

In formulating the cultural premises underlying speech enactments in both cases, we have pointed out the working of several discursive hubs identified by Carbaugh (2007), including *identity, dwelling, relation, feeling,* and mainly *action*. Our main theoretical contribution, however, is to propose an additional hub of *temporality* to the CuDA framework. The relevance of this proposed discursive hub to our particular case studies is quite evident, as they both thematize future-oriented action, though in quite different ways. In the 2011 summer protest, calls to "change the discourse" or to forge "a new discourse" were clearly future-oriented, as are all calls for change. These calls implied recognition of the action potential of discourse and of its formative role in social affairs. They were thus infused with a prefigurative temporality that found its expression in the alternative communicative landscape fostered within the protest's "tent republic." Talk about discursive change also allowed for flexibility in evaluating the protest's *achievements* in retrospect, since it was impossible to determine the degree to which a "change in discourse" had in fact occurred. This vagueness thus served to cultivate a sense that the protest was successful (see also Juris, 2012).

Second, and relatedly, talk about discursive change as a search for new forms of communicative encounters and public dialogue addressed a general sense of *political* inefficacy felt among a growing number of citizens. In particular, the protest arena attracted youth disenchanted with mainstream politics, who sought to disengage themselves from large-scale, highly bureaucratized and technologized state-related social processes in favor of the relative intimacy of personal encounters and face-to-face communal gatherings that could provide a sense of hope and possibility in a shared struggle for social change (Herzog, 2013).

In retrospect, while some commentators commended the Israeli 2011 summer protest's achievement as having succeeded in radically "changing the discourse," others highlighted its lack of significant concrete political accomplishments (e.g., Gordon, 2012). Others left the question open. Thus, journalist and activist Dror Feuer (2011, para. 8–9) noted that "what is defined as the protest's greatest victory thus far, changing the discourse, or the new discourse," remains unclear, and asked "what does it actually consist of, this new discourse? Has it really changed anything?" Similarly, evaluating the protest's achievements on its two-year anniversary, blogger-activist Shir Nosatsky (2013, para. 3, 5) wrote: "Everyone starts . . . by dramatically declaring 'there is no doubt that public discourse has greatly changed.' . . . But with discourse you can't go to the convenience store. We don't have the privilege of dealing with this only by talking." Looking back, then, it appears that the risk of an overreliance on discourse as a locus of change has led to a shift toward more concrete social and political initiatives, including the election of two of the protest leaders to Parliament, greater media emphasis on economic inequality and misconduct, the formation of new locally based partnerships, and so on.

In the case of Netanyahu's Congress speech, the heightened reflexive attention to discourse was an intrinsic part of the political process, and can be seen as an offshoot of a long-standing Western political tradition that places oratory at the heart of political action. Indeed, the metadiscourse surrounding political speeches is grounded in a language ideology that acknowledges the action potential of speech so that, in the words of political scientist Murray Edelman, "political language *is* political reality" (Edelman, 1964, p. 1, emphasis in the original). In this view, whether a speech performance is persuasive or not, even ineffective speeches do not compromise the potential value of doing political things with words. Since the use of persuasive language is the human way of forestalling and regulating violence, the effectiveness of political speechmaking is always both contingent and materially consequential. The case of Netanyahu's U.S. Congress speech is striking in that although it gripped public attention to an almost unprecedented degree, public commentary focused on the circumstances and potential consequences of its delivery rather than on its content (except to complain there was nothing new in it). Therefore, this speechmaking occasion needs to be considered in terms of the contextual dimensions of public speaking as a form of political action and symbolic display, not as a rhetorical-textual product.

The two case studies we have discussed demonstrate different ways in which the discursive hub of temporality may come to occupy center stage in a CuDA-oriented analysis, throwing new light on the nature of political action. Four aspects of temporality came to the fore in our analyses, as the temporality associated with discourses of social change was grounded in (1) a linear (rather than cyclical) view of time; (2) a future (rather than past or present) orientation, whether it is infused by a sense of hope as in the first case or by a sense of threat as in the second; (3) a concern with timing; and (4) a sense of urgency.

Addressing these temporally related issues, and linking them to issues of place, identity, and relations, our analysis has brought out the central role played by the discursive hubs of action and temporality in structuring our understanding of the rich metadiscursive commentary that surrounded both grassroots and institutional political discourse in the cases we studied. We believe that more concerted and systematic attention to temporality can provide new insights into the meaning of situated speech occasions of the kind addressed in many CuDA studies, and thus help to further illuminate the cultural worlds in which they find their place.

REFERENCES

Bing, E., & Wolfson, T. (June 17, 2012). The protest's most significant accomplishment is changing public discourse: An interview with Esther Dominicini. *The Economics and Society Program Magazine.* Retrieved from https://vanleerecon.wordpress.com/2012/06/17/ (Hebrew)

Calamur, K. (March 3, 2015). "Nothing new" in Netanyahu's speech, Obama says. NPR. Retrieved from http://www.npr.org/sections/thetwo-way/2015/03/03/390457724/praise-criticism-for-netanyahus-speech

Carbaugh, D. (2007). Cultural discourse analysis: The investigation of communication practices with special attention to intercultural encounters. *Journal of Intercultural Communication Research, 36,* 167–182.

Carbaugh, D. (2017). Terms for talk, take 2: Theorizing communication through its cultural terms and practices. In D. Carbaugh (Ed.), *The handbook of communication in cross-cultural perspective* (pp. 15–28). London: Routledge.

Carbaugh, D., & Cerulli, T. (2013). Cultural discourses of dwelling: Investigating environmental communication as a place-based practice. *Environmental Communication: The Journal of Nature and Culture, 7,* 4–23.

Channel 2 News (March 4, 2015). The poll after the Congress speech: The Likud and Netanyahu are stronger. Mako. Retrieved from http://www.mako.co.il/news-military/politics-q1_2015/Article-ea17ea292c5eb41004.htm

Dyer, G., & Reed, J. (March 3, 2015). White House pushes back on Netanyahu. *Financial Times.* Retrieved from http://www.ft.com/cms/s/0/b17c894e-c0f3-11e4-876d-00144feab7de.html#axzz3d1qIolp5

Edelman, M. (1964). *The symbolic uses of politics.* Urbana, IL: University of Illinois Press.

Eichner, I. (March 3, 2015). The speech is a distraction. *Yedioth Ahronoth,* p. 4 (Hebrew).

Enders, D., & Senda-Cook, S. (2011). Location matters: The rhetoric of place in protest. *Quarterly Journal of Speech, 97,* 257–282.

Feuer, D. (December 13, 2011). "The new Israelis?" Nothing's happened yet. Globes. Retrieved from http://www.globes.co.il/news/article.aspx?did=1000706496 (Hebrew)

Free in Israel (July 25, 2011). On indulgence [blog post]. Retrieved from https://freeisraeli.wordpress.com/2011/07/25/ (Hebrew).

Gordon, U. (2012). Israel's "tent protests": The chilling effect of nationalism. *Social Movement Studies, 11*(3/4), 349–355.

Herzog, H. (2013). A generational and gender view of the tent protest. *Theory and Criticism, 41,* 69–96 (Hebrew).

Juris, J. S. (2012). Reflections on #Occupy everywhere: Social media, public space, and emerging logics of aggregation. *American Ethnologist, 39*(2), 259–279.

Katriel, T. (1986). *Talking straight: Dugri speech in Israeli sabra culture.* Cambridge: Cambridge University Press.

Katriel, T. (2017). *"A day will come": Alternative temporalities in media activism projects.* Paper presented at the "Public Time and Accelerated Futures" Israel Science Foundation research workshop, March 14–16.

Laclau, E. (2006). Why constructing a people is the main task of radical politics. *Critical Inquiry, 32*(4), 646–680.

Landau, I. (August 8, 2011). Taming the struggle: Disturbances at the fence, committees in Jerusalem [blog post]. Retrieved from http://idanlandau.com/2011/08/08/68845/ (Hebrew)

Livio, O., & Katriel, T. (2014). A fractured solidarity: Communitas and structure in the Israeli 2011 social protest. In P. Werbner, M. Webb, & K. Spellman-Poots (Eds.), *The political aesthetics of global protest: The Arab spring and beyond* (pp. 147–176). Edinburgh: Edinburgh University Press.

Livio, O., & Katriel, T. (2015). Between nostalgia and utopia: Meta-communicative aspects of the 2011 Israeli social protest. In N. Elias, G. Nimrod, Z. Reich, & A. Schejter (Eds.), *Media in transition: In honor of Dan Caspi and his scholarship* (pp. 29–50). Tel Aviv: Tzivonim (Hebrew)

Matar, H. (August 18, 2011). Civil refusal in September. MySay. Retrieved September 30, 2011, from mysay.co.il (Hebrew)

Misgav, U. (October 26, 2012). The protest in service of Netanyahu. *Haaretz.* Retrieved from http://www.haaretz.co.il/opinions/1.1850228 (Hebrew)

Netanyahu, B. (February 10, 2015). *Statement by PM Netanyahu.* Prime Minister's Office. Retrieved from http://www.pmo.gov.il/English/MediaCenter/Spokesman/Pages/spokeusa100215.aspx

Nosatzky, S. (2013). Exactly two years since the start of the protest: What have we succeeded in changing? [blog post]. Retrieved from http://www.mako.co.il/video-blogs-shir-nosatzki/Article-5db4a8048fcdf31004.htm (Hebrew)

Nrg News (February 14, 2015). Poll: Most of the public—the PM should not speak before Congress. Nrg. Retrieved from http://www.nrg.co.il/online/1/ART2/676/312.html (Hebrew)

Oren, B., et al. (2012). The field of tents: Conclusions from the social protest. Retrieved from http://shakufbaohel.org.il/index.php?title

Ram, U., & Filk, D. (2013). Daphni Leef's July 14th: The rise and fall of the social protest. *Theory and Criticism, 41,* 17–43 (Hebrew).

Schechter, A. (2012). *Rothschild: The story of a protest movement.* Tel Aviv: Hakibbutz Hameuchad (Hebrew).

Shalev, C. (March 6, 2015). If the speech leads to confrontation, Israel will not have an alibi this time. *Haaretz.* Retrieved from http://www.haaretz.co.il/news/politics/.premium-1.2582373 (Hebrew)

Taub, A. (March 3, 2015). White House official on Netanyahu speech: "Literally not one new idea." Vox. Retrieved from http://www.vox.com/2015/3/3/8141157/netanyahu-congress-speech-whitehouse

Verter, Y. (March 4, 2015). The Congress speech: Netanyahu hopes to win the elections with words. *Haaretz.* Retrieved from http://www.haaretz.co.il/news/elections/.premium-1.2580431 (Hebrew)

Chapter Five

Cultural Discourse Analysis as Critical Analysis

A View from Twin Oaks and SuicideForum.com

Jolane Flanigan and Mike Alvarez

According to Philipsen (1989/1990), the task of the ethnographer is to understand and appreciate the discursive practices of the people they study. It is not for the ethnographer to judge but to interpret, to suspend judgment until the ethnographic work is finished, for judging too soon could limit the insights one attains. Huspek (1989/1990) concurs, in that the ethnographer should avoid the grievous error of imposing their criteria of truth and rationality and "foisting upon members of a culture foreign principles to live by" (p. 309). However, this does not mean there is no room for critique, for the critical mode is after all one of the five investigative modes of cultural discourse analysis (CuDA) (Carbaugh, 2007). In the critical mode, a practice is evaluated (judged good or bad) from an ethical juncture or standpoint; it may ask who is being privileged by a communicative practice, and who is being disadvantaged by it. Because the task of CuDA is to theorize, describe, and interpret such practices, critique is not essential, but neither is it excluded. As Carbaugh has stated (1989/1990), it does not mean systems of inequality must go unchallenged, only that they must not be assumed *a priori*. In fact, ethnography can be critical even when the intention is not to be so. By creating a "discourse of distance" (p. 276), the ethnographer might call attention to aspects of cultural life others might want to keep hidden, and "help correct misimpressions and oppressions by the 'other'" (ibid.).

The present chapter honors CuDA's critical mode by presenting two cases in which the communicative practices and expressive activities of marginalized communities open up dominant discourses to closer inspection and critique. Both began with the modest goals of description and interpretation, and with the assumption central to cultural discourse theory that when participants speak, they are not only saying something about the topic at hand, they are also making metacultural commentaries about how to act, how to feel, how to relate to others, how to be, and how to inhabit the world—what Carbaugh (2007, 2017) calls *radiants* of acting, feeling, relating, being, and dwelling, respectively. These radiants of meaning are activated every time *discursive hubs* are used, which are those words, phrases, gestures, symbols, and terms that are pregnant with meaning for participants, evidenced by their emphatic usage, frequency of use, and mutual intelligibility to said participants. Hubs and radiants are inseparable; they are always activated at the same time, though not all hubs are salient in every scene, and the activation of one hub can activate one or more of the other hubs. Over the course of tracking hubs of action of interest, however, we arrived not only at corresponding radiants of meaning, but at an indirect mode of criticism grounded in participants' own terms. We offer these in the form of *norms* and *cultural premises* (italicized throughout). The former are prescriptions for proper conduct or action. The latter are abstract formulations that capture taken-for-granted knowledge and participant beliefs about the current state of things, and their evaluative judgments about the ideal state of things (Carbaugh, 2007).

In the first case study, Flanigan presents findings from her fieldwork in Twin Oaks, an intentional community in Louisa County, Virginia.[1] With a corpus of thirty-seven field note entries, two group interviews, twelve individual interviews, and two naturally occurring conversations (all of which had been recorded), Flanigan used CuDA in tandem with Hymes's (1972) descriptive theory to formulate the norms, rules, and premises that give Oakian communicative practices form and meaning for its members. In the course of her analysis, she observed that the dominant styles of communicating on the farm privileged white middle-class members and discriminated against the communicative styles of working-class members and members of color. She confirms Huspek's (1989/1990) position that within a community, even one as egalitarian as Twin Oaks, practices of inclusion and exclusion may exist to confer advantages to some members and disadvantages to others.

In the second case study, Alvarez heeds Hecht's (2010) call to extend culture to entities not previously considered by studying the online communication of suicidal individuals, arguing that cyberspace presents us with a unique opportunity to discover how persons with *discreditable* stigmas (Goffman, 1963) coconstruct meaning outside of clinical contexts. In order to arrive at cultural premises and corresponding *radiants* of being, feeling, acting, and relating, he systematically tracked participants' usage of the word "suicide" (a hub of action) and other relevant hubs, including "suicidal" (a hub of identity and emotion), in 951 messages across 45 threads in SuicideF-orum.com, the communication scene (Hymes, 1972) in question. His findings reveal that the clinical portrait of suicidal persons does not always align with suicidal persons' grounded experiences, highlighting CuDA's applicability to clinical and therapeutic practice.

In our work, we endeavored to listen to cultural voices "from the standpoint of those who create them" (Carbaugh, 1989/1990, p. 279), to discover the worlds of communities "in their own terms and tensions" (p. 278). As such, the natural and cultural criticisms (Carbaugh, 1989/1990) that we offer stem not from us, the ethnographers, but from the interlocutors (the *locus* of criticism) themselves.

A GROUNDED CRITIQUE OF COMMUNICATION IN TWIN OAKS

Next to the South Anna River in Louisa, Virginia, are the more than four hundred wooded acres of Twin Oaks property. Tucked into these woods are the seven residences, the industrial buildings (saw mill, tofu hut, warehouse), the conference site, the dining hall, a retreat cabin, a dairy barn, three composting toilets, chicken coops, and two large gardens. I (Flanigan) spent nearly ten months in residence "on the farm" interested in and learning about their communication practices as they related to their egalitarian identity.[2] During my time on the farm, talk related to a normative Oakian style of communication permeated daily conversations. Much of this everyday talk critiqued the utility and function of what Oakers referred to variously as "the written culture," "passive aggressive communication," or a "middle class" style of communication on the farm. These terms were treated as key cultural symbols—defined as terms that are mutually intelligible, deeply felt, and widely accessible to a group of people—and became the focus of data generation (Carbaugh, 1988). The interpretive analysis of the cultural discourse being tapped in attending to these communication patterns focused on the hub of action with associated implicit and explicit meanings, with emotion being the key radiant (Carbaugh, 2007, 2017).

The distinction between public and private contexts as a dimension of interpersonal communication is necessary to understand before explicating normative communication practices on the farm. Weintraub (1997) argues that there are two fundamental distinctions made between public and private. One is the distinction between what is hidden and what is openly observable while the other is a distinction between what is individual and what is collective or communal. In terms of communication practices on the farm, the more public a space, the more Oakers could be seen and heard and the more communicative practices were expected to adhere to community norms. In private relationships and spaces, members were not (typically) seen or heard and there communicative practices could be idiosyncratic. While the only spaces defined as private were members' bedrooms, spaces such as the woods were understood to be more private than, for example, the Courtyard, which served as a primary hub of community activity.

Just as the public or private nature of spaces dictated appropriate ways of communicating, so too did the public or private nature of members' relationships dictate the kind of communication that took place in them. Members who had close personal relationships with one another had norms that governed communication that were sometimes distinct from the prevailing norms on the farm. These norms, then, were understood by the membership to be private, and unless the private relational communication violated Twin Oaks' core principles (e.g., nonviolence) or became public (e.g., due to loudness), it was left to relationship partners to work out their style of communication. Conversely, members who did not have close relationships tended to follow the normative patterns of communicating on the farm. These relationships took place in less private spaces and were more a part of the normative, public communication culture. Thus, normative communication patterns were found in these less private relationships, or when personal friends were in a public space.

Normative Styles of Communicating on the Farm

There were four key norms active on the farm. The first was that *members could communicate if they wanted to, but could also choose not to communicate if they did not want to do so.* This norm shaped everyday behaviors such as requesting to talk with a member rather than assuming it would be fine to do so or disengaging from a conversation before others were satisfied by it. Thus, a member would say, "Can I ask you a question?" rather than asking the question outright. Or a member could disengage from a conversation with another Oaker by simply stating, "I'm angry, too, and I'm hanging up now because I've already answered that question," as Dave, a member who lived in my residence, did. Because it was acceptable to choose not to discuss an issue with another member, a neutral third party would sometimes be chosen to engage in the communication deemed necessary to resolve the issue.

A second Oakian norm institutionalized confidential communication, which was understood to facilitate communication. Thus, *if the community wanted to promote the communication of honest opinions and feelings about potential members as well as existing members, then the community must allow this type of feedback to be confidential.*[3] Premised on a belief that constructive feedback can be received as positive criticism by some and as negative criticism by others, confidential communication enabled members to give feedback without fearing consequences that would make living on the farm with a disgruntled communard emotionally difficult. Tea, for example, explained the outcome of her decision not to remain confidential when veto-ing a person for membership.[4] In the end she said, "It was emotionally costly. It was really hard to live with the negative feedback I got from not supporting him for membership." While all members could waive confiden-tiality, the vast majority did not. Practicing confidential communication was generally unremarkable and expected, and for some, a highly celebrated way of communicating that enabled the honest communication of potentially hurt-ful observations and feelings by lessening the fear of retaliation or protracted conflict.

While confidentiality was generally understood on the farm as a practice that allowed members to give others constructive feedback without repercus-sions, it was also a practice that masked the identity of a member in a public conversation so that others would not have a negative evaluation of that member. I first noticed this practice during my visitor meetings when mem-bers used words such as "some members" and "co," a gender neutral pro-noun, in conversation (see Flanigan [2013] for an analysis of "co"). While related to the norm of confidential feedback presented above, this aspect of normative confidentiality could best be phrased as *in everyday public conver-sations about controversial topics or objectionable behaviors, members should maintain other members' confidentiality*. As with the aforementioned confidentiality norm, this norm enabled Oakers to preserve privacy and less-en the possibility of interpersonal conflict.

Analyzing norms for communication as a hub of action on the farm re-veals a key radiant of meaning: emotion. While the above norms regulated whether or not and how a member communicated, norms regulating the communication of emotion were perhaps the most vital for achieving an understanding of an Oakian style of communication. On the farm, members tended not to express strong emotion, especially those that were considered to evoke negative feelings in others, such as anger and rage. Instead, mem-bers promoted the explicit statement of their thoughts and feelings—articu-lating specific emotions experienced—rather than relying on the nonverbal communication of affect to convey emotion. This was also a norm governing Dave's choice to disengage from the phone conversation quoted above. Dave explicitly stated that he was "angry."

Of course, members did communicate in ways that were not understood to be calm, and these instances were generally chalked up to either a person having a bad day or, more than likely, that person's rather unfortunate per-sonality. On the farm, there were clear proscriptions on how emotion was communicated. The most strongly proscribed way was characterized as loud, and when a member did not disengage from communication to prevent a heightened expression of emotion, s/he was also understood to be aggressive and confrontational. Marked as violent and unsafe, this style of communicat-ing utilized the body as a medium for the expression of negative emotion (anger) or sentiment (disapproval of another's thoughts or opinions). While it was fine to have an argument "in the most quietest of terms," as Watermelon observed, it was strongly proscribed to yell. While it was celebrated to state verbally that one was angry, it was threatening to embody that anger and express it through raised voice or agitated movement. The link between loud, confrontational, and bodily emotional expression and violence was not, as will be discussed in the following section, held by all members, but it was a pervasive belief that was occasionally made explicit in conversation. "We're a nonviolent community. You can't yell at your partner while cooking dinner," Beth offered, explaining how Twin Oaks culture shapes interpersonal communication.

The proscriptions can be summarized in two norms: *On the farm, if one wants to be an effective and well-liked member, then one should not express negative emotion loudly—either vocally or with one's body. It is preferred that members articulate their emotional experiences with words, either in writing or in face-to-face communication, rather than to rely on their bodies to express emotion.* These norms were especially important in interpersonal conflict, but they also applied to situations where members were upset with community policy-making. In the next section, I discuss Oakers' race- and class-based critiques of normative Oakian communication.

Egalitarianism Doesn't Mean Equity: Raced and Classed Communication Practices

In many ways Oakers were a self-reflective lot who took their identity as an experimental community seriously. When members found a community practice objectionable, open communication was supported and effort was made to analyze issues and rectify problems. In my time on the farm there was no more hotly discussed issue than Oakian communication practices. While the above section worked to explicate a normative style of communicating on the farm, this section utilizes *naturally occurring criticisms* to develop a race- and class-based critique of this style of communicating (Carbaugh, 1989/1990).

Critiques of Oakian communication practices clustered around the terms "passive aggressive," "middle-class community," and "written culture." In the early months of my stay, I heard these critiques as general statements made about a "middle-class" communication system that relied heavily on personal choice, confidential feedback, calm emotional expression, and writing. Accordingly, the issues identified stemmed from the middle-class architects of the community who crafted a communication system that was biased toward a middle-class ideology. Toward the later months of my fieldwork, however, the critiques had come to identify normative Oakian communication practices not just as "middle class," but as racist. It was not just that

Oakers practiced a "middle-class" way of communicating; it was that the system, now also identified as a white system, marginalized people of color and the working class. These class- and race-based critiques pivoted on two key interrelated issues: directness and honesty.

Twin Oaks' elaborate system of written communication was often cited as the primary issue for members of color. According to Black members, Oakers' reliance on written communication perpetuated indirect and passive-aggressive communication. A stylistic difference identifiable in broader U.S. culture (Kochman, 1990; Spears, 2001), Black members rejected indirect, written communication, instead favoring direct, face-to-face communication. For example, April, a new member of color who identified as middle class, participated in a series of practical jokes that culminated in turning several items in a residence upside down. Because a residence was considered to be relatively private space, this type of practical joke was potentially problematic and could jeopardize April's acceptance into full membership. Concerned for April, Karl wrote her a note saying that he had "reason to believe that [she was] a member of the upside down club" and that he "suspect[ed] [she wouldn't] be accepted for membership." While Karl was motivated by a genuine fondness for April, she understood this note to be a part of Twin Oakian passive-aggressive culture. Wanting to make clear her position on written interpersonal communication, April took what was intended to be a private note and posted it on the O&I (opinions and information) board, a wall of clipboards that members used to discuss community issues, along with the explanation that members who had an issue with her or her behavior should talk with her face-to-face. The O&I conversation on this issue was short-lived and consisted mostly of public interpersonal repair work being done by both Karl and April. However, having violated an Oakian conceptualization of confidentiality, April's posting of Karl's note resulted in negative feedback for April that extended beyond the O&I conversation.

As part of the membership process, after three months of living on the farm, current members are asked to provide input on new members. Input could be either positive or negative—what was understood to be "constructive" insofar as it was meant to help a new member understand the behaviors others found troubling. In her three-month feedback, April was told that some members, who were to remain confidential, thought she was too loud and too aggressive in her communication style. Furthermore, she was told that at least one member no longer felt comfortable eating in ZK's lounge because of her style of communicating. Clearly hurt by this feedback, April tried to figure out who these members were so that she could talk directly with them in order to come to a mutually beneficial understanding. She reasoned that without more information on when she was being aggressive and loud, this feedback was not helpful. April asked a few members if they had given her feedback and on one of these occasions she approached Shena, who was finishing her lunch. Shena denied having given feedback but explained that it was likely the objection had to do with April's louder, heightened emotional expression. Hearing this, I asked Shena what was wrong with being emotionally expressive, especially since it was an honest way to communicate. Shena's demeanor changed; her eyebrows raised and moved slightly together while her eyes grew wider. Her smile changed to a frown as she stated that it was oppressive to others and was understood to be violent.

It was clear that April spoke from an orientation to communication that was distinct from what was normative on the farm—the position from which Shena spoke. April understood written communication to be indirect and hurtful and valued direct communication. When a member had issues with her, she believed that the member should talk with her face-to-face. This belief was in tension with the norm for confidentiality and the support the community afforded members who did not want to communicate. Operating from the belief that direct, face-to-face communication was less hurtful and more genuine, April was heard by members like Shena as being aggressive. That aggressiveness was attributed to her tendency to state her thoughts, feelings, and opinions without hedges or qualifiers, to her violation of interpersonal boundaries as a member of the upside-down club, and to her louder voice and emotional expression.

Like April, Watermelon Jenkins, a working-class Black woman, had also received negative "constructive" feedback during her three-month membership poll. This feedback included comments that she was too emotionally expressive and that she stated her opinions as fact. In her response to this feedback, Watermelon stated:

> My opinion don't count for shit and neither do any one else's. They're a drop in the bucket. I completely understand that. But if I'm goin' to have them, they are my personal facts. How dare I say something and then let someone sway me. And people here pretend—they give you lip service. I don't give a fuck about lip service.

According to Watermelon, all people had opinions, and these opinions may not matter, but they should not be denied. Like opinions, emotion should also not be denied—a point Watermelon made explicitly on a number of occasions and implicitly in her tone of voice and choice of words. While her words were delivered with animated (but not angry) emotion, the addition of obscenities marked it as a violation of the Oakian norm for the calm expression of emotion.[5] In contrast to Watermelon's preferred style of communicating, Oakers were understood to "give lip service" rather than honest and forthright communication. Watermelon found herself altering her communication style, and in the absence of honest and direct communication, she was finding it difficult to attend to other members' communication. "I used to be much more nice. I used to be much more, ya know," she said, and then, leaning forward in an exaggerated listening pose: "That's nice. . . ."

The heightened expression of emotion contrasted with the Oakian emphasis on quiet and verbal expressions of emotion that Stearns (1994) identifies as the dominant U.S. style of emoting—a style that he contrasts with more emotionally expressive working-class Americans as well as African Americans. Differences in how communicative practices were counted produced tensions between normative Oakian communication and the communication style normative for working-class members and members of color. Whereas the normative Oakian style supported confidential communication, quiet and calm communication, verbal rather than embodied expression of emotion, and the choice to not communicate, working-class members and members of color favored face-to-face communication and the forthright expression of emotion and personal opinions. Normative communication on the farm was premised on an understanding that honest and emotional interpersonal communication took energy, and that because people had no necessary relationship with other communards, members could choose in which relationships they communicated this way. Conversely, the communication style of working-class members and members of color was premised on an understanding that disingenuous and "passive-aggressive" communication took energy and was hurtful. Honest and direct communication was a preferred way of communicating that was not contingent on the quality of relationship—on whether or not the relationship was more private or more public. The tension between this marginalized style of communication and that of the normative style of communication on the farm finds parallels in the disjuncture between the clinical portrait of suicidal persons and suicidal persons' own terms and meanings explicated in the following section.

A GROUNDED CRITIQUE FROM SUICIDEFORUM.COM

Founded in 2005, SuicideForum.com is one of the largest and most visible sites tailored specifically for suicidal persons, a "peer to peer community support forum and chatroom for people in need" (www.suicideforum.com/about-sf/). Its members abide by a "Do no harm, promote no harm" principle; although they can discuss their history of suicidality and self-harm, they are prohibited from discussing or encouraging specific plans to commit suicide or solicit suicide partners—a rule strictly enforced by moderators. In the twelve years since its founding, it has grown to 120,000 discussion threads, 1.4 million replies, and 27,000 members from across the globe. Access to most of the site's content does not require formal membership. Visitors can see and read posts, but in order to post messages and participate in conversations, they must become registered members, which is free and requires no name or other personally identifying information. As previously mentioned, I (Alvarez) analyzed a purposive sample of messages (approximately 300 pages of data), tracking the hub of action "suicide" in order to arrive at cultural premises and corresponding radiants of being, feeling, acting, and relating.

The Ontology and Emotional Expressivity of Suicidality

When members speak of "suicide" they inevitably speak of *being* "suicidal," which is to suffer from a fractured identity.[6] This fragmentation has two key variants. There may be a profound disconnect between "inner" and "outer" parts of the self; in SuicideForum.com—or SF, as members like to call it— the metaphor of the ocean is often used. Like the ocean, one might appear "peaceful" or "quiet" on the surface, but underneath the calm veneer lies turbulence. In the words of one member: "it holds beauty within but dangers can also lurk deep inside." The outer self is often characterized as artificial or fake, while the inner self, which is hidden from others' view, is real and authentic (e.g., "I feel like I have to put on this metaphorical outfit and wear [a] fake smile just to fit in"; "I hide behind a mask"). Of course, one can argue that everyone experiences some discrepancy between public and private, "front stage" and "back stage" (Goffman, 1959), but in the case of SF members, the discrepancy is experienced immensely. The two parts are not congruent, and it is congruence that is wished for. Because the inner self contains that which is unacceptable by society's standards, it must be kept secret. "People tend to make public the things that society approves of, and then hide all the rest," wrote one member. Doing so, however, can cause one to "suffer in silence."

The fragmentation of self can also be experienced temporally. There may be a perceived discrepancy between past and present selves, between who one *was* and who one *is*. One member, who had been running for years and whose identity as a runner constituted a vital part of the self, "felt completely lost" after quitting the track and field team. Another member, who was suddenly thrust into the role of father, discovered that he "couldn't handle it." There may also be a discrepancy between present and future selves, between who one *is* and who one aspires to be, as in the case of an overweight member who wants so badly to be thin and gets "angry at myself for eating." At issue in both scenarios is a discrepancy between real and ideal(ized) selves, and falling short of the ideal creates a profound sense of "worthlessness." This deep dissatisfaction with the self also manifests among members who are unhappy with their sex at birth ("I didn't want to be a male"; "I hate being a woman!"). In sum, SF members' sense of self can be captured by the following cultural premise: *there is a self, and when this self is bifurcated into incongruent parts, great anguish is experienced.*

When SF members invoke the word "suicide" they also speak of *feeling* "suicidal," a necessary precondition to the act. Often, the word "depression" is invoked, referring to a "crippling" state that renders the world "bleak" and all manner of activity (e.g., getting up from bed, brushing one's teeth, stepping out of the house) seemingly impossible. However, "suicidal" and "depression" are not synonymous; when the words "suicide" and "suicidal" are used so too are affective states like "pain," "misery," "anguish," "loneliness," "sadness," "anxiety," "fear," "powerless," "useless," "worthless," "purposeless," "nervous," and "bored." What this suggests is that *to feel suicidal is to experience not one affective state but a complex of feelings*. Because so many powerful feelings are amalgamated, the experience of suicidality is difficult for SF members to articulate to those who "have not gone through them."

When one is in the grip of suicidality, the feelings seem interminable ("A never ending track of nothing"; "it isn't getting any easier") and ubiquitous, like an amorphous cloud that follows one everywhere ("Darkness seems to surround me all the time"). No source is too trivial or inconsequential for such feelings ("If it's causing you pain then it matters"). Phrased another way, members of the SF community do not view some sources as more legitimate than others; *every source of painful feelings is valid*. Lastly, no one deserves to experience what it is like to feel suicidal; "I wouldn't wish this on anyone (especially good people)," wrote one member.

Suicide, Agency, and Relational Failure

There is a deeply held belief, shared by clinicians and laypersons alike, that suicide is an impulsive act (Joiner 2005, 2011), the product of raw emotion. Contrary to this popular view is the belief shared by members of the SF community that suicide is volitional and agentic, the product of careful thought and deliberation. For instance, one member, who prayed to God to make her/him "disappear forever" due to the relentless sexual abuse s/he suffered at the hands of an uncle, described a past suicide attempt as follows: "he [God] didn't listen, so I figured I needed to get to work on it myself." With no reprieve in sight, this person resorted to suicide as a way of taking matters into their own hands. To underscore suicide's volitional nature, other members invoked the words "plan" (e.g., "I plan on not being alive to see my next birthday") and "decision" (e.g., "the decision to suicide"). The latter is particularly telling given the usage of "suicide" as a verb while keeping the focus on the agent rather than the act.

As further evidence, consider the following reactions to a member who had expressed wanting to kill her/himself as a way of seeking revenge on her/his oppressors. "Don't do things for other people," wrote one respondent. "'Revenge suicide'? No, nobody forces a person to commit suicide—it is based on your own choices and your own responses and actions," wrote another. "Choosing to end your life to make others feel bad is a false hope of martyrdom I am afraid." In other words, *suicide is committed by the self* for *the self*, and the transgressive member was brought into line for suggesting otherwise.[7]

The path to suicide consists of five sequential acts of variable length. First, there is a period of deliberation with no attempt: "I used to hang my Barbies and pretend it was me"; "I was already thinking about suicide during early teens"; "Started praying for it at 5." This period can span months or even years, and could take place at an age when the person did not yet fully comprehend what death or suicide meant, as the following comment suggests: "I was baffled afterwards because . . . couldn't recall ever hearing about death at that point, so I have no idea where the idea actually came from."

The second act involves the enactment of risky behaviors that are not necessarily suicidal in intent but nevertheless pose dangers to oneself. Such behaviors might include participating in criminal activities and gang life, having unprotected sex with multiple partners, abusing illicit drugs and substances, or in the case of one member, "riding a dirt bike recklessly." The connective thread is utter disregard for one's physical and biological safety.

During the third act, the person makes a "preliminary" attempt, or "practice run," as one member called it. Like the second act, there is no real intent to die ("less than earnest and more of a cry for attention"), but unlike the second act, harm is inflicted not by an external agent but by the person him/herself. The harm is also inflicted directly rather than indirectly.

In the fourth act, further attempt is made, this time with the intention of losing one's life. The attempt has been described by members as "active," "legitimate," and "serious," and is typically preceded by a period of research for the appropriate means to one's demise. Should the active attempt succeed—in the first try or after subsequent tries—the person is said to have "committed" suicide. Act five, then, is death, the cessation of one's existence, the termination of one's life. The five acts follow a loose sequence, and the periods separating each act are highly variable in length (e.g., "I was 10 when I first started to have daily thoughts about it, 14 when I made a 'gesture,' and 17 when I made a real attempt"; "it just clicked to end my life one day but it took me ages thinking about it and what I should do").

It is important to note that the fourth act's "active" attempt has a "trigger," referred to by some users as the "straw" that broke the proverbial camel's back, or that which "pushed" one over the precipice or "edge." The trigger is almost always relational; in other words, as a hub of action "suicide" taps into the radiant of relating. Triggers include the death of a parent or loved one; rejection by or separation from a significant other; bullying and harassment; physical, emotional, and/or sexual abuse—the list goes on. These sources of relational rupture call into question one's sense of connectedness with others. One feels "alienated," "profoundly alone," and "completely detached," as if one's "existence didn't mean anything to anybody."

The attribution of suicide attempts by SF members to relational causes, to factors extrinsic to oneself, runs counter to the view espoused in the clinical literature (Jamison, 2000) that suicide is the outcome of *endogenous* forces arising from within the individual. According to this view, biochemical imbalances produce the conditions (e.g., major depressive disorder) that we recognize as mental illness, which in turn may eventuate in suicides. However, SF members reframe the etiology of suicide by centering relational causes instead of medical causes. In doing so, suicide is transformed from a medical phenomenon into a human phenomenon; *instead of a (biologically) damaged human being, the culprit is damaged/damaging relationships*. This does not mean members of the SF community reject the medical model of mental illness entirely. In fact, many (but not all) identify as mentally ill, attribute their mental illness to biochemistry, and/or avail themselves to pharmacologic treatments. Rather, even those who subscribe to a medical view of mental illness do *not* necessarily subscribe to a medical view of suicide.

Invocation of the word "trigger" and similar other terms also suggests that from SF members' perspective, *suicide is multicausal rather than unicausal*. The trigger, the precipitating moment, is but one event in a long chain of unfortunate circumstances. Observe the following comments: "*Many* things triggered it but I think the main thing was my dad walking out on me"; "What triggered me, my family had *several* successful suicides in my/our history"; "it was building *over time*." From an outsider's point of view, the act of suicide might seem impulsive when only proximal factors are considered, but when one views a life through eagle eyes, it becomes apparent that *suicide is a culmination of events temporally distant and near*.

Suicide is seriously attempted only as a last resort, when pain has reached its highest pitch ("I couldn't take the pain any longer") and when no other options seem feasible or are forthcoming ("I've already tried getting help so see no other solution to my suffering"). In fact, *it is preferred that one "hang on to" life as fiercely as one could*. Within the pro-life context of the SF community, when a member confesses a desire for death or a loss of the will to live, it is customary for other members to acknowledge the feelings behind the message ("I am so sorry you are feeling this way"), then offer words of encouragement ("if you aren't around the world loses a caring soul") and concrete advice grounded in personal experience ("make a list throughout your day of the things that have gone right"), in the hopes that the distressed member will reconsider life.

Interestingly, the decision to die and the decision to continue living are both framed in terms of courage and fortitude. To "keep going" even when one wants to "give up" is courageous because it means actively resisting suicide at every turn. At the same time, SF members know all too well how frightening death and dying can be, even when the desire to die is strong. Therefore, *overcoming one's fear of death requires courage, albeit a different kind of courage than the one required by living.* In the words of one member: "Never attempted yet, I'm too coward." The idea that suicide is "courageous" flies in the face of popular discourse that suggests that suicide is a cowardly act, exclusive to those who are afraid to pull themselves up by the bootstraps and face life head-on (see Joiner [2011] for a discussion of this stereotype).

Once the option of suicide has been considered, it will never cease being an option. As one member writes, "one never lets that 'option' go, when things get hard it's a way out." Another member, who had deferred his/her decision to die, writes the following: "I went through the process of buying a somewhat expensive suicide method, truly believing I would use it soon. I never did of course, but it's hidden away in my closet should I ever choose to do so." These and other similar comments suggest a communal view that *the decision to live is impermanent and that one's stance on life is subject to ongoing renegotiation.* In this vein, past suicide attempts are reevaluated in light of present circumstances. When life seems hopeful, members are thankful that past attempts had failed: "Now, although my problems and difficulties in life still remain, I feel lucky and good that I am alive." On the flip side, when one's current predicament seems bleak, one wishes instead that past attempts had succeeded: "The greatest regret in my life is not getting it right"; "I was actually happy I didn't die. I look at that situation now and I really wish I did." But even those who are happy to be alive recognize how precarious such a state can be: "Glad I am here . . . but I swear some days are so bad I could do it again and the right way." Suicide is a door through which anyone could walk, and once opened, it remains perpetually ajar.

Therapeutic Implications Based on Grounded Discourse

Treating "suicidal" as a cultural rather than a diagnostic category, and valuing suicidal individuals' own terms and meanings, enables us to "help correct misimpressions" (Carbaugh, 1989/1990, p. 276) held by the dominant culture and imagine ways treatment regimens can incorporate suicidal persons' voices. This is especially important since many SF members have expressed dissatisfaction with mental health professionals, who are said to treat problems "like it's just a common cold." As one member caustically remarked, "I have yet to find a psychiatrist who actually does something aside from talking the same old methodologies that doesn't work and or apply to everyone."

First, clinicians need to recognize that depressed mood, though a cardinal feature of suicidality, is entangled with other affective states, to which they must also attend. Second, current treatment modalities, including psychopharmacology, are based on a model of expediency (Breggin, 2008; Reznek,

2016) whose avowed purpose is rapid symptom elimination. Such a model, however, is not flexible enough to accommodate the idea that suicide, once considered, remains lodged in the thoughts of suicidal persons. Longer-term care may be necessary. Third, biomedical models of mental illness and suicide, which locate the fault within the individual, need to be tempered with relational frameworks that view suicide as an intelligible response to painful circumstances. Fourth, it is important to recognize the agency of suicidal persons. There have been recent attempts by mental health professionals to police usage of the phrase "commit suicide" given its criminal implications (Hecht, 2014). However, the word "commit" remains deeply meaningful to SF community members, for it captures the agency and gravity of the act. Recognizing the agency of suicidal persons does not mean approving the choice to end a life, but rather, enlisting them as *active* participants in their own recovery, not passive recipients of intervention and care. Lastly, as the discourses of SF members illustrate, the path to suicide consists of five sequential acts; in other words, there are multiple junctures at which caregivers can meaningfully intervene.

SUMMARY AND CONCLUSIONS

The two cases in this chapter present studies explicating the hub of action. In Flanigan's case, the communication system on the farm is the focal hub and in Alvarez's case, the discursive hub focuses on "suicide." Both cases track emotion as a key radiant of meaning; however, Alvarez connects emotion to being and includes the radiants of acting and relating.

The two cases presented in this chapter are also examples of engaging with the critical mode of CuDA (Carbaugh, 2007). Flanigan's case explained how the normative communication system on the farm, as a raced and classed system, privileges those enacting white, middle-class communication patterns. Alvarez's case argued that clinical practitioners should consider how those with suicidal ideation make sense of suicide in order to assuage potentially harmful "misimpressions." Both cases described and interpreted cultural communication before engaging in a grounded critique of a normative system. However, a key difference between the two cases should also be noted: Flanigan's critique arose from *in situ* criticisms heard on the farm, while Alvarez's critique of normative therapeutic systems arose from immersion in two distinct cultural discourses: the clinical literature (from his training in psychology) and the grounded discourses of SuicideForum.com participants.

Both critical moves have utility in explicating a normative cultural system that implicates a nonnormative cultural system with its own deeply meaningful set of cultural premises. While ethnographers (Carbaugh, 1989/1990;

Huspek, 1989/1990; and Philipsen, 1989/1990) have argued that we should be wary of moving (too quickly) into the critical mode to avoid ethnocentrism, it is equally important to understand that where there is a normative cultural system, there are bound to be marginalized cultural systems. While we do not have to take up a critical analysis, this chapter suggests that we cannot adopt a neutral position either, because to do so is to participate in a normative discourse and to *not* participate in a marginal one. In other words, it is to privilege one discourse over another.

Beyond engaging in the critical mode, the two cases explored the public versus private dichotomy as a key feature of cultural discourses. According to the two cases, the public is the site of normative communication while private realms are sites of resistance, honesty, and authenticity. Both cases framed the public as that which is openly observable and the private as something that is hidden from those in broader (i.e., normative) culture. In Flanigan's case, the public/private dichotomy was active in defining both spaces and relationships. In Alvarez's case, the dichotomy was active in defining an inner and outer self. Interestingly, Flanigan looked to the public to identify normative communication while Alvarez looked to the private to identify critiques of normative cultural discourses.

In both cases, emotion was also a key feature of communication that was comported in public/normative culture. Attempts to comport emotional expressivity led to isolation of an aspect of self from normative culture and to attendant negative affect (e.g., anger, frustration, sadness, helplessness). With restraints on emotional expressivity, marginalized people were compelled to seek and find understanding and acceptance in marginalized communities that share their cultural understandings and ways of communicating.

NOTES

1. There were approximately 100 members that lived and worked in the community at the time of fieldwork. Most members chose to live in community because of their interest in the communities movement, living sustainably, or living with others who supported a way of life that was counter to dominant U.S. culture.

2. Twin Oaks was frequently referred to as "the farm" by members. Frequent terms used by members to refer to themselves included "Oaker" and "communard." Members also used the adjective "Oakian" to refer to something understood to be unique to the farm. All terms, including identity terms, used in this analysis are native terms.

3. Community feedback was a part of the membership process. People wanting to join the community first had to complete a three-week visitor period after which current members would offer feedback and recommend or reject the person for membership. Feedback was also given after a three-month provisional membership so that provisional members could correct behaviors, and so that they would not be blindsided when their full membership poll was taken at six months.

4. All names have been changed and all pseudonyms were either self-selected or agreed upon by the member. It was a common practice on the farm for members to change their

names. During my stay, some members of color changed their names to draw attention to the underlying racism and white normativity. For example, a Black member changed her name to Watermelon Jenkins.

5. Spears (2001) identifies "cussin' out (cursing directed to a particular addressee)," along with "going off on someone (a sudden, often unexpected burst of negatively critical, vituperative speech), getting real (a fully candid appraisal of a person, situation, event, etc.), and trash talk (talk in competitive settings, notably athletic games, that is boastful and puts down opponents)" as features of African American verbal culture (p. 240).

6. Identity here is defined as an interactional achievement (Carbaugh, 1996), mutually constituted rather than intrinsic to individuals.

7. It is interesting to note the orientation to individualism active in these responses, which are characteristically very American (Carbaugh, 1996). Even marginal discourse, then, is constrained by dominant culture(s).

REFERENCES

Breggin, P. R. (2008). *Medication madness: The role of psychiatric drugs in cases of violence, suicide, and crime.* New York, NY: St. Martin's Griffin.

Carbaugh, D. (1988). Comments on "culture" in communication inquiry. *Communication Reports, 1,* 38–41.

Carbaugh, D. (1989/1990). The critical voice in ethnography of communication research. *Research on Language and Social Interaction, 23,* 261–282.

Carbaugh, D. (1996). *Situating selves: The communication of social identity in American scenes.* Albany, NY: State University of New York Press.

Carbaugh, D. (2007). Cultural discourse analysis: Communication practices and intercultural encounters. *Journal of Intercultural Communication Research, 36*(3), 167–182.

Carbaugh, D. (2017). Terms for talk, take 2: Theorizing communication through its cultural terms and practices. In D. Carbaugh (Ed.), *The handbook of communication in cross-cultural perspective* (pp. 15–28). New York, NY: Routledge.

Flanigan, J. (2013). The use and evolution of gender neutral language in an intentional community. *Language and Gender, 36*(1), 27–41.

Goffman, E. (1959). *The presentation of self in everyday life.* New York, NY: Anchor.

Goffman, E. (1963). *Stigma: Notes on the management of spoiled identity.* New York, NY: Simon & Schuster.

Hecht, J. M. (2014). *Stay: A history of suicide and the arguments against it.* New Haven, CT: Yale University Press.

Hecht, M. (2010). The promise of communication in large-scale, community-based research. In D. Carbaugh & P. M. Buzzanell (Eds.), *Distinctive qualities in communication research* (pp. 53–72). New York, NY: Routledge.

Huspek, M. (1989/1990). The idea of ethnography and its relation to cultural critique. *Research on Language and Social Interaction, 23,* 293–312.

Hymes, D. (1972). Models of interaction of language and social life. In J. Gumperz & D. Hymes (Eds.), *Directions in sociolinguistics: The ethnography of communication* (pp. 35–71). New York, NY: Holt, Rinehart & Winston.

Jamison, K. R. (2000). *Night falls fast: Understanding suicide.* New York, NY: Vintage.

Joiner, T. (2005). *Why people die by suicide.* Cambridge, MA: Harvard University Press.

Joiner, T. (2011). *Myths about suicide.* Cambridge, MA: Harvard University Press.

Kochman, T. (1990). Force fields in black and white communication. In D. Carbaugh (Ed.), *Cultural communication and intercultural contact* (pp. 193–218). Hillsdale, NJ: Erlbaum.

Philipsen, G. (1989/1990). Some initial thoughts on the perils of "critique" in the ethnographic study of communicative practices. *Research on Language and Social Interaction, 23,* 251–260.

Reznek, L. (2016). *Peddling mental disorder: The crisis in modern psychiatry.* Jefferson, NC: McFarland.

Spears, A. (2001). Directness in the use of African American English. In S. L. Lanehart (Ed.), *Sociocultural and historical contexts of African American English* (pp. 239–260). Philadelphia, PA: John Benjamins Publishing.

Stearns, P. N. (1994). *American cool: Constructing a twentieth-century emotional style.* New York, NY: New York University Press.

SuicideForum.com (n.d.). About SF. Retrieved September 30, 2016, from https://www.suicideforum.com/about-sf/

Weintraub, J. A. (1997). The theory and politics of the public/private distinction. In J. A. Weintraub & K. Kumar (Eds.), *Public and private in thought and practice: Perspectives on a grand dichotomy* (pp. 1–23). Chicago, IL: University of Chicago Press.

Chapter Six

Cultural Variation in End-of-Life Conversations

Using Cultural Discourse Analysis to Inform Case Studies Designed for Professional Military Education

Lauren Mackenzie and Kelly Tenzek

A fundamental assumption undertaken by many communication scholars is that quality of life can be enhanced by meaningful conversation (Stewart, 1973). The current chapter offers a unique educational context in which conversations, such as those that occur at end of life (EOL), can be explored through case study creation and cultural discourse analysis (CuDA).

Recent EOL research has revealed two important trends: (1) that most individuals feel ill-equipped for conversation at end of life (Hamil, Wu, & Brodie, 2017) and (2) that "cultural differences must be considered if end-of-life care is to be delivered in an accessible, interdisciplinary fashion across health settings to relieve distress among vulnerable and diverse populations" (Boucher, 2016, p. 1000). The current study aims to reduce students' uncertainty with regard to EOL communication, specifically final conversations (Keeley & Generous, 2017), and increase intercultural communication self-efficacy. This is the belief that "you will be effective in a cross-cultural encounter" (Van Dyne, Ang, & Livermore, 2010, p. 135) and is a powerful type of motivation for educators and trainers to consider as they develop intercultural curricula. Creating teaching and learning tools that instill confidence in students' ability to engage in intercultural communication, especially at EOL, is a key learning objective in the diverse communication courses taught by both authors.

In an attempt to create a meaningful learning experience specifically for professional military education,[1] we have created a case study that situates instances of EOL communication and cultural variation into a military context. The case study was constructed for integration into Intercultural Communication Competence courses at Marine Corps University and uses CuDA to highlight the ways in which a primary focus on action renders the content and context relevant for military students.

The initial intent in using a CuDA approach to develop case studies for use in military education was prompted by Carbaugh and Lie's (2014) description of competence as:

> housed in actual communication practice, in situated interactional lives of people. Communication practice is lived at least partly and prominently, at a local level, through local means of expression; local means of expression carry deep cultural meanings; these meanings revolve around dimensions of appropriate and effective conduct; these meanings reveal a cultural discursive commentary, or coding, about being a good person, doing the right actions. (p. 75)

The current chapter responds to the necessity of *action* and *application* in a competence-based course in an effort to (a) initiate conversations related to EOL, (b) illustrate the impact of cultural difference on expectations and appropriateness regarding EOL communication, and (c) focus on military-relevant contexts. An analysis of the case study highlights cultural premises that can be used to render EOL content relevant for professional military education students. The end of the chapter will summarize the case study themes and provide recommendations for engaging in EOL conversations and suggests ways such recommendations can be incorporated into diverse educational contexts. Before introducing the case study and analysis, we briefly review pertinent literature related to CuDA, final conversations, and professional military education.

CUDA CONNECTION

Locating and analyzing cultural ideals found in salient features of EOL communication has the potential to be a transformative means for developing relevant interpersonal and intercultural skills and competencies for military students. We draw from Carbaugh's (2007) explanation of CuDA as an investigative stance for understanding culturally distinctive communication practices and argue that CuDA provides a platform to connect intercultural communication with EOL communication. To this end, military students will have the opportunity to reflect on and discuss the importance of such conversations in their personal and professional lives.

One of the recurring themes in Carbaugh's program of research over the past several decades has been the focus on communication as both a practice and a perspective on that practice. Carbaugh and Buzzanell (2009) explain that "In this way, communication is not just the topic of concern, or a description of a social and cultural process, but offers a way of accounting for that concern and those processes" (p. 116). The theoretical foundation provided by CuDA (Carbaugh, 2007) underscores the ways in which communication is shaped as a cultural practice and responds to at least one of the following research questions:

1. What is getting done when people communicate in this way?
2. How is this communication practice put together?
3. What act sequence constitutes this communication practice?

The current project responds to the second research question in both its creation of a case study for a particular group of students in a particular context and in its use of the hub of action to illustrate what such conversations "should" entail. CuDA offers five discursive hubs—action, identity, feeling, dwelling, and relating—which help us locate meaning in communication practices. In his recent work, Carbaugh (2017) notes that a discursive hub "is an item—word, phase, form, gesture—in social discourse that participants use to make sense of their communicative action" (p. 19). We focus on EOL as a key "form" of communication and examine how the cultural premises surrounding "action" can be used to construct a case study that connects cultural variation and final conversations. The notion that when we communicate, we are not only saying something, we are also *accomplishing* something has been reiterated in countless studies ranging from sociolinguistics (e.g., Hymes, 1964) to anthropology (e.g., Schiefflin & Ochs, 1986), to communication (e.g., Pearce & Cronen, 1980), and linguistics (e.g., Wierzbicka, 1997) across both decades and methodological vantage points. This chapter underscores the importance of communication as action for military students. That is, for communication education to be perceived as meaningful and relevant, it must be applicable and actionable.

The hub of action has been studied in diverse communication contexts (see, for example, Katriel & Livio, Flanigan & Alvarez, and Wilkins, Gulinello, & Wolf, this volume). This chapter aligns with Carbaugh's (2017) definition of cultural terms for communicative action as "terms and phrases that are used prominently and routinely by people to characterize communication practices that are significant and important to them" (pp. 15–28). Analyzing the key cultural terms and premises revolving around the hub of action serves to both *contribute* to Carbaugh's increasingly diverse CuDA research program and *advance* professional students' understanding of final conversations as a rich communication practice. We now turn to a brief overview of EOL communication, specifically final conversations.

END-OF-LIFE COMMUNICATION

The results of a recently published study by the *Economist* and the Kaiser Family Foundation suggest that many U.S. Americans still view end of life as a topic that is avoided (Hamil, Wu, & Brodie, 2017). EOL scholars have encouraged more public dialogue and education for health care participants to normalize EOL conversations and reduce the stigma and taboo nature related to EOL, leading to a good death experience (Meier et al., 2016; Tenzek & Depner, 2017). Therefore, creating educational opportunities to prepare individuals for dialogue at EOL becomes even more important. For the purposes of the current study, we focus on one specific thread of EOL scholarship, final conversations.

Final Conversations

Keeley's (2004a, 2004b, 2007; Keeley & Generous, 2017) work has focused on final conversations as an integral part of the EOL experience that focuses on the survivors' experience of communicating with a loved one during the dying process. This thread of research illustrates five themes that are present in final conversations and include (a) love, (b) identity, (c) religious/spiritual messages, (d) everyday talk, and (e) difficult relationship talk (Keeley, 2007; Keeley & Generous, 2017). Similar to EOL conversations, in general, final conversations can be challenging and complex—especially regarding the timing of when to engage in conversation with a terminally ill person and the tensions surrounding how to have these conversations (Keeley & Generous, 2015, 2017). One area in which final conversation research has called for further study is cultural variation, as the previous studies have included a predominantly Caucasian sample (Keeley & Generous, 2017) and have oc-curred primarily with populations in the United States. We aim to extend the work on final conversations into the military educational context including cultural variation. We argue that the combination of increased awareness surrounding final conversations (and the potential for cultural variation in associated communication preferences) sets the stage for patients to (1) feel some sense of control in their dying experience and (2) recognize that the inclusion of family through communication can enable a positive EOL pro-cess. The next section delves into the specific context of professional military education.

PROFESSIONAL MILITARY EDUCATION (PME) AND CULTURAL PREMISES

Several scholars have written about the intersection of academic and military cultures, calling for the importance of sharing teaching strategies that help manage potential tensions between them (see Higbee, 2010; Johnson-Freese, 2013; Steen, Mackenzie, & Buechner, 2018). Specifically, Carter (2010) refers to a "culturally specific way of teaching" in PME that emphasizes the question "Now that you know this, how might this apply to your military career?" (p. 171). He uses midwifery as a metaphor to suggest that the PME faculty member's role is often to "enable experience-based knowledge to give birth to usable education" (p. 174). One way of capturing the students' desire for usable, applicable knowledge in the PME classroom is through the use of case studies.

Case study analysis is a primary educational tool used in professional military education to situate concepts and skills into specific military contexts. The current chapter draws from the numerous publications devoted to best practices for teaching culture in the military; notably, the prescriptive framework put forth by Abbe and Gouge (2012) that suggests focusing on interaction between members of cultures rather than on the cultures themselves; devising techniques to transfer the intercultural skills learned during training to the real world; and comparing optimal with ineffective performances to give trainees a basis for evaluating their own behavior in similar circumstances.

The cultural premises that inform the creation of the current case study draw both from the general literature related to PME and the specific literature devoted to the Marine Corps. Holmes-Eber's (2014) six-year anthropological study addresses specific aspects of Marine Corps cultural identity and describes ways in which culture training and education is "Marinized . . . to make it look, sound, smell and taste Marine" (p. 6). In particular, she discusses how the Marine Corps bias for action manifests itself in language and, to quote one of her in-depth interviews, "The general Marine ethos is about doing and acting" (p. 97).

The case study was thus created to illustrate the following cultural premises drawn from existing literature as well as from the first author's teaching and research:

1. *PME should provide knowledge that is actionable*
2. *PME should prepare students for the unknown*
3. *PME is meaningful if the information students receive is applicable and relevant*

Using these premises as a guide in the creation of our case study, we asked:

1. How can CuDA be used to create an applicable teaching tool for PME students?
2. How does the hub of action render new EOL and culture content relevant and meaningful for military students?

Similar to the work by Boromisza-Habashi, Hughes, and Malkowski (2016) and Wilkins (2017), who seek to understand ideal forms of communication and compare them across cultures, the current chapter views *preparation for action* as an optimal form in the PME classroom.

CASE STUDY

The following case study was created for the PME classroom to introduce cultural variation in a particular relational context: final conversations. The scenario and accompanying discussion questions illustrate the impact of culture on the EOL process in the life of a Marine. The context of the final conversation involves middle-career Major Simon, who is faced with the final stage of his wife's terminal cancer diagnosis. We base the scenarios on research, experience, and voices in the EOL and Marine Corps community. It is important to emphasize here that although conversation is only one aspect of EOL care,[2] it is fundamental to the assumption that relationships begin and end, succeed or fail "one conversation at a time" (Scott, 2004, p. 97). The following scenario highlights the impact of cultural complexity on one such conversation.

Major Simon

1   Major (Maj) Simon is midway through his Marine Corps career and has been happily
2   married for 15 years. He met his wife, Yuna, while stationed at Camp Hansen in
3   Okinawa, Japan. They had traveled all over the world as a couple and were thrilled with
4   their current assignment in residence at Command and Staff College (CSC) in Quantico,
5   Virginia. Last month, however, they received the devastating news that Yuna was in the
6   advanced stage of terminal breast cancer. Yuna and Maj Simon left the doctor's office
7   feeling confused and overwhelmed by the details of the terminal diagnosis. On the car
8   ride home, Maj Simon wanted to talk about what just happened, but didn't know how
9   to begin. About three weeks later, the doctor asked them both to come back in and he
10 explained it was time to start making arrangements. Maj Simon was in complete shock.
11 As ashamed as he was to admit it, he had been enjoying the distractions that came with
12 being a CSC student and all the seminars, lectures, and staff rides that filled up his weeks.
13 Now, he had to make a choice: he could face the truth and come to terms with the
14 diagnosis or continue on in denial. Despite how sad he was, he knew he needed to start
15 somewhere and find out what Yuna wanted him to do. He didn't want any regrets about
16 what they did/didn't talk about, so he took out a notebook and started writing some
17 questions down on paper. He didn't have the exact words to say but knew he needed to sit
18 down with her and talk through things while they still had some time alone.
19 That night at dinner, he wasn't sure how to begin, but he took a deep breath when there
20 was a break in the conversation and told Yuna how happy he was that they were married.

21   This opened the conversational door and they began to talk about how they first met, how
22   they relied on one another, and the day-to-day activities that they enjoyed together. Yuna
23   seemed relieved when he brought up the conversation and asked that he invite her parents
24   to come to the States because she wanted them there before she died. He was anxious
25   about this because he and her parents didn't always see eye-to-eye—especially regarding
26   their decision not to practice Buddhism and not to have children. Although Maj Simon
27   knew his in-laws didn't agree with their choices, both Yuna and Maj Simon had always
28   been happy supporting each other's individual careers and personal goals. He only
29   wanted what was best for Yuna and made the call. Her parents said that although they didn't
30   want to be a burden, they would come and make sure Yuna experienced a proper death.
31   Over the next couple of days, they had many more conversations; some were happy and
32   some were sad as they reflected on the difficult times in their marriage including her
33   loneliness during deployment and trouble transitioning once he returned home. But they also discussed
34   the good times, such as the first time she was able to use Skype to communicate with
35   him while he was deployed. They talked about their different views of "what happens
36   next?" after she dies, the difficulty of involving her parents in the EOL process since they
37   live in Japan, and some of the ways she wanted to be remembered. She expressed her
38   fears associated with being in pain, but also didn't want to spend her final days hooked
39   up to machines. As Yuna became weaker, the conversations decreased, but they were
40   still able to hold hands, and eye contact was their main form of communication. They
41   had told each other what they wanted to say days ago, however, and accepted in the last
42   few days that words were no longer necessary. The one thing that he was still uncertain
43   about, though, was what her parents were expecting and how Japanese ideas of funerals
44   and mourning might be very different from his own. Maj Simon remembered a Buddhist
45   saying that he once saw framed on his in-laws' wall: "In the end, only three thing matter:
46   how much you loved, how gently you lived, and how gracefully you let go of things not
47   meant for you." He started to wonder what more he could do to learn about Buddhist
48   rituals at end of life. His conversation with Yuma's parents on the phone later that day
49   confirmed his concern that their ideas about preparing for death conflicted with his own.
50   They were on their way to the States and he needed to prepare for the long conversation
51   with them that was to come in hopes of finding a way to recognize and respect their
52   different, and sometimes contradictory, expectations surrounding a good death. He was
53   embarrassed that he had not taken the time to do this before, but hoped that one day he
54   could use this experience to ensure that his fellow Marines were aware of what he had not,
55   until now, taken the time to consider.

Discussion Questions

1. What particular aspects of final conversations were present in the scenario?

2. What do you think are the most important topics to be included in final conversations?
3. What steps could Maj Simon have taken to learn about Japanese cultural preferences surrounding EOL as he prepared for the arrival of Yuna's parents and the funeral?
4. How do you define a good death?
5. Are there actions you can take now to make loved ones aware of your EOL preferences?

ANALYSIS

The current analysis calls attention to cultural differences in EOL conversations, which are viewed here as highly relevant forms of communication for military personnel. The questions after the case study suggest a frame for communicative action, that is, "what we should be doing." The premise at work as the authors sought to bring together insights from the EOL literature in such a way that would align with military culture in the form of a case study was indeed "action" focused. Questions posed to students after reading the scenario include "What steps can be taken?" and "What action can be performed?" Giving the students a military-relevant context combined with some culture-specific variation in a prominent feature of EOL communication serves as an educational jumping-off point for professional military students.

This section is divided into parts that help the reader understand the how, who, where, what, and why of the case study creation process and analysis in an attempt to address the following premises:

1. *PME should provide knowledge that is actionable*
2. *PME should prepare students for the unknown*
3. *PME is meaningful if the information students receive is applicable and relevant*

The "How?"

The process of creating the case study began by using Hymes's (1972) SPEAKING framework to begin to structure the content in a way that would both meet the expectations of PME students and connect EOL and culture content. The first four elements of the SPEAKING framework were used in the creation of the case study and are summarized as follows:

Setting. The case study consists of different contexts in which EOL communication often occurs: at the doctor's office and at home.

Participants. The case study illustrates several kinds of interpersonal relationships for Marines: romantic partner, health care provider, and family.

Ends. The case study was designed to put the following desired outcomes of EOL communication into narrative form: participate in meaningful final conversations; avoid regret; continue to build the relationship; take steps to ensure a good death as defined by the cultural values of participants involved.

Acts. The case study was created to underscore a common American Marine sentiment surrounding cultural complexity: What can I *do* to better understand, plan, and prepare? Ask what themes should be included in an ideal final conversation; create interpersonal "scripts"; learn about cultural differences in expectations surrounding preparation for EOL and mourning; find out from the loved one what they would consider a good death; write down wishes of your own.

This "acts" framework is mirrored in the Conversation Project (conversationproject.org) starter kit, which provides checklists and questions to consider in EOL communication. The questions ask us to consider:

1. Who do you want to talk to?
2. When would be a good time to talk?
3. Where would you feel comfortable talking?
4. What do you want to be sure to say?

The conversation starter kit offers suggestions for breaking the ice, specific topics for beginning the process, as well as websites that link to each state's "advance directives" forms. It is a practical tool for self-reflection and a means for taking action. The kit does not delve into the complexities of intercultural differences in communication preferences, however, which is where this chapter adds to the existing literature.

The "Who?" and the "Where?": Course Context

The 230 students at the U.S. Marine Corps Command and Staff College consist of military personnel from all branches of service (Marine Corps, Navy, Army, and Air Force), civilian students from a variety of government agencies (such as the FBI, Department of State, and CIA), as well as international officers from dozens of different countries. Like most professional schools, the students in each seminar represent wide diversity in communication styles and cultural preferences, and each class session can be thought of as an intercultural communication context.[3] The elective (in which the case study developed for this chapter will be included) provides an overview of the communication skills that are enablers of intercultural competence along with a variety of culture-specific, military-relevant applications.

The specific goals of the course in terms of student outcomes include:

- Understand and apply the skills and concepts associated with intercultural communication competence
- Develop increased ability to create multiple explanations for confusing intercultural behaviors
- Explore and analyze a variety of culturally complex case studies

Situational judgment tests (SJTs), case studies, as well as pre- and postcourse scenario-based tests have been used to assess intercultural competence since the course was first developed. A recent chapter (Mackenzie & Wallace, 2015) discusses how SJTs were used to create a more effective and meaningful educational experience for students in an online, asynchronous Introduction to Cross-Cultural Communication course that has been completed by more than 2,000 Community College of the Air Force students. The current study extends that work by looking at cultural variation and communication practices in EOL case studies for an in-residence, graduate-level course offered to PME students.

The "What?"

The assumptions that inform CuDA—first, that communication is cross-culturally variable, and second, that people invent their own means and meanings of communication that are distinctive and should be analyzed as such (Carbaugh & Cerulli, 2013), also informed the creation of this case study for the professional military education classroom. The scenario illustrates differences in ideals surrounding communication preferences—with a focus on military context and culture. Previous research has explored the influence of culture on EOL decision making (Bullock, 2011) and categorized variant cultural beliefs according to views on reality (structured versus spontaneous), views on autonomy ("master of my fate" versus "fate of my master"), and views on advance directives (written versus oral).

The current analysis explores relevant cultural assumptions and expectations imminent in the American, Japanese, and Buddhist ideals associated with end-of-life communication. We highlight the hub of action as displayed in each scenario's cultural ideal and discuss the various ways in which EOL conversations are interpreted as appropriate and meaningful.

Specific topics were introduced into the case study that reflect the content of EOL research and literature:

1. Taboo nature of and difficulty associated with talking about death (lines 8–9)
2. Starting the conversation (lines 19–20)
3. Avoiding regret (lines 15–17)
4. Cultural variation in terms of what is considered a "proper" death (line 30)
5. Expectations surrounding funeral/mourning (line 43–44)

Several instances in the scenario aim to be consistent with a military preference for preparation, planning, and action, such as (line 13) "Now, he had to make a choice"; (line 47) "He started to wonder what more he could do to learn"; and (lines 16–17) "he took out a notebook and started writing some questions down on paper." This was written in such a way as to resonate with the cultural upbringing of many Marines officers who are primed from their earliest days in training to be able to answer the question, "What next, Marine?"

The "Why?"

This scenario and ensuing discussion questions were designed to use a situated marital context in which a terminal diagnosis was received and ensuing actions needed to be considered to prepare for and participate in a series of final conversations—thus highlighting the cultural premise *PME should prepare students for the unknown.*

The participants involved consisted of husband, wife, health care provider, and parents. The action-related themes involved how to begin a final conversation, recognizing cultural variation in appropriate planning for death and mourning, and common final conversation topics (Keeley & Koenig Kellas, 2005). The interactions between Maj Simon and his wife and the questions Maj Simon asks himself are consistent with themes in the literature devoted to final conversations, for example, When is the right time to say "goodbye"? How do you begin such a conversation? What topics should be included in final conversations?

At the middle point of the case study, the reader learns that Yuna's parents "would come and make sure she experienced a proper death" (line 30). Recognizing that *PME should prepare students for the unknown*, the students will be given readings that explore cultural variation in expectations regarding a "good death," such as the articles "Concept Analysis of a Good Death in a Japanese Community" (Hattori, McCubbin, & Ishida, 2006); "Good Death in Japanese Cancer Care" (Hirai et al., 2006); and "Cultural Scripts for a Good Death in Japan and the U.S." (Long, 2004). The following excerpt from the case study, "The one thing that he was still uncertain about, though, was what her parents were expecting and how Japanese ideas of funerals and mourning might be very different from his own" (lines 42–44), encourages students to reflect on and discuss the Japanese perspective about being a "burden" (line 30) at EOL as well as appropriate arrangements for funerals and expectations surrounding mourning. Additionally, the Japanese cultural preference for family presence at EOL is reinforced by Yuna, who asks Maj Simon to communicate with her parents "because she wanted them there before she died" (line 24).

The introduction of Yuna's parents highlights cultural variation (both Japanese and Buddhist) in religious and family practices as well as in preferences surrounding a "good death." The couple's "decision not to practice Buddhism and not to have children" (line 26) is recognized by Maj Simon as a source for why they haven't always seen "eye-to-eye" (line 25). Maj Simon realizes that although he takes on some preferences associated with U.S. American values—for example, the individualist tendency to prioritize "each other's individual careers and personal goals" (line 28)—he is open to learning more about other ways of thinking about death. Recalling a Buddhist quotation he once read on the wall of Yuma's parents' home, "In the end, only three things matter: how much you loved, how gently you lived, and how gracefully you let go of things not meant for you" (lines 45–47), he becomes curious to learn about different ways of thinking about EOL. Maj Simon then begins to connect thinking to action: "He started to wonder what more he could do to learn about Buddhist rituals" (lines 47–48).

In an effort to acknowledge that *PME should provide knowledge that is actionable* the discussion questions posed to students after they review the case study reflect the cultural premise of using knowledge to prepare for action, such as "What steps could Maj Simon have taken to learn about Japanese cultural preferences surrounding EOL as he prepares for the arrival of Yuna's parents and the funeral?" (Discussion question #3) and "Are there actions you can take now to make loved ones aware of your EOL preferences?" (Discussion question #5). These questions extend the focus on what can be *done* during such a difficult time in Maj Simon's life—to include steps that can be taken to learn more about diverse meanings derived from cultural values—and how they manifest themselves in communication behavior. Within the scenario itself, several final conversation topics are included to echo those found in the EOL literature. Specifically, they talked about their different views of "what happens next?" (lines 35–36); the fact that she "didn't want to spend her final days hooked up to machines" (lines 38–39); as well as "some of the ways she wanted to be remembered" (line 37). This particular content was designed to mirror several themes in final conversations, including verbal and nonverbal messages as summarized by Keeley & Generous (2017), such as love (line 20), everyday talk (line 22), and difficult relationship talk (lines 32–33). This aspect of the case study was designed to introduce some potential topics for students to consider as they prepare not only for discussion about the case study in class, but also for their own personal relationships.

After reading the scenario, students are also encouraged to ask questions about Buddhist understandings of what constitutes a "good death" (they will read, for example: "Buddhist families' perspective of a peaceful death in ICUs" (Kongsuwan, Chaipetch, & Matchim, 2012). Students will reflect on and respond to the questions "How do you define a good death?" (Discussion question #4) and "What do you think are the most important topics to be included in final conversations?" (Discussion question #2) so as to encourage reflection on and discussion about this commonly avoided communication context.

At the end of the case study, emphasis on action is once again reinforced and brought back to the Marine Corps, acknowledging that *PME is meaningful if the information students receive is applicable and relevant* as Maj Simon reflects back on his EOL experience with his wife and considers how it might be used to help others. For example, he "hoped that one day he could use this experience to ensure his fellow Marines were aware of what he had not, until now, taken the time to consider" (lines 53–55). The case study concludes with the point that Maj Simon's future actions will reflect what he learned from his wife and her family, specifically:

- taking the time to initiate meaningful conversations: "Despite how sad he was, he knew he needed to start somewhere and find out what she wanted him to do" (lines 14–15); "He wasn't sure how to begin, but he took a deep breath when there was a break in the conversation and told Yuna how happy he was that they were married" (lines 19–20);
- anticipating cultural differences in EOL expectations: "what her parents were expecting and how Japanese ideas of funerals and mourning might be very different from his own" (lines 43–44);
- preparing to learn from varying definitions of a good death: "He needed to prepare for the long conversation with them that was to come in hopes of finding a way to recognize and respect their different, and sometimes contradicting, expectations surrounding a good death" (lines 50–52).

This scenario will be used as a catalyst to discuss that as a result of cultural variation in EOL communication preferences, there is no one universal way to experience or define a good death. What then becomes important is the opportunity to communicate with loved ones and health care participants at EOL in a manner that supports cultural beliefs and values.

As with all forms of communication, EOL communication happens in context, and preferences can change depending on a range of variables. Accordingly, there may not be one ideal for EOL communication but rather a range of actions that can be considered, depending on the circumstances.

This chapter set out to illustrate how the use of a case study that features communication (as both a topic and process), culture (both military and national), as well as key components of EOL literature (final conversations) can open the aperture to different possibilities and outcomes that can be achieved through conversation across relational contexts.

The scenario included three types of relationships in Maj Simon's life: romantic (wife), familial (in-laws), and professional (his Marines). He hopes that the knowledge gleaned from this EOL experience is ultimately going to be able to help his Marines prepare in ways that he had not. The case study begins with Maj Simon choosing to "face the truth" (line 13) about the diagnosis and learning what Yuna "wanted him to do" (line 15). He knew he did not want to have any regret about what he did or did not say during these final conversations and decided to start the process by taking out his notebook and "writing some questions down on paper" (lines 16–17) so he would be prepared to sit down and talk with her. This led to the beginning of a series of final conversations that were both relationally focused on their marriage and concerns they both had about "what happens next" (line 35). The actions Maj Simon took to prepare for these final conversations led to a sense of acceptance and a degree of closure: "they had both told each other what they wanted to say days ago . . . and accepted in the last few days that words were no longer necessary" (lines 41–42). In line with the research devoted to final conversations, the actions Maj Simon took to prepare for and participate in these final conversations with his wife were important steps in the healing process.

Along with the relationship with his wife, Maj Simon is also concerned with how his actions impact the relationship with his wife's Japanese Buddhist parents. He recognizes that they "didn't agree with [his and Yuna's] choices" (line 27) and is uncertain about their expectations of and ideas about a "proper death" (line 30). He decides to take steps to educate himself on "Buddhist rituals at end of life" (line 48) and "prepare for the long conversation with them that was to come" (lines 50–51). Maj Simon does this "in hopes of finding a way to recognize" (line 51) their cultural values so as to respect them and improve their relationship. Although there are national, religious, and cultural differences to bridge in this conversation to come, anticipating this challenge and preparing for it is a key component associated with the Marine ethos of "doing and acting" (Holmes-Eber, 2014, p. 97).

Finally, the case study concludes with Maj Simon thinking about how his experience with Yuma and his in-laws can be used to help his Marines be better prepared than he was when it comes to EOL communication. His logic was that "one day he could use this experience to ensure his fellow Marines were aware of what he had not, until now, taken the time to consider" (lines 53–55). This point emphasizes a common sentiment that Marines are always looking out for one another and reflects the Marine Corps motto and core value: "Semper fidelis"—always faithful.

The case study was created with the assumption that, for PME students, preparing for EOL conversations is *doing* something, and thus the educational process is more meaningful and relevant when acting is the focus. The intent of the analysis was to demonstrate how final conversations and cultural variation in expectations surrounding such conversations can be incorporated into a teaching tool that emphasizes the intersection between communication and action—which then paves the way for a discussion about relational maintenance.

CONCLUSION

The current study is one aspect of an ongoing effort by the authors to incorporate diverse intercultural communication practices into an existing framework for teaching culture in a way that is relevant and meaningful for military students. It is hoped that the process described here of creating and analyzing this teaching tool can be used in other educational contexts including public university course curricula related to EOL and health communication as well as medical school. As discussed previously, there has been ample research to support the claim that there is value in the process of preparing for, conducting, and reflecting back on final conversations (see, for example, Keeley & Koenig Kellas, 2005). Specific benefits include learning tools for communicating more effectively in the present, reconstructing relational identities, and making sense of death in different ways—which has the potential to contribute to the healing process.

The case study serves as a teaching tool designed to be in line with the premises *PME should provide knowledge that is actionable, PME should prepare students for the unknown,* and *PME is meaningful if the information students receive is applicable and relevant.* Using these premises as a guide in the creation of our case study, we asked, how can CuDA be used to create an applicable teaching tool for PME students? How does the hub of action render new EOL and culture content relevant and meaningful for military students? To respond to these questions, the case study created for this chapter integrated the following elements of final conversations: taboo nature of and difficulty associated with talking about death (lines 8–9); starting the conversation (lines 19–20); avoiding regret (lines 15–17); cultural variation in terms of what is considered a "proper" death (line 30); and expectations surrounding funerals/mourning (lines 43–44). We then added several elements of cultural variation into the scenario through the introduction of Yuma's parents as Buddhist and Japanese to create teachable moments for students (assigning readings in advance of class discussion devoted to ideas surrounding a "good death" in Japanese and Buddhist culture). Finally, we focused on how communication (in the form of preparing for and participating in final conversations) can be viewed as action for Maj Simon in a way that supports several key relationships in his life: marital, familial, and professional.

Based on the process of constructing and analyzing the case study, we offer several recommendations for educators, scholars, and health care professionals who are also routinely charged with navigating through thick layers of cultural complexity:

- Recommendation 1: Be aware of the importance of EOL conversations in military education, service, and life outside of the military. Additionally, while awareness and knowledge are very important, we also want to increase the self-efficacy of students who will inevitably be discussing end of life with loved ones. In doing so, EOL can be a less stigmatized and more normalized topic.
- Recommendation 2: Recognize that intercultural considerations are key to improving the quality of EOL experiences, including final conversations. Expose students to various contexts in which communication resourcefulness and adaptability can be used to inform how questions are asked, how active listening is demonstrated, and how nonverbal cues can aid in preparing for and engaging in EOL situations.
- Recommendation 3: Understand the importance of final conversations and differences in cultural considerations for each individual and relationship. As such, through competent intercultural communication, a window of opportunity is opened for constructing a quality EOL experience, including bereavement (Keeley & Generous, 2017; Tenzek & Depner, 2017).
- Recommendation 4: Incorporate case studies into curricula as a way to initiate the conversation and allow students to become more familiar with cultural variation at EOL. It is important to continue with EOL and intercultural communication courses in higher education, including curricula in professional schools. Furthermore, for practitioners, there should be more opportunities for continuing education units related to the impact of cultural differences on expectations of appropriateness at EOL.

The case study created for this chapter will be featured in the forthcoming Intercultural Communication Competence course at Marine Corps University and serves as a key communication practice that is not only personally and professionally relevant to Marines, but also as a means for students to reconsider previously held assumptions about what is possible through conversation.

NOTES

1. The first author teaches intercultural communication courses at Marine Corps University, which is where this case study will first be piloted.

2. See Shrank et al. (2005) for focus group findings on the influence of culture on communication preferences in EOL care.

3. The 10-month program runs annually from August to June, is located in Quantico, Virginia, and offers students a master of military studies. The program is selective and typically attracts the top 15% of field grade officers (O-4) in each branch. The electives program offered by the Marine Corps CSC gives students the opportunity to choose two, 20-contact-hour elective courses of their choice. The first author is a faculty member who has been teaching Intercultural Communication Competence elective courses for the military since 2009.

REFERENCES

Abbe, A., & Gouge, M. (2012). Cultural training for military personnel. *Military Review, 92*(4), 9–17.

Boromisza-Habashi, D., Hughes, J., & Malkowski, J. (2016). Public speaking as cultural ideal: Internationalizing the public speaking curriculum. *Journal of International and Intercultural Communication, 9,* 20–34. doi:10.1080/17513057.2016.1120847

Boucher, N. A. (2016). Direct engagement with communities and interprofessional learning to factor culture into end-of-life health care delivery. *American Journal of Public Health, 106*(6), 996–1001.

Bullock, K. (2011). The influence of culture on end-of-life decision making. *Journal of Social Work in End-of-Life and Palliative Care, 7,* 83–98.

Carbaugh, D. (2005). *Cultures in conversation.* Mahwah, NJ: Erlbaum.

Carbaugh, D. (2007). Cultural discourse analysis: Communication practices and intercultural encounters. *Journal of Intercultural Communication Research, 36*(3), 167–182. doi:10.1080/17475750701737090

Carbaugh, D. (2017). *The handbook of communication in cross-cultural perspective.* New York, NY: Routledge.

Carbaugh, D., & Buzzanell, P. (2009). *Distinctive qualities of communication research.* New York, NY: Routledge.

Carbaugh, D., & Cerulli, T. (2013). Cultural discourses of dwelling: Investigating environmental communication as a place-based practice. *Environmental Communication: The Journal of Nature and Culture, 7*(1), 4–23.

Carbaugh, D., & Lie, S. (2014). Competence in interaction: Cultural discourse analysis. In X. Dai & G. Chen (Eds.), *Intercultural communication competence: Conceptualization and its development in cultural contexts and interactions* (pp. 69–81). Newcastle: Cambridge.

Carter, B. (2010). No "holidays from history": Adult learning, professional military education, and teaching history. In D. Higbee (Ed.), *Military culture and education* (pp. 167–182). Burlington, VT: Ashgate.

Feldstein, C. B. D., Grudzen, M., Johnson, A., & LeBaron, S. (2008). Integrating spirituality and culture with end-of-life care in medical education. *Clinical Gerontologist, 31*(4), 71–82. doi:10.1080/07317110801947185

Hamil, L., Wu, B., & Brodie, M. (2017). Views and experiences with end-of-life medical care in Japan, Italy, the United States, and Brazil: A cross-country survey. Henry J. Kaiser Family Foundation.

Hattori, K., McCubbin, M., & Ishida, D. (2006). Concept analysis of good death in the Japanese community. *Journal of Nursing Scholarship, 38,* 165–170.

Higbee, D. (2010). *Military culture and education.* Burlington, VT: Ashgate.

Hirai, K., et al. (2006). Good death in Japanese cancer care: A qualitative study. *Journal of Pain and Symptom Management, 31*(2), 140–147.

Holmes-Eber, P. (2014). *Culture in conflict: Irregular warfare, culture policy, and the Marine Corps.* Redwood City, CA: Stanford University Press.

Hymes, D. (1964). *Language in culture and society: A reader in linguistics and anthropology.* New York, NY: Harper and Row.

Hymes, D. (1972). Models of the interaction of language and social life. In J. J. Gumperz & D. Hymes (Eds.), *Directions in sociolinguistics: The ethnography of communication* (pp. 35–71). New York, NY: Holt, Rinehart and Winston.

Johnson-Freese, J. (2013). *Educating America's military.* London: Routledge.

Keeley, M. P. (2004a). Final conversations: Messages of love. *Qualitative Research Reports, 5,* 48–57.

Keeley, M. P. (2004b). Final conversations: Survivors' memorable messages, concerning religious faith and spirituality. *Health Communication , 16 ,* 87–104.

Keeley, M. P. (2007). Turning toward death together: The functions of messages during final conversations in close relationships. *Journal of Social and Personal Relationships, 24*(2), 225–253. doi:10.1177/0265407507075412

Keeley, M. P., & Generous, M. A. (2015). The challenges of final conversations: Dialectical tensions during end-of-life family communication from survivors' retrospective accounts. *Southern Communication Journal, 80,* 377–387.

Keeley, M. P., & Generous, M. A. (2017). Final conversations: Overview and practical implications for patients, families, and healthcare workers. *Behavioral Sciences, 7*(2), 17. doi:10.3390/bs7020017

Keeley, M., & Koenig Kellas, J. (2005). Constructing life and death through final conversation narratives. In L. Harter, P. Japp, & C. Beck (Eds.), *Narratives, health and healing* (pp. 365–390). Mahwah, NJ: Erlbaum.

Kongsuwan, W., Chaipetch, O., & Matchim, Y. (2012). Thai Buddhist families' perspective of a peaceful death in ICUs. *Nursing in Critical Care, 17*(3), 151–159. doi:10.1111/j.1478-5153.2012.00495.x

Long, S. (2004). Cultural scripts for a good death in Japan and the U.S.: Similarities and differences. *Social Science and Medicine, 58,* 913–928.

Mackenzie, L., & Wallace, M. (2015). Intentional design: Using iterative modification to enhance online learning for professional cohorts. In T. Milburn (Ed.), *Communicating user experience: Applying local strategies research to digital media design.* Lanham, MD: Lexington.

Meier, E. A., Gallegos, J. V., Thomas, L. P. M., Depp, C. A., Irwin, S. A., & Jeste, D. V. (2016). Defining a good death (successful dying): Literature review and a call for research and public dialogue. *American Journal of Geriatric Psychiatry, 24*(4), 261–271. doi:10.1016/j.jagp.2016.01.135

Pearce, W. B., & Cronen, V. (1980). *Communication, action, and meaning: The creation of social realities.* New York, NY: Praeger.

Schiefflin, B., & Ochs, E. (1986). *Language socialization across cultures.* Cambridge and New York, NY: Cambridge University Press.

Scott, S. (2004). *Fierce conversations: Achieving success at work and in life one conversation at a time.* New York, NY: Berkley.

Shrank, W. H, Kutner, J. S., Richardson, T., Mularski, R. A., Fischer, S., & Kagawa-Singer, M. (2005). Focus group findings about the influence of culture on communication preferences in end-of-life care. *Journal of General Internal Medicine, 20* (8), 703–709.

Steen, S., Mackenzie, L., & Buechner, B. (2018). Incorporating cosmopolitan communication into diverse teaching and training contexts: Considerations from our work with military students and veterans. In D. Becker & J. D. Wallace (Eds.), *Handbook of Communication Training.* New York, NY: Routledge.

Stewart, J. (1973). *Bridges not walls: A book about interpersonal communication.* New York, NY: McGraw Hill.

Tenzek, K. E., & Depner, R. M. (2017). Still searching: A meta-synthesis of a good death from the family perspective. Special issue: Family communication at the end of life. *Behavioral Sciences, 7.* Available online, http://www.mdpi.com/2076-328X/7/2/25. doi:10.3390/bs7020025

Van Dyne, L., Ang, S., & Livermore, D. (2010). Cultural intelligence: A pathway for leading in a rapidly globalizing world. In K. M. Hannum, B. McFeeters, & L. Booysen (Eds.), *Leadership across differences: Cases and perspectives*. San Francisco, CA: Pfeiffer.

Wierzbicka, A. (1997). *Understanding cultures through their key words: English, Russian, Polish, German and Japanese*. New York, NY: Oxford University Press.

Wilkins, R. (2017). The optimal form and its use in cross-cultural analysis: A British "stiff upper lip" and a Finnish matter-of-fact style. In D. Carbaugh (Ed.), *The handbook of communication in cross-cultural perspective*. New York, NY: Routledge.

Chapter Seven

Museum Tour Talk

Communicative Acts, Associated Identities, and their Idealizations

Richard Wilkins, Fran Gulinello, and Karen Wolf

> I am going to stop talking; who wants to hear me talk the whole time?
> —Docent, museum tour, June 2014

In certain contexts, these words might have provided a welcome end to a boring event, but ironically they were uttered by a docent during an observation of a guided museum tour. Ironically, because many museum visitors take guided tours specifically to hear a docent talk and because the museum tour itself is a historicized site for speaking dating back to the early 1900s. This historicized sense of the guided tour is illustrated by an announcement in the August 1910 *Museum of Fine Arts Bulletin* (Boston) for free docent service. The brief article explains that speakers "act as guides to those seeking information about the exhibits or they lead a circuit of about an hour through the galleries of department with remarks" (Museum of Fine Arts, Boston, 1910, p. 28). The announcement ends with a call for volunteers:

> The hope of the Museum is that people of culture will be willing to put their attainments at the service of visitors, speaking familiarly to them on any subject—artistic, literary, historical, technical, scientific, moral or religious—that the works of art shown in the galleries may suggest. (p. 28)

Thus, the docent and the guided tour—in their original construction—were intended to be an agent and a site for speaking about art and culture. More than a hundred years later, the docent is curiously regretful for *talking*.

TERMS FOR TALK

Part of Carbaugh's cultural discourse theory is his (1989) terms for talk framework, which suggests ways of formulating research questions about the ways in which docents go about evaluating their talk in the scene of the guided museum tour. Induced through a comparative study of several ethnographic case studies, terms for talk not only identify and label highly indigenous processes of communication, but can also imply an indigenous sequencing and framing within which the talk is performed (Carbaugh, 1989; Wilkins, 2007). An examination of cultural terms for talk in the initial descriptive stage receives four levels of application. These are at the level of act, event, style, and function (Carbaugh, 1989, pp. 97–103). The first three describe some native organization of the means of speech. The fourth, the functional shaping of speech, addresses itself to some indirect outcome of a cultural term for talk. In order to understand the larger set of communicative acts within which the evaluations of the docents are framed, the task here is to identify the terms for talk that reside within this speech community through an analysis of the communal understandings of the kinds of speech practices that are important enough to receive a label. The central question for our study was the following: what communicative action is accomplished in verbal performance of cultural labels?

Further to these levels of application there are messages that are active in these terms for talk that say something about communication itself, social relations, and personhood (Carbaugh, 1989). One of the threads woven throughout much of Carbaugh's scholarship is the important link between communication and the cultural identity of a particular situated community of people. Throughout much of our research we have taken as the central problem of concern the way in which a community of speakers communicate to construct for themselves and others a cultural understanding of who they are. We start with the notion that communication is cultural and that through describing the repertoire of communicative acts we can identify patterns of communication that say something about the beliefs and values of a people, ultimately conveying a deeper understanding of the premises that guide communicative acts and give focus to a community of speakers. Carbaugh (1996) explains:

> that we think of identities as dimensions and outcomes of communication practices; second, that we think of each identity as a system of communicative practices that is salient in some but not (necessarily) all social scenes; third, that we think of communication, as a cultural accomplishment. (p. 24)

In any study of communication and culture, the theme of identity and identification contributes to a greater conceptualization of the important ways a group uses communication to convey to both insiders and outsiders who they think they are as a people. In studying culture this way one can gain insight into why groups choose to use certain expressions and communicative actions to accomplish tasks, goals, and relate to nature. Cultural discourse analysis (CuDA) provides a way to investigate and explain "culturally distinctive practices" of communication including talk, nonverbal, and technological communication (Carbaugh & Cerulli, 2017).

Many studies have explored the role of communicative acts as a means toward identification. For instance, Carbaugh and Wolf (2000) explored the way some Apache argued through acts of *silence* for the protection of a sacred mountain, as compared to a verbal act of *argument* used by scientists. The silent act of communication was misperceived by scientists as a lack of knowledge, when in fact silence was employed as a cultural strategy for demonstrating respect for the land for which they fought. Basso (1990) has also shown how the Apache use acts of *silence* prominently in events of meeting strangers. Warm Springs Indians have also used communicative acts of *silence* in classrooms (Philips, 1983). Carbaugh (1999) has shown how the Blackfeet use acts of *listening* to connect with a specific physical place. Studies in Anglo American communication have found that some North Americans identify with one another through the communicative acts of *being honest* (Carbaugh, 1994), *communication* (Katriel & Philipsen, 1990), and *sharing* (Michaels, 1981; Carbaugh, 1988). Baxter (1993) has shown how members of an academic institution identify with themselves as colleagues through the acts of *talking things through*, whereas *putting it in writing* identifies with professional management. The act of *brown-nosing* in American organizations is "linked to the ulterior goals of getting attention or advancement" (Hall & Valde, 1995, p. 399). *Communitas*—the valorization of community at Hampshire College in Massachusetts—is instituted through a variety of communicative activities found in the discussion events in classroom scenes (Gibson, 1995). Sabra Israelis assert their identity through the act of *dugri* [talking straight] (Katriel, 1986). More recently Block (2003) has shown how, when faced with the possibility of being labeled a *Freier* [sucker], Israelis will "refrain from voluntarily undertaking any activity that would entail an effort not resulting in the actor's own immediate interests or not taking advantage of a situation that presented itself" (p. 131). Acts of *confianza* [trust] for Colombians (Fitch, 1994, 1998) lays down the basis for a sociocentric model of personhood as does the term *musayara* [going with or accompanying one's partner in conversation] for Arabs in Israel (Griefat & Katriel, 1989). A form of wit practiced in China from 200 to 600 C.E. called *pure talk* enabled community, ego reinforcement, and a potential weapon for hostile encounters with the outside world (Garrett, 1993).

If a docent refrains from talk, this act may demonstrate to those present that a docent's knowledge is shared in more ways than through talk; knowledge is not transferred, but is communally constructed. In this way, choosing to speak or refrain from talk serves as a basis for affirmation, validation, negotiation, and ultimately denial of an identity. We can look at communication practices, then, to get at a particular group's cultural identity, and how group members create and maintain their identity through communicative acts. As Carbaugh (1996) aptly states, "together, then, and in summary, one might think of social identities as a dimension and outcome of communication performances, as more salient in some scenes than others, and as socially negotiated and culturally distinct" (p. 27). By applying Carbaugh's (1996) definition of identity, one can look at how a group's communicative actions constituted a sense of what it means to be a member of this group; the appropriate ways for communicating action in that particular scene; the cultural premises of belief and value that are deeply meaningful throughout communicative enactments; and the rules for communicating throughout symbolic rituals. Clearly, there is much to be learned about cultural identity by analyzing a community of speakers in this way. "It is to know ways to express that identity efficaciously, that is, to express it and have it validated, through a variety of actions, in a variety of scenes" (Carbaugh, 1996, p. 25).

METHOD

Data collection involved participation in tours of nine New York City museums and four galleries over a period of two years from January 2013 to January 2015. Multiple visits were made so that the content, the guides, and the visitors varied with each observation. Audio recordings were taken for most of the observations and supplemented with field notes to capture non-verbal messages and descriptions of the settings and participants. While the majority of the data for this study is based on the interactions between visitors and docents in museums, we also examine cultural texts to demonstrate that patterned communication inside the museums has been carried over from the patterned communication outside of the museums and vice versa. Cultural terms for talk by definition will have a pervasive quality and not only will be found in the scenes marked for participant observation, but will often punctuate a variety of scenes found in the community of speakers of which these scenes are a part. With this in mind, blogs, social media, and newsgroup postings were also consulted to understand better the performance of communicative acts found at the museum tours (e.g., Cora-Garcia, et al., 2009; Boretree, 2005; Wittel, 2000).

The analysis begins in the descriptive mode presenting the words of the docents themselves as a way of answering the question "What actually happened as a practice of communication?" (Carbaugh, 2007, p. 173). It then moves to the interpretive mode exploring the meanings of the practice to the participants and to the community. Here we discuss an idealized form of communication practice that holds significance to educators and their identities as good docents, teachers, and guides. Finally, in the critical mode—a form of natural criticism—we look at how idealized practices of communication inform both a set of deficiencies and excessive qualities of communication in public settings as participants struggle to seek a balance in what Wilkins (2005) refers to as an optimal form. We ask what meanings are articulated when docents and visitors seek a balanced form of interaction. Or more simply put, we answer the question, why would a docent regret talking?

Wilkins (2005) introduced the optimal form in his study of the *asiallinen* [matter-of-fact] nonverbal style in Finland. This nonverbal style has identifiable features, such as a concentrated silent attitude and the moderation of facial movements, but as Wilkins notes, it is best defined by what it is not. It is best defined by the nonverbal elements that are stigmatized. For those Finns that idealize the *asiallinen* [matter-of-fact] style they will reject those that are "quick to answer." A long period of silence is expected as one reflects upon possible responses and answers to questions and makes certain that any response is well reasoned or accurate. Also stigmatized are excessive facial and bodily movements that reveal too much emotion. This does not mean that Finns do not use the face to show emotion; rather, the movements are moderated according to the scene and the social roles. The *asiallinen* [matter-of-fact] style will encourage a range of moderated gestures such as hands held close to the body and no large grins or excessive head bobbing. Individuals are also expected to restrict their nonverbal behaviors that interrupt the flow of information such as excessive eye contact by a public speaker.

Wilkins interpreted the underlying meanings of this style by introducing the concept of an optimal form. An optimal form refers to an ideal style within a community, "where participants evoke a standardized quality in communication" (2005, p. 396). This evocation of the standardized quality takes place at various levels. At the first level the participants are cognitively aware that their actions are framed by a standardizing work of excess and defect. At the second level the participants of a community will categorize relevant lexical items, what Wilkins (2005) calls the "indigenously named elements of communication," into "clusters of excess and defect and a favored standard" (p. 396). At the third level the optimal form is an interpretive device that shows how elements of a style or form can best be used to "serve a community's rhetorical ends" (Wilkins, 2005, p. 397). In later work Wilkins (2009) shows *infocentrism* as the communicative ideal where a speaker code is constructed through a preference for an informational face; a *kuulija* [listener] and *sanomakeskeinen* [message centered] orientation motivates participants to listen and understand; and simplicity in expression marks the preferred performance in speech.

FINDINGS

The practice that was immediately apparent in the museum scene was a labeling of talk that the docents engaged in as they discussed how communication on the guided tour should proceed. To be clear, we do not mean that docents gave instructions on how to interpret art (brushstroke, perspective, object placement, or curator's vision). The docents specifically discussed what a guided tour should be called, who should talk on a guided tour, and what would happen if the talk were to be one-sided. We begin by presenting excerpts that illustrate the presence of this pattern in museum discourse and then ask the analytically relevant question posed by Carbaugh, "What cultural commentary is eminent in this practice?" (2007, p. 168).

The pattern began during the earliest observation with a docent who discussed naming practices with the tour group.

Extract 1. Field Notes, January 2013

The tour participants assembled outside the exhibit in a small seating area just above the main lobby on the second floor. The docent was male, in his late twenties or early thirties by best estimation, and was dressed in a shirt and tie but no jacket. He announced the beginning of the session and asked the participants to gather closer to him. The group initially consisted of twelve to fifteen people; seven were from a university class. In his introduction the docent explained:

> Docent 1: This is a conversation not a guide and it took a long time for the museum to come up with that name.

Notice that the docent (and presumably the museum curators and administrators) renamed the tour, calling it a "conversation." Implicit in the renaming and the "long time" it took to find the right name is careful thought into how communication should ideally be practiced in the museum setting and what that practice should be called. In doing so, beliefs regarding effective communication about art were expressed to visitors. As docents labeled their communication as a *conversation* they also referred to their goals of evoking a less formal experience and one of equal participation. The renaming of things in modern museums has become commonplace. In some museums, the "gallery session" has replaced the "daily tour" with the former distancing itself from connotations of a walking lecture. New York's Museum of Modern Art (MoMA), for example, describes gallery sessions on their website as "lively conversations and engaging activities, facilitated by museum educators."

The "docent," a term originally used for a teacher in a religious or university setting, has given way to "gallery guide." Blogger and author Maeve Maddox comments on this naming practice at the Crystal Bridges Museum of American Art in Arkansas. He reminds us that the word *docent* has its roots in Latin *docere*, "to teach," and suggests that museum directors made this change because they felt that the word was too off-putting for potential visitors and were giving in to "sophophobia." One respondent to the blog explains why her museum uses "guide" and not "docent":

> This is a wonderful conversation. I've worked as a museum educator for more than 25 years. Here at my museum we've used "Guides" since the opening. The story is that the volunteers in the first guide training discussed what they should be called. The decision to be called "Guides" came after a fevered pitch by an older man. I paraphrase, "Did DOCENTS guide people West? NO! Sacagawea was a GUIDE. She wasn't a Docent. We aren't docents, we are guides!" And that's how it went down in history about 21 years ago. (Cathy, April 25, 2011, What's so hard about docent?)

New labels are intended to create a more visitor-friendly, accessible art experience, but are deeply connected to identity and specifically address the way people should talk in museums.

Whereas the first docent implied ideal communication via naming practices, the following docent explicitly laid out the parameters of communication on the tour.

Extract 2. Field Notes, June 2014

> Docent 2: So we are here today to . . . we are going to go through the Polke Show. But if you've been through the show already this is going to be a very different kind of experience. I am not just talking and you're listening, anybody can do that, right? You can get information in many many ways. But what's different about what we are going to do today is we are doing it together and it's going to really depend on all of us participating.

The docent in this observation describes the tour as a "very different kind of experience," and that experience is situated mainly in communicative practice. She describes a traditional notion of a guided tour in which one person talks and the others listen and promptly dismisses that as less than ideal. She then describes the ideal as "doing it together," and the success of the tour as depending on "all of us participating." Evident in her description are values about the way art education should proceed. It is the process that is worthwhile, not the outcome, and that process is one in which everyone participates by talking. Other docents confirmed these expectations by prompting those who were not participating or not wholly participating.

Extract 3. Field Notes, January 12, 2015

1	Docent 3:	Without knowing too much about Siqueiros, what kinds of
2		feelings come to mind?
3	Visitor 1:	War
4	Docent 3:	War, okay excellent
5	Visitor 2:	Grim, dark
6	Docent 3:	OK, what else, without censorship
7		(No response)
8	Docent 3:	(looking at a visitor) Do you have something for me?

Although the docent in this excerpt did not explicitly describe how one should communicate, the expectations of participation were clear. She suggested that the group was holding back in some way, monitoring or "censoring" their responses. The docent specifically called on one visitor, who had not participated at all, and her question implied that everyone had a responsibility to say something.

The following extract exemplifies the preferred participation on the part of the docent. The communication of the docent should be minimal in proportion to the communication of the visitor. The visitor is expected to participate and is evaluated by that participation. One feature of that participation is that it should not dominate the participation of other visitors. The acts of communication in this scene should not be telling, but they should be *asking*, *involving*, and *precipitating*. This vocabulary and associated gestures facilitate its function. It has identifiable features and it has meaning to its participants and their identities as good educators and good students.

Extract 4. Observation of Schoolchildren, January 2015

A teacher had just begun discussing the painting *Birth of the World* by Joan Miró with a class of young schoolchildren. In front of the painting about eighteen children sat on the floor. The teacher stood near the painting asking them questions. There were other adults that may have been with the class (perhaps parent chaperones). Museum visitors moved in and out of the scene, stopping to look or read the nearby plaque. Briefly listening to the teacher and the children. (Ethnographer's note: It is quite common on school days to see classes at the museum. They often sit in front of a painting or sculpture and sometimes even have sketch pads where they draw the piece. Some interaction took place in another language. This is an excerpt from the portion that was in English.)

1	Teacher:	What do you see?
2	C1:	A balloon
3	C2:	A spider
4	C3:	I see darkness
5	C4:	The spider only has five legs
6	Teacher:	Yes, the spider only has five legs. What do you think
7		happened to the other legs? Do you think they blew away?
8	C5:	I see a person.
9	Teacher:	Where do you see the person?
10		(Several children call out)
11	Teacher:	Raise your hands to speak. (Children raise their hands and
12		the teacher calls on one)
13	C6:	I see a flag.
14	Teacher:	You see a flag? But (C5) said she sees a person? Does
15		anyone else see a person?
16	C7:	(Calls out loudly) I see a person with his leg broke.
17	Teacher:	(Addressing C7 by name and speaking sternly) I will not
18		recognize you unless you raise your hand.
19		(C7 raises his hand and the teacher says his name)
20	C7:	(More meekly) I see a person with his leg broke
21	Teacher:	It looks like his leg is broken like this? (She does a comical
22		imitation of the figure in the painting)

The teacher begins with the discourse initiator, an open-ended question: "*What do you see?*" Four children give comments, but only one receives feedback. The comment "the spider has five legs," gets an affirmative response and is repeated. It is then followed up with another open-ended question to encourage interpretation. The teacher's question is ignored by the next child who is allowed to shift the topic away from the spider's five legs to the human figure. Another child tries to shift the topic again, to the flag. The teacher brings the conversation back to the human figure. Children call out and speak over each other. They are asked to raise their hands even though they had not all raised their hands previously. A child calls out loudly and is admonished for his behavior. The child then raises his hand and says, "I see a person with his leg broke." The teacher affirms his observation with a humorous rendition of the figure in the painting. This scene does not simply illustrate the teacher's philosophy about learning and knowledge or a preferred pedagogy, it exemplifies a communicative practice.

REPORTS ABOUT EXCESS AND INADEQUACY

Understanding the communicative practices of the docents, teacher, and visitors to a gallery as being bound to an idealized construction of communicative acts gives some insight into the question posed at the beginning of the chapter. What brought the docent to evaluate her own participation? How does the act of talking or refraining from talk frame the docent in a way that allows her to identify as the one with knowledge while at the same time constructing knowledge with those in her group?

The critical mode in its strictest interpretation responds to questions about how a practice advantages some over others and the relative worth of this practice among its participants (Carbaugh, 2007, p. 173). Natural criticism is heard when "the communication system under investigation evaluates itself, or some aspect of itself, on the basis of one of its moral system(s)." Here, the emphasis of criticism is derived from the "indigenous cultural practice" (Carbaugh, 1989/1990, p. 267). The ethnographer here is responsible for describing the communication patterns through which the community members evaluate their own cultural practice. The optimal form was developed through the observation that speech communities will often naturally reference both the excessiveness and shortcomings of various speech and nonverbal activities. In so doing they invoke an idealization—a middle path, a golden mean, a balance—of some deeply held belief about persons, their relationships, their communication, and their feelings. The analytical task is (a) explore clusters of terms, (b) identify possible optimal strategies in the clusters through an analysis of indigenously named excessive or substandard communication practices, and (c) explicate the types of persons, their actions, their feelings, and their understandings of sociality that can exist based on an optimal performance of the activity in question (Wilkins, 2005; Wilkins and Wolf, 2014).

Docents and educators are faced with the situational constraints of daily communication. They may be guided by beliefs about successful communication practices and want to maintain them but are constrained by practical issues of time, group size, and by individual learner characteristics. We recall the story of a well-respected scholar in the field of active learning who had been lecturing to an audience of educators for over an hour, despite admonishments that the "old paradigm of lecturing was out." Upon realizing the contradiction of communication ideal versus practice, he said to his audience, "what I'm doing here is passive (learning), but I have a lot of information to give you so I'm stuck with it." It is not a matter of being a "hypocrite" or a "bad teacher," rather it reflects the complex interaction between a culturally idealized communication practice and the realization that in practice one's communication may not live up to the understood ideal.

Applying Wilkins's first level—that participants are cognitively aware that their actions are framed by a standardizing work of excess and defect—to the words of the docents in this case, one could conclude that the docents are aware because they explicitly refer to it. Museum staff meet about the exhibit tours, about engaging the visitors, and about the relevance of these interactions with respect to the museum's place in art education. The guests at the museum had been made cognitively aware of the optimal form by the docents' explicit discussion of the parameters of the gallery sessions but also by educational norms that have been culturally transmitted. Americans have been made aware that communication in educational settings is framed by a standardizing work via cultural texts. The droning teacher played by Ben Stein in *The Wonder Years* or the unintelligible "Mwah Mwah" of Charlie Brown's teacher are reminiscent of a time in education where the students were given information with little thought to what they could create or discover. Online universities entice the modern student with ad campaigns that promise "no more boring lectures." As a testament to how deeply ingrained ideals have become to the average American, we can look at a contest held by an organization called Students First (Weasler, 2012). The contest asked people to write a six-word description of what it means to be a good teacher. One finalist wrote these six words: *all thirty students raised their hands* (Murray, 2012). It almost does not matter what the students said, just that the teacher got them to say it. For many American educators, communication has become the hallmark of a good education. Not just any or all communication but that which takes a specific form.

Educators, parents, and students have come to categorize the communicative practices of good teachers using relevant lexical items. The familiar adage not a "sage on the stage" but a "guide on the side" juxtaposes the defect and the favored standard (in Ackerman, 2004). To the layperson, the favored communication style in education is categorized by lexical items such as engaging, passionate, and interactive, the defect by lecture and spoon-feeding, and the excess by "freedom without focus" (Bronson & Merryman, 2010). These terms embed either one-sidedness or equality of talk in their connotations. The communicative practice regarding participation became apparent in the museum scene, but calls to mind cultural expectations outside of the museum in modern classrooms. Educators may relate the docents' practices to their own during which expectations about participation and its value to a successful class are implicitly or explicitly expressed to students. Recall the saying "tell me and I forget, teach me and I may remember, involve me and I learn." The theory of knowledge and learning reflected in those words is often referred to as constructivism. The constructivist perspective holds that knowledge is not stored information but the organization and interpretation of experience. People therefore gain knowledge or learn most effectively by working through problems, engaging with authentic materials, discovering and incorporating, not by being told principles or truths that someone else has discovered. Kai-Kee (2011) explains the constructivist perspective in *A Brief History of Teaching in the Art Museum*:

> Constructivism describes knowledge as comprising not of truths about an independent reality to be discovered and transmitted but explanations constructed by humans engaged in meaning making in cultural and social communities of discourse. Learning takes place as individuals struggle to make meaning, assimilating and adapting conceptual schemes and structures into new experience. (Kai-Kee, 2011, p. 46)

While the constructivist perspective is a theory of knowledge per se, it drives classroom practice and is often associated with theories of pedagogy. Many museums have adopted constructivist ideologies in their approach to art education to various extents (Rice & Yenawine, 2002; Kai-Kee, 2011; MoMA, *Five Tips to Teaching Art*, MoMA video), and these approaches were directly observed in museum discourse.

To simply remark that museums have adopted constructivist ideas may not in itself be the concern of the ethnography of communication and cultural discourse analysis. What is important to this study is that so many of the explanations of constructivism as a pedagogy are couched in labels of discourse that constructivism has come down to educators not just as a theory of knowledge or a pedagogical methodology but as a communication practice. Creating a constructivist educational setting is dependent on the way teachers and students communicate. It is the communication practice that is of interest here, specifically how constructivist ideologies have altered the speaking roles in the classroom, have developed into a standardized communication form, and have impacted how some American educators and students feel about talk.

The relationship between theories of knowledge and classroom practice is a familiar one. Ways of thinking about knowledge and learning, from behaviorism, to cognitivism, to constructivism, to humanism, inform instructional design and classroom practices. To understand how constructivism came to be a style of communication, we must look at how the epistemology and pedagogical ideas have been presented to educators. Consider the explanation of constructivism from a PBS workshop for teachers:

> In the classroom, the constructivist view of learning can point towards a number of different teaching practices. In the most general sense, it usually means encouraging students to use active techniques (experiments, real-world problem solving) to create more knowledge and then to reflect on and talk about what they are doing and how their understanding is changing. (Educational Broadcasting Corporation, 2004, para. 2)

The sequence described in the PBS workshop can be parsed into its key elements. It begins with "the constructivist view," which points to "different teaching practices" and culminates in "talk." As individuals struggle to make meaning in a classroom they must "talk about what they are doing and how their understanding is changing." If you are not talking about what you have learned then the paradigm fails. Learning is thus situated in a community discourse (Kai-Kee, 2011), which can mean the museum community, the classroom community, or the community at large. Participants in the discourse have expected roles. Specifically, the educator speaks primarily to encourage the learner to speak.

Since learning and knowledge in this view are dependent on this community discourse, it makes sense that individuals who identify as part of this community will have ideas about how the discourse should proceed, what form it should take, and how it is done correctly or incorrectly. Such standardizing elements were expressed explicitly and implicitly by the docents in this study but are also evident in pedagogical texts. For example, teacher education materials focus on who should talk and who should not talk in a constructivist's classroom. If an educator is talking, students are passive and not actively making meaning, not constructing knowledge, and not transforming input. In fact, by talking an educator takes talk away from the learner, the very thing the learner needs to gain knowledge. This is poignantly expressed in a quote attributed to Piaget: "Whatever you tell a child you won't allow her to discover herself" (Ackerman, 2004, p. 17). At least some educators have come to believe that when they talk, they deprive the learner of precious discoveries. It is no wonder that the docent seems apologetic for speaking too much. She may believe that by talking she is depriving the visitors of their own discoveries about art.

Pedagogical texts center on how to facilitate the community discourse on which constructivism relies. For example, one way of encouraging students to talk about their understanding is through open-ended questions such as "What happened?" and "What did you observe?" We can refer back to the docents and teacher asking, "(w)hat do you see?" or "what kinds of feelings come to mind?" Inquiry and response is discussed at great length in the constructivist literature. Teachers are encouraged to permit topic shifts based on student responses—recall the children at the Miró exhibit shifting from the spider to the person to the flag. Educators are also advised to use "cognitive terminology" such as "classify, analyze, predict and create" (Grennon-Brooks & Brooks,1999, p. 104).

Facilitating constructivism as a communicative ideal extends beyond the *words* educators use and includes *nonverbal* cues as well. Mike Watts and Di Bentley wrote about constructivism in the late 1980s in their article subtitled "Enabling Conceptual Change by Words and Deeds." They argued that in a constructivist classroom, children risk exposing their existing ideas. In order to encourage students to take such a risk, teachers must build trust in the classroom by becoming "skilled in the verbal and non-verbal cues they initiate" (1987, p. 121). Their detailed interviews indicate that students judge when a teacher is enthusiastic (by the quickness of movement), when a teacher likes a student (by movement in the corners of the mouth), and when a teacher is sympathetic to a student who does not understand (by the tone of voice). The teacher speaking to the children at the Miró painting mimicked a broken leg. Her nonverbal message communicated forgiveness to the student who called out so he would trust her and continue to participate.

To say that constructivism is a communicative ideal is to say that it has features that repeat, are recognized, and are transmitted to others but also that its use has meaning to participants. If one were to list the features of the constructivist communicative ideal they would include inquiry though open-ended questions, topic shifts guided by response, the use of cognitive terminology, and nonverbal cues to build rapport and trust. Implicit in the constructivist communicative ideal are standardizing elements about the correct way to communicate in an educational setting and the incorrect way. Knowledge is not a reality transmitted but meaning that is assimilated, adapted, and coconstructed. In simple language, teacher workshops present this dichotomy in terms of active and passive learning.

> Constructivism transforms the student from a passive recipient of information to an active participant in the learning process. Always guided by the teacher, students construct their knowledge actively rather than just mechanically ingesting knowledge from the teacher or the textbook. (Educational Broadcasting Corporation, 2004, para. 6)

It is not difficult to see how this dichotomy has come to educators, students, and parents through heuristically encoded concepts such as *participation* and *lecture.* These are set against each other in evaluations of *good teaching* and *bad teaching.* We see this opposition play out in the research literature, in the classroom, and in popular culture.

> A good teacher, in this sense, is one that helps learners explore, express, exchange—and ultimately expand—their views, from within [not a sage on the stage, but a guide on the side]. (Ackerman, 2004)

"Good teachers" in U.S. educational contexts are defined as those that help the student "express"; they are not the ones doing the talking.

The constructivist ideal was revealed in the patterned communication of the participants on guided museum tours and provides a lens for understanding this particular aspect of museum talk and the way we communicate in broader educational settings. It offers insight into what some Americans who identify as educators consider to be the ideal when it comes to teaching and learning, but also provides an understanding of why educators, students, docents, and visitors often struggle against this ideal. Specifically, it offers insight into why an individual who identifies as a docent would regret talking too much.

REFERENCES

Ackerman, E. (2004). Constructing knowledge and transforming the world. In M. Tokoro & L. Steels (Eds.), *A learning zone of one's own: Sharing representations and flow in collaborative learning environments* (pp. 15–37). Amsterdam, Berlin, Oxford, Tokyo, Washington, D.C.: IOS Press.

Basso, K. (1990). "To give up on words": Silence in Western Apache culture. In D. Carbaugh (Ed.), *Cultural communication and intercultural contact* (pp. 303–320). Hillsdale, NJ: Erlbaum.

Baxter, L. (1993). "Talking things through" and "putting it in writing": Two codes of communication in an academic institution. *Journal of Applied Communication Research, 21,* 313–326.

Block, L. (2003). Who's afraid of being a Freier? The analysis of communication through a key cultural frame. *Communication Theory, 13,* 125–159.

Boretree, D. (2005). Presentation of self on the web: An ethnographic study of teenage girls' weblogs. *Education, Communication and Information, 5*(1), pp. 25–39. doi:10.1080/14636310500061102

Bronson, P., & Merryman, A. (July 27, 2010) The creativity crisis. *Newsweek.* Retrieved from http://www.newsweek.com/creativity-crisis-74665

Carbaugh, D. (1988). *Talking American: Cultural discourses on Donahue.* Norwood, NJ: Ablex.

Carbaugh, D. (1989/1990). The critical voice in ethnography of communication research. *Research on Language and Social Interaction, 23,* 261–282.

Carbaugh, D. (1989). Fifty terms for talk: A cross-cultural study. *International and Intercultural Communication Annual, 13,* 93–120.

Carbaugh, D. (1996). *Situating selves: The communication of social identities in American scenes.* Albany, NY: State University of New York Press.

Carbaugh, D. (1999). "Just listen": "Listening" and landscape among the Blackfeet. *Western Journal of Communication, 63,* 250–270.

Carbaugh, D. (2007). Cultural discourse analysis: Communication practices and intercultural encounters. *Journal Intercultural Communication Research, 36*(3), 167–182. doi:10.1080/17475750701737090

Carbaugh, D., & Cerulli, T. (2017). Cultural discourse analysis. In Y. Y. Kim (Gen. Ed.) & K. L. McKay-Semmler (Assoc. Ed.), *The international encyclopedia of intercultural communication* (pp. 1–9). Hoboken, NJ: John Wiley & Sons. doi: 10.1002/9781118783665.ieicc0117.

Carbaugh, D., & Wolf, K. (2000). Situating rhetoric in cultural discourses. *International and Intercultural Annual, 22,* 19–30.

Cora-Garcia, A., Standlee, A., Bechkoff, J., & Cui, Y. (2009). Ethnographic approaches to the encounters. *Journal of Intercultural Communication Research, 36*(3), 167–182. doi:10.1080/17475750701737090

Educational Broadcasting Corporation. (2004). Constructivism as a paradigm for teaching and learning. Retrieved from http://www.thirteen.org/edonline/concept2class/constructivism/index.html

Fitch, K. (1994). A cross-cultural study of directive sequences and some implications for compliance-gaining research. *Communication Monographs 61,* 185–209.

Fitch, K. (1998). *Speaking relationally: Culture, communication, and interpersonal connection.* New York, NY: The Guilford Press.

Garrett, M. (1993). Wit, power, and oppositional groups: A case study of "pure talk." *Quarterly Journal of Speech, 79,* 303–318.

Gibson, T. R. (1995). The liminal institution: An ethnography of communication at Hampshire College. Unpublished master's thesis, University of Massachusetts Amherst.

Grennon-Brooks, J., & Brooks, M. (1999). *In search of understanding the case for constructivist classrooms.* Alexandria, VA: ASCD Publications.

Griefat, Y., & Katriel, T. (1989). Life demands musayara: Communication and culture among Arabs in Israel. *International and Intercultural Communication Annual, 13,* 121–138.

Hall, B., & Valde, K. (1995). Brown-nosing as a cultural category in American organizational life. *Research on Language and Social Interaction, 28,* 391–419.

Internet and computer-mediated communication. *Journal of Contemporary Ethnography, 38*(1), 52–84. doi:10.1177/0891241607310839

Kai-Kee, E. (2011). A brief history of teaching in the art museum. In R. Burnham & E. Kai-kee (Eds.), *Teaching in the art museum.* Los Angeles, CA: The Paul J. Getty Museum.

Katriel, T. (1986). *Talking straight: Dugri speech in Israeli Sabra culture.* Cambridge, UK: Cambridge University Press.

Katriel, T., & Philipsen, G. (1990). What we need is communication: "Communication" as a cultural category in some American speech. In D. Carbaugh (Ed.), *Cultural communication and intercultural contact* (pp. 77–94). Hillsdale, NJ: Erlbaum.

Maddox, M. (April 21, 2011). What's so hard about docent? [Blog post]. Retrieved from https:/ /www.dailywritingtips.com/whats-so-hard-about-docent/

Michaels, S. (1981). "Sharing time": Children's narrative styles and differential access to literacy. *Language in Society, 10,* 423–442.

Murray, D. (June 22, 2012). What makes a great teacher? You have 6 words to describe one. MLive. MLive Media Group. Retrieved from http://www.mlive.com/education/index.ssf/ 2012/02/what_makes_a_great_teacher_you.html

Museum of Fine Arts, Boston. (1910). Free docent service. *Museum of Fine Arts Bulletin, 8*(46), 28.

Philips, S. U. (1983). *The invisible culture: Communication in classroom and community on the Warm Springs Indian Reservation.* New York and London: Longman.

Rice, D., & Yenawine, P. (2002). A conversation on object centered learning in art museums. *Curator: The Museum Journal, 45*(4), 289–299.

Watts, M., and Bentley, D. (1987). Constructivism in the classroom: Enabling conceptual change by words and deeds. *British Educational Research Journal, 13*(2), 121–135.

Weasler, S. (January 28, 2012). 27,000 ways to describe a great teacher. Studentsfirst. [Blog post]. Retrieved from https://www.studentsfirst.org/blogs/national/27000-ways-to-describe-a-great-teacher

Wilkins, R. (2005). The optimal form: Inadequacies and excessiveness within the Asiallinen [matter of fact] nonverbal style in public and civic settings in Finland. *Journal of Communication, 55*(2), 383–401.

Wilkins, R. (2007). Cultural frames: Loci of intercultural communication asynchrony in a CBS 60 Minutes news segment. *International Journal of Intercultural Relations, 31,* 243–258.

Wilkins, R. (2009). Celebrating infocentrism through the Asiasta Puhumisen event: A term for talk in settings for adult education in Finland. In P. Isotalus & R. Wilkins (Ed.), *Speech Culture in Finland* (pp. 63–84). University Press of America.

Wilkins, R., & Wolf, K. (2014). *Culture in rhetoric.* New York, NY: Peter Lang.

Wittel, A. (2000). Ethnography on the move: From field to net to internet. *Forum Qualitative Social Research, 1*(1).

Part III

Relating

Chapter Eight

"Talking" and *Tapailla* ("Seeing Someone")

Cultural Terms and Ways of Communicating in the Development of Romantic Relationships in the United States and Finland

Michelle Scollo and Saila Poutiainen

Amber,[1] a 28-year-old female from the United States, recounting her current romantic "situation," explained:

> We've been friends now for four years, but this whole time he's been pursuing me. And recently I kind of gave him an inch, you know, like we've been kind of talking now, so like the label that's been put on that was friends, and then friend zone, for a couple years . . . and now like there's potential and so it's like a positive situation.

When asked why she calls it a "situation," Amber further explained:

> Because I wouldn't say that we are dating. I wouldn't say that . . . I would say that he's my friend and now we're talking I guess.

What does it mean that Amber has given "him an inch," so now they are not just "friends," or in the "friend zone,"[2] nor "dating," but are friends that are "talking"?

In Finland, a participant in a *Vauva* online discussion forum,[3] responding to a question on the difference between *tapailu* and *seurustelu*, noted:

Well, I have *tapaillut* more men in my lifetime than what I've eventually *seurustellut* with. Even with my current husband we *tapailtiin* for some time before we started to call it *seurustelu.*

Tapailu is lighter than *seurustelu.* It is precisely that, that you don't know yet, whether you want to commit with the other one. *Tapailu* is about getting to know the other and figuring out the chemistry. If two people are on the same page regarding *tapailu,* you wouldn't think it bothers anybody if you want to call it that (August 17, 2017).[4]

Although the Finnish writer clearly distinguishes between *tapailu* and *seurustelu* in her response, the differences between the two terms and relationship stages being up for discussion in an online forum and her last claim suggest that there is ambiguity and tension between them in Finland. Similarly, in Amber's example above, there is ambiguity and tension between the emerging term and relationship stage of "talking" and "dating" in the United States.

These examples suggest not only that ways of identifying and developing romantic relationships are in transition today, but also that they are culturally situated processes. We are interested in the communicative process of romantic relationship development across cultures, with attention to both the cultural terms participants use to identify ways of communicating, relating, and feeling in them, as well as those very ways (Carbaugh, 2005).

Research and theorizing about interpersonal communication has long focused on communication and relationships in the United States and only marginally addressed the influence of culture (Scollo & Carbaugh, 2013; Fitch, 1998; Poutiainen, 2009; Gudykunst, Ting-Toomey, & Nishida, 1996; Gudykunst & Ting-Toomey, 1988). Romantic relationship research has also been critiqued for being largely focused on the Western context and ignoring cultural differences regarding love (Baxter & Akkoor, 2008; Goodwin, 1999; Dion & Dion, 1996; Jankowiak, 1995).

Despite this, research on romantic relating in different cultures has been on the rise, with the ethnography of communication (EC), the research program within which this study is situated,[5] offering some notable contributions. Early on in EC, Basso (1970) studied silence among the Western Apache and found that *zééde* ("sweethearts") who are in the beginning stages of *líígoláá* ("courting") spent time together in a variety of settings yet were often silent and talked little until after several months when they felt more comfortable. Later, Katriel and Philipsen (1981) examined the importance of "communication" and Carbaugh (1988) "self" as cultural categories in the domain of interpersonal communication in the United States. Fitch Muñoz has perhaps most extensively studied interpersonal communication and relationships in the EC program, examining multiple forms of interpersonal communication in Columbia including directives, leave-taking, personal address, politeness, and narratives, also introducing the concept of "interpersonal ideology" (2009, 2006, 1998, 1994, 1991a, 1991b).

Poutiainen (2009, 2005) examined romantic relationship development in Finland and found at the time that some relationships began with a period of *kattelu*, meaning to observe or watch someone that one has romantic interest in for a period of time, before a committed relationship (*seurustelu*) ensues.[6] There is also a burgeoning area of research on culture, weddings, and marriage, with Sandel's (2015, 2011) work on cross-border marriage in Taiwan, Leeds-Hurwitz's (2002) study of intercultural weddings in the United States,[7] and Baxter and Akkoor's (2008) study of East Indian arranged marriages.

Although "dates" and "dating" have also been most extensively studied in the United States (e.g., Mongeau & Wiedmaier, 2012; Mongeau, Jacobsen, & Donnerstein, 2007; Roses, 2006), dating and romantic relationships in different cultures have intrigued scholars doing qualitative research in different disciplines in recent years. Some noteworthy examples include Jyrkiäinen's (2016) study of Egyptian females' negotiation of identity profiles on Facebook as part of their dating practices and Farrer, Tsuchiya, and Bagrowicz's (2008) study of *tsukiau* dating relationships in Japan. There is also a nascent area of research on online dating applications and sites in different countries including China (Liu, 2016; Pan & Lieber, 2008), Iran (Golzard & Miguel, 2016; Shakoori & Shafiei, 2014), and the Netherlands (Sumter, Vandenbosch, & Ligtenberg, 2017; Ward, 2017).

While research on romantic relationship development in different cultures is growing, we aim to illustrate what a cultural discourse analysis approach, a research method and theory in EC, can offer to studies of interpersonal communication in the development of romantic relationships in different cultures today (Carbaugh, 2007, 2005).

METHOD

We take relationships to be constructed via communication and, following Fitch (1998), "that personal relationships are, like speaking more generally, culturally situated processes" (p. 14). As such, relationships are not only constructed through communication, culture is at the root of that very communication and re-created in the process. Likewise, relationships are both cultural and communicative processes.

We are particularly interested in the role of communication in the development of romantic relationships in different cultures. We are drawn to Knapp's long-standing model of interaction stages in relationships (Knapp, 1978; Knapp, Vangelisti, & Caughlin, 2014) in this endeavor due to its popularity, focus on communication in the development of relationships, yet its common presentation in introductory communication texts and research without attention to culture. The model is a descriptive model of communication patterns in the development of relationships such as romantic relationships and friendships that is organized into five progressive stages each of "coming together" and "coming apart." Our focus is on the stages of "coming together," which include (1) "initiating" (greeting); (2) "experimenting" (small talk); (3) "intensifying" (self-disclosure, expressions of commitment, personal idioms); (4) "integrating" ("two become one" in communication and relationship); and (5) "bonding" (public institutionalization of the relationship such as marriage) (Knapp, Vangelisti, & Caughlin, 2014).[8] Following our own and others' research, we argue that this may be a cultural model of communication in relationship development that is not applicable to all cultures (Poutiainen, 2009, 2005; Scollo & Poutiainen, 2006; Basso, 1970).

To begin exploration of this with preliminary cultural cases, we interviewed adults ages 22 to 38 about their experiences in developing romantic relationships from first meeting to establishment of a serious relationship, including ways of communicating involved in them, in the United States[9] and Finland.[10] We also took field notes on naturally occurring talk and interaction about the development of romantic relationships in our everyday lives in the United States, for Scollo, and Finland, for Poutiainen. Lastly, we searched for and examined online articles, discussion forums, and videos about recurrent, prominent terms in our initial data, such as "talking" in the United States and *tapailu* in Finland, to round out our data and analysis.

While it would be ideal to observe all the varied communication involved in the development of romantic relationships, this is likely not possible. Moreover, *how people talk about* relationship development can be an equally important window into how cultural members develop such relationships and make sense of them in their own lives. Toward this end, to analyze our data we conducted a cultural discourse analysis (CuDA) concerning the communicative process of romantic relationship development in the United States and Finland according to members' perspectives (Carbaugh, 2017, 2005; Scollo, 2011).

CuDA, a theory and method within EC, conceptualizes cultural discourse as "a set of communication practices—acts, events, and styles—which is treated as a historically transmitted expressive system of symbols, symbolic forms, norms, and their meanings" (Carbaugh & Cerulli, 2013, p. 7). Cultural discourses may be topical (e.g., discourses of romantic relating or health), and multiple, intertwined discourses comprise cultures.[11] Cultural discourses are systems of associated communication practices and norms that are symbolic in the sense that while our communication may say something explicitly about, for example, communication or relationships, it also implicitly says something about who we are and should be, how we can and should act, relate to others, feel, and live in place (Carbaugh, 2017, 2005). As such, "communication presumes and creates a rich meta-cultural commentary," radiating a web of symbolic meanings about being, acting, relating, feeling, and dwelling (Carbaugh, 2017, p. 19).

Using CuDA to unravel this web, there is dual attention on identifying and describing explicit communication practices, or "discursive hubs," such as cultural terms for types of communication or relationships, while also interpreting the implicit meanings radiating through them or "radiants of meaning" (Carbaugh, 2017). These are "part of an unspoken coherence participants take-for-granted in order to understand their communication," often formulated into statements of cultural premises, which are combinations of deeply held beliefs and values (Carbaugh, 2017, p. 19). A cultural discourse is likewise typically comprised of multiple "discursive hubs," associated communication practices, and norms, whose deep meanings are interpreted through cultural premises.

In the spirit of CuDA, our study follows its four modes of analysis—descriptive, interpretive, comparative, and critical—as we describe, interpret, and compare communication practices and cultural discourses of romantic relating in the United States and Finland (Carbaugh, 2017, pp. 17–18). We also include two forms of critical analysis, "natural" and "academic" criticism (Carbaugh, 1989/1990). In the U.S. case, some participants employ "natural criticism" as they critique the emerging term for and relationship stage of "talking," while in the Finnish case, the data includes criticism of the tone of the relationship stage, *tapailu.* We also engage in "academic criticism" as we use a cross-cultural comparative analysis to critique potential Western bias in Knapp's model.

For our study, we analyzed our interview transcripts, field notes, and online articles, videos, and discussions for recurrent, prominent cultural terms, associated practices, and norms that feature in the process of romantic relationship development in the United States and Finland today. Inspired by Knapp's model—since some of these terms identified relationship stages, ways of communicating in those stages, and participants' recognized stages—we identified stages of romantic relationship development from initial meeting to declaration of a serious relationship in both cases. Lastly, we interpreted the key cultural terms—often identifying stages and ways of communicating, relating, or feeling in them—for cultural premises of being, acting, relating, feeling, and dwelling that radiated through them.

In our analysis, we found differences in the ways the process of romantic relationship development was discoursed[12] in each case. In the U.S. case, the process of developing a romantic relationship was discoursed by participants as primarily one of communication, and secondarily of relating; thus, we have discursive hubs of acting (or communicating) and relating. In the Finnish case, the process of romantic relationship development was discoursed as one of both relating and feeling; thus, we focus our analyses on these discursive hubs. In what follows, we present U.S. and Finnish cultural discourses of romantic relating, each comprised of a system of cultural terms, associated practices and norms, and a constellation of cultural premises radiating through them.

U.S. DISCOURSE OF ROMANTIC RELATING

The process of developing a romantic relationship in the United States was discoursed by our participants as primarily one of communication, and secondarily of relating. In what follows, we delineate three prominent stages in the communicative development of romantic relationships in the United States up to being in a serious "relationship"—Initiating, "Getting to Know Each Other," and "In a Relationship"—with their associated terms, practices, norms, and cultural premises.

Initiating

Similar to Knapp's model, "Initiating" is our term[13] for the first stage of romantic relationship development in the United States, though we broaden it to include a series of communicative means that initiate romantic relationships, including (1) meeting, (2) social media "stalking," and (3) contacting.

Meeting. Our participants noted a number of settings and scenes where they meet potential romantic interests, including school, work, school clubs, athletic activities, bars, through friends, and mobile dating apps, with Tinder being most popular.[14] While some of our participants were using dating apps and there were varying degrees of comfort with them, most noted that they were especially useful for older people (typically 30 and older) since they have more difficulty meeting people due to being out of school and potentially living in new areas for work. As such, one can meet romantic interests in a variety of physical settings and mediated scenes, suggesting an expanded notion of space and important cultural premises of dwelling and relating: *Space in the United States includes physical place and cyberspace. Both are places to meet potential romantic interests.*

If there is romantic interest, our participants noted the importance of initiating some sort of communication with the person. Here there was a gender norm, that in heterosexual relationships, males should make "the first move," though several females and males said they would be fine with females doing so. For homosexual and lesbian relationships, participants noted that whoever is more romantically interested should make the first move.

For participants, this "first move" depended on the context or scene. If in a physical setting such as a bar, participants noted that they or the other person would "strike up a conversation," buy the other person a drink if in such a setting, and eventually exchange mobile phone numbers, Instagram,

Facebook, or Snapchat names, often calling, texting, following, or friending each other right then on their phones. Younger participants preferred to exchange social media handles, while older participants tended to prefer mobile numbers. For those meeting on dating apps, conversation began on private messaging through the app, following the same norms as above for first contact, eventually moving to following on social media or exchanging mobile numbers.

"Stalking." Most of our participants noted that after meeting someone they were romantically interested in, they immediately started social media "stalking" the person. That is, they would look them up on Facebook, Instagram, and/or Twitter (e.g., "a thorough Facebook stalking"; "I'm that Instagram stalker") to learn more about them, depending on if their pages are set to public (and therefore open to everyone to see) or private (for only friends/followers). Several participants said they would not friend or follow someone right away, but rather after time if the relationship developed. Participants noted looking for various information while "stalking," including if they were a real person; if they were in a relationship; last time in a relationship; ratio of female to male "likes" on photos; if they were safe to go out with; what their interests were; their photos; and, for older participants, if they had children.

Importantly, much of this "learning" about the other person is quick and *visual*, done by examining photos and posts. This not only helps one decide if there is romantic interest, but also speeds up the process of getting to know the person. As one participant, John, age 23, noted, he "stalked" his current girlfriend:

> Just to kind of see what she was into, see what she was doing and seeing her or her interests. . . . I was trying to kind of see what she was, what she liked doing. And turns out she had a lot of pictures of nature and hiking. I saw she ice skates, so I like that too about her. . . . And I just got to know her a little bit better through social media before I even started dating her. [15]

Contacting. Lastly, if one party decides after meeting and likely "stalking" the other that they are romantically interested, they may contact the other person. This followed the same norms above for first contact. Depending on the setting or scene where participants first met, as well as what medium of contact was exchanged upon first meeting, this could be a direct message on social media or a dating app, a text message, or, though rare, a phone call. [16]

At this point we can ask, what must be presumed for participants to discourse the initiation of romantic relationships in the United States in this way? A set of cultural premises can be formulated that helps unravel this rich complexity: *Being romantically involved with another is, at times, a desirable state. As all people are free and equal, people have a right to choose their romantic partners. Potential partners can be met in a variety of places, both physical and online, and through relationships such as friends. Since people are separate, unique individuals, each with their own thoughts, feelings, and experiences, communication must be used to learn about the other person to see if there is romantic interest. This communication may be conducted through a variety of channels such as face-to-face interaction, social media, or mobile texts and calls.* [17]

If all goes well and there is reciprocal contact after the first meeting, participants move to the next stage of romantic relationship development, "getting to know each other."

"Getting to Know Each Other"

"Getting to know each other" is a native phrase that captures much of what this stage of developing romantic relationships is about, using various ways of communicating to get to know the other person more deeply to determine if one is romantically interested in them.

There is a system of cultural terms, associated practices, and norms in this stage, some currently emerging and in tension as new ways of communicating and relating take shape and transform over time. Specifically, the cultural term "talking" has emerged in approximately the past five years, which identifies a *relationship stage* (e.g., "we're talking"). This is in tension in this discursive system with "dating," an older term, which our older participants tended to prefer for identifying this stage, yet they used, understood, and often critiqued the more recent term "talking." Most of our younger participants would use the term "talking" to identify this stage of romantic relationships. We have used the broader native phrase "getting to know each other" instead, as it captures the heart of this stage, while encompassing participants who prefer the term "talking," "dating," or no term at all.

"Talking" identifies a relationship stage in which participants are trying to get to know each other through various communicative means and can include "meeting up," "hanging out," or "dates," as well as sexual activity. This generally is not exclusive; one can be "talking" to multiple people. As one of our participants, Jordan, age 23, explained:

> It's like you're not *really* dating yet, but you're just testing each other I guess. . . . You're not committed though. . . . You're kind of like trying to see if it will go there.

"Talking" can last for a few days up to a few months, until participants decide if they want to move to the next, more serious relationship stage, just be "friends," or end their "talking." That this stage is identified with the verbal communication term "talking" points to the primary goal of this stage:

using various communicative means to "talk" to get to know the other person to decide if you want to pursue a more serious relationship. We argue, following our participants, that "talking" follows a loosely structured sequence of five communicative activities: (1) "talking"; (2) asking out; (3) going out; (4) more "talking"; and (5) having a "conversation."

"Talking." Beginning "talking" often follows "a level of progression" in terms of medium, for example, from directing messaging on a social media site to asking for the other person's number, to texting. "Talking" at this point can include social media direct messages and posts (e.g., Facebook, Instagram, Snapchat, Tinder), texts, and possibly phone calls or "FaceTiming."

The tone of early "talking" is "casual" and "informal." Social media and text messages are often funny and flirtatious (e.g., "flirtatious Snapchats back and forth"), while seeking out potential common interests. As Eve, age 28, Lara, age 23, and Mia, age 26, explain after being asked what role texting and social media play in the beginning of romantic relationships:

1	Eve:	I think texting is huge
2	Lara:	Yeah
3	Eve:	Which I hate
4	Lara:	To be able to hold a conversation
5	Mia:	That's the whole beginning now
6	Eve:	Like I don't, I can't (.5) I can't date a bad texter. Like if you can't like
7		make me laugh via text or like play off mine, it's *not* gonna work
(. . .)		
8	Mia:	Give me like a hello, give me a good morning
9	Eve:	A joke
10	Lara:	Absolutely, yeah
11	Eve:	Thought of you when I saw this
12	Lara:	Exactly
13	Mia:	No like I want, yeah absolutely, like if I'm gonna like, when I wake up in
14		the morning I'm thinking of you, like I wanna make sure that it's the same
15		thing on your side too
16	Eve:	Send me a funny meme
17	Lara:	Yeah
18	Mia:	One hundred percent, yeah, flirt
19	Lara:	Yes
20	Mia:	Be a goofball

Notice here that the developing relationship and romantic feeling are located *in communication*—in texts of different kinds—between interlocutors. Even an important model of personhood—being a good "texter" (and thus potential romantic partner)—is located in communicative action, that is, the ability to craft good texts.

The goal of "talking" at this point is to get to know the other person to see if there is romantic potential. This may include who the other person is, potential common interests, and career and life goals. According to participants, this can last for a few days to a few weeks.

Asking Out. At this point, if there is interest, one person will ask the other person, or they may mutually decide, to "meet up," "hang out," or go out on a "date." This follows the same gender norms as above. Interestingly, our younger participants treated such events informally, not wanting to call this a "date," but rather "meeting up" or "hanging out." A "date" for them is much more formal, involving dressing up and something more serious and planned in advance such as a nice dinner out, and should be built up to over time. For several of our older participants, a "date" was seen as more casual yet necessary to move relationships forward. There was a certain sense of frustration among them that there is a reluctance to call this a "date" or "dating." For many of our younger participants, however, "dating" is seen as the next, more serious stage of relationships.

Some of our participants suggested that this is "generational." Many of our older participants grew up with the terms "date" and "dating," while for our younger participants, "talking" has emerged during their formative years of developing romantic relationships. Thus, we can see how the terms would be in tension for older participants, as new ways of communicating and relating in the development of romantic relationships emerge.

Going Out. At this point, the participants "meet up," "hang out," or go out on a "date." It should be "casual" in nature, one-on-one so that participants can talk, and likewise in a setting that enables talking. Participants noted going out for a drink, coffee, or dinner as good first dates. Several also noted doing a "fun" activity such as hiking, bowling, or mini golf as good first dates, since they enable participants to have fun, while giving them something to talk about during the date. Several participants noted that going to a "movie" should *not* be a first date, since you cannot talk. As Eddie, age 22, noted: "Definitely not the movies. . . . You can't *speak*. You can't talk, can't talk at all."

The goal of the first "meet-up" or "date" is to talk to get to know the other person to see if there is romantic interest for both parties. This involves learning more about the other person than in the initial "talking" phase over social media and text. Topics may include work, common interests, and life in general. Some of our older participants that wanted to be in a serious relationship preferred to discuss more personal topics and life goals on the first date as they did not want to waste time, whereas younger participants preferred keep first "meet-ups" light.

Participants also noted the importance of being "fun" and "interesting" and not "boring" on first "meet-ups" or "dates," which is gleaned through conversation. Likewise, romantic interest and feeling are located *in conversation*. As John, age 23, noted:

> I went on a date with another girl from the college . . . and it just wasn't there. We went to Outback and we ah, it just wasn't there. It was slow conversation the whole entire time, no laughs. She was a nice girl but it just wasn't there, really dull the entire time like I could tell I wasn't having a good time. And I think you could just see it wasn't going anywhere, there was no laughing. It was kind of just slow, like really nice girl, but it just wasn't there.

Notice here that "it"—presumably romantic interest or "chemistry"—is located in "conversation" that is not "slow" or "dull," but rather in which you have "laughs" and "a good time." Unfortunately, for John, "it just wasn't there." Participants noted in such cases that they would not see the other person again. They may say they could be "friends" or, more likely, not continue "talking" after the first "date" or "meet-up."

More "Talking." If both parties are romantically interested in each other after the first "meet-up" or "date," more "talking" ensues. This includes more "talking" over social media and texts, "FaceTiming," and phone calls, more "meet-ups," "hanging out," or "dates," as well as sexual activity. The goal here is to get to know the other person more deeply, to see if one wants the relationship to evolve to the next, more serious stage.

A few of our participants noted that there may be "stages" to "talking" and that there is "talking" and "talking talking." "Talking" is the beginning stage and not exclusive, whereas "talking talking" is a later stage and exclusive. This is where some of the natural critique of "talking" comes in—that it is an amorphous stage where one does not really know where one stands in the relationship. Several of our younger and some of our older participants liked this, as they were interested in more casual relationships, and if interested, wanted to take time to develop a more serious relationship. For many of our participants who were seeking serious relationships, the term and stage of "talking" frustrated them as it seemingly prolonged the development of relationships as well as declaration of their status and exclusivity.[18]

Having a "Conversation." After "talking" or "getting to know the other person" for a period of time, one or both parties may be interested in moving to the next, more serious stage and, if not already, becoming exclusive. At this point, one or both parties may initiate and "have a conversation." This "conversation" is more serious in tone, where both parties are working out what they would like their relationship to be. If both are interested in deepening their relationship, "talking" or this stage of relationships ends, and they move to the next more serious stage.

"In a Relationship"

According to our participants, there are several terms for couples who reach this more serious, exclusive stage of romantic relationships, including: "dating," "in a relationship," "boyfriend girlfriend," and "they're" or "we're together." Interestingly, for our participants who used the term "talking," "dating" was seen as the next, more serious stage of romantic relationships, equivalent to "in a relationship," "boyfriend girlfriend," or "we're together." For participants who preferred "dating" to label the stage of "getting to know each other," the next stage of romantic relationships was identified as "in a relationship," "boyfriend girlfriend," or being "together."

Analysis

With the communicative process of developing romantic relationships in the United States, including the three primary stages of (1) Initiating, (2) "Getting to Know Each Other," up to (3) "In a Relationship," now delineated, we can ask, why are romantic relationships discoursed as developing in these ways? What must be presumed for participants to make sense of the process in this way? A set of cultural premises regarding being, acting, relating, and feeling can be formulated that helps unravel this rich complexity: *People are separate, unique individuals, each with their own passions, interests, thoughts, feelings, and experiences. Due to this, if one is interested in another romantically, one must use communication to learn about the person, to connect to them, and to develop romantic feelings. This communication should be fun and interesting in the beginning, as it is an expression of self and develops the relationship and romantic feelings. Time should be taken in this process, since relationships are a serious commitment. People are and should be independent; thus, any relationship impinges on both parties' freedom. Thus, time and care should be taken in getting to know someone to develop the relationship to see if they are a good match. There are a variety of communication channels today, including the Internet, mobile phones, and face-to-face interaction, that offer more ways and time to get to know another person and develop relationships. This should be taken advantage of so that one can make a good choice.*

FINNISH DISCOURSE OF ROMANTIC RELATING

In contrast to the U.S. case in which the process of developing a romantic relationship focused largely on communication, in Finland the focus was more on relating and feeling. In this cultural discourse of romantic relating, a system of cultural terms for relating, feeling, and communicating, as well as associated practices and norms, came into view as participants made sense of their romantic lives. The Finnish participants were clear in their responses that the beginning of romantic relating had stages. Throughout the interviews and in other data as well, people analyzed, told stories, and stated beliefs and opinions about these stages. Most of the participants—but not all—expressed hope and longing for meeting potential partners and for long-term relationships.

In what follows, we delineate three current prominent stages in the communicative development of romantic relationships in Finland up to being in a serious relationship—*Tapaaminen* ("Encounter"), *Tutustuminen* ("Getting to Know Someone"), and *Seurustelu* ("Romantic Relationship"). In the following, we discuss in detail the first two stages with their associated terms, practices, norms, and cultural premises.

Tapaaminen ("Encounter")

The two most prevalent first encounters that were described by participants were meeting face-to-face and meeting on Tinder.[19] Meeting someone for the first time face-to-face was described as coincidental and unpredicted—one could meet new people at unexpected times and in unexpected places. Yet some scenes or ways were described as more typical, such as bars, events, parties, the work environment, and hobbies. First encounters were either followed by interaction via technology (Excerpt 1), or technology was already entwined within the first encounter (Excerpt 2).

Excerpt 1

1	Interviewer:	*Tai tyypillisesti. Miten parisuhteet tyypillisesti alkaa?*
2		Or typically. How do relationships typically begin?
3	Maija:	*Mä kertoisin oman tarinan ja sä sanoisit et se on tyypillinen, koska*
4		*baarissa tavattiin ja hävettää myöntää muille, koska kaikki*
5		*muutkin aina tapaa baarissa tai siis silleen, niin.*
6		I would tell my own story and you would say it's typical, because
7		we met in a bar and I'm ashamed to admit to others because all the
8		others also always meet in a bar or so.
9	Interviewer:	*Joo, joo. Ja siihenkin liittyy teknologiaa sitten?*
10		Yes yes. And technology is related to that as well then?
11	Maija:	*Joo, sen jälkeen sit oltiin yhteydessä. Ensin katottiin et kumpi lisää*
12		*kumman Facebookissa ja sit et kumpi alottaa keskustelun ja*
13		*tämmöstä.*
14		Yes, after that we were in contact. First we checked out which one
15		adds which one in Facebook and then which one begins the
16		conversation and so on.

Excerpt 2

Roosa (age 33): *Että mulla on ainaki monesti sit ku on laitettu Facebook-kaveriks, ni sitten on käyty siinä jo läpi, esims jos baarissa on et ootsä hei Facebookissa. Aa, ni sitte tavallaan niinku käyä jo läpi et aa, nää on yhteisiä, että mistä sä tän tunnet ja näin, ni sit, sit-siitä saa jo semmosen niinku, alku-keskustelun aikaseks että.*

For me at least many times when you have accepted each other as Facebook friends then you have already there, for example in a bar, [asked] are you on Facebook. Aaa, you kind of go through them, and aaaah, these are common [friends], how do you know this one, and then you kind of get the early conversation going.

The first face-to-face encounters vary. Length of time does not define the actual act or account of *tapaaminen* face-to-face. It could be a short encounter, as described by Sini, age 33. She had had a short but meaningful first meeting, a 15-minute conversation in a daytime outdoor event that was followed by a "friend request" on Facebook, an exchange of messages the day after, and an agreement to meet sometime in the future in the city where the other party lived. Further, first encounters may or may not include sexual activity or romantic feelings. Some of the first *tapaaminen* were described with expressions such as *meillä synkkasi* ("we hit it off"), *hän oli kiinnostava* ("he was interesting"), *hän teki itseään tykö* ("he put himself forward"), and *me juteltiin koko ilta* ("we talked the whole night"). These expressions suggest that the speaker has met an interesting person, that they have possibly experienced mutual interest toward each other, and expressed that by having an extended conversation and moment of enjoying each other's company.

The first face-to-face encounter—or the first few—in interviewees' descriptions included an exchange of contact information. Friending on Facebook or using Facebook Messenger were the primary channels for first contact. If phone numbers were exchanged, typically messaging then moved from Facebook Messenger into the WhatsApp service.[20]

The participants discussed who initiated friending on Facebook, time between the first encounter and first message, and the amount and content of first messages as points for making interpretations of the other person, possible romantic interest, and compatibility. However, when discussing the amount and kinds of messages, there was not a strong consensus or shared norms for messaging. What participants seemed to agree on was that Facebook is a source of potentially meaningful information. In Excerpt 2 above, Roosa described how during the first face-to-face encounter parties would bring up their Facebook pages on their phones, friend each other, and examine each other's contact list. To have common friends on Facebook is not rare in Finland or Helsinki. Participants mentioned, for example, that sometimes it is refreshing to meet someone who does not have shared friends on Facebook. On the other hand, participants also suggested that if the other party shared several friends, he or she could not be that dangerous or strange.

Tutustuminen ("Getting to Know Someone")

Although we have separated the first stage of *kohtaaminen* ("encounter") from the stage of *tutustuminen* (literally translated as "getting to know someone"), the transition from one stage to another is not always clear. The very first *kohtaaminen* could already contain deep and long conversations, high self-disclosure, sexual activity, and romantic feelings—all of which certainly lead into getting to know someone. Martta, age 33, described the beginning of her current relationship as:

> *Meil ei kyl ikinä oikeen ollu treffejä ku me tavattiin silloin yöl, yöl Mustas Häräs ja sit vietettiin se yö yhdes. Ja sit seuraavan viikonloppun, no me, oli se tavallaan treffit ku me oltiin sovittu tapaaminen, mut siis mun luo. Me käytiin vaan kävelee ja sit Jussi tuli heti mun luo yöks ja sit me ollaan siit lähtien aina oltu toistemme luon yöt. Et ei me olla ikin oikee käyty missää kahvil tai mitään.*

> We never really had any *treffit* when we met that night at the Musta Härkä [a restaurant] and then spent the night together. And then the next weekend, well, it was kind of *treffit* as we had agreed to meet but at my place. We just went for a walk and then Jussi came over right away for the night and then we've then on been at each other's place the nights. So we have not really ever gone out for coffee or anything.

Although Martta's relationship began swiftly and without *treffit* ("dates"), participants in her group interview stated that typically, at the stage of *tutustuminen,* there would be face-to-face meetings (*deitti* or *treffit* in Finnish, translated as "a date" or *hengailu,* "hanging out").[21] As Maria, age 32, explained, "There needs to be *treffit,* so that the thing starts developing to some direction," and then laughed. *Treffit* could follow, for example, after meeting someone for the first time at a party or bar. An invitation to meet up would be presented, and the parties would agree on a time, place, and activity for the meeting. During the first few meetings (or *treffit*) an evaluation of the connection takes place, as noted here in Roosa's, age 33, words: "*Jaksaaks rueta tapailee tai kohtaako intressit tai onko kemiaa?*" ("Do I feel like starting *tapailee* or do our interests meet or do we have chemistry?"). If two people end up having multiple meetings and occasions of getting together, even lasting for months, these meetings or activity could be called *tapailu* (ongoing meeting-up).[22] *Tapailu* is also part of the *tutustuminen* stage. In the following, we describe in detail the ways in which participants talked about two significant cultural terms in this stage, *Tinder-treffit* and *tapailu.*

Tinder-Treffit ("Tinder Dates"). Some participants had single *Tinder-treffit* occasionally, while some described phases in their lives during which they could have five or six *Tinder-treffit* in one week with different individuals. Participants also knew of others who had had multiple *Tinder-treffit* in one day. An invitation to a *Tinder-treffit* would follow a shorter or longer period of exchanging messages on Tinder. Participants had different opinions on whether the male or female should present an invitation and whether the invitation should always be accepted or not. A typical *Tinder-treffit* was going for a drink or coffee. The emphasis here is on "typically"—a drink or a coffee were discussed as safe and easy activities, but also as predictable or unimaginative suggestions.[23] Participants also expressed frustration regarding unimaginative opening lines for chats on Tinder, and on patterns of communication during *Tinder-treffit*, such as questions and topics for conversation.

On the stage of getting to know someone, for example during *Tinder-treffit*, the parties interact when they meet up. In addition to getting to know one another, parties explore, evaluate, and reflect on the potential for their own and the other's romantic interest. However, participants described not only the content of the conversations, but also the gaze and physical appearance as meaningful sources of information. To the interviewer's question on how do you know, in addition to self-disclosure, whether there is romantic interest, Leena (33), Saimi (32), and Martta (33), replied:

1	Leena:	*Jotain vaan puuttuu.*
2		Something is just missing
3	Saimi:	*Niin*
4		Right
5	Leena:	*Et ei oo, ei oo kemiaa*
6		There is no, there is no chemistry
7	Martta:	*Nii, se kemia*
8		Right, the chemistry
9	Leena:	*Eikä se ihminen kiehdo jotenki välttämättä.*
10		Nor does the person fascinate somehow necessarily
11	Saimi:	*Niin, et tietenki se voi, ihan niinku siis, ihan tosi karua, että näki*
12		*jostain ihmisistä että kun olit sopinut treffit niinkun Tinderissä tai*
13		*Tinderissä oot jutellut jonkun aikaan ja vaikutti hyvältä ja näin. Ja*
14		*sitten ku se käveli sua koh, niinkun kohti ni se olemus ja kaikki*
15		*kerto ja niinkun itelle tuli saman tien semmonen [olo, tunne] et ei.*
16		*Sit vaan silleen et fuck, et no okei istutaan tässä ja juodaan nää*
17		*kahvit tai kaljat.*
18		Well, of course it can be, very harsh, that you saw in someone,
19		when you had agreed on *treffit* on Tinder, or on Tinder you have
20		talked for a while and he appeared good. And then when he walked

21		towards you, the appearance and everything told you and you got
22		that [feeling] right away that no. Then you just go oh fuck, okay,
23		let's sit here and drink these coffees or beers.

In a similar manner, in another interview, Liila, age 31, responds as follows to the interviewer's clarifying questions: "What was the word you used, did you talk about chemistry?" and "How do you know that the other one is interested in you?" Note at the end of her turn, how all the participants agree with her:

1	Liila:	*Et se, se toinen, kat-, se katse, että [kyllä mä sen tiedän et onks se*
2		*toinen kiinnostunu vai ei*
3		The other one, the the gaze, I do know whether the other is
4		interested in or not
5	Sini:	*[Kyllä, kyllä. // Ja kaikki eleet siis sellaset*
6		Yes, yes. And all the gestures those
(. . .)		
7	Liila:	*Se on paljon niinku sellasta . . . no vet-vetovoima*
8		It's a lot that kind of . . . well gravity
(. . .)		
9	Liila:	*Mut tässä jos, ihan niinku miettii ni, ihan et mitä siellä silmissä*
10		*näkyy, se semmonen tietynlainen pilke // sellanen // ni se kertoo*
11		But here if you think about it what do you see in the eyes, it's the
12		certain kind of twinkle, that, so that tells you
13	Sini, Roosa:	Mm, mm

From these utterances, we see that chemistry or fascination—or lack of them—is something that can be observed without engaging in verbal interaction. This does not mean, however, that on *Tinder-treffit*, there would be no talk, or that silence would be important, not to mention preferred. Our aim here is simply to underline that it is not only verbal communication that is observed, interpreted, and evaluated by participants. Occasionally, as in the excerpts earlier, it is also difficult to verbalize what is the source or channel from which the interpretations are drawn.

Tapailu. The phase of *tapailu*, in practice, consists of a number of meetings (meet-ups, dates, rendezvous) that could be regular, but go on without an agreement of a set time period or set requirements, for example, for the frequency of the meetings. *Tapailu* most likely would include sex, and it could go on only for sex. For example, Liila, age 31, described her current relationship as *tapailu*: she is single, but meets with a particular man five or six times a week. They are attracted to each other, enjoy each other's company, and the sex is "great"; however, they are not in a committed romantic relationship (*seurustelu*), and she would not want to have one with him.

Earlier Roosa stated that the first few *treffit* are a point to evaluate whether to start *tapailu*. During *tapailu* the partners get to know each other, and they evaluate, further, the level of romantic interest and the need and possibility for a monogamous relationship (*Et onks tässä jotain?*, "Is there something going on here?"). *Tapailu* either develops into *seurustelu* (romantic partnership) or eventually ends.

Participants were keen on analytically evaluating the expectations, beliefs, and values surrounding *tapailu*. Participants also discussed changes, and some of the participants stated as natural criticism that in current times, *tapailu* is preferred over "serious" relationships. Commitment (to one person) was considered to be rare, and there was an expectation to enjoy Tinder and *tapailu* lightly and playfully. Tinder, in particular, creates the impression that there are multiple possible people to meet, and thus committing to someone becomes more demanding. In other words, *tapailu* is not necessarily assumed as a monogamous stage. At least monogamy is not agreed upon once in this stage (although *tapailu* could move into monogamy without an explicit agreement). As Sini, age 33, explains:

> *Mun mielestä // esmes parisuhde on jo sit tosi vakava jo nykyaikana et jos jotkut sanoo et ne on parisuhteessa niinku me nyt sanotaan ni se on jo melkeen niinku avoliitto . . . sitte // niinku tapailusuhde, se voi kestää x määrän aikoja riippuen niist henkilöist mitä ne haluu mut parisuhde on jo sellane et sit niinku esittäydytään vanhemmille // ja sit ku jos ollaan tän ikäsii [kolmekymppisiä] ni sit siinä on niinku jo se optio niinku tosi vahvana siihen että // pitäs ehkä niinku mennä naimisiin ja sitte niinku tehä niitä asioita et, tietysti on erilaisia pariskuntia et jotkut ei haluu ees lapsia tai näin mutta //*

> In my opinion for example *parisuhde* [romantic relationship] is already really serious nowadays. If someone says that they are in *parisuhde*, like we are now saying, then it is already almost like *avoliitto*[24] . . . that *tapailusuhde* (*tapailu* relationship), it can last x amount of time depending on the people what they want, but *parisuhde* is already that, that in it you introduce yourself to the parents and when you are at this age [around 30s] there is that option, very strong, that maybe we should get married and do those things, of course there are different kinds of couples, not all even want to have children, but like this.

Participants also discussed romantic relationships as a bonus. Some participants suggested that instead of looking at committed romantic relationships as the aim, those relationships are seen as a bonus in the process of getting to know new people, and in the process of *tapaileminen*. In the end, participants' experiences and discussion were full of contradictions. In addition to describing lightness, playfulness, and staying noncommitted, the participants described heartaches, tears, disappointments, fears for expressing romantic interest, and difficulties in experiencing rejection.

Participants recognized *keskustelu* ("the conversation") as the turning point, which moves *tapailu* into a committed relationship. In the conversation, the couple defines the relationship. They could, for example, acknowledge their mutual feelings (or lack of them) and agree on monogamy. Some of the participants describe *keskustelu* as scary or risky. Roosa, age 33, suggested that both parties might be afraid of initiating *keskustelu*, being worried about getting rejected, and thus *tapailu* could go on for a long time.

Seurustelu ("Romantic Relationship")

If *keskustelu* is successful and both parties want to move forward to the next, more serious stage of romantic relationships, they move into *seurustelu* ("romantic relationship"). Synonyms for *seurustelu* from participants included *tyttöystävä, poikaystävä* ("girlfriend, boyfriend"); *naisystävä, miesystävä* ("womanfriend, manfriend"; equivalent for "girlfriend, boyfriend," but used in relationships of older partners, in middle age and up); and *varattu* ("to be taken"). Other expressions used were *olla yhdessä* ("to be together"), *olla jonkun kanssa* ("to be with someone"), or to be *(pari)suhteessa*, which is the expression used also on Facebook, "in a relationship."

Analysis

When listening to these men and women in their 20s and 30s living in Helsinki, we can ask, why are romantic relationships discoursed as developing in these ways, through the three stages of (1) *Tapaaminen* ("Encounter"), (2) *Tutustuminen* ("Getting to Know Someone"), up to (3) *Seurustelu* ("Romantic Relationship")? The most prevalent premise is about communication, relating, and feeling happening *luonnollisesti* ("naturally"). This could be considered an ideal, which participants reflected upon regarding their experiences. When something happens *luonnollisesti*, it could be explained as follows: *Participants engaging in romantic relating prefer, emphasize, hope for, trust, and believe in communication, relating, and feeling that is effortless, not forced or artificial, just happening, happening easily, without work or trying, comfortable, happening without noticing, happening on its own pace—be it fast or without rush—and without feeling too anxious about or insecure of the other's behavior or feelings.* In addition, the following premises are active: *Individuals can have periods of time when they wish for and actively aim to engage in romantic relationships, and periods when they do not wish for or want to engage in one. The feeling of being in love is wonderful but it can be rare. Sometimes it can be difficult to verbally express romantic feelings or the reasons for lack of them. Romantic interest does not only lie in the individual feeling the feeling, but it should also be observable or felt between the parties, in the chemistry that is shared by the parties. An individual should listen to his or her feelings, and she or he can and must trust one's own feelings. Potential for romantic relating is observed and evaluated not only in one's feelings, but also in the interaction of the parties. In interaction, nonverbal communication is meaningful—the other's gaze, presence, and appearance affect romantic interest in someone.*

DISCUSSION

We have painted, albeit partially, U.S. and Finnish discourses of romantic relationship development, each including a system of cultural terms for relationship stages and types, communicative activities and events, and romantic feeling, as well as associated practices, norms, and their meanings.

While on the surface, the three relationship stages in each case may seem similar, as well as the three initial stages of "coming together" in Knapp's (1978) model, as illustrated below in table 8.1, beneath the surface there are deep cultural differences.

While the first stage for all three is some sort of initial meeting, in Knapp's model the sole focus is on the communication pattern of "greeting," while Initiating in the U.S. case and *Tapaaminen* ("Encounter") in the Finnish case include multiple communicative activities and potential romantic feelings, often identified by cultural terms rich with potent meaning. In fact, aspects of the first stage in the U.S. and Finnish cases would likely be part of Knapp's second and third stages, illustrating variance in relationship development culturally and over time, as well as potential bias in Knapp's model.

On the surface, the second stage looks similar for all three, all focusing on getting to know the other person, but deep differences abound. For Knapp, this stage of "Experimenting" focuses on "small talk," a cultural term for and way of communicating that may not be present in all cultures.[25] Indeed, a cultural premise runs through Knapp's model that small talk is the way to get to know people, develop, and maintain relationships.

Table 8.1.   Relationship Stages in Knapp's Model, U.S. and Finnish Cases

	STAGE 1	STAGE 2	STAGE 3
Knapp's Model	Initiating	Experimenting	Intensifying
U.S. Case	Initiating	Getting to Know Each Other	In a Relationship
Finnish Case	*Tapaaminen* (Encounter)	*Tutustuminen* (Getting to Know Someone)	*Seurustelu* (Romantic Relationship)

In the U.S. case, the second stage of "Getting to Know Each Other" is discoursed as largely focusing on conversing through multiple channels and meetings to get to know the other person more deeply to see if there is romantic potential. Here we also see a cultural discursive system in motion, as new terms for and ways of communicating and relating emerge and are in tension, with participants having competing preferences and opinions about the new term for and relationship stage of "talking" versus "dating." Regarding this, there has been a proliferation of mediated technologies such as cell phones, text messaging, Twitter, Facebook, Instagram, Snapchat, online dating sites, and apps that enable people to talk to romantic interests in multiple, new ways. As such, "talking" may have emerged as a relationship stage in concert with—or precisely because of—these technologies.[26] In a similar manner, in the Finnish case, participants' talk was filled with technology language and loan words such as *swaipata Tinderiä* ("to swipe Tinder"), *Tinder-treffit* ("Tinder-dates"), and *laittaa viestiä* (literally, "to put message"), and there seems to be a recent change in approaching romantic relating more playfully, lightly—more superficially. Thus, new technologies are likely transforming how we communicatively develop romantic relationships today, and concomitantly, those very relationships.

In contrast, in the Finnish case, the second stage, *Tutustuminen* ("Getting to Know Someone"), is discoursed as much more amorphous and largely focused on *relating* and *feeling*. Interestingly, feeling is linked to communication: participants talked about the importance of determining romantic "chemistry," and on the ways in which it is focused not only on verbal but also on nuanced interpretations of nonverbal communication such as "gaze," "appearance," presence, and "gestures." This is perhaps one of the most significant differences between the two cases, that in the Finnish case, romantic relationships and feelings should ideally develop "naturally" and are interpreted also via subtle nonverbal (and verbal) cues, while in the U.S. case, the developing romantic relationship and feelings are located more explicitly in verbal communication between interlocutors (e.g., texts or talk). This is not to say that Finns do not talk in the beginning stages of romantic relationships. The difference is that when Finnish and U.S. participants *talk about* developing romantic relationships, they focus on different things, suggesting deeper and differing cultural premises grounding the development of romantic relationships.

While there are differences, there were also many commonalities across the cases, which we do not want to diminish. Though we spent the majority of our analysis on the first two stages, we did discuss cultural terms for relationships once both parties had "a conversation" or *keskustelu* and decided to move to a more serious, monogamous relationship ("In a Relationship" or *Seurustelu*). For Knapp, this is the "Intensifying" stage, which is marked by a number of communication patterns distinctive to and constitutive of this stage.[27]

While Knapp's model is a long-standing and important one in the field of interpersonal communication, we hope to have illustrated that the model, though useful, may be culturally biased and not applicable to how all cultures develop romantic relationships today. Additionally, we hope to have illustrated how a cultural discourse analysis approach focused on key cultural terms and their meanings can bring a more in-depth and culturally situated view to the study of romantic relationship development and interpersonal communication more broadly. In both the U.S. and Finnish cases, cultural terms for communicating, relating, and feeling were portals into the deep meanings as to how and why participants develop romantic relationships in the way they do. We hope to have provided two such windows into cultural worlds of interpersonal communication and romantic relationships today.

NOTES

1. Names have been changed for all research participants to protect anonymity.

2. The "friend zone" refers to a relationship in which one person is romantically interested in another, but the other is not, so they are placed in a "friend zone," meaning the other person does not think of them in any other "zone" than friends, nor want to be more than friends.

3. *Vauva* online discussion forum (www.vauva.fi/keskustelu) is one of the most active and popular in Finland. It is connected to *Vauva* magazine (in English, "Baby") that publishes on family, children, pregnancy, health, home, and so forth. The discussion forum is not moderated; however, discussants need to register (*Vauva,* October 15, 2017).

4. This excerpt is translated from Finnish into English by the second author, with key Finnish terms included in the English translation, as for all other Finnish interview quotes and transcripts in the chapter. The original Finnish online discussion transcript can be obtained from the authors.

5. The ethnography of communication (EC) research program, originally the "ethnography of speaking," was originated by linguistic anthropologist Dell Hymes in a 1962 article and developed further in a series of articles (e.g., Hymes, 1964, 1967, 1972). Gerry Philipsen brought EC to the communication field with a series of articles on communication practices in Teamsterville, Chicago (e.g., Philipsen, 1975, 1976, 1986). EC is an approach to the study of human communication with its own philosophy, theory, and methodology that aims to study communication in local contexts of use and in cross-cultural perspective. See Philipsen (1990), Carbaugh (1995), and Carbaugh and Hastings (1995) for more on the EC research program and its methodology.

6. Note that in our current research, *kattelu* is no longer talked about as part of the beginning stages of romantic relationship development in Finland.

7. See also Riley (1996) on courtship, marriage, intermarriage, and divorce in the American West.

8. The stages of "coming apart" are (1) "differentiating" (communication focused on differences); (2) "circumscribing" (decreased communication, more superficial); (3) "stagnating" (little communication); (4) "avoiding" (avoidance of communication); and (5) "terminating" (communication that ends the relationship) (Knapp, Vangelisti, & Caughlin, 2014).

9. For the U.S. data, 4 individual interviews and 5 group interviews with 2 to 7 participants each were conducted in the northeastern United States. There were 22 participants ranging in age from 22 to 38, with an average age of 25, including 15 female and 7 male participants. Seventeen identified as White/Caucasian, 2 as Asian/Pacific Islander, 2 as Black or African

American, and 1 as Hispanic or Latino. Fifteen identified themselves as heterosexual, 3 as homosexual, 3 as bisexual, and 1 as other. All had bachelor's degrees except for 4 who were working toward them; 4 were working toward or had master's degrees. All interviews were audio-recorded and transcribed. We are grateful to research assistant Jaclyn Hahn for invaluable help with data collection.

10. For the Finnish data, 1 preliminary group interview and 4 group interviews with 3 to 4 participants each were conducted in Helsinki. There were 14 participants ranging in age from 22 to 33, including 11 female and 3 male participants. All participants were Finnish, Finnish speaking, heterosexual, and currently living in Helsinki. All but two participants had completed or were currently studying toward a graduate degree. All interviews were audio-recorded and transcribed. Research assistant Salli Kolehmainen's work on transcription and some analysis was invaluable.

11. Note that, following Carbaugh (2005), we locate culture in communication practice and are making claims about discourse concerning practices prominent in some scenes of social life in the United States and Finland, particularly in the Northeastern United States and Helsinki areas. Our claims are thus about cultural discursive practices, not populations of people. Following Carbaugh (2005), we may call practices in the U.S. case "USAmerican," meaning "practices prominent and potent in some scenes of the United States" (p. xxiv), while practices in the Finland case, experienced while living in Helsinki, we refer to as "Finnish." Several Finnish participants noted that the experiences in, beliefs about, or practices of developing romantic relationships would not be similar outside the capital area of Helsinki.

12. Note the dual meaning of the term "discoursed" here, meaning (1) how the process of romantic relationship development was discussed by participants and (2) the system of cultural practice and meaning that was brought into view during this, or "cultural discourse."

13. "Initiating" is also the first stage in Knapp's interaction stages of relationships model. While that stage is marked by the communication pattern of "greeting," our stage includes first meeting (likely involving "greeting"), social media "stalking," and first contact after meeting (Knapp, 1978; Knapp, Vangelisti, & Caughlin, 2014).

14. A mobile dating application ("app") is accessible via mobile phone or tablet, whereas online dating sites use a desktop site. Many dating sites now also have apps, so these terms are becoming more interchangeable. In the U.S. case, of our participants who used this technology, they only used dating apps, but did give examples of older family and friends that used dating sites. A few noted that they used dating apps because they were free (whereas dating sites often have a fee). The dating apps our participants used included Tinder, Bumble, Coffee Meets Bagel, Grindr, Jack'd, OK Cupid, and Plenty of Fish, with Tinder being most popular.

15. Note that the native term "stalking" denotes that one is almost lurking privately in a public space, anonymously learning more about the person rather quickly without them knowing. Users enable this possibility if they set their social media as open to the public, but it nevertheless carries some negative connotation.

16. Many of our younger participants noted that they were uncomfortable with phone calls early in a relationship and waited to talk on the phone until they had met in person once or a few times. Conversely, a few of our older participants sought to talk to romantic interests right away on the phone as a way to more quickly see if they were romantically interested in the other person.

17. See Carbaugh (1988, 2005) for similar symbols and premises concerning "rights," "choice," the "individual," and "communication" in "USAmerican" culture.

18. Part of this natural critique can be heard in the phrase "just talking," e.g., "we're just talking." The qualifier "just" denotes this as a less serious relationship, which often frustrates those who want to be in a more serious relationship and want the exact nature of the relationship clarified. Conversely, for those who do not want such a relationship, "we're just talking" becomes a way to claim or account for a less serious relationship.

19. According to some estimates, Tinder has about 100,000 Finnish users (www.väestöliitto. fi). Participants were aware of some other applications as well, but did not use them as frequently or could not remember the names of the applications available. Tinder was by far most recognized, used, and described by participants. This is apparent in media data as well; media

discourse focuses on Tinder. For example, *Tinder-treffit* (a Tinder date) is a widely recognized and used expression in the media.

20. WhatsApp is an Internet-based messaging application through which text-messaging is free. WhatsApp is connected to the parties' phone number, while Facebook Messenger is connected to one's Facebook account. Facebook recently bought WhatsApp.

21. These two terms are loan words. *Deitti* originates from English ("a date") and *treffit* is a loan word from Swedish (*träff*), for which meanings in English are, e.g., a date, a meeting, an appointment, a rendezvous.

22. *Tapailla*, a verb, is derived from *tavata* (to meet). When adding the ending *-illa* or *-ella* to a verb, the meaning changes into action that is ongoing and that is done lightly, or is done only a little, or in passing. In other words, *tapailla* is that kind of meeting that is ongoing, light, and in passing. In addition to *tapailla*, participants used expressions such as *olla jotain* (to have something) or *nähdä toista* (to see one another).

23. Participants listed other, less typical activities as well. These were, e.g., rock climbing, going for a walk, paddleboarding, having dinner at home or a restaurant, and washing windows together.

24. In addition to *avoliitto* (marriage), *avoliitto* (common-law-marriage, cohabitation) is recognized both socially and legally (including taxation, marriage law, social welfare) in Finland. *Avoliitto* is described as two people living indefinitely together without marriage. With some few exceptions, couples live together (they are in *avoliitto)* before marriage. It is also common that a child or children are born to parents who live in *avoliitto*, and who only later marry.

25. The cultural discourse of Finnishness (e.g., Poutiainen, 2015) includes a notion of Finns lacking skills in "small talk" (see also, e.g., Salo-Lee, 1993). These notions emphasize cultural differences in what counts as meaningful communication.

26. We would also suggest that "talking" may mark the ethos of a new generation, i.e., that these technologies are not only changing the way romantic relationships develop, but the very desire for or creation of new types of relationships. As such, new technologies could be changing ways of being, relating, acting, feeling, and dwelling in the world (Carbaugh, 2005).

27. One important note here is that Knapp's model focuses on interaction stages of development across relationship types (e.g., romantic, friendship); therefore, it would be more difficult to focus on terms for relationship types and types of communication specific to certain types of relationships (e.g., romantic, friendship, family). Thus, the model is broader, to encompass interaction in multiple types of relationships.

REFERENCES

Basso, K. H. (1970). "To give up on words": Silence in Western Apache culture. *Southwestern Journal of Anthropology, 26*(3), 213–230.

Baxter, L. A., & Akkoor, C. (2008). Aesthetic love and romantic love in close relationships: A case study in East Indian arranged marriages. In R. C. Arnett & K. G. Roberts (Eds.), *Communication ethics: Between cosmopolitanism and provinciality*. New York, NY: Peter Lang.

Carbaugh, D. (1988). *Talking American: Cultural discourses on Donahue*. Norwood, NJ: Ablex.

Carbaugh, D. (1989/1990). The critical voice in ethnography of communication research. *Research on Language and Social Interaction, 23*, 261–282.

Carbaugh, D. (1995). The ethnographic approach of Gerry Philipsen and associates. In D. Cushman & B. Kovacic (Eds.), *Watershed research traditions in human communication theory* (pp. 269–297). Albany, NY: State University of New York Press.

Carbaugh, D. (2005). *Cultures in conversation*. New York, NY: Routledge.

Carbaugh, D. (2007). Cultural discourse analysis: Communication practices and intercultural encounters. *Journal of Intercultural Communication Research, 36*(3), 167–182.

Carbaugh, D. (2017). Terms for talk, take 2: Theorizing communication through its cultural terms and practices. In D. Carbaugh (Ed.), *The handbook of communication in cross-cultural perspective* (pp. 15–28). New York, NY: Routledge.

Carbaugh, D., & Cerulli, T. (2013). Cultural discourses of dwelling: Investigating environmental communication as a place-based practice. *Environmental Communication: The Journal of Nature and Culture, 7*(1), 4–23.

Carbaugh, D., & Hastings, S. O. (1995). A role for communication theory in ethnographic studies of communication. In W. Leeds-Hurwitz (Ed.), *Social approaches to communication* (pp. 171–187). New York, NY: Guilford Press.

Dion, K. K., & Dion, K. L. (1996). Cultural perspectives on romantic love. *Personal Relationships, 3,* 5–17.

Gudykunst, W. B., & Ting-Toomey, S. (1988). *Culture and interpersonal communication.* Newbury Park, CA: Sage.

Gudykunst, W. B., Ting-Toomey, S., & Nishida, T. (Eds.). (1996). *Communication in personal relationships across cultures.* Thousand Oaks, CA: Sage.

Hymes, D. (1962). The ethnography of speaking. In T. Gladwin & W. Sturtevant (Eds.), *Anthropology and human behavior* (pp. 13–53). Washington, D.C.: Anthropological Society of Washington.

Hymes, D. (1964). Introduction: Toward ethnographies of communication. In J. J. Gumperz & D. Hymes (Eds.), *The ethnography of communication* (pp. 1–34). Washington, D.C.: Blackwell Publishing on behalf of the American Anthropological Association. *American Anthropologist 66*(6), part 2.

Hymes, D. (1967). Models of the interaction of language and social setting. *Journal of Social Issues, 23*(2), 8–38.

Hymes, D. (1972). Models of the interaction of language and social life. In J. J. Gumperz & D. Hymes (Eds.), *Directions in sociolinguistics: The ethnography of communication* (pp. 35–71). New York, NY: Holt, Rinehart & Winston.

Farrer, J., Tsuchiya, H., & Bagrowicz, B. (2008). Emotional expression in tsukiau dating relationships in Japan. *Journal of Social and Personal Relationships, 25*(1), 169–188.

Fitch, K. (1991a). The interplay of linguistic universals and cultural knowledge in personal address: Colombian madre terms. *Communication Monographs, 58,* 254–272.

Fitch, K. (1991b). *Salsipuede*: Attempting leave-taking in Colombia. *Research on Language and Social Interaction, 24,* 209–224.

Fitch, K. (1994). Culture, ideology, and interpersonal communication research. In S. Deetz, Ed., *Communication Yearbook 17,* 104–135. Beverly Hills, CA: Sage.

Fitch, K. (1998). *Speaking relationally: Culture, communication and interpersonal connection.* New York, NY: Guilford Press.

Fitch, K. (2006). Two politeness dilemmas in Colombian interpersonal ideology. In M. E. Placencia (Ed.), *Politeness in the Spanish-speaking world* (pp. 239–254). New York, NY: Guilford Press.

Fitch, K. (2009). Culture and interpersonal relationships. In S. Wilson and S. Smith (Eds.), *New directions in interpersonal communication research* (pp. 245–263). Thousand Oaks, CA: Sage.

Goodwin, R. (1999). *Personal relationships across cultures.* London: Routledge.

Golzard, V., & Miguel, C. (2016). Negotiating intimacy through social media. *Middle East Journal of Culture & Communication, 9*(2), 216–233.

Jankowiak, W. (Ed.). (1995). *Romantic passion: A universal experience?* New York, NY: Columbia University Press.

Jyrkiäinen, S. (2016). Online presentation of gendered selves among young women in Egypt. *Middle East Journal of Culture and Communication, 9*(2), 182–198.

Katriel, T., & Philipsen, G. (1981). "What we need is communication": "Communication" as a cultural category in some American speech. *Communication Monographs, 48*(4), 300–317.

Knapp, M. L. (1978). *Social intercourse: From greeting to goodbye.* Needham Heights, MA: Allyn & Bacon.

Knapp, M. L., Vangelisti, A. L., & Caughlin, J. P. (2014). *Interpersonal communication and human relationships* (7th ed.). Boston, MA: Pearson.

Leeds-Hurwitz, W. (2002). *Wedding as text: Communicating cultural identities through ritual.* Mahwah, NJ: Erlbaum.

Liu, T. (2016). Neoliberal ethos, state censorship and sexual culture: A Chinese dating/hook-up app. *Continuum: Journal of Media and Cultural Studies, 30*(5), 557–566.

Mongeau, P. A., Jacobsen, J., & Donnerstein, C. (2007). Defining dates and first date goals: Generalizing from undergraduates to single adults. *Communication Research, 34*(5), 526–547.

Mongeau, P. A., & Wiedmaier, B. (2012). How to have better first dates (Even if people don't have first dates anymore). In A. K. Goodboy & K. Shultz (Eds.), *Introduction to communication studies: Translating scholarship into meaningful practice* (pp. 217–224). Dubuque, IA: Kendall Hunt.

Pan, J., & Lieber, P. S. (2008). Emotional disclosure and construction of the poetic "other" in a Chinese online dating site. *China Media Research, 4*(2), 32–42.

Philipsen, G. (1975). Speaking "like a man" in Teamsterville: Culture patterns of role enactment in an urban neighborhood. *Quarterly Journal of Speech, 61*, 13–22.

Philipsen, G. (1976). Places for speaking in Teamsterville. *Quarterly Journal of Speech, 62,* 15–25.

Philipsen, G. (1986). Mayor Daley's council speech: A cultural analysis. *Quarterly Journal of Speech, 72,* 247–60.

Philipsen, G. (1990). An ethnographic approach to communication studies. In B. Dervin, L. Grossberg, B. O'Keefe, & E. Wartella (Eds.), *Rethinking communication, V. 2, paradigm exemplars* (pp. 258–268). Newbury Park, CA: Sage.

Poutiainen, S. (2005). Kulttuurista puhetta deittaamisesta [Cultural talk about dating]. *Puhe ja kieli, 3,* 123–136.

Poutiainen, S. (2009). Do Finns date? Cultural interpretations of romantic relating. *Interpersona, 3,* 38–62.

Poutiainen, S. (2015). Myths about Finnishness: On cultural mobile phone discourses. In T. Milburn (Ed.), *Communicating user experience: Applying local strategies research to digital media design* (pp. 133–154). Lanham, MD: Lexington Books.

Riley, G. (1996). *Building and breaking families in the American West.* Albuquerque: University of New Mexico Press.

Roses, D. C. (2006). "I could say I am 'dating,' but that could mean a lot of different things: Dating in the US as a dialogical relational process" (Unpublished doctoral dissertation). University of Iowa, Iowa City, IA.

Salo-Lee, L. (1993). 'Teillä on kaunis nappi'–Small talk: Tyhjänpuhumista vai mielekästä viestintää [You have a beautiful button–Small talk: Empty talk or meaningful communication]. In J. Lehtonen (Ed.), *Kulttuurien kohtaaminen. Näkökulmia kulttuurienväliseen kanssakäymiseen* (pp. 77–90). J Viestintätieteiden julkaisuja, 9. Jyväskylän yliopisto.

Sandel, T. L. (2011). Is it just cultural?: Exploring (mis)perceptions of individual and cultural differences of immigrants through marriage in contemporary Taiwan. *China Media Research, 7*(3), 43–55.

Sandel, T. L. (2015). *Brides on sale: Taiwanese cross- border marriages in a globalizing Asia.* New York, NY: Peter Lang.

Scollo, M. (2011). Cultural approaches to discourse analysis: A theoretical and methodological conversation with special focus on Donal Carbaugh's cultural discourse theory. *Journal of Multicultural Discourses, 6*(1), 1–32.

Scollo, M., & Carbaugh, D. (2013). Interpersonal communication: Qualities and culture. *Russian Journal of Communication, 5*(2), 95–103.

Scollo, M., & Poutiainen, S. (August 2006). "A cultural critique of relationship stage models." World Communication Association, North America, Springfield, MA.

Shakoori, A., & Shafiei, Z. (2014). An analysis of the reproduction of conservative values in mate selection in Iran: A case study of Toba online dating site. *Global Media Journal: Persian Edition, 9*(1), 231–260.

Sumter, S. R., Vandenbosch, L., & Ligtenberg, L. (2017). Love me Tinder: Untangling emerging adults' motivations for using the dating application Tinder. *Telematics and Informatics, 34*(1), 67–78.

Ward, J. (2107). What are you doing on Tinder? Impression management on a matchmaking mobile app. *Information, Communication and Society, 20*(11), 1644–1659.

Chapter Nine

"Fellow Hunters" and "Humans of the Ocean"

Identity and Relations across Species

Tovar Cerulli and Tema Milstein

For centuries, Euro-Americans have depicted large carnivores as demonic, destructive threats. On land, the wolf has been called "the beast of waste and desolation" (Roosevelt, 1893, p. 386). At sea, orcas have been called "merciless destroyers" and "wolves of the ocean" (Scammon, 1874, p. 90). These two top predators often have been seen—especially by communities engaged in hunting and animal husbandry, and whaling and fishing—as intolerable competitors.

As a result, both have been heavily persecuted. From the earliest days of colonization through the 1960s and 1970s, Euro-Americans used all available methods, including traps and poison, to wage war on the wolf; today, despite federal protection in many places, wolves are often killed illegally. At sea, orcas have been assaulted by North American militaries, including the 1940s Royal Canadian Air Force, which reportedly used orca family pods as bomber-training targets, and the 1950s U.S. Navy, which used machine guns, depth charges, and rockets to kill hundreds of Icelandic coastal orcas to protect the fishing industry from damage orcas ostensibly did to nets. Today, embedded bullets believed to be fired by North American fishermen are still found during orca autopsies.

Wolves and orcas also both illustrate dramatic shifts in North American understandings of, and ways of speaking about, nature and wildlife. Over the past century, popular perceptions and depictions of these animals as competitive threats to be eliminated have, in part, been replaced by perceptions and depictions of them as symbols of ecological wholeness and as endangered species to be protected. Their declines are now often depicted as representative of anthropogenic harm to ecological systems and their comebacks, in the case of wolves, as recovery from such harm. Less prominently, over the past several decades both species also increasingly have come to be understood in Western[1] culture as intelligent, communicative beings who interact with one another in social and familial ways (Milstein, 2008).

Though these two predominant depictions of top predators—as demonic threats and as endangered symbols of ecological wholeness—stand in apparent opposition to one another, they share a common foundation. Whatever our ideas about wolves and orcas, and whatever lenses or languages (e.g., scientific, legal, popular) we use to think and speak of them, dominant Western discourses have long depicted these and other wild species primarily as parts of "*nature*" subject to programs and policies of human *action* (e.g., extirpation, management, conservation, protection). In the terms proposed by cultural discourse analysis, we can say that Euro-American discourses, which continue to dominate in North America, depict wildlife primarily in terms of *dwelling* and *acting*.

Here, a few words on cultural discourse analysis (CuDA) are in order. In using CuDA as a theoretical and methodological framework, we understand communication (cultural discourse) as a historically transmitted and evolving cultural practice in which deep meanings are both presumed and created. In communication, such meanings can be made quite explicit or they can be left more or less implicit. In CuDA, this spectrum of explicitness is described in terms of *hubs* and *radiants*, with particular attention devoted to five discursive themes that resonate across a wide range of ethnographic sites: being/identity, acting, feeling, relating, and dwelling. When one or more themes are made explicit in communication, we conceptualize them as *discursive hubs*. When other themes and meanings tag along as implicit threads in a cultural web of meaning-making—taken-for-granted, but no less powerful—we conceptualize them as *discursive radiants* (Carbaugh, 2007; Carbaugh & Cerulli, 2013).

With these hubs and radiants in mind, CuDA analysts can examine participants' communicative practices for *cultural terms* (key symbolic terms), especially as they appear in clusters, and then seek to formulate *cultural propositions* (arrangements of cultural terms that express taken-for-granted views) and *cultural premises* (statements that capture the essence of participants' beliefs). These examinations draw our attention to ways discourses comprise systematic statements about beliefs and values. That is, cultural discourses are morally infused. In creating and using cultural discourses, we tell ourselves and each other how we should be, relate, act, feel, and dwell (Carbaugh, 2007).

In commenting on ways Euro-American discourses explicitly and implicitly characterize wildlife as part of "nature" and as objects of human action, we are noting that (1) dominant communication practices depict these beings primarily in terms of *dwelling* and *acting* and, moreover, that (2) these discourses evoke only a specific and narrow range of many possible meanings about *dwelling* and *acting*. In this chapter, drawing on two distinct corpora of data, we examine instances in which *identity* and *relationship* are also central themes in meaning-making about wildlife, and in which *dwelling* and *acting* are activated in ways that contrast remarkably with dominant discourses.

The first corpus—on cultural discourses about wolves, constituted and used among hunting communities—comes from the western Great Lakes region of the United States.[2] In 1974, when the federal Endangered Species Act first protected wolves, northern Minnesota was home to the only remaining population in the contiguous states. Since then, wolves have recovered dramatically, returning to significant portions of that state and also to Wisconsin and Michigan's Upper Peninsula.

In January 2012, after many years of legal battles, the U.S. Fish and Wildlife Service removed the region's wolves from the threatened and endangered species lists. In December 2014, a federal court returned them to those lists. This first data corpus was gathered across that unique three-year period, during which the western Great Lakes population segment of wolves was not on the federal lists and was subject to state management, including regulated public hunting and trapping seasons. At the time of writing this chapter in 2017, the region's wolves remain on the federal threatened and endangered species lists.

The second corpus—on cultural discourses about cetaceans, produced among tourists, the tourism industry, island locals, and cetacean researchers and advocates—comes from the Pacific transborder region of the United States and Canada.[3] This site, which hosts the highest concentration of whale watching in the world, is home to an abundance of interconnected oceanic life, including the top predators and main tourism draw, orcas or killer whales.[4] The Southern Resident killer whales, often regionally present in the summer, are the first orcas in the world to be declared endangered and were declared so on both sides of the border in the mid-2000s due to risks to their individual health and collective existence posed by pollution, increased vessel traffic, and overfishing of salmon (their main prey) by humans. The ethnographic data that make up this second corpus were gathered from just before the endangered species rulings until present. Today, orca deaths continue to climb and successful births continue to drop. At time of writing, the Southern Resident killer whales had not shown signs of recovery and their population is on a declining trend (U.S. EPA, 2013) with only 76 individuals remaining in the oceans.

Our investigation of instances of speech from these two data sets is guided by two questions: Broadly, what expressive means are used and what meanings created as case study participants speak about wolves and orcas?

Specifically, what means and meanings are used and created concerning the identities of—and relationships between—wolves and humans and whales and humans?

As scholars, we take different approaches to CuDA and to our data. Cerulli adheres more closely to the tools of CuDA and, in this chapter, takes a focused look at a few selected utterances.[5] Milstein adheres to general tenets of CuDA but takes a looser approach to its application as a methodology and, in this chapter, applies a wider scope on data, bringing in an array of speakers and contexts in conversation.[6] We both use CuDA in our work, largely to illustrate ways in which human relations with the wider ecological world are discursively constructed. Despite our different approaches, we believe—to paraphrase Carbaugh (1996a)—that comparisons across these case studies enable assessment of available means for conceiving of and evaluating human ecological situatedness, as well as the attendant attitudes and ways of being that these means both cultivate and constrain.

"THE RELATIONSHIP THERE BETWEEN WOLVES AND HUMANS"

Cerulli begins with an extended excerpt in which a Euro-American hunter in Minnesota speaks of relations between wolves and humans:

> You think about wolf and human history and we have many many many many thousands of years where I really think sometimes we made the kill, sometimes they made the kill. I mean you're living in close company with large game, basically. We're all hunting the same large game. And, you know, I think there was some sort of relationship there between people and wolves that's very different than the European relationship between people and wolves, which developed with agriculture.
>
> I don't know, there's a guy out in British Columbia, on the coast of British Columbia. He's done a lot of wolf photography with these packs, these coastal packs. What he found was a lot of the wolf denning areas were old long houses from a hundred and fifty years ago. And it got him wondering why is this, what's the relationship there between wolves and humans.
>
> But he had a feeling that wolves have a much longer memory than we do. And a lot of the wolf behavior, especially in Minnesota that we see now, where people talk about wolves being "bold" or not having the fear and all that, they're really just behaving like wolves have always behaved. 'Cause they look at us more as fellow travelers than they do as predators. And they've lost the memory—of being hunted and trapped, or relentlessly hunted and trapped—over the past forty years. But they have the longer, you know, instinctive memory of this relationship between us and them, humans as fellow hunters.

A minute later, discussion of this topic continued:

I've just noticed, like when you do encounter wolves, the way they behave, other than if you startle them. . . . I was deer hunting a few years ago and it was early in the morning and the snow was kind of crunchy, and I was walking into where I was going to hunt and just kind of walking and stopping and walking and stopping and all of a sudden I hear something walking towards me so I just stopped and waited.

Here was a black wolf and he came out. I was on a road through an old cutting and he walked out and he stepped out on the road, looked at me, you know he was about fifty yards away. And he just looked at me and I looked at him, turned around—he knew what I was then, 'cause he had heard that noise and he was coming over to check out what that sound was—once he saw what I was, he turned and went back the way he came and made a big arc around me, just totally nonchalant, and just went on his way. You know, you have that happen to you a couple, three times, you're just like, well, obviously they're not that afraid of me and they don't look at me as a threat.

Early in this excerpt, the discursive hubs of relationship and action are explicitly activated as "some sort of" ancient "relationship" between "people and wolves" is linked to engaging in a parallel, mutually beneficial activity ("hunting the same large game," "sometimes we made the kill, sometimes they made the kill") in shared places ("in close company") over an extended period of time ("many thousands of years"). This relationship is said to be "very different" from that which developed with "agriculture."[7]

Describing photographer Ian McAllister's observations of wolves in British Columbia, this hunter makes dwelling a resounding hub by depicting a striking overlap in dwelling space: wolves living and making dens in the same places where indigenous human inhabitants lived and built structures. And he ties this to the hub of "relationship there." The radiant of action remains implicitly alive for listeners who wonder what interactions occurred in those places, centuries ago, between wolves and humans.

The interpretation ascribed to McAllister, and avowed by this speaker, is that "wolves have a much longer memory than we do." During four decades of U.S. federal protection, wolves have forgotten Euro-American persecution of them and have returned to an "instinctive memory" of a more ancient wolf-human "relationship," on this continent and perhaps others. This is said to explain wolf behavior in Minnesota today; wolves who are "bold" and do not display "fear" are "just behaving like wolves have always behaved."[8] As this speaker recounts one experience of wolf behavior, action becomes explicit ("I just stopped," "he came out," "looked at me," "went on his way") and is closely linked to relationship and shared identity. Through "nonchalant" action, it is said, wolves indicate their memory and perception of a "relationship" between "fellow travelers" and "fellow hunters."

To further interpret meanings expressed and created here, and to make their semantic logic more scrutable, we can formulate cultural propositions:

- In "hunting" the same "large game" for millennia, "people" and "wolves" developed a "relationship" as "fellow hunters" and "fellow travelers."
- As "fellow hunters," "wolves" and "humans" inhabit the world in similar ways and have long "lived" and "hunted" in "close company."
- In "Minnesota" and elsewhere, "wolves" have recalled their "memory" of this "relationship" and do not see humans as a "threat."

"Not a Lot of Folks You Can Talk to about Stuff Like That"

At one point, this speaker indicated difficulty in discussing these ideas:

> There's not a lot of folks you can talk to about stuff like that really. You know, [another local hunter] would be one of the few people I know that would grasp that, and be able to grasp it from an experiential sense as well. I talked to [a senior wolf biologist] about that, and definitely it's something he'd thought about. It wasn't a new idea to him by any means.

How does he, and how might we, account for this constraint on communicative possibility—this lack of "folks you can talk to about stuff like that"? Why might it be difficult for this speaker to identify people who, he thinks, would "grasp" the notion?

The discourse employed by this hunter is not uncommon. Like him, other hunters in the region speak and write of the wolf as a fellow predator to be appreciated—"a fellow hunter on the trail" (Weber, 2011)—and as a symbol of wildness and ecological wholeness. Yet this discourse is not publicly prominent. Unlike more widely audible discourses used by the region's Euro-American hunting communities—one depicting wolves as a manageable threat to deer and deer hunting, another depicting wolves as an out-of-control threat to local autonomy and ways of life, both depicting wolves as "predators" in competition with human "hunters"—this one has not been used by hunting organizations active in wolf-related debates (Cerulli, 2016). If this speaker knows or presumes that most local people tend to speak in ways that differ from his—and that echo traditional Western discourses about predator control—he might indeed find it difficult to find "a lot of folks [he] can talk to" about his understandings.

Another likely factor is suggested by his mention of having spoken to a senior wolf biologist. Above, he states that this ancient wolf-human relationship "wasn't a new idea" to him: "definitely it's something he'd thought about." At another point, he described the biologist's response: "I could tell it was a topic that he didn't hear about very often."

This turns our attention to the discourse that dominates most contemporary, public discussions of wolves and other wildlife in the United States. This institutional, professional discourse—employed by representatives of state and federal wildlife agencies, among others—identifies and defines wolves (1) in scientific terms as a biological species with particular physical, genetic, and behavioral characteristics, and as part of ecological systems and (2) in legal terms as a species with federal and state statuses that change over time. In scientific and legal terms, emphasis is placed on wolves as a population.[9]

With its focus on technical "management" and "conservation" of "nature," this dominant discourse sets the context for other ways of speaking about wolves and other wildlife, censuring some, including those said to "anthropomorphize" animals. In this context, it is not surprising that a biologist who had thought about ancient wolf-human relationships (and the possibility that wolves remember them) might not speak or write or even hear about such ideas much. Nor is it surprising that this speaker senses that he can discuss such things with relatively few people.

"They Traveled Together"

Intriguingly, however, this speaker's understandings resonate with another discourse employed in the region. Though they stand on different cultural and historical ground, Ojibwe elders speak about wolves in a way that encompasses similar ideas and beliefs (Cerulli, 2017). Their understandings—which include an awareness that wolf and Ojibwe have long been treated similarly, as competitive threats to be controlled or eliminated—are often expressed by telling a creation story. Consider, for example, a portion of a telling by one elder:

> Original Man and the wolf were brothers. And the Great Spirit told them, He said, "Original Man, Anishinaabe, the wolf, Ma'iingan." He said, "In many ways, you are alike." He said, "When you take a mate, you mate for life." He said, "Your social structure will be the clan system." He said, "Both of you will be good hunters."

Consider, too, how a leader from another community began the story:

> When the Creator, we call him Gitchie Manitou, put man on this earth, he walked and he was lonely. And as he walked, it was the Ma'iingan that walked with him, kept him company, and they traveled together.

And consider something said by a leader from a third Ojibwe community:

> When you see a wolf now in the north woods of Wisconsin, they stop and they look. They stop and they watch you go by. They look back at you. And it makes you wonder, "Okay, well, what's going through their mind?" This is part of their territory, part of their life, and they have to deal with us as human beings there too.

Though brief—and representative of only a small part of a broader discourse in which harmony, rather than conflict and control, is said to be the norm in wolf-human relations[10]—these excerpts communicate essential ideas. Wolf and human, it is said, are "brothers" who are "alike in many ways." We are, for instance, "hunters" with similar "social structures." Wolf and human, it is said, have "walked" and "traveled" in one another's "company" in the past. Today, when you see wolves, they "watch" and "look back at" you. Such experiences make you "wonder" about wolves' thoughts about us, as "part of their territory, part of their life."

Premises for "Fellow Hunters"

With both of these discourses in mind—one used and created by some Euro-Americans, the other by many Ojibwe—we can propose cultural premises, illuminating core threads common to these ways of speaking:

- Humans and other kinds of beings can be alike; humans and wolves are alike.
- Relationships develop through (inter)acting and dwelling in company with one another; through such, wolves and humans developed a relationship.
- Other-than-human beings can perceive, think, and remember; wolves perceive, think, and remember.

In these premises, and in the excerpts above from two different discourses, note how wolves are understood and depicted as agents of action and interaction. Wolves are not mere objects of human agency; they are subjects who act and interact for their own reasons—denning at old long house sites, for example, or stopping and looking at humans—based on their own perceptions, thoughts, and memories. In past and present alike, wolf-human relationships are not said to be shaped solely by us. *They* also approach, circle, watch, and look at *us*. *They* perceive and are curious about *us*. *They* see and remember *us*.

Carbaugh (1996b) proposed that our notions of "persons," "agents," and "consciousness" are created and maintained through communication. Employing "various cultural codes of the agent," we make claims about identity and personhood and assign these to various entities, places, and beings, including—in some cultural contexts—members of species other than our own (pp. 148–149). And it has long been recognized that the Ojibwe (among other cultural groups) understand the identity category of "person" to include not only humans but also a wide range of beings, including other animals. In such understandings, the defining characteristic of personhood is not human form but rather ability and willingness to enter into relationships (Hallowell, 1960; Overholt & Callicott, 1982).

These excerpts, and the discourses of which each is part, suggest that some Euro-Americans—dwelling and hunting in the company of wolves—have developed and articulated a similar understanding and sense of relationship. The historical roots of this Euro-American discourse (see Cerulli, 2016) can be traced back to a number of notable voices, including Henry David Thoreau, Sigurd Olson, and Aldo Leopold (1949) who famously wrote of the "fierce green fire" he saw in the eyes of a dying wolf, of "something known only to her and to the mountain" (p. 138), and of human "kinship with fellow-creatures" (p. 117). In this way of speaking, the wolf is an agent who is conscious of having a relationship with humans, even if "there's not a lot of folks you can talk to about stuff like that."

"HUMANS OF THE OCEAN"

Milstein now turns to a corpus of data concerning endangered wild orcas. Though contexts and participants in these two North American case studies differ, overlaps and consistencies regarding wolves and whales are striking. This section takes the premises introduced in the wolf-human section above as points of comparison and introduces an array of discourses in this whale-human site to illustrate and examine ways the above premises are further substantiated and complicated within another site of interspecies relations.

"If They're Just Like *Us* in Other Words They *Humble* Us"

The first premise established in the wolf-human site—that humans and other beings (in this case, orcas) can be and are alike—serves as the entry point of comparison. In this whale-human site, it is common in the contexts of tourism for those introducing the orcas (tour boat naturalists) to visitors (tourists) to point to sameness and similarities between orcas and humans. Similarities presented range from the biological (similar life spans and stages and, in the case of Southern Resident orcas, similar diets of salmon) to the familial (both humans and orcas form families who live and stay together, though orcas are decidedly matriarchal) to the cultural (as with humans, different orcas have different foods, languages, and ways of behaving). In addition, tour naturalists often discuss ways both orcas and humans are self-aware, are highly social and always in communication, and have large brains (though naturalists sometimes also point out that orca brains proportionally are far larger than human brains). Tour naturalists commonly point out similarities to provide points of connection for tourists; for instance, orcas have unique saddle patches and dorsal fin markings that, "just like the human fingerprint," can be used to identify individuals (Milstein, 2011).

Yet the notion in this North American site of humans and orcas being alike can go deeper than pointing to specific indications of similarity. Consider this excerpt from an interview with a Euro-American orca researcher:

> For me orcas have always been basically humans of the ocean. And basically extraterrestrials if you will. Because they're filling the same evolutionary niche I think in the ocean that we are on Earth on the terrestrial. They're long-lived big-brained social predators and so they're a wonderful anthropological model for human evolution. . . . They have a lesson for us that is much bigger than what the culture is actually selling us right now. And that particular message isn't necessarily out as much as it could be. In other words these are organisms that should be respected like another human culture. You know I mean if they're just like *us* in other words they *humble* us. We just aren't this special because evolution produced something almost very very similar—same principles in another media.
>
> But I haven't seen that happen yet. The culture hasn't seen what I see. There's small groups of us out there but you know. And a lot of it becomes religious and superficial you know and people start worshipping them and that's not right either. . . . The idea is they're just like us you know we're all in this together. And so that to me is what motivates me. But I don't see the culture getting it. *But* because the orcas are so popular the culture is being drawn to them anyway for these sort of superficial reasons. And so the true lesson will probably eventually work its way in culturally. But you know we've got a ways to go.

Similar to the Euro-American hunter with the wolves, this speaker notes that his view is different from most ("The culture hasn't seen what I see") and that his view, based on a sameness between humans and orcas, results in a humbling of humanity, an understanding that "we just aren't this special" and orcas are "just like us." In contrast to the Euro-American hunter, in this site and context the speaker feels he must do work to undo elevation in either direction (neither human nor whale is superior) and, from his positionality, instead of feeling he can't talk to many others about what he sees as his unique views, he asserts an authority that he knows the "true lesson" that must reach the broader culture.

Indeed, dominant Western views of human exceptionalism or mastery over "nature" or of being smarter or better than other animals are rarely communicated by the wide array of participants in this site (e.g., locals, researchers, tour industry, tourists, orca advocates). Instead, when orca and human differences come up, they often are presented as a critique of humanity (as destructive, controlling, hierarchical in contrast to orcas) and to illustrate a superiority of orcas (as more evolved, sexually progressive, peaceful, egalitarian, sustainable in habits of consumption, physically and mentally advanced). This superiority assertion likely represents what the speaker frames as the culture "selling us," which relates to his typifying of some people "worshipping" orcas in a "superficial" way.

The first premise established in the wolf-human site was that humans and other beings can be and are alike. The relationship asserted in this site between orcas and humans perhaps is more abstracted (that humans and orcas fill "the same evolutionary niche," and, from tour naturalists, that orcas and humans are biologically, culturally, and socially similar) than the more personal relationship asserted between wolves and humans ("fellow hunters"). This difference may in part be due to dwelling in different (oceanic and terrestrial) environments. At the same time, statements of alikeness are prevalent and persistent across differently positioned speakers in this site, pointing to a broad cultural formation of identity based on relating to orcas in social, embodied, and ecological terms.

"This Is Part of *Their* Culture Too Now"

The second premise is that interspecies relationships develop through (inter)acting and dwelling with one another. In this site, various participants articulate ways orcas and people have developed their relations, as well as their identities, in interaction with one another in shared spaces. Similar to but also different from the wolf-human historical relationship of hunting and living side by side, participants in this site at times speak of shared spatial meanings and processes of intense orca-human fishing and dwelling.

As with hunting and wolves, with fishing, local people often described orcas and humans fishing in proximity and, on good salmon run years, this was visible to any observant person, with commercial and private fishing boats and orcas intermingled, all fishing for the same prey. This relationship has not always been a peaceful one. For instance, there was often talk of Euro-American fishermen historically (and in contemporary times in secret) shooting at orcas as orcas "steal" salmon from their nets. At the same time, there were contrasting stories of First Nations fishermen laughing and taking photos as orcas picked salmon from their nets, illustrating differing cultural interspecies relationships based on differing histories and knowledges of interacting and dwelling together.

During private and commercial fishing seasons, marine monitors—who monitor the whale tourism industry and private boaters around the orcas and provide on-water education to private boaters about whale-safe boating regulations—often were called upon by private boaters to address this parallel fishing relationship. One marine monitor described orcas as "just looking for fish, like everyone else; they're working the area. The commercial fishing boats and the whales are often fishing in the same good spots." Another marine monitor responded to a private boater's concern about commercial fishing boat nets amidst the orcas by explaining that the fishing industry and

orcas "have been working it out for a long time" to which the boater, highlighting a view of the orcas' primacy in this place of dwelling, responded,
"All I know is who was here first."

Marine monitors publicly described humans who were fishing as part of
the orcas' environment, and orcas as having "lived with fishing boats and
grown up with fishing lines all their lives." By doing so and letting "the
fishing boats do what they do as long as they follow the guidelines coming to
and from their fishing spots," monitors strategically and actively avoided
fishing community backlash against both the monitors and the orcas. At the
same time, monitors privately described an individual blindness among those
who fish when orcas are present to the reality that the orcas' environment has
been drastically changing even solely in terms of the density of human presence: "They don't realize it's not just them—it's more of them, it's commercial fishing, it's whale watching boats, and there's more of us than there ever
were."

Indeed, increased pressure on Southern Resident killer whales from humans overfishing wild salmon (and from other anthropogenic destructive
impacts on wild salmon and their habitat such as damming rivers, farming
salmon, developing coastlines, and agricultural runoff) runs parallel to increased pressure on the water's surface from tourism. Many orca researchers
and advocates in the site describe whale-watch boat tourism interaction with
orcas as "at capacity" or out of balance. In addition to overall risks of stress
to an endangered population, researchers have found orcas are making longer
calls to one another and "shouting over the noise" of vessel engines as they
must during heavy rains, and they are sleeping less during the day as a
suspected result of increased boat presence. In this shared space of dwelling,
some locals speak of a personal aversion to tour boats ("It's hard not to have
a visceral reaction to the boats coming. I mean it is serenity here.") and
describe mounting human interactions with orcas as "loving the orcas to
death" or as being "insane." One spoke of wanting "to mount a howitzer and
blow those zippy Canadian (tour) boats out of the water" (alluding to and
contrasting with a mid-20th-century act of government-placed machine gun
mounts on the coast to shoot orcas) and another spoke of avoiding boating
when orcas are around ("It's too crazy with all those boats out there surrounding the whales").

These types of observations of human relations with orcas as out of balance are repeated regularly in the news media, but are regarded as cliché by
on-the-water orca advocates who monitor the whale watch industry and focus
on encouraging humans to interact with orcas more wisely and from greater
distances. Indeed, in dwelling together, many in this site now work to emphasize that human visitors are in the orcas' home (e.g., kayak guide to tourists:
"We do know that we are paddling in their home") and, at the same time, that
humans constitute part of the orcas' home (e.g., orca advocate: "We are as

much their environment as anything else that's out there"). In humans being both visitor and dwelling space, orcas at once are viewed as hospitable or at least tolerant hosts and as captive to humanity's continual reconstitution of their home.

Still there are those who see the orcas as enjoying increased human presence and this increased intensity of interaction as forming not only human but also whale culture. For instance, one local islander described the annual cycles of summer tourism of the past 30 years as creating a shared seasonal urban culture for the whales within their "traditional" space of foraging and dwelling:

> Just the intensity of all the traffic and you know I mean I look at these guys as urban whales. You know during the day it's busy, there's lots of traffic, there's a lot of noise, there's lots of people, and then at night it gets quiet just like any city. And it has its season, and when you're here they *know* it's summer, it's urban, and they're going to have a lot of activity. And then they have all winter where it's completely quiet, and they're hardly ever here. So even though it's their traditional feeding grounds I think that they really enjoy being around the people, and this is part of *their* culture too now you know? It's very much part of their culture. A lot of these calves you know they've had boats with them every year of their lives.

The speaker's assertion—that the "intensity of all the traffic" is part of "*their* culture" and that increased human presence communicates to orcas that it is summer—is a positioning of humans as both visitors and as constituting orcas' dwelling space. Yet in many ways, of which the speaker appears only partly reflective, his assertions overshadow the orcas' sustenance-based need to be present in the local waters during summer (the presence of their main diet of salmon, who are returning to the rivers to spawn). Whereas the hunter in the wolf site speaks of historical mutually beneficial activity, the island local asserts a mutual enjoyment of intensive shared seasonal presence that ignores the endangered species rulings highlighting increased vessel traffic as one of the anthropogenic risks contributing to orca endangerment.

As stated at the beginning of this section, the second premise established in the wolf-human site is that interspecies relationships develop through (inter)acting and dwelling with one another. In the orca-human site, we find this premise characterized in similar and different ways. Similarities include shared spatial meanings and shared processes of intense orca-human fishing and dwelling. Differences include an emphasis on stresses on the endangered orcas, expressed in phrases such as "at capacity" and "out of balance," describing increased human presence in the forms of fishing and tourism. In addition, in this site, speakers often characterize orcas as having primacy in their ocean home and humans as being at once guests, environment, and makers of orca culture.

"They Must See Something in Us"

The third premise articulates that, in past and present alike, the wolf/orca-human relationship is not said to be shaped solely by us. *They* approach, circle, watch, and look at *us*. *They* perceive and are curious about *us*. *They* see and remember *us*. Indeed, in this scene of high-intensity whale watching, orcas are often said to watch or seek out humans. One local who moved to the San Juan islands to live near the orcas described a time when orcas purposefully looked at her:

> It's almost like you're not in their world but you're as close as you're ever going to get to their world. And you're almost making a connection. I've had actually two spy hop right at me off the kelp and I was the only one here—they came up to take a look.

Spy hopping, the name given to whales pushing their heads and some of their bodies vertically out of the water, signals to the speaker orca curiosity in her not just as a human but also as an individual ("I was the only one here"). In this site, these oceanic beings often are positioned as creating connections based on a mutual interest instead of indifference. Similarly, a tour boat naturalist, in explaining his bond with orcas, described orcas visiting tour boats:

> I'm convinced there's some days they come right by the boat. You see their eyeball and they're just "We know you, we know who you are." There's people on this island who think these whales are just big dumb animals. I just don't understand that.

Here, the naturalist describes not only orca curiosity but also knowledge about humans ("We know you, we know who you are"). As with the Euro-American hunter and the orca researcher, this naturalist points to his views being in contrast to some others'—in this case, those who are dismissive of orcas as sentient actors.

Another parallel with wolves is found in complications of the idea of orcas seeking out humans. One marine monitor focused on orcas as subjects and agents in their own right, not in serving human desires but instead in just going on their way (like the wolf above "just went on his way"):

> I do think that they are interested in boats and I think they're interested in people, but I also think they are doing their thing . . . that they may not be actually picking people on boats to come up to all the time, that they may be going about their business and we happened to be there. . . . I wouldn't want to take the magic out of that experience by saying "oh the whale was just chasing a fish underneath the boat and that's why they went there" because I don't always believe that but I don't always believe that they came up to people. So

it's hard for me to take people entirely seriously when they tell me stories about whales doing something amazing *for them* [*laughs*]. But on the other hand I also have seen whales definitely leave the groups and beeline to boats and I've had people on our boat whistle and had a whale whistle back and I definitely have had enough stuff that I do think that there are things that happen occasionally and I also think it's important to keep the mystery and magic of it all.

Whereas this speaker downplays the notion that humans are a high priority for orcas, she also does not take away their interactional intent. This speaker communicated with me on different occasions that she, like most advocates, tries to counter expectations of orcas seeking out humans—expectations shaped by particular contexts. Through captures and marine park captivity, orcas (and Southern Residents in particular, having been captured and their population decimated in order to supply SeaWorld's first "Shamus") have been brought into the center of Western culture in one way wolves have not, as captive entertainment. This perception often transfers to the ocean in shaping false expectations and interpretations of wild orca actions that emphasize satisfying Western human needs for entertainment or an anthropocentric sense of importance (Milstein, 2016).

In this way, speakers at times posed the idea that it is through what wild orcas *choose not to do to us*—which at times their captive counterparts do (e.g., there are no known killings of humans by orcas in the wild whereas there are several by captive orcas)—that they shape the human-orca relationship despite what they remember. Similar to speakers in the first case study describing wolves as relating to humans in ways that do not reflect our "relentless" hunting and trapping of them but instead earlier more instinctual relational memories, two orca advocates in conversation stated:

1	Advocate 1:	I wonder why they don't do anything to us because we've
2		done really crummy things to them. The older ones were
3		around for the captures. They remember us capturing them
4		and taking away their young ones. They remember us
5		corralling them. They swim by the capture coves all the
6		time. And we've shot at them from boats.
7	Advocate 2:	And it looks sometimes like we're corralling them with the
8		whale watch boats.
9	Advocate 1:	. . . One thought is they trust these boats. Another thought is
10		they may not have a fear response—that they're a top
11		predator and simply had no need for one. I don't know.

These advocates point to orca memories of human actions and their lack of fear in ways comparative to those speaking about wolves above. Another study participant, a summer research volunteer, described orcas as being victims of other systemic human destructive actions yet still having "unconditional love for us" based on "seeing something in us":

> Our research has shown there are high levels of PCBs and flame retardant materials (in the orcas). And we're taking their food. I feel so bad. They're so innocent and humans just control their world. We're the main reason for their decline and yet they kind of still have unconditional love for us. In the human world, if someone did that to me, forget it. . . . They're filled with love. *They must see something in us*. They forgive and forget.

The third premise emanating from the wolf-human site is that, in past and present alike, the interspecies relationship is not shaped solely by us. In the orca-human site, speakers articulate key notions rooted in this premise: *They* approach, circle, watch, and look at *us*. *They* perceive and are curious about *us*. *They* see and remember *us*. Orcas are described as knowing who and what humans are, as seeking humans out, and—similar to the Euro-American hunter's description of his encounter with the wolf—as having interactive intent but at times also just "going about their business and we happened to be there." Also, as in the wolf-human site, orcas are described as retaining memories of human violence on their kind but attending to deeper relational memories. In this way, orcas are characterized as taking the high road, as choosing to forgive and forget. In choosing not to return the violence that humans have done to them (but that some of their captive orca counterparts have returned), free wild orcas also are framed as shaping human-orca relations through their intentional and loving interactions.

SPEAKING OF WOLVES AND WHALES

Early in this chapter, we noted that dominant Euro-American discourses have long depicted wolves, orcas, and other wildlife—both explicitly and implicitly—as parts of nature subject to human action. In the analyses and reflections above, we have investigated instances of speech that express (1) meaningful elements of identity shared by wolves and humans, and by orcas and humans, (2) the development of mutually meaningful relationships between wolves and humans, and orcas and humans, through interacting and dwelling together, and (3) the identities of wolves and orcas as agents who—like us—perceive, think, know, remember, and act for their own reasons.

In the utterances we have examined—and in the root premises formulated in the wolf site and explored as they extend and surface in the orca site—the hubs and radiants of *being* and *relating* are foregrounded. *Acting* plays a vital role in the webs of meaning presumed and created in the instances described and interpreted, but emphasis is placed on *inter*-action between subjects, rather than on animals as objects of human action. *Dwelling* is likewise vital, but emphasis is placed on coinhabitation of places and natural systems, rather than on animals as part of "nature," separate from human "culture."

These two case studies, drawn together here within the framework of CuDA, illustrate related ways of speaking that are, in many ways, at odds with dominant Western discourses about wild animals, especially large predators. Some speakers offer metadiscursive commentary on the differences—and the difficulties that can emerge—between their understandings and dominant understandings. After speaking of wolves' "instinctive memory of this relationship between us and them," one speaker tells us that "there's not a lot of folks you can talk to about stuff like that." After speaking of orcas as beings who are "just like us," another speaker tells us that "the culture hasn't seen what I see." Such utterances speak not only of wolves and orcas, but also of diverse patterns of meaning-making and of relationships between dominant and subordinate Euro-American discourses.

Critiques of Western understandings of nature often contrast them with indigenous beliefs and knowledge systems. Making such comparisons in Australia, for instance, Howitt and Suchet-Pearson (2006) argue that the idea of wildlife "management," often presumed to be universally relevant, is culturally specific and problematic. The idea of management, they write, is a virtually "invisible foundational concept" that is "intimately woven into the twin Eurocentric notions of development and conservation." They note that the ideas of development and conservation, in turn, "assume not only separation between society and nature . . . but also superiority of society and humans over nature and animals" (pp. 324–325). Such ideas, they argue, have "marginalized" and "overruled" indigenous understandings, including "the idea of people as kin to other species and sentient entities, as co-equal occupants of places" (p. 328).

Central to their critique, in other words, is the observation that Western ideas of management, development, and conservation are rooted in thinking and speaking of wildlife species as parts of *nature* subject to programs and policies of human *action*. Central to the marginalized indigenous understandings they discuss are ideas rooted in the foregrounding of *identity* and *relationship*, in thinking and speaking of wild animals and humans as kin and as mutually aware sentient agents.

In this chapter, we have heard how—largely based on years of personal observation and interactive experience—some Euro-Americans formulate and articulate understandings rooted in similar premises. According to the meanings they create and presume, wolves and orcas are not merely parts of "the environment" that can be wholly understood in biological or ecological terms, and are not merely objects to be "managed." Rather, these "fellow hunters" and "humans of the ocean" are like us and in relationship with us.

In listening closely to such voices, we can cultivate deeper understandings both of the diverse patterns of meaning-making within and among human communities, and of the other beings alongside whom we dwell. By attuning our listening to commonalities among ways of speaking, for instance, we can hear how dominant Western discourses concerning wildlife—the discourses that drive policy formulation and implementation—marginalize not only indigenous understandings but also some Euro-American understandings. As articulated by Rudnick, Witteborn, and Edmonds in this volume, policy discourses are cultural discourses that reflect particular assumptions: assumptions not always shared by those whom policies affect. The dominant legal and scientific discourses that shape wolf- and orca-conservation planning do not make their central assumptions explicit, and policymaking processes rarely encompass concerted efforts to comprehend and include alternative or radically different understandings. For those interested in remedying these disconnects, CuDA offers a powerful set of tools for practicing inclusivity both across and within cultures, for hearing and honoring the diverse voices that constitute our overlapping and intersecting worlds.

NOTES

1. In this chapter, we use the terms "Western" and "Euro-American" somewhat interchangeably, to refer to patterns of cultural meaning-making and, at times, to North American people of European descent.
2. This body of data encompasses audio recordings of dozens of in-depth interviews, audio and video recordings of dozens of public events, field notes on more than 100 hours of informal conversation and participant observation, and approximately 200 publicly available texts related to wolves in the region, including newspaper and magazine articles, letters to the editor, written testimony, organizational websites, and wolf management plans written by state and tribal agencies (see Cerulli, 2016).
3. This body of data comprises hundreds of pages of field notes collected between 2005 and 2017 during on-shore and on-water field observations, as well as transcribed audio recordings of in-depth interviews and public meetings, and publicly available texts related to orcas in the region, including news articles, whale watch tour brochures and websites, museum texts, educational signage, and governmental websites (see Milstein, 2008, 2011, 2016; Milstein & Dickinson, 2012; Milstein & Kroløkke, 2012).
4. Orcas, the largest dolphins, are commonly referred to as whales, so we use this cultural moniker.
5. CuDA was the central framework for the study from which wolf-related data and interpretations are drawn. This study employed descriptive (e.g., transcription), interpretive, and comparative modes of analysis. Core to the study's interpretive analyses were (1) identification of communicative practices and meanings constellated around themes of central import for participants, (2) identification of key *cultural terms* and phrases, (3) formulation of *cultural propositions*, using participants' own words to articulate the range of meanings audible in uses of key terms and phrases, and (4) formulation of *cultural premises*, capturing the essence of key terms and propositions, with attention to discursive *hubs* and *radiants*. These interpretive analyses yielded a model of five prominent and distinct cultural discourses among western Great Lakes hunting communities. These were then compared, with attention to similarities, connections, and overlaps—as well as distinctive differences—among the five, as well as dynamics apparent among them (Cerulli, 2016).

6. Early data analysis in the orca-human site was done using interpretive and critical discourse analysis approaches. Later analysis in this long-term study site has employed CuDA as an additional well-suited frame of analysis.

7. As used here, in contrast with "hunting," the term "agriculture" can be heard as a catch-all, encompassing herding and farming and, most specifically, protecting livestock. Historically, there appears to be a strong link between attitudes toward wolves and primary means of subsistence. Around the globe, traditional hunting cultures have honored the wolf as a hunter. Nomadic shepherding cultures have been consistently hostile toward wolves, which threatened their mobile and relatively vulnerable livestock. Farming and sedentary shepherding cultures, where livestock could be more easily protected but could fall prey to wolves on occasion, have typically held mixed and ambiguous views (Boitani, 1995).

8. This hunter, like others who speak in this way, also said that "people aren't going to tolerate" excessively "bold" and potentially dangerous wolf behaviors (such as hanging out near a school bus stop), and that people must refrain from activities (such as feeding wolves) that habituate wolves to areas densely populated by humans. There are, he said, "some logical lines to draw." Though he noted that "wolves don't attack people" as a rule, he spoke of how wolves may perceive children: "If you think about how little kids run, they fall down, they squeal, they make noises, you know, they look like prey." In virtually all the very rare, recent, and credibly documented cases where wild, healthy (nonrabid) wolves have attacked humans, the victims have been children. These incidents have occurred in places—mainly in India—where wolves "commonly frequent villages and sometimes even enter huts" and encounter "many small children in heavy cover" (Mech, 1998).

9. This institutional discourse has been identified and interpreted through careful CuDA-based analyses of historical and contemporary data, including books on and plans for the scientific "management" and "conservation" of wolves and other species, state and federal laws concerning the "recovery" of threatened and endangered species, and public presentations by wildlife professionals (Cerulli, 2016).

10. Interpretation of this prominent Ojibwe discourse has been based on tribal wolf plans, instances of public talk, and interviews with tribal elders and tribal natural resources employees, among other data. In this discourse, Ma'iingan is spoken of as a member of a natural and cultural community, as one who—like the Ojibwe—belongs in that community and should flourish there in harmony with others. The people are bound to honor and respect wolves, and to protect them against those who do not. The roots of this historically transmitted expressive system are audible both in Ojibwe (and, more broadly, American Indian) cultural traditions and in their long political history of interaction with Euro-Americans (Cerulli, 2016).

REFERENCES

Boitani, L. (1995). Ecological and cultural diversities in the evolution of wolf-human relationships. In L. N. Carbyn, S. H. Fritts, & D. R. Seip (Eds.). *Ecology and conservation of wolves in a changing world* (pp. 3–11). Edmonton, Alberta: Canadian Circumpolar Institute.

Carbaugh, D. (1996a). Naturalizing communication and culture. In J. G. Cantrill & C. L. Oravec (Eds.), *The symbolic earth: Discourse and our creation of the environment* (pp. 38–57). Lexington, KY: University Press of Kentucky.

Carbaugh, D. (1996b). *Situating selves: The communication of social identities in American scenes.* Albany, NY: SUNY Press.

Carbaugh, D. (2007). Cultural discourse analysis: Communication practices and intercultural encounters. *Journal of Intercultural Communication Research, 36,* 167–182.

Carbaugh, D., & Cerulli, T. (2013). Cultural discourses of dwelling: Investigating environmental communication as a place-based practice. *Environmental Communication, 7*(1), 4–23.

Cerulli, T. (2016). *Of wolves, hunters, and words: A comparative study of cultural discourses in the western Great Lakes region* (Doctoral dissertation). University of Massachusetts, Amherst.

Cerulli, T. (2017). "Ma'iingan is our brother": Ojibwe and non-Ojibwe ways of speaking about wolves. In D. Carbaugh (Ed.), *The handbook of communication in cross-cultural perspective* (pp. 247–260). New York, NY: Routledge.

Hallowell, A. I. (1960; repr. 1981). Ojibwa ontology, behavior, and world view. In S. Diamond (Ed.), *Culture in history: Essays in honor of Paul Radin* (pp. 19–52). New York, NY: Columbia University Press; repr. by Octagon Books.

Howitt, R., & Suchet-Pearson, S. (2006). Rethinking the building blocks: Ontological pluralism and the idea of "management." *Geografiska Annaler: Series B, Human Geography, 88*(3), 323–335.

Leopold, A. (1949; repr. 1970). *A Sand County almanac with essays on conservation from Round River.* New York, NY: Ballantine.

Mech, L. D. (1998). Who's afraid of the big bad wolf? *International Wolf, 8*(1), 8–11. Retrieved September 9, 2017, from http://www.wolf.org/wolf-info/basic-wolf-info/wolves-and-humans/whos-afraid-of-the-big-bad-wolf/

Milstein, T. (2008). When whales "speak for themselves": Communication as a mediating force in wildlife tourism. *Environmental Communication, 2*(2), 173–192.

Milstein, T. (2011). Nature identification: The power of pointing and naming. *Environmental Communication, 5*(1), 3–24.

Milstein, T. (2016). The performer metaphor: "Mother Nature never gives us the same show twice." *Environmental Communication, 10*(2), 227–248. https://doi.org/10.1080/17524032.2015.1018295

Milstein, T., & Dickinson, E. A. (2012). Gynocentric greenwashing: The discursive gendering of nature. *Communication, Culture and Critique, 5*(4), 510–532.

Milstein, T., & Kroløkke, C. (2012). Transcorporeal tourism: Whales, fetuses, and the rupturing and reinscribing of cultural constraints. *Environmental Communication, 6*(1), 82–100.

Overholt, T. W., & Callicott, J. B. (1982). *Clothed-in-fur and other tales: An introduction to an Ojibwa world view.* Lanham, MD: University Press of America.

Roosevelt, T. (1893). *The wilderness hunter: An account of the big game of the United States and its chase with horse, hound, and rifle.* New York, NY: G. P. Putnam's Sons.

Scammon, C. M. (1874). *The marine mammals of the north-western coast of North America.* San Francisco, CA: John H. Carmany and Company.

U.S. EPA, R. 10. (April 29, 2013). Southern Resident killer whales [reports and assessments]. Retrieved August 21, 2017, from https://www.epa.gov/salish-sea/southern-resident-killer-whales

Weber, R. (December 30, 2011). Confessions of a wolf lover. *Rice Lake Chronotype.* Retrieved September 30, 2017, from http://www.apg-wi.com/rice_lake_chronotype/opinions/confessions-of-a-wolf-lover/article_95094425-f9a6-56ac-8ccf-92d9db9d5899.html

Part IV

Feeling

Chapter Ten

Symbolic Agonistics

Stressing Emotion and Relation in Mexican, Mexican@, and Japanese Discourses

Patricia Covarrubias, Dani S. Kvam, and Max Saito

> *¡El que no entiende eres tú porque yo ya entendí perfectamente bien! . . . !El que no entiende es usted ! . . . ¡Quiero cumplimientos, quiero resultados!* [You (using *tú*) are the one who doesn't understand because I understood perfectly well. . . The one who doesn't understand is you (using *usted*)! . . . I want follow-through! I want results!].

And so, in this Mexican social scene, within a sudden pronominal shift, shouted in a burst of anger, the relationship between a particular speaker, in this case a Mexican construction company manager, and his listener, a labor contractor, was transformed. What had begun as a calm and amiable conversation culminated as one where not only their communication was punctuated with tension, anger, and hostility, but also their interpersonal relationship suffered similarly.

In a second example, heightened emotions were seen, heard, and felt as Mexican@ immigrants marched for equality.

> "*¡El pueblo unido, jamás será vencido!¡El pueblo unido, jamás será vencido!*" [The people united will never be defeated! The people united will never be defeated!] and "*¡[Nombre de la gobernadora] escucha, estamos en la lucha!¡[Nombre de la gobernadora] escucha, estamos en la lucha!*" [(Name of governor) listen, we are in the fight! (Name of governor) listen, we are in the fight!][1]

These chants were among those heard in a Mexican@ scene where marchers advocated for immigration law reform. In a sonorous chorus marchers moved through city streets, asserting their legitimacy, humanity, and presence.

In a third example, in the Japanese film *Okoge*, a mother covered her daughter's eyes at a beach where LGBTQ people gathered, saying, *"Micha dame. Mietemo, mienakattano. Souiukotoni shiyoune. Wakatta."* [Don't look. Even if you saw it, you did not see anything. We'll pretend it never happened. Understood?] In Japanese cultural scenes, the mother's utterance is understood as the communicative practice of *"mizaru, kikazaru, iwazaru"* [see no evil, hear no evil, and say no evil], whose use enables all involved to go on as if their encounter had never happened.

What do the three culture-rich social scenes above have in common? Individually and jointly they offer evidence that the human experience calls on us to confront poignant moments of dissonance, struggle, and combat in our everyday lives. In these moments social interactants activate agony "as both a particular and a universal force in cultural communication systems" (Carbaugh, 1988/1989, p. 182). As this chapter will show, although anguished social interaction is universal, the means and meanings for its use are experienced locally in distinctive ways. In the spirit of Hymes's (1972) appeal for comparative work using ethnographies of communication, we use extant empirical inquiries to examine cultural symbols and their meanings in order to abstract understandings about agonistic communication across interactional levels. In particular, we investigate more micro-level interpersonal interactions, meso-level communal protests, and more macro-level mass-mediated communication. Cross-cultural comparison of these corpora of data provide the foundation for the introduction of an interpretive tool to account for emotion in cultural texts and productions. Specifically, we introduce the construct we name, *symbolic agonistics*.

Our reasons for choosing to focus on agonistic—combative, painful, tense, hostile, and strained—communication are manifold. The ubiquity of agonistic communication across cultural scenes in our everyday lives confirms its relevance to social actors. Randomly tuning in to nightly news, for example, certainly attests to the recurrent displays of adversarial emotion in private as well as public milieu. Yet curiously, despite its social currency, emotion is an undertheorized area in communication studies, with the study of anguish-charged communication yet rarer. Perhaps it is because of deeply rooted cultural orientations that privilege, at least ideally, sanguine and validating forms of communication that expressions about pain, travail, suffering, grief, and distress are unattractive. Some cultural communication scholars, however, have made moves to underscore the centrality of emotion in its diverse expressions in human conduct. For example, Carbaugh (2005) prioritized the role of emotion through his definition of culture as "a system of expressive practices that is fraught with feeling, and grandly implicates beliefs about persons, places, and practices of living" (p. 60). In the present essay, we seek to affirm this emphasis on emotion in the study of cultural communication undertaken by Carbaugh (2005, 2007) and others (Boromisza-Habashi, 2013; Covarrubias, 2002, 2017). To understand emotion, we draw from Wierzbicka (1999), who holds that emotion resides in feelings, thoughts, and within the body, and Lutz (1986/2013), who suggests that emotion should be examined explicitly and within its sociocultural contexts (p. 288). As scholars of cultural communication, we contend that because of its relevance to the human experience, agonistic displays put in relief the connection between emotion, culture, and communication, and thus offer exceptionally rich loci for inquiry. These communicative displays become available to onlookers as well as participants in the interaction. From a communication perspective, then, we treat the verbal and nonverbal displays or observable manifestations of emotion as an important form of cultural communication.

In the spirit of this book, which celebrates the utility of Carbaugh's cultural discourse analysis (CuDA) (2007) for understanding situated communicative conduct, we first frame our discussion of agonistic communication as the communicative practice that locates the pertinent hub for our metacommunicative commentary. Our ultimate goal in examining CuDA along with key literature pertaining to the agon is to provide a definition for symbolic agonistics. With this definition we contribute a useful and relevant construct to theories of cultural communication while expanding understandings about the linkages between culture, communication, and emotion.

In the pages that follow, we use Carbaugh's (2007) CuDA as a methodological approach for detailing the particular elements of agonistic communication that function as means for interlocutors to shape particular culturally informed social relationships. Although his etic framework consists of five "radiants" of meaning—personhood, relation, action, emotion, and dwelling—our emic abstraction focuses on the radiant of relation as it emerged as the most salient in our joint corpora of data. Again, careful scrutiny of our data revealed emotion, specifically as agon-charged communication, as the discursive form or "hub" around which relation radiates (Carbaugh, 2017). Isolating this hub and its attendant radiant of relation enabled us to examine aspects of the cultural nature of talk that too often are left unarticulated (Carbaugh, 2007, 2017). As loci for inquiry we used the contexts of a Mexican workplace, a Mexican@ social support center in the U.S. Southwest, and a Japanese film and television talk show. We begin by presenting materials grounding the notion of agonized communication. Then we present a definition for symbolic agonistics, along with our theoretical assumptions and methodological procedures. Finally, we apply our definition to our combined data and conclude with the articulation of cultural propositions that cut across these diverse cultural scenes (Carbaugh, 2007).

THE AGON ACROSS CONTEXTS

The term *"agón"* [ἀγών], or agon as it is used contemporarily, appears in a variety of contexts starting in ancient Greece, where it was used as a cultural form to encompass the struggle between opposing participants, principles, desires, and even a struggle in the soul (Bible Hub, 2011). The Greek agon was enacted in competition pertaining to public athletics, music, literature, or religion. In drama, it was a theatrical form that presented the conflict between characters and their ensuing argument. Later, in the social sciences, Scott and Fredericson (1951), who observed animal behavior to later offer insights into human behavior, coined the term "agonistic behavior." According to Barratt (2001), this term signified "adaptive acts which arise out of conflicts between two members of the same species" (p. 326). The term agonistic behavior was meant to embrace broader meanings beyond aggression to include interrelated behaviors such as passive acts of submission, flight, and even playful behaviors involving physical contact (Barratt, 2001). Although in its original meaning playful pushing and shoving would still be noted as agonistic behavior, as time passed, agonistic and aggressive behaviors became interchangeable (p. 326).

Huizinga (1955) used the *agon* (contest) to distinguish between *ludus* (free or unstructured play), with the former serving as a situated societal tool for creating music, drama, dance, and poetry. Later, Ong (1981) argued that the notion of "contest" could be mapped through human intellectual history. He contended that as societies transitioned from orality to technology, and academic instruction changed from Latin to English and from male-only to coeducational, the role of contest continued to be of paramount importance for humans. During these societal shifts, contests began appearing in different places. In particular, as academia, an important site for the creation of knowledge, became more "irenic" and less contested, sports, politics, and religion developed into the principal arenas for humans to enact agonism (Ong, 1981).

Contemporarily, we also see the agon woven into political and social theory (Mouffe, 2000). Mouffe (2000) proposed *agonistic pluralism* as an approach to democracy that allows its users to "construct the 'them' in such a way that it is no longer perceived as an enemy to be destroyed, but an 'adversary,' i.e., somebody whose ideas we combat but whose right to defend those ideas we do not put into question" (p. 15). This approach did not champion apathy or concession, but rather suggested that dueling parties often have common ground, differing in the value placed on means to achieve political and social ends. Agonism, then, is not something to be eradicated, but to be "tamed" (p. 15).

THE AGON IN COMMUNICATION STUDIES

In the study of human communication, and cultural communication in particular, the agon can be heard across everyday life scenes in the discursive practices of people in diverse cultural contexts. Philipsen (1986) introduces the terms "agonistic sequences," "agonistic encounter," and "deep agony" in his notable study about the controversial speech presented by then-mayor of Chicago Richard J. Daley (pp. 254–255). With this move, then, Philipsen makes available the accounting of emotion in studies of culture. Carbaugh (1988/1989) showed how for interactants on the *Donahue* television show, the agon involves humans in a fight for the expression of a self *vis-à-vis* society where communication served as fundamental tool for enacting the fight and for articulating the fight's outcomes. Studying interpersonal interactions at a Mexican construction company in Veracruz, Mexico, Covarrubias (2002) argued that via the very uttering of particular pronominal shifts, agonistic discourses can be and are activated. Such shifts are shown to cohabit with emotions of anger and antagonism resulting in the amending of human connections from positive to agonistic realignments. As Covarrubias noted, pronominal shifts have the potential to damage and even permanently sever existing generative rapports.

Further, investigating a Finnish adult education center, Wilkins (2006) conceptualized *vaikeneminen* [silence] and *puhuminen* [speaking] as agonistic or "competing" modes of communication. In this case, participants experienced a conflict between desires to maintain "a silent listener orientation" that valued speaking to present information and an "expressive speaking orientation that animates individual purpose, meaning, and intention" (p. 249). These two understandings of communication were shown to compete with one another, for example, when an instructor asked students to present publicly an idea that they had been taught to keep private, resulting in a norm violation. Wilkins (2006) explained this norm violation resulted in feelings of unease for the students.

And exploring *gyűlöletbeszéd* or hate speech in Hungary, Boromisza-Habashi (2013) described "agonistic discourse" as "a way of speaking that members of a given cultural community see as presenting irreconcilable, conflicting worldviews" (p. 49). He maintained that opposition allowed communicators to speak from "social personae" that served as meaningful representations of particular identities. In other words, agonistic discourse not only shaped what one said, but also, the kind of person one enacted while saying it (p. 49). Ultimately, Boromisza-Habashi (2013) argued that agonistic discourse was present in a number of cultural scenes (public, private, societal, interpersonal), that they were often related to other extant social fissures, and that they were not a result of a "lack of understanding," but disagreement about the possible outcomes of a course of action (p. 62).

From this literature we see that across sociocultural contexts enactments of the agon are imbued with variant expressions of emotional distress and pain. Emotions such as strife, anger, hostility, embarrassment, and animosity, among other possibilities, reveal themselves to be inseparable from their meanings. It is within the expression of emotion that ardent meanings are best apprehended. Within the combination of agonized emotion and semantic resources social actors fashion the discursive economy for managing (or not) competing and even clashing perspectives, attitudes, principles, goals, motives, or sociocultural imperatives.

Symbolic Agonistics

The presence of agonistic interaction in diverse domains of the human experience and the constitutive and reflective functions of communication in it exacts the need for a communication-centered approach. To that end, we offer the following definition for the construct we name "symbolic agonistics": *The discursive practice involving the strategic use of symbolic resources for activating agony-laden social distancing that can and does forecast the emotive frames of subsequent interactions among the original or alternative social actors.* In this definition, we assume that humans are purposeful and artful users of communicative means (words, phrases, nonverbal cues, and silence) (Philipsen, 1992) and that those means and their derived meanings emerge from the cultural context in which they are deployed (Covarrubias, 2007; Hymes, 1972). We hold humans to be users (and abusers) of symbols for meaning-making (Burke, 1969). Symbolic agonistics is fundamentally concerned with the concrete, relational outcomes of communication, because communication itself has force and bears social consequences. For example, communicative phenomena can and do offer the means for mediating social distancing (Brown & Gilman, 1960; Brown & Ford, 1961), for disrupting relational alignments (Covarrubias, 2002), and for infusing communication with meaningful emotion (Carbaugh, 2007; Covarrubias, 2002, 2017), whether intentional or not. When symbolic agonistics are manifest, an originating communicator triggers an act sequence with a verbal and/ or nonverbal expression of contest, which, in turn, aligns participants into nonproductive social configurations. This centering of emotion in studies of cultural communication differs from Philipsen's (1986) terms "agonistic sequences," "agonistic encounter," and "deep agony" (pp. 254–255) in that our focus is on the relational alignments (Covarrubias, 2002) among social actors themselves and the potential for future agony-laden emotive framing of unproductive outcomes.

For purposes of transparency and specificity, it is important for us to differentiate symbolic agnostics from hate speech (Boromisza-Habashi, 2013; Waltman & Haas, 2010) in four ways. First, in some cases, symbolic agonistics mediate culturally valuable and affirming social ends. For example, Mexican female interlocutors may use *usted* [formal "you"] strategically as a pronominally mediated distancing device to deflect men's sexual advances (Covarrubias, 2002). Other interlocutors may use *usted* to sidestep interpersonal abuses (i.e., lending of money, requesting special favors, or overlooking professional infractions) (Covarrubias, 2002).

As a second point of differentiation, symbolic agonistics is more dialogic than hate speech. In other words, interactants at dyadic (Covarrubias, 2002) or communal levels (Kvam, 2017) are more likely to engage give-and-take conversational rhythms. For example, phrases yelled by Mexican@ immigrants during protest marches can serve as a means for asserting their visibility and personhood to those for whom immigrants too often are invisible. Marchers produce these chants to respond to negative characterizations of immigrants deployed in interpersonal and mass-mediated interactions, as well as invite a response from outsiders (Covarrubias, 2017). In the Japanese scene below, a lesbian couple asserted their right to become parents while opposing those they perceived to deny them this right. Their appearance on a talk show directly implicated real-time give-and-take.

A third differentiation resides in the idea that symbolic agonistics can and does occur at micro, meso, and macro levels of human expression. Although not absolutely, hate speech implicates a more public and even institutional expression. Fourth, symbolic agonistics focuses, intentionally and purposely, on the affective components of a particular key or tone of communication, which hate speech does not necessarily do despite its label "hate" speech. Moreover, symbolic agnostics points to a broader range of possible emotions and feelings beyond hatred.

METHODS

To abstract the construct of symbolic agonistics, we studied our cumulative data line-by-line to isolate moments of verbal and nonverbal communication that were punctuated by key (Hymes, 1972) or emotion (Jakobson, 1960), such as fear, stress, anger, or pain. We looked for recurring and co-occurring terms (Covarrubias, 2017). For example, screening data for expressions of emotion, Kvam found repeated mentions of *miedo* [fear] as in: "Yo quiero compartir algo que cuando fuí a pedir unos papeles a la corte, tuve mucho *miedo*" [I want to share that when I went to court to get some papers, I was very *frightened*], "Me daba miedo platicar con personas en inglés, me daba *miedo* porque me decía se van a reír de mi" [I was *afraid* to speak English with people, I was *afraid* because I told myself, "they're going to laugh at me"], and "Cuando yo llegué aquí yo no quería salir de mi casa. Yo tenía mucho *miedo* de salir a la calle y que me preguntaran de algo" [When I first arrived here I didn't want to leave my house. I was very *frightened* to go out in the street and that someone might ask me something].

Also, we scrutinized data for expressions that resulted in the social distancing of interactants. Covarrubias, who has native knowledge of Mexican Spanish, screened for enactments of *tú* and *usted* whose consequences shaped or reshaped relationships into alignments characterized by combat, distress, enmity, and the like. For example, the Mexican construction worker's utterance *"El tú murio para nosotros"* [(The use of the pronoun) *Tú* died for us] revealed that the highly charged emotional exchange with a coworker brought about the death of the use of the pronoun *tú* while simultaneously announcing a reformulation of a relationship once characterized by harmony to one marked by antipathy and by possible permanent estrangement.

Kvam, a native English speaker born in the United States, has developed agility for conducting and analyzing ethnographic observations and interviews in Mexican Spanish. She scanned her data for talk that revealed the myriad emotions experienced by Mexican@ immigrants as they struggled to reestablish lives for themselves and their families. This analytic move brought to light talk about fear and intimidation of interaction with police and with other U.S. Americans owing to the countless new rules, expectations, people, and situations intrinsic to resettling in a new country. She was alert for expressions of emotion such as hope to *"salir adelante"* [come out ahead] and satisfaction when one or a member of one's community wins a fight in the ongoing *"batalla"* [battle] of immigration.

Saito, who has native knowledge of Japanese, reviewed research data pertaining to the Japanese LGBTQ community by studying the film *Okoge* and the TV talk show *Watashi no naniga ikenaino?* He used the film and the TV talk show for two reasons. First, his research interviewees asked him not to include actual interactions and interviews especially when he observed actual LGBTQ-related communicative practices. Second, the segments in the media indicated intersections between actual and mass-mediated communication regarding LGBTQ issues. With *Okoge*, he also studied data from interviews with research participants for their interpretations of the film and about the salient concept of *"mizaru, kikazaru, iwazaru"* [see no evil, hear no evil, speak no evil]. With *Watashi no naniga ikenaino?* he explored discourses pertaining to LGBTQ identity and parenthood while applying his previous findings (Saito, 2009) and participant observations. In 2015, Shibuya ward in Tokyo started issuing same-sex marriage certificates. Still many people, both heterosexual and LGBTQ, are concerned about potential discrimination against LGBTQ individuals.

We used Carbaugh (2007) to isolate the relevant hub and radiant. Our initial open-ended codings exposed the prominence of emotion. From repeated and systematic codings, we became aware that focusing on emotion would allow us to apprehend meanings in the data that otherwise would remain hidden. To locate our understandings of these data, we turned to Hymes's (1972) notions of the "key" or tone of the interaction and Jakobson's (1960) perspective on the affective function of language. Our analysis put in relief emotion as the hub around which other elements actuated, specifically the radiant of relation (Carbaugh, 2007).

HUB IN (E)MOTION

For "symbolic agonistics," we center emotion as the core or basis for shaping culturally informed sociality. Given the corrosive content of the interaction, symbolic agonistics has a heightened potential for transforming social alignments as our data show. Returning to the Mexican social scene that introduces this chapter, Covarrubias overheard the saying between a company manager and a labor contractor during a telephone conversation (see Covarrubias, 2002). A careful listening to the manager's utterance revealed the insertion of a sudden and attention-grabbing pronominal shift; attention grabbing not only to the addressee but also to bystanders as the rate of speech quickened and the loudness rose to an agitated shout. As that conversation heated up because the contractor had not delivered the expected services, the manager suddenly and unexpectedly switched from a composed *tú* (informal "you") to a fuming *usted* (formal "you"). With the combination of the amended pronoun along with attendant paralinguistic cues, the manager fashioned strategically the social distance necessary to voice a harshened reprimand, and literally spoke into being a reformulated social relationship. In this instance the combatants each understood that their new relationship and likely their future encounters would be punctuated by deeply felt stress and strain via the turn of uttered pronouns. Covarrubias (2002) titled exemplars of this type of anguished enactment, "agonistic provisional realignments" (p. 68). The notion of "provisional" refers to the idea that such realignments might or might not be permanent, leaving open the possibility of reconciliation with the formerly generative relationship.

It is worthy of note that pronominally mediated shifts in agonistic provisional realignments can and do accommodate variances in emotion-laden displays while potentially activating an array of agonistic metapragmatic alternatives. Depending on their emotive intensity, reprimands can and do range from "softened" to "harshened" varieties (Covarrubias, 2002). Indeed, other workers shared stories with her about workday moments involving deeply felt and expressed aggressions wherein temporary distancing and even permanent severances replaced previously amicable relationships. In each of these latter instances, expressions of agonistic relational realignments were declared by sudden shifts from *tú* to *usted*. As a study participant who was involved in a workplace brawl that escalated into physical violence put it, *"El 'tú' murió para nosotros"* [(the use of the pronoun)*"Tú"* died for us]. For these interactants, in a culturally recognized and upheld interpersonal enactment, a pronominal semantic served to punctuate relational agony and literally speak into being the extinction—nonexistence—death of a once fruitful bond.

Agony also is seen, heard, and felt in scenes involving Mexican@ immigrants in and to the United States. To enhance understanding, we offer some details about the backdrop against which the data to follow can be understood. As we write in 2018, immigrants continue to dwell in agonistic environments created and maintained by their U.S. American neighbors, politicians, and news media, among others. This claim is perhaps best illustrated by President Donald Trump's description of some Mexican immigrants as "rapists," people "bringing drugs," "not their best," and "not you" as he announced his candidacy in June 2015 (Time Staff, June 16, 2015). When Trump used depreciatory language to describe Mexican immigrants to his U.S. American audience, he reinforced a long-standing narrative about the alleged inferiority of Mexican immigrants (Flores, 2003). Such talk enhanced adversarial alignments between Mexican immigrants and others in the United States, producing symbolic agonistics. Certainly, the fight for the rights of Mexican immigrants in the United States is not new. The opening exemplar in this essay, which unfolded on the celebration of César Chávez Day in 2013, attests to this claim. This commemorative day is a time to honor the struggles and victories spearheaded by labor leader and civil rights advocates César Chávez and Dolores Huerta, cofounders of the National Farm Workers Association in 1962 (United Farm Workers, 2017). For the community the annual march in a traditionally Mexican neighborhood makes public and visible their often private, invisible, and agonizing battle (i.e., discrimination, civil rights violations, and familial separations provoked by differing legal statuses of family members). In 2013, the chants echoed through the streets as protesters held signs demanding, *"¡No más familias divididas!"* [No more divided families!], *"¡Mira tu alrededor, somos una gran familia!"* [Look around you, we are a big family!], and *"¡Todos somos seres humanos, nadie es ilegal!"* [We are all human beings, nobody is illegal!]. Protesters of all ages wore butterfly wings on their backs to emphasize that humans are not the only migrating beings, but that movement from place to place is natural, expectable, and beautiful. When Kvam asked a member of this community what she wanted others to know about the experiences of immigrants, she replied, *"Qué es batalla, es batalla bastante, pero . . . al último puedo beneficiar mucho de estar aquí y que hecho las ganas y salir adelante."* [That it's a battle, it's a significant battle, but . . . in the end I can benefit a lot from being here and I can put effort into it, succeed, and come out ahead].

These chants and sign artifacts are among the communicative cultural resources used to fight immigrant battles for civil rights in this agonistic environment (Covarrubias, 2017) against both human and nonhuman combatants. In particular, through an alliterative chant, "*¡[Nombre de la gobernadora] escucha, estamos en la lucha!¡[Nombre de la gobernadora] escucha, estamos en la lucha!*" [(Name of governor) listen, we are in the fight! (Name of governor) listen, we are in the fight!] marchers concomitantly decried a human opponent as well as the abstract, nonhuman governmental entity that the governor represented. In other instances, nonhuman adversaries manifested in the form of news media, regulatory policies and laws, and access to institutional supports. Moreover, whether combating human and nonhuman opponents, immigrants bear the brunt of costly emotional and interpersonal tolls. Kvam (2017) argued that agonistic environments posed threats to Mexican@ immigrants' ability to create and maintain *confianza*-based relationships (confidentiality, trust, and interpersonal closeness). We see, then, that symbolic agonistics is not experienced fleetingly with a single opponent, but rather in sustained combat with human and nonhuman antagonists alike.

Agony also is present in mass-mediated Japanese social scenes involving LGBTQ and heterosexual people discussing LGBTQ realities. In the summer of 2015, the TV talk show "*Watashi no naniga ikenaino?*" [Is there something wrong with me?] featured a Japanese lesbian couple, Hiroko and Koyuki. The program included reenactments of LGBTQ people coming out or revealing their sexuality to parents, as well as situations addressing the legal obstacles confronted by same-sex couples seeking marriage. At one point, Hiroko said, "*Rezubian dearukotowo nakattakotoni suru. Himitsuni shinakyaikenai kurushimiga sugoku aru*" [It is excruciating to pretend as if my being lesbian were nothing and to have to keep it secret]. With this utterance she explicitly acknowledged the agonistic experience of societal pressures to keep her *honne* feelings (her true feeling as a lesbian) nullified while consciously affirming her *tatemae* feelings (how she is supposed to feel as heterosexual when she is not) even when she cannot tolerate the incongruity. Hiroko goes on to express her desire to live with Koyuki as their true selves, an action that necessarily required making public their sexuality despite the potential for painful sociocultural ramifications.

As the story progressed, viewers learned that Koyuki's family members had refused to attend her wedding held at Tokyo DisneySea. The refusal by Koyuki's family to attend the wedding was contrasted by the presence and support of Hiroko's family. The show's narrator remarked on the feelings of pride displayed by Hiroko's father, whose tearful speech during the reception invoked sympathetic reactions among the attendees. He stated, "*Honrai hito ga hito wo aisurukotoni seibetsuha arimasen. Sono kotowo ookuno hitotachiga rikaidekiru jidaiga menomaeni kiteirunowo kanjimasu.*" [Fundamentally, gender is irrelevant when people love one another. I feel that the era where people understand and accept it is right here in front of our eyes]. The narrator informed the audience that for ten years prior to the wedding, Hiro-ko's parents had refused to talk about her sexuality, but now respected her sexual orientation.

The show's conversation then shifted to talk about LGBTQ parenthood, illustrating another site for societal strife and marginalization of this commu-nity. This conflict was broached when a panelist remarked that the human rights of a child also should be taken into consideration, implying that LGBTQ people should not become parents. Hiroko, however, responded calmly, saying that denying anyone potential parental rights constituted hu-man rights violations. For her, this included the ability to pursue happiness (*shiawase*), a stable life (*anteishita seikatu*), legal protections (*houtekihogo*), and living as who they are (*jibunrashiku ikiru*). This exchange illustrated the chasm separating supporters and opponents of same-sex marriage and recon-firmed the ongoing, often painful struggles of LGBTQ communities. Finally, Hiroko's public and direct presentation of her real self explicitly contests the Japanese cultural communicative practice of "*mizaru, kikazaru, iwazaru*" [see no evil, hear no evil, and say no evil] discussed next.

In the Japanese mass-mediated example noted in our introduction, in the film *Okoge*, a mother covered her daughter's eyes at a beach where LGBTQ people gathered, telling her children, "*Micha dame. Mietemo, mienakattano. Souiukotoni shiyoune. Wakatta.*" [Don't look. Even if you saw it, you did not see anything. We'll pretend it never happened. Understood?]. This enactment of "*mizaru, kikazaru, iwazaru*" [see no evil, hear no evil, and say no evil] presumably enabled those present to proceed as if they had never encoun-tered one another. Yet the mother's action was fraught with a distressing paradox for all involved. On one hand, the communicative practice osten-sibly allowed the people at the beach to exist undisturbed and without their sexuality singled out, and for the mother to avoid further discussion. A contrasting perspective suggests that the mother's actions also can be con-strued as agonistic. For some, this practice is interpretable as means for silencing, nullifying, and even demonizing LGBTQ interactants by rendering them socially invisible (Saito, 2009). Without doubt, Hiroko's wedding, shared publicly on a television program, served to challenge notions of *miza-ru, kikazaru, iwazaru* and thereby made available alternatives for communi-cating with and about members of LGBTQ communities.

Carbaugh's (2007) CuDA facilitated assessing the confluences of sym-bolic agonistics across micro-, meso-, and macro-level cultural scenes. Across levels, interactants showed themselves to be skillful users and abusers of symbols (Burke, 1969) to animate combative interactional sequences. These sequences can and do result in the transformation of relationships, the death of relationships, the assertion of individual and communal personhood, the identification of human and nonhuman combatants, the pressing for vis-ibility within societal mainstreams, and the pressing for the maintenance of societal mainstreams that render some communities invisible, among other possibilities. Our cross-cultural examination points to convergences that are expressible as shared cultural propositions. We now turn to the presentation of those six cultural propositions.

The Comparative Mission

Key to the study of cultural communication is the abstraction of the complex linkages among culture, communication, and emotion. Building on the efforts and traditions of Hymes (1972), Philipsen (1992), Carbaugh (2007), and Covarrubias (2002, 2017) among others, we center an ever-present and undertheorized phenomenon. To remind the reader, symbolic agonistics references *The discursive practice involving the strategic use of symbolic resources for activating agony-laden social distancing that can and does forecast the emotive frames of subsequent interactions among the original or alternative social actors*. Now, we elaborate on this definition by discussing its grounding propositions.

Proposition One: Symbolic agonistics can and do summon communicative defenses to communicative offenses of self and community.

Across Mexican, Mexican@, and Japanese contexts, symbolic agonistics shows people activating defensive communicative sequences (Hymes, 1972) to counter perceived challenges to their personhood(s). The nature of symbolic agonistics can be understood to be as generative, performative, and socially consequential as a physical and/or emotional confrontation.

Proposition Two: Symbolic agonistics forecasts diminished communicative options.

For example, by employing the Japanese communicative practice of *"mizaru, kikazaru, iwazaru"* [see no evil, hear no evil, and say no evil], users announce an inherently limited scope of available communicative practices. Disconfirming LGBTQ people by pretending not to see or hear them damages and perhaps even destroys the potential for interaction and connection at the heart-to-heart communication level.

Proposition Three: Symbolic agonistics inhere in and across multiple levels of interaction, including relational, communal, and mass-mediated.

Our data reveal that this mode of communication does not occur solely at a single level, but also across multiple levels. That is, agony, combat, and contest in communication infect a range of actions from dyadic (Covarrubias, 2002) to communal (Kvam, 2017) to mass media (Saito, 2009) intersections.

Proposition Four: Symbolic agonistics forecasts the construction of potentially unproductive relational alignments that can and do lock interactants into either/or existential schemes.

Once symbolic agnostics were activated, Mexican construction workers' relational options became polarized; they could be either close or distant; amiable or hostile; harmonized or discordant. Mexican@ community members could be either visible or invisible; individuated or generic; like you/not like you. Japanese LGBTQ people could live either in happiness or in pain; included or marginalized. These binaries lock communicators into relational impasses that thwart the possibility of more generative options for interrelating.

Proposition Five: Symbolic agonistics announces social distancing that transcends the moment of its initial uttering to an undefined period of time.

When the Mexican interactant uttered "*El 'tú' murió para nosotros,*" explicitly marking an interpersonal shift from harmonization to dissonance, unless an explicit action aimed at resurrecting rapprochement, future relationships likely would be characterized by distance or even their severance, thereby transcending the particulars of their real-time extemporizations.

Proposition Six: Symbolic agonistics forecasts adversarial emotive frames.

The emotional currency of symbolic agonistics persists beyond their real-time instantiations. The transformed selves, the reformulated relationships, the fractured communities, and the memory of viscerally felt emotion are all outcomes that can and do extend beyond the moments of their manifestation. That is, symbolic agonistics sets up a social dynamic and digs an emotional terrain marked by combativeness, anger, fear, animosity, and enmity among other possibilities that likely will extend beyond the moment of their first enactment.

In sum, as users and misusers of communication (Burke, 1969), our three sets of interlocutors showed themselves strategically to use emotion-laden communication to achieve their social ends. Using CuDA, we echoed the idea that universally and locally, cultural meanings reside within situated emotion and relations (Carbaugh, 2007). To extend this claim, we presented *symbolic agonistics* to show that this practice involves communicative defenses of perceived offenses, manifests at different interactional levels, limits relational options, limits communication options, and has potential for persisting beyond its initial enactment well into the future. Therefore, symbolic agonistics offers an interpretive tool to account for emotion across cultural scenes and productions.

Finally, attending to and understanding situated emotion holds the promise of a generative yield. First, it would cue outsiders to the communal beliefs, values, goals, intentions, and imperatives that are privileged (or not) in a given society, as well as to the intensity with which they are held. Examining emotion in context would help avert easy generalizations and foster more nuanced and precise understandings. Moreover, insights gleaned from inquiry into deep emotion would illumine the possible social consequences of particular communicative actions. Such insights not only would contribute to conceptual knowledge, but also, perhaps more importantly, could help us all enact productive strategies and circumvent those with potential for unnecessarily producing agony.

NOTE

1. The quotes in the first and second examples were recorded as field notes in their respective social scenes. In the first example, names of participants have been omitted. The second example occurred as a collective, public chant.

REFERENCES

Barratt, E. S. (2001). Agonistic behavior. In *International encyclopedia of the social and behavioral sciences* (1st ed., pp. 326–329). Retrieved from http://www.sciencedirect.com/science/article/pii/B0080430767035762

Bible Hub. (2011). Strong's Concordance. Retrieved from http://biblehub.com/greek/73.htm

Boromisza-Habashi, D. (2013). *Speaking hatefully: Culture, communication, and political action in Hungary.* University Park, PA: The Pennsylvania State University Press.

Brown, R., and Ford, M. (1961). Address in American English. *Journal of Abnormal Psychology, 62,* 375–385.

Brown, R., and Gilman, A. (1960). The pronouns of power and solidarity. In P. P. Giglioli (Ed.), *Language and social contexts* (pp. 252–282). London: Cox & Wyman.

Burke, K. (1969). *A rhetoric of motives.* Berkeley, CA: University of California Press.

Carbaugh, D. (1988/1989). Deep agony: "Self" vs. "society" in Donahue discourse. *Research on Language and Social Interaction, 22,* 179–212.

Carbaugh, D. (2005). *Cultures in conversation.* Mahwah, NJ: Erlbaum.

Carbaugh, D. (2007). Cultural discourse analysis: Communication practices and intercultural encounters. *Journal of Intercultural Communication Research, 36*(3), 167–182. doi:10.1080/17475750701737090

Carbaugh, D. (2017). Terms for talk, take 2: Theorizing communication through its cultural terms and practices. In D. Carbaugh (Ed.), *The handbook of communication in cross-cultural perspective* (pp. 15–28). New York, NY: Routledge.

Covarrubias, P. (2002). *Culture, communication, and cooperation: Interpersonal relations and pronominal address in a Mexican organization.* Lanham, MD: Rowman & Littlefield.

Covarrubias, P. (2007). (Un)biased in Western theory: Generative silence in American Indian communication. *Communication Monographs, 74*(2), 265–271.

Covarrubias, P. (2017). *Respeto* [respect] in disrespect: Clashing cultural themes within the context of immigration. In D. Carbaugh (Ed.), *The handbook of communication in cross-cultural perspective* (pp. 208–221). International Communication Association Series. London: Routledge.

Flores, L. A. (2003). Constructing rhetorical borders: Peons, illegal aliens, and competing narratives of immigration. *Critical Studies in Media Communication, 20*(4), 362–387. doi:10.1080/0739318032000142025

Huizinga, J. (1955). *Homo ludens: A study of the play-element in culture.* Boston: Beacon Press.

Hymes, D. (1972). Models of interaction of language and social life. In J. J. Gumperz & D. Hymes (Eds.), *Directions in sociolinguistics: The ethnography of communication* (pp. 35–71). New York, NY: Basil Blackwell.

Jakobson, R. (1960). Closing statements: Linguistics and poetics. In T. A. Sebeok (Ed.), *Style in language*, pp. 350–377. Cambridge, MA: MIT Press.

Kvam, D. S. (2017). Supporting Mexican immigrants' resettlement in the United States: An ethnography of communication approach to building allies' communication competence. *Journal of Applied Communication Research, 45*(1), 1–20. doi:10.1080/ 00909882.2016.1248469

Lutz, C. (1986). Emotion, thought, and estrangement: Emotion as a cultural category. *Cultural Anthropology, 1*(3), 287–309.

Mouffe, C. (2000). Deliberative democracy or agonistic pluralism. *IHS Political Science Series, 72.* Retrieved from http://irihs.ihs.ac.at/1312/1/pw_72.pdf

Ong, W. J. (1981). *Fighting for life: Contest, sexuality, and consciousness.* Ithaca, NY: Cornell University Press.

Philipsen, G. (1986). Mayor Daley's council speech: A cultural analysis. *Quarterly Journal of Speech, 72,* 247–260.

Philipsen, G. (1992). *Speaking culturally: Explorations in social communication.* Albany, NY: SUNY Press.

Saito, M. (2009). *Silencing identity through communication: Situated enactments of sexual identity and emotion in Japan.* Saarbrücken, Germany: DVM Verlag Dr. Müller Aktiengesellschaft & Co. KG.

Scott, J. P., & Fredericson, E. (1951). The causes of fighting in mice and rats. *Physiological Zoology, 24*(4), 273–309.

Time Staff. (June 16, 2015). Here's Donald Trump's presidential announcement speech. Retrieved from http://time.com/3923128/donald-trump-announcement-speech/

United Farm Workers. (2017). The story of Cesar Chavez. Retrieved from http://ufw.org/ research/history/story-cesar-chavez

Waltman, M., & Haas, J. (2011). *The communication of hate.* Language and social action series (vol. 9). New York, NY: Peter Lang.

Wierzbicka, A. (1999). *Emotions across languages and cultures: Diversity and universals.* Cambridge: Cambridge University Press.

Wilkins, R. J. (2006). Agonistic depictions of communication: Vaikeneminen [silence] versus puhuminen [speaking] in classroom settings for adult education in Finland. *Atlantic Journal of Communication, 14*(4), 247–266.

Chapter Eleven

Policing the Boundaries of the Sayable

The Public Negotiation of Profane, Prohibited, and Proscribed Speech

Brion van Over, Gonen Dori-Hacohen,
and Michaela R. Winchatz

What can be said, and what cannot, is a problem peculiar to the metadiscursive capacity of language tangled up in the human mandate for a world of moral order. Kenneth Burke captures this tension in his definition of man as "the symbol-using (symbol-making, symbol-misusing) animal, inventor of the negative (or moralized by the negative), separated from his natural condition by instruments of his own making, goaded by the spirit of hierarchy (or moved by the sense of order), and rotten with perfection" (Burke, 1966, p. 16). Similarly, Becker states that what is not said and what cannot be said is one of the central elements of language use (Becker, 1988, p. 25). Both agree that we make and remake our social worlds, take up residence in them, moralize their righteousness, forget we made them (Carey, 2009), and, as Nietzsche (1977) worried, ultimately go to war over them.

However, the question of what can and cannot be said does not always enter the realm of public moral deliberation. Carbaugh (2007) suggests that cultural norms for speaking are not always well established, clearly defined, or broadly adopted. Some norms, for instance, may "crystallize" in a discursive community to a greater or lesser extent. Norms for speaking that are well crystallized may never be brought to the level of explicit verbal reflection because their prohibition is self-evident and entrenched in cultural practice in that what cannot be said is simply not. Conversely, certain sayings take on such cultural force that they must be said, lest the failure to speak be marked as a violation of the moral order, e.g., a husband who fails to wish his wife a "happy birthday." In the murky middle ground of norms for speaking lie those norms in a given speech community that are yet undecided and subject to public negotiation, wherein the future adoption of the norm, or not, is determined.

Wittgenstein (1922) in his Tractatus also takes up the issue of what can and cannot be said when he declares in the last sentence of the work, "whereof one cannot speak, thereof one must remain silent" (p. 90). Wittgenstein does not appear to be addressing the normative dimensions of speech, but rather the philosophical possibilities of expression in language, the potential limits of what language can or cannot accomplish. Wittgenstein claims that language does what it can, and what it can not is ultimately impossible to explore because language would *a priori* be incapable of doing it. While this claim may be philosophically defensible, van Over (2012), in studies of talk about the inexpressible in moments of everyday life, suggests that interactants are likely to hit the presumed and negotiated cultural boundaries of expression before the limits of linguistic or neurobiological capacities are reached. Van Over's work (2012) demonstrates the fundamentally cultural and negotiated nature of the limits of the "sayable" as interactants enact, maintain, and transform local and distinctive cultural premises about the uses and capabilities of linguistic expression.

Nor are these the only possible conceptualizations of the unsayable. To these we might add things that cannot be said because of a claimed capacity of a *particular* language, as in, "there's no word for it in English, but there is in German"; or things that cannot be said because of a temporary failure of competence: "I can't remember the word right now, but give me a minute, it'll come to me"; or things that cannot be said because of a presumed nontemporary failure of competence: "he lacks the verbal prowess to describe it."

Taken together, these considerations raise questions about the negotiation of the sayable, the premises of communication, emotion, place, personhood, and relations (Carbaugh, 2007) that are presumed and enacted in that negotiation, and the moral and normative dimensions of speaking. This means that interactions where the sayable is made a topically relevant discursive problem are of particular interest as they index the ongoing negotiation of the normative moral order while illustrating the potentially competing taken-for-granted cultural premises that inform any given debate about what can or cannot be said.

Below we examine three cases wherein a public negotiation of the normative dimensions of speaking are at play and analyze them from the vantage of cultural discourse analysis (Carbaugh, 2007). We expose the *agonistic discourses* (1988/1989) that dramatize, here, competing premises of communication and emotion with particular implications for the practice of political speech. First, we explore talk about "race" and "racism" as politicians and pundits admonish or praise talk about race as either a *reification* of the social relevance of race or as the means to *transform* racial inequality. Second, we examine the professional provocateur Milo Yiannopoulos and the controversy surrounding his various university speaking engagements, where Yiannopoulos and protesters clash over the potential harm of speech. Third, and in keeping with CuDA's comparative mode (2007), we examine the negotiation of the moral order in Israeli talk radio as callers and hosts draw and redraw the boundaries of culturally appropriate speech surrounding the Holocaust.

In each case we conclude that in the ongoing public performance of deliberation over race, the speech of a provocateur, or the Holocaust, conversation on the purported topic is eschewed by an ongoing metadiscourse that draws in agonistic premises of communication and emotions. These agonistic discourses betray a fragmented cultural landscape lacking shared premises about the nature of communication. The analysis points to the tension between individual agency and the structuring force of culture as interlocutors employ cultural premises of communication and emotion that enable particular political behavior in accomplishing the sometimes strategic ends of interlocutors.

STUDYING THE UNSAYABLE

Research on the culturally distinctive ways communities have imagined communication to work and the different forms presumed to accomplish that work has been central for ethnographers of communication (Hymes, 1964). Numerous theoretical developments have evolved from that concern including speech codes theory (Philipsen, Coutu, & Covarrubias, 2005), cultural communication (Philipsen, 1987), and cultural discourse analysis (CuDA henceforth, Carbaugh, 2007). These developments have benefited as well from complementary approaches like conversation analysis, and discourse analysis broadly conceived.

In our chapter, CuDA forms the conceptual lens and analytical tool. The adoption of this approach is ideal for explicating sets of competing cultural premises in our three cases, which play a role in the ongoing maintenance of entrenched political discourse. To conceptualize and draw attention to the particularly agonistic nature of these premises when they are played dialectically against one another, we draw on the concept of "agonistic discourse" (Carbaugh, 1988/1989; 1996).

Agonistic discourse serves a variety of analytical purposes, prominently including the demonstration of how focused attention on cultural discourses that play on a "deep agony" between discursive symbols can "add to an understanding of its production, performance, and moral assessment" and can "show how a single agonistic form constitutes a cultural communicative system of symbols and meanings" (Carbaugh, 1988/1989, p. 182). Carbaugh demonstrates the utility of the concept in his articulation of competing cultural symbols of "self" and "society." He demonstrates that these terms are drawn into discursive moments, implicating both the cultural value and mandate of "individuality," but also function as a performance of community, as interlocutors participate in a "system of contrastive meanings" (p. 197).

Carbaugh draws on Burke's (1969, pp. 19–23) formulation of the tension between "division" and "identification," which we attend to here in our use of the concept to draw attention to the ways the enactment of cultural premises of communication and emotion can function to member speakers of particular discursive communities, or as commonly aligned with particular principles, while also by the inverse highlighting and contrasting those we are not like.

However, Carbaugh reminds us that at base the concept is a cultural one as "the functions and structures of the agonistic form may be identifiable generally, its cultural contents—its local radiants of meaning—vary cross-culturally" (1988/1989, p. 206). Thus, we employ the concept as a means of discovery of the local meanings and enactments of a system of symbols that pits interlocutors' premises of communication and emotion against one another in a set of agonistic exchanges.

The relevance of the broader CuDA approach to a study of the (un)sayable has been demonstrated in previous research with great utility. One such exploration attends to enactments of silence performed by some American Indian students in a largely white U.S. university setting. Covarrubias and Windchief (2009) argue that American Indian silence, in some contexts, can be understood as an empowering and generative communicative action that serves to "particularize," "perpetuate," and "protect" cultural practices from non-Indians.

This identification of the use of a common cultural communicative practice, silence rather than the "telling of sacred stories" (p. 345) to outsiders, can then further serve to bond these students together in an enactment of communal membership and maintenance. We join this line of work investigating the meaningfulness of the boundary between speech and silence (Basso, 1996; Braithwaite, 1990; Carbaugh, Berry, & Nurmikari-Berry, 2006; Carbaugh, 1999; Milstein, 2008; Molina-Markham, 2014; Scollo, 2004). The cultural boundaries of what can and ought be communicated, to whom, and with what consequences are explored in the following analysis, first in two different cases that investigate public political discourse in U.S. contexts, and then in the speech of public Israeli political radio call-in shows.

THE CASE OF SPEAKING ABOUT RACE: TRANSFORMATION VERSUS REIFICATION[1]

First, we study a number of instances where public discourse about racial inequality and discrimination, and appropriate verbal or nonverbal actions for addressing these, are deployed in conversation with particular premises about the nature and function of communication taken-for-granted in the saying. These premises presume the very act of speaking to be either a transformative act that can be used to remake an unjust world through the power of speech, or a reifying one, where to speak at all merely infuses existing conditions with greater strength and persistence. We present instances of talk where each of these premises is evident as well as a blended instance where an agonistic discourse pitting these premises against each other is enacted.

1: President Obama: White House Convening on Building Community Trust, 4/13/16

After meeting with a variety of constituents, including police chiefs from various communities, Obama offered an address summarizing his sense of the consensus on how best to move forward on improving race relations in policing.

1	And finally, there was broad agreement that this needs to be sustained. I didn't
2	hear anybody around this table suggest that this problem is going to be solved
3	overnight. Because the roots of the problems we saw this week date back not just
4	decades, date back centuries. There are cultural issues, and there are issues of race
5	in this country, and poverty, and a whole range of problems that will not be
6	solved overnight. But what we can do is to set up the kinds of respectful
7	conversations that we've had here—not just in Washington, but around the
8	country—so that we institutionalize a process of continually getting better, and
9	holding ourselves accountable, and holding ourselves responsible for getting
10	better.

President Obama notes that the problems highlighted by recent tensions between police and members of the African American community are the result of issues that "date back not just decades, date back centuries" (1:3–4). He continues that these problems "will not be solved overnight," contributing to his framing of the issues as particularly entrenched, presumably requiring powerful and sustained methods to address. His solution (1:6–7) is "respectful conversations," but not conversations that can be had only once, or only in one place, but ones that must be had "around the country." President

Obama moves to forward "conversations," a deeply cultural form of communicative practice (Carbaugh, 2007), as a powerful way of addressing historical issues of "race" and "poverty."

Obama's proposed solution of "conversations" relies on the premise that no singular communicative act is powerful enough to affect the required change, but perhaps "conversations" that continue across time and space can be leveraged to create transformative change, to make sure things are "continually getting better" (1:8). It is not necessarily given that communication be conceived as a proper and appropriate means of addressing "race" and "poverty"; in fact, as we see in later instances, other opposing premises can be and are invoked. However, Obama's approach is not surprising either, given the centrality of "communication" in many U.S. cultural scenes (Katriel & Philipsen, 1981).

In the following instance, the agonistic nature of these cultural discourses is analyzed as Howard Schultz, CEO of Starbucks, announces a plan to write "race together" on coffee cups as a way of stimulating conversation about racism. Audio of the announcement is played on Fox's TV show *The Five*, where pundit Greg Gutfeld reacts. We first analyze Schultz's announcement, followed by Gutfeld's reaction.

2.1: Fox, *The Five*, 3/17/15

1	What can we do to create more empathy, compassion, more understanding, not
2	only within our own company but how can we do it so that we elevate that sense
3	of humanity inside our stores with our customers. . . . So what if we were—what if
4	we were to write "race together" on every Starbucks cup. And if a customer asks
5	you what this is, try and engage in the discussion, that we have problems in this
6	country with regard to race and racial inequality. You can do that with one
7	customer a day, then we're making significant progress as we go forward.

Schultz states as his explicit goal the creation of "empathy, compassion, understanding," (2.1:1) and "humanity" (2.1:3). This can be accomplished, in his view, by "engaging in discussion" (2.1:5) on the "problems" of "race and racial inequality" (2.1:5–6) in the service of "making significant progress" to go "forward" (2.1:7). Schultz then employs a term for talk (Carbaugh, 1989) cast here as "discussion" and related to Obama's "conversation." His talk, like Obama's, shares in the premise that talk can not only transform powerful social issues like "race and racial inequality," but also the very personhood of those who engage in the "discussion," as they become more "human" through the discursive process.

Also, similarly to Obama, Schultz formulates "discussion" as a force productive of a new future, which can help "make progress as we go forward," or as in Obama's talk, "continually getting better." "Discussion" or "conversations," then, are the preferred tools for producing personal and social change, and are the primary and appropriate means conceived for doing so. Conversely, silence is the perpetuation of the status quo, where inaction, a refusal to speak, is a tacit agreement to continue as we are, to not "get better." Note here that the generative and transformative capacity of speech in "conversations" or "discussion" is not seen as something dangerous, or in need of control, as it might be (see below).

In the service of exposing the premises informing the above instances for explicit comparison with the instances that follow, and in keeping with the "comparative" analytical mode of CuDA, we offer the following articulation of cultural premises derived from the above analysis.

Cultural Premise 1: Talk can transform our reality into something better.

Cultural Premise 2: Difficult and persistent social issues, like racism, are best addressed through sustained conversation about the issue.

The instance below is Gutfeld's reaction to Schultz's announcement (2.1). Gutfeld enacts an agonistic discourse that challenges the presumed nature of communication that informs Schultz's talk.

2.2: Fox, *The Five*, 3/17/15

8	When anybody ever says that they want to start a conversation, what they're
9	saying is I want you to agree that we are right and you are wrong. So I will bet
10	you the conversation on race will come down to you're probably an unconscious
11	racist. You live in a racist country. And there needs to be change from within.
12	But do not berate me on race while I'm holding a cup of hot coffee, because
13	then it's going to be on you.
14	[. . .]
15	And also, there's a fundamental misunderstanding here with what—what
16	Americans conceive in the world of conversation where race lies. We're not like
17	the media. We don't like to sit around and talk about race, because frankly, most
18	of us don't give a damn. We go on and do—look at St. Patrick's Day right now.
19	I'm seeing every color drunk out there, having a good time. They don't—if you
20	think Ferguson is emblematic of the United States, then you're an idiot who only
21	listens to CNN and MSNBC, because it's not. The only time race ever comes up
22	is when somebody is looking for a fight. That's all it is.

For Gutfeld, racism is not the problem Schultz and Obama assert it is. Racism exists in the minority, in "Ferguson" (2.2:20), and "conversation" (2.2:8) about race is for those "looking for a fight" (2.2:22). For him, only those who want to live in a world where race continues to matter would talk about it, because the rest of us "don't give a damn" (2.2:18). For Gutfeld, *talk about race* is the real problem. "Conversation" does not serve the purposes Obama and Schultz presume of "getting better" but rather serves to transform the identity of your conversational partner into that of an "unconscious racist" (2.2:10–11). In this way, both Schultz and Gutfeld presume talk to have transformative power over identity; however, "conversation," a term for talk also employed by Obama, where talk is presumed to be transformative of social life, is here problematized as a practice akin to media dramatization, where "conversation" as conceived by "Americans" (2.2:16) means "sitting around talking about race" (2.2:17), and hence worsening a problem where only a marginal one exists. In this instance, the taken-for-granted nature of "conversation" about race is one of reification, rather than transformation.

3: Fox, *Hannity*, 3/20/15

Here, Jason Riley, Sean Hannity, and Deroy Murdock discuss Dick Durbin's criticism of the Senate for delays in Loretta Lynch's confirmation to attorney general. Durbin is accused of "playing the race card" and a discussion about motivations for Democrats' talk about race ensues.

1	The Left is obsessed with identity politics. They want to divvy us up by race and
2	gender and so forth and then play us against one another. They claim, as Al Gore
3	did, that they want a colorblind society. That's the last thing they want. They
4	want to drag race into our national discussions, keep it front and center. That's
5	what they depend on to garner votes from their constituents.

Riley attributes particular motivations to "the Left" (3:1) for continually "dragging race into our national discussions" (3:4). The purported goal of "the Left" in having these ongoing discussions is not, according to Riley, to achieve the "colorblind society" (3:3) they presumably desire, but rather to "play us against one another" (3:2) in order to "garner votes" (3:5). The ongoing "conversations" and "discussions" about race so fiercely advocated in the previous instances are not presumed to be productive of the purported goal of a postracial world. Talk about race is presumed to be strategic, something that keeps race in the public consciousness, that reifies existing divides and boundaries, and that does so for political ends.

We can hear a competing premise of communication in strong contrast to the premises above.

Cultural Premise 3: Talk reifies conditions in their existing composition and may worsen an existing problem.

Presumably, then, the best and most appropriate way to address race in U.S. society is silence. Because talk continually speaks race into being, silence is necessary and is the only response that serves the counterpurpose of moving beyond the problems of racial division; hence:

Cultural Premise 4: Difficult and persistent social issues, like racism, are best addressed through sustained silence about them.

Having explicated a set of agonistic premises of communication that formulate conversation as either transformative or reifying, we next present an analysis of premises, again as in the first case, entwined in an agonistic discourse that formulates speech as harmless and provocative versus powerful and dangerous.

THE CASE OF SPEAKING AS A PROFESSIONAL PROVOCATEUR[2]

We turn to Milo Yiannopoulos—a self-proclaimed "professional provocateur," British journalist, and former senior editor of the conservative website Breitbart News. Between 2015 and 2017, Yiannopoulos embarked on his "Dangerous Faggot" tour that included stops at universities across the United States, with the goal of talking about his views on free expression and entertainment.

His appearance at DePaul University—a private Vincentian and Catholic university in Chicago, Illinois—was spurred by an invitation from the DePaul College Republicans. Prior to this, there were various events on the DePaul campus that had led to racial tensions (Chang, 2016), leading to strong opposition from Black Lives Matter supporters regarding Yiannopoulos's upcoming talk. These events resulted in a change.org petition ("Stop hate speech") that called for the administration to cancel the talk. The "Yiannopoulos event at DePaul" reportedly had 550 audience members in attendance with hundreds more outside of the event space who protested the speaker's presence on the campus. Approximately 15 minutes into the event, Black Lives Matter protesters took over the stage and did not allow the event to continue. Despite the presence of security and the arrival of the Chicago Police Department, the protesters were not removed. After approximately 25 minutes, Yiannopoulos stopped the event.

Our analysis shows that there exists an agonistic discourse between Yiannopoulos and the protesters regarding the cultural premises that underlie communication itself (Carbaugh, 2007). Yiannopoulos is known for making controversial statements, e.g., calling feminism a "cancer" (Yiannopoulos,

2016), Black Lives Matter "the last socially accepted hate group" (Kew, 2016), and has called for President Trump to deport "fat people" (Mauff, 2017). In a CNN report (Lieberman and Urbany), when asked if he believes what he is doing is dangerous (a probable reference to his "Dangerous Faggot Tour" title), Yiannopoulos responded:

4: Yiannopoulos in CNN Interview, 2/2/2017

1   No, it's a joke. Do I look dangerous to you? Do I look like somebody that
2   students need to be protected from? I don't think so. The whole point of it is
3   to draw attention to the absurdity of what the Left has been doing.
4   Muddying the waters between language and action, you know? You hear on
5   college campuses a lot these days threats to students "safety." Well there is
6   no threat to student safety from people who have different political opinions
7   or different ideas. That's ridiculous.

Similarly, on Bill Maher's *Real Time* (2/17/17) he said:

8   What actually hurts people is things that actually happen in the real world. I
9   mean, I don't go on about it because I'm not a professional victim . . . But—
10   what actually hurts people is like murder, violence—you know, that kind of
11   stuff—mean words doesn't [*sic*] hurt people.

Yiannopoulos characterizes his goal (4:3): "to draw attention to the absurdity of what the Left has been doing." He thus creates oppositional identities between himself and "the Left."[3] This opposition is based on what he ascribes to the Left, i.e., an expansive view of the unsayable. For him, the Left censors speech due to "safety" and in order to not "hurt" people, which his premises of communication reject.

Yiannopoulos's premises of communication differentiate speech and action as completely separate and distinctive entities. For him, words are not "things that actually happen in the real world" (4:8). Further, the things that happen in the real world are the only things that can do harm to individuals; specifically, such things as "murder" and "violence" (4:10). Concomitant to casting the activity in which he engages—public speaking appearances—as a "joke," he simultaneously characterizes jokes as a type of activity from which students (his target audience) need not be protected. Students' "safety" (a term he uses nonverbal "air quotes" to mark in the video) is then noted as something that gets talked about on university campuses. Finally, the term "hurt" (4:8,10,11) points to premises of feeling, emotion, and affect (Carbaugh, 2007). For Yiannopoulos, there is "real world" hurt, which includes harm that can be done to a person's physical self, and the hurt that "mean words" (4:11) may cause to a person's feelings. The latter of these does not count nor concern Yiannopoulos, which is made evident when he famously yelled "fuck your feelings" to a female protester at a University of Houston event (Yiannopoulos, 2016).

We have gleaned from the propositions found in Yiannopoulos's utterances the following premises of communication:

Cultural Premise 5: Speech is innocuous and because no speech should be censored, everything falls within the realm of the sayable. And, Cultural Premise 6: Speech and action should not be equated. [4]

Yiannopoulos understands himself to be undertaking innocuous, nonharmful, nonthreatening activity when he speaks, and he is not dangerous. Hence, these cultural premises, while not necessarily aligned with how communication theorists and practitioners understand the power or force of communication (see Philipsen et al., 2005), are central to Yiannopoulos's understandings of what he is (and is not) doing when he speaks. It is a cultural premise that encounters a deep agony (Carbaugh, 1988/1989) in the discursive struggles between the provocateur and his protesters.

In contrast to Yiannopoulos's premises, those who protest him as a public speaker engage in the counter to the first half of this agonistic dialogue by deeming his communication as anything but innocuous and sayable.

5: change.org petition to DePaul administration, 5/24/2016

1   The problematic and xenophobic statements and ideologies promoted by Milo
2   Yiannopoulos are outraging. He perpetuates the dangerous systems of
3   oppression that exist in our world and, as a result, on our campus. From the
4   name of his tour which includes a homophobic slur—to the violently oppressive
5   commentary he has made in the past, it is our belief that his presence will
6   ultimately bring harm to the students on our campus. . . . What makes Milo
7   Yiannopoulos' presence as a speaker on campus particularly violent is the fact
8   that he promotes—and attempts to legitimize many of the systems of oppression
9   that currently affect marginalized communities, as well as being a vocal
10 proponent of ideologies that constitute as hate speech. . . . The systemic
11 oppression of these communities is not a form of "intellectual thought," nor is it
12 just "someone's opinion." It is not a tool for an entertainer to use and classify
13 as "pop culture" or "sensationalism" to turn a profit. . . . It is real, it hurts people,
14 and it kills.

6: Female student on DePaul Campus at live-streamed interview, 5/24/2016 (Tubesocks, 2016)

1   He is violent. The words that he says—the rhetoric—racist, sexist bullshit—that is
2   violent.

Protesters and petitioners alike characterize Yiannopoulos's practice of communicating as "xenophobic" (5:1), "homophobic" (5:4), "racist," "sexist" (6:1), "oppressive" (5:4), "violent" (6:2), and "hate speech" (5:10). They also state what Yiannopoulos's speech is *not*: "a form of 'intellectual thought'" (5:11); "just 'someone's opinion'" (5:12); a "tool" for him to use (5:12); "pop culture"; or "sensationalism" (5:13). Beyond the characterizations of his speech are descriptions of what Yiannopoulos's speech accomplishes in the world with various actions (e.g., "perpetuates" (5:2), "promotes" (5:8), and "attempts to legitimize" (5:8) the "dangerous systems of oppression" (5:2–3) that "currently affect marginalized communities" (5:9). Premises of feeling, emotion, and affect also play a role here, in that the petitioners call Yiannopoulos's communication "outraging" (5:2), which seems to be combined with a sense of urgency by the petitioners to have him barred from speaking at the campus. Also, premises of relating and relationships are at play since petitioners place in contrast the "students on our campus" (5:6) and "marginalized communities" on one side and Yiannopoulos, an "entertainer" (5:12), who will "ultimately bring harm" (5:6), on the other.

The protesters' cultural premises can be summarized in the following premises:

Cultural Premise 7: Speech is hurtful and not everything is sayable.

Cultural Premise 8: Speech and action should be equated.

This interpretive move references a clear counter in this agonistic discourse to Yiannopoulos's premises (CP5 and CP6 above). Unlike Yiannopoulos's clear separation and distinction between speech and action, the protesters and petitioners do not share this cultural premise. According to them, the provocateur's speech may commit heinous acts in the real world. Further, the protesters' premise 7 also points to Covarrubias, Kvam, and Saito's (this volume) premise six of "symbolic agonistics"; specifically, that these "forecast adversarial emotive frames." That is, the discourse between Yiannopoulos and the protesters clearly marks combativeness, anger, and "dig an emotional terrain" that will extend beyond this one moment in time.

Further, while the petitioners labeled Yiannopoulos as one who engages in "hate speech" (5:10), there appears to be no distinction made by the petitioners between the interpretation of his speech as a *direct* cause of harm, hurt, or even death to certain individuals and what Boromisza-Habashi (2013) terms an "audience-oriented interpretation" (p. 33). Specifically, an audience-oriented interpretation of hate speech is one that points to a third party, in that the speaker may persuade and/or incite a third individual or group to commit real-world acts of violence on others. In this data segment, rather than make the claim that Yiannopoulos's speech may incite others to commit heinous and harmful acts, the protesters and petitioners equate his speech with the act of violence. Here, the topic addressed or the arguments made by Yiannopoulos are not the focus of the talk; rather, for the speakers holding these cultural premises (CP7,8), the act of Yiannopoulos communicating is itself so destructive and violent to "students" and "marginalized communities" that it must be stopped.

We turn to our final case wherein the normative propriety of talk about the Holocaust, and what is presumed and enacted when speaking about it publicly, are foreground.

THE CASE OF SPEAKING ABOUT THE HOLOCAUST[5]

When discussing the boundaries of what is allowed to be said (or the sayable) in Israeli radio phone-ins, we explore cultural premises of communication that inform the production and interpretation of talk in this context. In studying these premises, we can see a recurrent pattern regarding the setting of boundaries of communication as these are negotiated between the participants. Additionally, in our data, the negotiation of the sayable often leads to a performance of extreme emotions from the host, which is not the usual case in these shows; as such, the sayable and the unsayable in this scene are part of the symbolic agonistics (Covarrubias, Kvam, & Saito, this volume) of the Israeli culture. In the following interaction, the caller begins criticizing left-wing supporters, which leads to the following exchange:

7: TTST, Host, Dalik Volinitz; Caller, Yehoshu, 12/13/2004

1	Host:	you despise it for its political opinions.
2		great part of it, in your opinion
3	Caller:	why do you insert words in my mouth?
4	H:	wait, sec let me wait a sec wait
5	C:	I am a Holocaust remnant ((sarid))
6	H:	I—
7	C:	I don't despise any Jew.
8	H:	but but wait wait. wait.
9	C:	I—I'm against

10	H:	Yohoshua, do me a favor. Goddam—took you two minutes and you
11		brought in the Holocaust. Do me a favor. Leave the a— pay respect
12		to the Holocaust. And don't get it into this conversation.

The host describes the caller's position as hateful toward certain parties in Israeli politics. The caller then protests this characterization, amid interruption and overlaps. The caller continues to hold the floor and uses his identity as a Holocaust survivor (although he refrains from this term and uses a different one in Hebrew) as the basis for his rejecting the host's characterization. The host succeeds in securing the floor and then with extreme language (Goddam-, 7:10), which includes requesting a favor, he asks for the caller to "leave a— pay respect to the Holocaust." The host then requests, directly, that the caller not use the Holocaust in the interaction.

The caller makes relevant his identity as a "Holocaust remnant" in support of his claim that he doesn't "despise any Jew" (7:7). This talk presumes the relevance of his identity and personal experiences to whatever follows, and enacts a premise that talk about the Holocaust is permissible, relevant, and necessary for a proper hearing of the meaning of his claim. For the caller, identity and meaning are intertwined, and he appears to fear that his prior utterances will be misunderstood by the host ("I don't despise any Jew," 7:7) if not put in context with his claim to identity, "I am a Holocaust remnant" (7:5). This premise can then be formulated as:

Cultural Premise 9: Identity and meaning are tightly connected in communication.

Yet the host enacts the opposite premise. His talk presumes that the identity of a Holocaust survivor is not pertinent or allowable in the discussion, and that meaning can be expressed and interpreted without reference to this identity, "don't get it into this conversation" (7:12). These are competing premises for communication and personhood, which are tightly connected to the boundaries of what is allowed to be said.

Although the segment includes references to emotion from the beginning ("despise" 7:1,7), performance of emotion is limited. Yet when the caller mentions the Holocaust, the host reacts with a performance of emotion by using the explicative "goddam" (7:10). That the host's performance of emotion is not problematized or called into question in the interaction is suggestive of the appropriateness of such a response to mention of the Holocaust, and the legitimacy of the normative prohibition on such speech. The host provides an account for why such a reaction is justified and why such speech ought be prohibited—out of respect, although it is unclear respect toward whom. The following agonistic premise can then be formulated:

Cultural Premise 10: Talk about the Holocaust is connected to powerful emotions, which may be harmful if spoken.

This premise appears further connected to a norm for speaking in this context that might be articulated in the following way: *Some topics, such as the Holocaust, should be treated with respect, demonstrated through silence.*

This segment also suggests that the mere invocation of the Holocaust is outside the realm of the sayable, yet this boundary is negotiable, and can be set at a different location in the talk as the following excerpt shows.

8: TSTT, Host, Ehud Graf; Caller, Ben David, 1/31/2005

1	Caller:	And I as a Holocaust survivor,
2	Host:	Yes,
3	C:	Come and ask, why did it need to take sixty years.

(A) Later in the interaction:

4	H:	As someone who tries uhm to look on thing uhm in a way, a fuller way.
5		Although I of course, was not (living) in the era, that you,
6		unfortunately, had to experience.

And later:

7	C:	Maybe a blunt sentence, but I have no choice.
8		That what, in the Holocaust, we had kapos, and here we have
9	H:	David. David. David. I really request. Please. Let's not let
10	C:	No no. there are here pre-Kapos.
11	H:	No no no no no.
12	C:	They act like Kapos.
13	H:	No.
14	C:	By the way.
15	H:	David. David. No. No more. No more (ad kan, ad kan). I also have some
16		kind of a role, uh, god forgive me,
17	C:	Ok. I thank you
18	H:	A humble.
19	C:	For letting me talk.
20	H:	No no no. I—no no. I want to ask you an additional thing.

The caller also establishes an identity of a Holocaust survivor (8:1). The host then accepts the invocation of this identity (8:2), unlike the instance above.

Then, the caller brings up the Holocaust again (8:8), likely with some sense it may be provocative as he provides a disclaimer "but I have no choice" (8:7). The caller, then, appears to understand this use of the Holocaust is not the same as his initial claim to the survivor identity, as he invokes the Holocaust to compare some Israeli politicians to the pre-Kapo and Kapo—the Jews who cooperated with the Nazis at the different concentration camps (8:8,10,12). Indeed, the caller's concerns are justified and the host rejects this comparison. He emphasizes his role as a host (8:18), while using strong repetitive language to prevent the caller from presenting this comparison. Moreover, he invokes a divinity plea in his efforts to stop this line of talk (8:18). The caller takes this stopping to be an end to their conversation, yet the host continues their discussion (not shown here).

This use of the Holocaust in comparing a current politician to someone who cooperated with the Nazis, rather than as a personal claim to identity, is cast as unsayable here. Although the caller may work on the premise that being a Holocaust survivor allows him to say difficult and blunt things, the host rejects this position. The caller's premise of communication appears to be shared with the prior caller (7), and while the host in this instance also appears to share in the premise that *identity and meaning are connected in communication*, he appears to share a premise of emotion with the host from the prior instance that *talk about the Holocaust is connected to powerful emotions, which may be harmful if spoken.*

The host's premises for speaking in this instance allow for the Holocaust to be invoked as a personal identity claim, but they become a normative violation when used as a means to degrade the identity of another, i.e., the politician in question. This norm might be formulated as: *One ought not use the Holocaust to impugn the character or motives of another.*

As in the other cases, saying the unsayable leads the host to set strong boundaries by using his role as host to empower his demarcation of the normatively sayable in this context. In both interactions, host and callers negotiate the boundary of the sayable as it relates to Holocaust discourse. In each instance, the normative boundary of the sayable is shifted, with the legitimacy of invoking a "survivor" identity informed by differing premises on the interconnectedness of identity, personal experience, and meaning. However, norms also emerge for how the Holocaust might be invoked in discourse with one drawing the boundary at any mention, and the other drawing the boundary at its invocation for political or social ends, rather than as a deeply felt claim to personal experience.

DISCUSSION

While spatial limitations preclude a complete reprinting of cultural premises identified throughout, we draw attention to the overarching themes, where each case deals in some central way with *the consequentiality of speaking*. In the first case, agonistic premises of communication were enacted in discourse surrounding whether the very act of speaking reified social conditions or transformed them. This discourse is usefully understood as "agonistic" in the "system of contrastive meanings" that inform and motivate it. In this case, these contrastive meanings include prominent cultural symbols of "conversation" and "discussion," which are meant in the premises of some members of the community to create identification and unity, while in others are presumed to be divisive when the topic is race. Race as a symbol is also part of this contrastive system as its invocation for some members is connected to the ongoing reality of poverty, oppression, and material inequality, while for other members it is a specious strategic manipulation meant only for political gain. This discourse then shares common features of other agonistic discourses employing Burke's conceptualization of division and identification as in the "self" versus "society" agon identified by Carbaugh (1988/1989).

In the second case, similarly agonistic premises of communication and emotion were enacted surrounding whether speaking functioned as an intellectual *and* emotional act with harmful consequences or as a purely intellectually innocuous engagement. Here, the function of division and identification can also be located in this system of contrastive meanings as Yiannopolous and his supporters identify through the divisiveness of his rhetoric. Premises of communication then become a means by which to highlight membership in this community and bound those who are not alike.

In the third case, agonistic premises of communication and emotion were enacted surrounding whether speaking about the Holocaust was a necessary part of the meaning-making of the interaction or could be left out with no detriment, and whether speaking about the Holocaust was so emotionally powerful that its potential harm to listeners was unacceptable. Again, functions of identification and division in the contrastive symbol of the "holocaust" as its public deployment members those "remnants" as having shared powerfully meaningful and relevant experience while also creating division in the apparent violation of the public moral code characterized as a "disrespectful" use.

In each case, then, the normative boundary of the sayable is shifted as interlocutors negotiate the meaning of the act of speaking at all. The question of what it *does* to speak is negotiated in interaction as cultural interlocutors bring differing premises to bear in the local enactments of the answer to this question. We propose this agon over *the consequentiality of communication* and the power it is presumed, or not, to yield as a broader question, agonized over in multiple cultural and cross-cultural contexts, akin to Carbaugh's (1988/1989) identification of the "self" versus "society" agon.

The analyses of the cases above suggest three main conclusions. The first of these stems from our noticing that agonistic discourse between and within speech communities oftentimes appears to be about a particular topic, e.g., race or the Holocaust; however, the real deep agony ends up being about what the members of each speech community understand the communication about the topic to be doing (or not doing). Communication about the topic becomes the focus rather than the topic itself, which points to competing cultural premises of and for communication and emotion that underlie the agonistic discourse between interlocutors.

This potential obfuscation over whether we are debating the topic, or communication itself, obscures a potentially productive conversation examining members' taken-for-granted assumptions about the workings of communication, out of which might emerge an intersubjective consensus that allows debate about the actual topic to proceed. We recognize it is possible that the persistent shift of topical debate to metadiscursive commentary may be a strategic avoidance. Nevertheless, we conclude that there is a lack of common social consensus about the function of communication in social life. One can simply look at the stark distinction between the popular children's limerick "sticks and stones may break my bones but words will never hurt me," juxtaposed with the infamous biblical declaration, "in the beginning was the Word . . . and the Word was God" (John 1:1, The New King James Version) for evidence of this rift.

Our second conclusion, and following from the first, is that the field of communication, as compared to disciplines like psychology, has not well disseminated to the public what of our theories we are generally quite confident about. For instance, while Yiannopoulos frequently asserts the inactive nature of his speech, numerous theorists in the discipline have demonstrated the inherent connection between speech and action (e.g., Austin, 1962; Schegloff, 1995). Communication research suggests that talk has both the power to reify and transform; to be exploratory and consequential; to be a deeply personal testimony and a violation of fair play (as seen in our data). All communication serves multiple simultaneous functions of relational and cultural maintenance, as well as transformation—this is a dialectic, not a dichotomy (Bakhtin, 1992). The question, then, whether in a debate on race, the speech of a provocateur, or the Holocaust, is most usefully formulated as, what are we making of this talk, to what purposes is it put, and toward what future does that lead us? What matters in determining whether a given communication act reifies or transforms, offends or identifies, harms or explores, are the participants, setting, topic, ends, and the sequential organization of previous acts to which the act in question is understood as relevant and responsive to, among others. Perhaps a better understanding about the practice of communication might allow us to focus instead on questions about the consequences of *particular* speech rather than on debates about speech itself.

Our final conclusion addresses the tension between agency and structure in our discussions of culture, cultural premises, and action. The notion of the cultural premise as a preconscious implicit taken-for-granted piece of a shared cultural symbolic system can seem to strip the agency of interlocutors as they produce their own meanings and interpret the speech of others. And while this is not the way we use the concept here, it may seem, upon first glance, that a cultural premise functions something like a coding system in this machinery, passively sitting behind the scenes furthering the process of meaning-making. However, while cultural premises certainly can be said to form a shared foundation for the production and interpretation of speech, this work seeks to yield some agency back to interlocutors as the analysis presented here suggests that, in each case, the premises that are informing the discourse of each speaker also enable and complement both their larger ideological positions and the accomplishment of their local strategic ends for the interaction. For example, Yiannopoulos's cultural premises of communication that *speech is innocuous and everything is sayable* enable his particular brand of provocation and serve as a defense to those who would problematize the consequences of his speech, and which further provides him direct financial benefits. In the case of speaking about the Holocaust, the radio host's premises of communication enable him to assert a local enactment of his authority as "host" to silence the caller, and in the talk of speakers aligned with conservative ideologies adopt premises of communication that enable the promotion of silence in response to racism as well as attacks on political opponents. A similar finding regarding the strategic use of agonistic discourse is articulated in Covarrubias, Kvam, and Saito's work in this volume.

This means that cultural premises ought not be treated as simply lurking behind the cultural scene, but may be (dis)aligned from a field of alternate premises precisely because they enable the kind of ideology and action desired by the speaker. To be clear, we do not mean to suggest that speakers choose premises from a cultural salad bar to suit their momentary strategic ends, but rather to point to the tension between the structuring force of culture and human agency within which cultural premises, and all human social life, exists.

Lastly, we adopted cultural discourse analysis as our primary lens and analytical tool, but space limited our ability to fully explore other radiants that were active in our data. In retrospect, we find the particular strength of the approach in connecting discourse to the cultural environment in which it is produced, which is often drawn outside of the focal range of other approaches to the analysis of interaction. We thus find the flexibility of the approach to be productively put to a range of data whether gathered through ethnographic participant observation, or public mediated texts, to be of superior utility.

NOTES

1. The data for the section titled "The Case of Speaking about Race: Transformation vs. Reification" are conceptually bound by talk designed for public audiences and disseminated through mediated channels that include explicit reference to "race," or "racism," or "color-blind," and "communication," and/or "politics." Data were collected through a search of these keywords in popular search engines and private news media databases such as LexisNexis. Data were then included on the basis of explicit verbal attribution of racism, behavior characterized as racist, or the continuing social relevance of race to communication practices. Data were collected and reviewed until a saturation of the diversity of characterizations of the relationship between race and talk were achieved. Data from each of the available characterizations of the relationship between race and communication were included in equal number here, though no claims are made as to an equivalent regularity in discourse of these characterizations. Textual data that were already transcribed were not modified and include a sufficient level of paralinguistic features for the purposes of this analysis. Data where audio sources could be located were transcribed in accordance with the practices of conversation analysis.

2. The data for the section titled "The Case of Speaking as a Professional Provacateur" centered on an event that took place on May 24, 2016, on the campus of DePaul University—a Catholic and Vincentian private university located in Chicago, Illinois. Milo Yiannopoulos—British journalist, then senior editor for Breitbart News, and professional provocateur—was invited by the College Republicans of DePaul University to present as part of his "Dangerous Faggot" tour. A transcription was completed of a 25-minute video that was available online and began with Black Lives Matter protesters taking over the DePaul stage until Milo Yiannopoulos called for the event to end. A second transcription was completed of segments of a 1-hour podcast (Episode 10 of the *Milo Yiannopoulos Show*) during which Yiannopolous interviews two of DePaul's College Republicans who were present during the DePaul event and protest. Two transcriptions of interviews with Milo Yiannopolous that took place on February 2, 2017, and February 29, 2017, respectively were also completed. These transcripts as well as approximately 12 articles that featured news coverage of the DePaul event and its aftermath from news outlets that are on the continuum between conservative (Breitbart) and liberal (ThinkProgress) complete the data set for this section of our study.

3. On this opposition between "right" and "left" in a different context, see Dori-Hacohen and Shavit (2013).

4. We note here that the formulation of cultural premises in this case reflect an innovative use of CuDA to discern the premises implicitly formulated in Yiannopolous's speech, which are ratified in his followers' celebration of this discourse. Often premises are formulated initially through study of a given speech community, but in the case Yiannopolous's speech may function to call a community into being.

5. The data collection for Case 3 was part of a larger project discussing the public sphere in Israel as it is constructed by radio phone-in programs (see Dori-Hacohen, 2014, for more details). Out of that corpus, all mentions of the Holocaust were collected, and the clearest are presented and discussed here.

REFERENCES

Austin, J. L. (1962). *How to do things with words*. Oxford, UK: Clarendon Press.
Bakhtin, M. (1992). *The dialogic imagination: Four essays*. Austin, TX: University of Texas Press.
Basso, K. H. (1996). *Wisdom sits in places: Landscape and language among the Western Apache*. Albuquerque, NM: University of New Mexico Press.

Becker, A. L. (1988). Language in particular: A lecture. In D. Tannen (Ed.), *Linguistics in context: Connecting observation and understanding* (pp. 20–29). Norwood, NJ: Ablex.

Boromisza-Habashi, D. (2013). *Speaking hatefully: Culture, communication, and political action in Hungary*. University Park, PA: The Pennsylvania State University Press.

Braithwaite, C. A. (1990). Communicative silence: A cross-cultural study of Basso's hypothesis. In D. Carbaugh (Ed.), *Cultural communication and intercultural contact* (pp. 321–327). Hillsdale, NJ: Erlbaum.

Burke, K. (1966). *Language as symbolic action*. Berkeley and Los Angeles: University of California Press.

Cameron, D. (1998). "Is there any ketchup, Vera?": Gender, power, and pragmatics. *Discourse and Society, 9*(4), 437–455.

Carbaugh, D. (1988/1989). Deep agony: "Self" and "society" in *Donahue* discourse. *Research on Language and Social Interaction, 22*, 179–212.

Carbaugh, D. (1989). Fifty terms for talk: A cross-cultural study. *International and Intercultural Communication Annual, 13*(93), pp. 93–120.

Carbaugh, D. (1996). *Situating selves: The communication of social identities in American scenes*. Albany, NY: SUNY Press.

Carbaugh, D. (1999). "Just listen": "Listening" and landscape among the Blackfeet. *Western Journal of Communication, 63*(3), 250–270.

Carbaugh, D. (2007). Cultural discourse analysis: Communication practices and intercultural encounters. *Journal of Intercultural Communication Research, 36*(3), 167–182.

Carbaugh, D., Berry, M., & Nurmikari-Berry, M. (2006). Coding personhood through cultural terms and practices: Silence and quietude as a Finnish "natural way of being." *Journal of Language and Social Psychology, 25*(3), 1–18.

Carey, J. W. (2009). A cultural approach to communication. In *Communication as Culture* (pp. 13–36). New York, NY: Routledge.

Chang, S. H. (June 7, 2016). Trump supporter Milo Yiannopoulos furthers racial hatred at DePaul University. ThinkProgress. Retrieved from https://thinkprogress.org/trump-supporter-milo-yiannopoulos-furthers-racial-hatred-at-depaul-university-ac5468a9e436

Covarrubias, P., & Windchief, S. (2009). Silences in stewardship: Some American Indian examples. *The Howard Journal of Communications, 20*(3), 1–20.

Dori-Hacohen, G. (2014). Establishing social groups in Hebrew: "We" in political radio phone-in programs. In T.-S. Pavlidou (Ed.), *Constructing collectivity: "We" across languages and contexts* (pp. 187–206). Amsterdam: John Benjamins.

Dori-Hacohen, G., & Shavit, N. (2013). The cultural meanings of Israeli *Tokbek* (talk-back online commenting) and their relevance to the online democratic public sphere. *International Journal of Electronic Governance, 6*(4), 361–379.

Hymes, D. H. (Ed.). (1964). *Language in culture and society: A reader in linguistics and anthropology*. New York, NY: Harper & Row.

Katriel, T., & Philipsen, G. (1981). "What we need is communication": "Communication" as a cultural category in some American speech." *Communication Monographs, 48*, 302–317.

Kew, B. (December 13, 2016). Milo: Black Lives Matter is "the last socially acceptable hate group." Breitbart. Retrieved from http://www.breitbart.com/milo/2016/12/13/milo-black-lives-matter-last-socially-acceptable-hate-group/

Lieberman, D., & Urbany, B. (February 2, 2017). Milo Yiannopoulos is trying to convince colleges that hate speech is cool. CNN. Retrieved from http://www.cnn.com/2017/02/02/us/milo-yiannopoulos-ivory-tower/

Maher, B., Carter, S. Griffiths, S., & Martin, B. (writers), & Maher, B., Gurvitz, M., & Martin, B. (producers). (February 17, 2017). *Real Time with Bill Maher* [Television series episode]. In Real Time with Bill Maher, Los Angeles, CA: HBO.

Mauff, J. (June 25, 2017). Milo Yiannopoulos rails against liberals, Muslims, feminism, and "fat acceptance" at CU Boulder. *CU Independent*. Retrieved from https://cuindependent.com/2017/01/26/yiannopoulos-speaks-cu-boulder-feminism-muslims-fat-acceptance-liberals-alt-right-brietbart/

Milstein, T. (2008). When whales "speak for themselves": Communication as a mediating force in wildlife tourism. *Environmental Communication: A Journal of Nature and Culture, 2*(2), 173–192.

Molina-Markham, E. (2014). Finding the "sense of the meeting": Decision-making through silence among Quakers. *Western Journal of Communication, 78*(2), 155–174.

Nietzsche, F. (1977). On truth and lie in an extra-moral sense. In W. Kaufman (Ed.) & W. Kaufman (Trans.), *The portable Nietzsche* (pp. 42–46). New York, NY: Penguin Books.

Philipsen, G. (1987). The prospect for cultural communication. In D. Kinckaid (Ed.), *Communication theory from Eastern and Western perspectives* (pp. 245–254). New York, NY: Academic Press.

Philipsen, G., Coutu, L. M., and Covarrubias, P. (2005). Speech codes theory: Revision, restatement, and response to criticisms. In W. Gudykunst (Ed.), *Theorizing about intercultural communication* (pp. 55–68). Thousand Oaks, CA: Sage.

Schegloff, E. A. (1995). Discourse as an interactional achievement III: The omnirelevance of action. *Research on Language and Social Interaction, 28*, 185–211.

Scollo, S. M. (2004). Nonverbal ways of communicating with nature: A cross-case study. In S. L. Senecah (Ed.), *The environmental communication yearbook, 1* (pp. 227–249). Mahwah, NJ: Erlbaum.

"Stop hate speech on DePaul University's campus." (2016). [Online petition]. Retrieved from https://www.change.org/p/dennis-holtschneider-stop-hate-speech-on-depaul-university-s-campus

Tubesocks, J. (May 30, 2016). Black Lives Matter activists and other protesters out in force at DePaul University. [YouTube video]. Retrieved from https://www.youtube.com/watch?v=nJ9UfoNcqHc

van Over, B. (2012). *"Beyond words": Exploring the cultural limits of the communicable* (Doctoral dissertation). Retrieved from https://search.proquest.com/docview/1033341726

Wittgenstein, L. (1922). *Tractatus logico-philosophicus* (C. K. Ogden, Trans.). London: Routledge & Kegan Paul.

Yiannopoulos, M. (September 19, 2016). Milo to protester: "Fuck your feelings" [YouTube video]. Retrieved from https://www.youtube.com/watch?v=e8chEy9rwL4

Yiannopoulos, M. (October 7, 2016). Full text: On how feminism hurts men and women. Breitbart. Retrieved from http://www.breitbart.com/milo/2016/10/07/full-text-milo-feminism-auburn/

Chapter Twelve

"We Know How to Cry Out"

Emotion Expression at an African American Funeral

Danielle Graham and Sally O. Hastings

FOREWORD FROM GRAHAM

Despite having been to numerous funerals before, the first time death seemed real to me was at the funeral of my friend. He was nineteen at the time of his passing, and his death was completely unexpected. The day of the funeral I watched from a distance as people stepped up one by one to the open casket before the funeral started. Some people just looked at his body, while others placed their hand on his chest and silently wept. Then the processional started and the family began to walk through the church doors and make their way down the middle aisle to say their last goodbyes to their loved one. As the mother of the deceased slowly made her way down the aisle, her crying went from soft sobs to distraught wailing. She approached the casket and began to touch the body of the deceased and kiss the body of the son she had lost. The mother nearly passed out as she began hyperventilating and had to be helped to her seat by the funeral ushers. As I watched the family of the deceased walk up to the casket one by one to say goodbye, the sorrow in the church became heavier.

I had encountered scenes like this many times before, but because this funeral was the first in which I was personally affected by the person who was deceased, I was intrigued by the things I was seeing and pondered the deeper meaning of each of these actions for the first time. I wondered why there seemed to be such a deep-seated need to touch the body of the deceased. I questioned why the casket needed to match the suit my friend was being buried in and why all the flowers seemed to meld perfectly with the chosen color scheme. I wondered why the ushers made the mother of the deceased and his siblings get back up to close the casket, especially since this seemed to be such an emotional trigger. I looked at these actions and could not wrap my head around why these things were necessary. From that experience forward I became keenly aware of the actions that surrounded a funeral, and what intrigued me most was that these actions and sentiments remained consistent across many of the funerals I attended. Once I realized these similarities, I began to wonder what their significance was and what bearings these rituals had on the expression of grief within the African American community.

INTRODUCTION

Carbaugh's (2007) cultural discourse analysis (CuDA) provides an approach through which Graham's questions in the above narrative can be answered. As she asked "why" funeral attendees are performing the actions they are performing, she began a journey toward trying to understand "When people are engaged in communication, what significance or meaning does it have for them?" (p. 168). When Graham approached Hastings to direct her thesis on African American funeral practices, she expressed two important concerns. First, she wanted to make sense of her observations. Second, she recognized generally at the outset and more specifically as her thesis delved deeper into the literature that the scholarship on grief was very White. The research was primarily conducted by White researchers investigating White populations. A recent systematic content review of bereavement literature involving African Americans supports Graham's assessment noting "significant problems in number, content, and rigor when it comes to this study population" (Granek & Peleg-Sagy, 2015, p. 627). The recognition of this imbalance in the literature fueled her desire to give voice to an understudied population.

This desire to "give voice" was an influential force in determining the initial theoretical direction for the study. After reviewing a range of possibilities, we chose ethnography of communication (EoC) to guide the conceptualization of the study because it is ontologically geared toward promoting understanding of communication practices and giving voice to speech communities about which limited knowledge exists (Hymes, 1972). After a data collection process guided by the Hymesian perspective, we then turned to address one specific portion of the research: the expression of emotion. At this juncture, cultural discourse analysis (CuDA) (Carbaugh, 2005, 2007, 2017) was invoked in order to more carefully analyze the discursive data, yielding insights into participant meanings.

We recognize that an introduction to this theoretical and methodological framework has been presented earlier in the book; hence, we do not define key terms in EoC and CuDA. Despite this overview, however, we begin with a brief discussion of the theoretical perspective with an eye focused specifically on the challenges and affordances of the theoretical framework in the context of this study. We then review literature addressing African American emotion expressions at funerals.

THEORETICAL PERSPECTIVE

In addition to building upon Hymes as a foundation, the analysis draws upon Carbaugh's (2005, 2007, 2017) cultural discourse analysis. The study was broadly guided by the view of African Americans as composing a speech community that could be interrogated for its culturally informed ways of speaking through the use of Hymes's heuristic SPEAKING mnemonic (Hymes, 1972). This chapter originated from Graham's interest in the cultural norm of effusive emotion expression evident in African American funerals. The choice of this point of interest led to the examination of two hubs that serve as concentric circles guiding the analysis: feeling and acting. We then sought to find the cultural premises associated with these hubs. CuDA centers on "describing and interpreting communication practices in situated scenes with attention to the cultural discourses that animate them" (Scollo, 2011, p. 20). The communication practice that bridged the hubs of feeling and acting involved the act of "crying out" or displaying strong emotions.

The chapter assumes a critical perspective, which calls for explanation. Carbaugh (2017) advises caution in assuming a critical stance in CuDA, saying that standards of judgment must be "carefully formulated in order to serve purposes of social justice. One challenge in such a study is making the ethical standard of such judgment explicit and deeply considered" (p. 25). The critical voice was deeply considered and remains consonant with the use of critical voice described by Carbaugh's (1989/1990) three types of critical voice that may be usefully included in ethnographically informed research: natural criticism (voiced by participants), academic criticism (critique of scholarly practices), and cultural criticism (evaluation of the community studied). This chapter invokes two forms of critique that Carbaugh identified as falling within the realm of academic criticism: the use of ethnographic data to clear up cultural misconceptions about a cultural minority and a critique of the scholarly community.

First, we adopt a critical stance similar to the one Carbaugh (1989/1990) attributes to Keith Basso's work on the Western Apache. Carbaugh characterizes the critical approach assumed by Basso as one in which he "begins by noting misperceptions of Apache as reticent" then proceeds to examine Apache uses of silence (p. 274). The aim of such research, Carbaugh explains, is to serve as "a correction of stereotypical images" (p. 274). In this chapter, we adopt a focus on misperceptions surrounding displays of grief at funerals in order to dispel stereotypes.

Emotion expression in African American funerals has been a subject in the comedy routines of Richard Pryor, Bernie Mac, and Rod Allison, all of whom contrast emotion expression at Black and White funerals. While these comedians are African American and speak to a predominantly African American audience, when the routines cross cultural boundaries, they do little to promote understanding. For example, a part of Allison's routine includes the statement, "And we do a little hollerin' at our funeral. We say crazy stuff. Like 'Take me Lord.' (Audience laughs)." Within the context of Whiteness, the "crazy stuff" expressed at a funeral may assume a more pejorative perspective. That pattern of difference is devoid of cultural meanings when it extends beyond the African American community. A motivating factor guiding the authors' interest in this study involved including African American communication practices as an important concern for scholarly interest and promoting broader appreciation and understanding.

The second critical element of the study involves critique of the scholarly community. As noted previously, this study responds to the paucity of research on African American bereavement. This paucity symbolizes more to the authors than just a random "gap in the literature." Because basic assumptions of the researcher should receive careful consideration (Carbaugh & Hastings, 1992), clarification is warranted. African Americans have experienced a long history of racial discrimination, and a parallel form of racial discrimination has inadvertently emerged from scholarly literature on bereavement. Research on Whiteness has helped develop an understanding of why ethnic minorities in the United States become marginalized in powerful and diverse ways.

One aspect of the prominence of Whiteness in research can be seen through its power to normalize that which it studies. Levine-Rasky (2013) describes the process whereby Whiteness assumes this power, saying, "Whiteness is a normalized category. It functions a good deal of the time in Western (and non-Western) societies as 'normal' against which difference is contrasted. . . . If whiteness is normalized, it is also naturalized" (p. 44). Although Levine-Rasky does not address academic research specifically, the same process whereby Whiteness gets naturalized in society can also be seen in much academic research. Experiences, in this case the bereavement experiences, of White America are normalized, and "other" "unnatural" practices get contrasted. Van Over, Dori-Hacohen, and Winchatz (this volume) point to ways in which racial discourses can become silenced. This silence between racial groups places those who are marginalized without any voice through which to promote understanding.

EMOTION EXPRESSION AT AFRICAN AMERICAN FUNERALS

Several scholars have already drawn a historical link between African funeral practices and those evident among African Americans (Armstrong, 2010; Ntloedibe, 2006; Ukaegbu, 2011). These scholars point to expressive practices evident throughout different tribes on the African continent. Some have also noted the funeral practices evident among slaves in early American history (Armstrong, 2010). Despite these important contributions, little scholarship has been devoted to understanding and appreciating modern-day African American funeral practices. Many of those who do address current African American bereavement experiences focus on the societal context of bereavement, such as heightened infant mortality or homicide rate (Armstrong, 2010; Granek & Peley-Sagy, 2015). This limited scope can be seen as further contributing to negative stereotyping. Extant literature has done little to address questions of "what system of symbolic meanings or what cultural commentary is immanent in practices or communication? When people are engaged in communication, what significance and meaning does it have for them?" (Carbaugh, 2007, p. 168).

The study that most closely parallels the present one was completed by McIlwain (2002), who interviewed pastors and funeral directors in African American funeral homes to explore the rituals involved in funerals. His first finding addressed freedom of expression. He reports that "extreme emotion expression is not only customary such that church workers and funeral directors prepare to deal with such situations, but funeral directors have explicit policies for what to do when it occurs" (p. 2). For example, one pastor described a fraught woman who tried to pull the deceased from the casket and, finding that she could not, tried to crawl into the casket with the deceased. Funeral homes have plans of action for dealing with such occurrences. McIlwain's research provided a solid starting point for this study; however, he explicitly calls for research that explores the motives for such behavior. Pastors and funeral home directors provided useful insights into how the funerals were managed; however, they did not offer the "native's point of view" espoused by ethnographic researchers. By contrast, the present study aims to provide insight from the perspective of those who participate in the communicative practices. The research question guiding the analysis is, what cultural premises do participants describe in association with emotion expression at African American funerals?

METHODS

The primary method of data collection involved focus groups held with members of an African American Baptist church located in the southeastern

United States. The data and the interpretation of data were reflexively informed as the first author, Graham, is a longtime member of the church and serves as the audio technician for Sunday services and for funerals. As a member of the church and community of study, Graham also drew upon her insights provided through her role as audio technician, which allowed her to assume the role of participant observer, as she physically occupied a space in which she was "part of" funeral services, yet simultaneously removed from direct involvement with others. Her role provided an ideal vantage point for observation.

Focus groups were conducted at Graham's church with volunteers from her church family. Graham is not only a member of the speech community, but is also someone with whom they have worshipped and grieved. All focus group participants were over eighteen, were African American, and had attended funerals in predominantly black churches. Graham chose to interview her own church family for two key reasons. First, she would be able to gather sufficient participants to hold well-populated focus groups. Second, the decision to use existing social groups engaged existing familiarity and trust among participants, thereby creating lively and enthusiastic participation (Kamberelis & Dimitriades, 2013). The focus groups exemplified the kind of free-flowing discussion that embodies the ideal of focus group discussion. The discussion was so open and active that overlapping talk and supportive vocalizations were heard throughout all four focus groups. In some sense, the call-response pattern associated with the church became evident during focus group discourse (Daniel & Smitherman, 1990). In other words, the focus group discourse paralleled naturally occurring discourse more so than in focus groups held among strangers.

In total, 25 church members participated in one of 4 focus groups. The first focus group had 7 participants, the second had 8, the third had 4, and the final one had 6 participants. Participants varied in age; however, nearly half were over 55 years old. Almost all acknowledged having attended numerous funerals. All focus group data were transcribed, yielding 78 pages of single-spaced data.

The data underwent multiple rounds of analysis. The data were first analyzed by applying the Hymesian SPEAKING mnemonic to the data, searching for patterns within each part of the mnemonic. Although multiple norms emerged in characterizations of funeral conduct, one communicative norm was isolated for more focused examination: that of a high level of expressiveness. When all data discussing the norm of emotion expression were identified, Carbaugh's CuDA approach of examining a hub (or hubs) and radiants was applied. Our goal was to respond to an important missing piece in the literature by addressing cultural premises that informed the norms. We wanted to know what sense African American funeral goers made of the actions they performed and observed from others.

DATA ANALYSIS

The "hubs" of the analysis involve the "feeling" and "acting" components of Carbaugh's model as well as the cultural premises associated with these linked hubs. The discourse also linked these hubs with the "being" and "dwelling" radiants, adding further layers of cultural meaning to the emotion expression. The experience of feeling grief after a loss is common to many cultures; however, for many African Americans emotions are figuratively worn on a person's sleeve. The aforementioned comedy routines referencing African American bereavement stem from the ways in which this emotion is acted out. The title of this chapter is derived from one example of a participant discursive device used to characterize the emotional display of "crying out."

African Americans express a greater level of comfort with showing pain (Rosenblatt & Wallace, 2005). This stands in stark contrast to the normative actions described by Flanigan and Alvarez (this volume) for Oakian preferred norms for self-expression. African American ways of acting at a funeral suggest an auditory element of using the voice and an active bodily component of increased action (e.g., throwing up, touching the body of the deceased, visibly crying). We believe that much of the stereotyping and mocking of this hub derives from the fact that, while African Americans are known to express emotion in this way, little has been made available regarding the cultural premises guiding this form of action. Previous research (e.g., Kochman, 1990) has discussed the higher level of expressiveness of African Americans in general, or the tendency to engage in more emotional, vocal behaviors in church (e.g., Battle, 2006; Best, 2005; Daniel & Smitherman, 1990); however, little has been said about the ways that these behaviors apply in the context of bereavement.

The grief experienced by African Americans can find expression during the funeral service. Participants described various actions observed at an African American funeral, including "crying," "wailing," "screaming," and in extreme instances "passing out" and "throwing up." These data were not surprising because they matched with existing research on African American bereavement. Although people from different American co-cultures may experience similar internal feelings following the death of a loved one, they may differ greatly in terms of "appropriate" outward expression (McIlwain, 2002).

A Deeper Connection between "Feeling" and "Acting"

The very study of emotion expression begins to link together notions of "feeling" and "acting," presuming of course that the emotions expressed are the actual emotions experienced. For the African Americans interviewed, the "acting" involves much more transparent, raw emotional portrayals. Participants describe the strength of emotion expression as indicative of an African American cultural identity. All focus groups included a question asking why African Americans were more expressive in funerals. The below example describes the deep connection between feeling, acting, and being.

> Kate: I think because we are a people of passion. We show our emotion. African-Americans, we have such a very rich culture. I think it's just embedded in us to embrace and portray our emotion and our passion. To portray our grief. We don't try to . . . I'm just going to be honest. African American people don't try to cover up much, but you have a lot of . . . I'm not racial, but I notice that in the Caucasian community, their families are jacked up, but you would never know it. When our families are jacked up, you know it, and it's because we have . . . I don't know. It's just this embedded passion in us that has to come out in one extreme or another I think that's one of the reasons.

In many ways the outpouring of emotion is used to show the authenticity of grief and Blackness. Kate links feeling and acting with African American identity. Others also described the strong emotion expression as "innate" and noted that "we know how to cry out." "Crying out" becomes a communicative form that is expressive of a group identity (the *we*). The emotion expression deeply connects *acting* and *feeling* in a way that contrasts with Caucasians. Caucasian may be "jacked up" but their *acting* does not reflect their *feeling*. This connection between the feeling and the acting is how the *we* gets accomplished.

Cultural Premise 1: The bereaved can get the grief "out" by expressing it through actions.

Cultural Premise 2: Open expression of emotion comprises an important aspect of African American identity.

Participants also tied this response to grief to a specific place or "dwelling." The focus group participants were churchgoers who generally attended funerals at church. Some drew the connection between the physical location, the identity, and the emotions.

1   Tyson: I was just going to say it's like an extension of what we see every Sunday.
2   We're not quiet at church. If we're happy about something, we're happy
3   Cam: Yes, man, there you go.
4   Tyson: If we're sad about something, we cry. We laugh. I just think we're an
5   expressive people. It's just an extension of that.

Tyson's remarks perfectly sum up why African Americans can be seen as highly expressive at funerals. The *dwelling* where many funerals occur has a pattern of *acting* already associated with it. The outward display of emotions is an extension of how African Americans experience life, and according to Tyson this need for expression leaks into every event surrounding the African American experience.

The Black Church comprises an important *dwelling* for many African Americans. Dr. Martin Luther King noted that "it is appalling that the most segregated hour of Christian America is eleven o'clock on Sunday morning." Many churches remain, to a large extent, segregated today. This is significant because the church provides a unique setting in which African Americans can readily portray an African American identity among others who share their cultural codes. The church holds deep meanings as a cultural scene. The fact that many African American funerals take place in churches invites participants to engage in patterns of action evident in many Black churches. Just as funerals often get characterized as highly emotional, this "caricature" or "stereotype" of African American emotionality has also been associated with worshippers in Black churches (Battle, 2006).

The heightened emotionality evident in church on Sundays was referenced by the participants, and they noted how it carries over into the funeral. It can be argued that the scene that is set for the funeral provides a context that invites and makes emotion expression sensible. McIlwain (2002) explains the role of the domain in facilitating certain kinds of acting: "while whites are every bit as emotional as blacks, the scene of most white funerals, including slow organ music, the singing of solemn hymns and the steady tone of speaking, make extreme emotional expression incompatible with the mood of the surroundings" (p. 3). By contrast, the scene in the African American funeral is more engaging in much the same way as the Sunday church service engages the congregation (McIlwain, 2002). The church provides a place where this identity can be openly expressed, understood, and appreciated. Rosenblatt and Wallace (2005) affirm the important role the church plays in African American grief. The church becomes a site where an African American identity can be safely and genuinely expressed.

The understanding of the cultural premises about "getting out" emotions and expressing identity through emotional displays may be deepened through examination of disconfirming instances. Not all emotion expressions receive validation and are viewed as getting grief out and reflecting an African American identity. Dawn characterized a typical funeral program, stating, "Somebody walks in, somebody cries over the body, somebody needs to be dragged away from the body because somebody can't stop crying over the body (group laughs) (group responds yea), somebody pulls themselves together." The way that the sequence of events gets characterized suggests a sense of predictability with extreme behavior. The series of events is presented as though it is a routine. The focus group became quite noisy with laughter and supportive back-channeling when this sequence was described. The group response suggests that this pattern is subject to derision from others.

If the cultural premise involves getting emotions out as a desired form of action while grieving, it becomes sensible to examine why the strongest emotion expressions are not always affirmed. Participants expressed a more critical view of emotion expression when seen as inauthentic or detracting from honoring the deceased.

> Kate: The second one is we like to be the C.O.A., the center of attention. That is always going to be, and we know this. There's always going to be that one member of the family, that one girlfriend in the group, that one homeboy in the group that has to be the center of attention that has to make something about them.

Kate's depiction received enthusiastic affirmation from others in the group. In her depiction of "that one" who takes emotion expression to an extreme, it is framed as making the event about themselves and becoming the center of attention rather than getting grief out.

Grief is not the only emotion about which extreme emotion expression gets called into question. A parallel perspective was provided by Faith, who described excessive positive emotional displays:

> Yes. It was supposed to have been a celebration but to see them like jumping up and down and doing praise dances, that's not why we are here. You could tell that it was just for show the way that they came in, what they wore, it was sad. Taking the focus off of the person that's deceased and the reason why you are there to me I think is so disrespectful. Talking about the antics that's the difference.

This segment offers several cues that point to the reasons for the disapproval. Faith suggests that the person drawing attention through highly expressive behavior came into the funeral with a purpose. Their actions were "just for show" and were thus labeled "antics." Regardless of the type of emotion expressed, if the expression lacks authenticity, it is viewed as attention-seeking rather than performing the expressive function of acting upon a truly passionate cultural identity.

Functional Accomplishment

Overt grief expression is described as a form of purging or "letting out" that emotion. Participants described this as preferable to other forms of grief management. The below exchange demonstrates how expressing grief is seen in contrast to other modes of grieving. They begin by discussing Caucasian funerals.

1	Dana:	Theirs is a little quiet
2	Ms. D:	It is very quiet
3	Dana:	But the thing about it is the thing that I see to that they don't let it out and
4		then they turn to the bottle.
5	Ms. D:	That's right, in another way
6	Dana:	They turn to other things to soothe that pain cause they hadn't released it
7		cause it's not their thing to be at the funeral you know screaming and
8		crying you know
9	Lady K:	And I see that in the Black culture as well you have your ones that don't
10		grieve and like you say they turn to other things you know to help them.

This exchange reveals another cultural premise associated with actions. The expression of emotions or "letting it out" has positive connotations within the African American culture because showing emotions within the context of a funeral shows that the person is dealing with their grief. A recurrent theme in discussing grief expression among participants was that the grief "came out." Rather than describing grief expression as a performance, grief was released through the act of visibly grieving. When one participant described the closing of the casket as a particularly poignant part of the ceremony, she explained, "it is that outpouring of emotion." Releasing the grief is associated with removing bad feelings from the body. The perception of how White people behave is not seen as healthy, which causes them to turn to detrimental alternatives to deal with their grief. This premise points to the "functional accomplishment" of the emotion expression: healing or closure (Carbaugh, 2007, p. 169).

Cultural Premise 3: Letting the grief "out" promotes healing and coping.

DISCUSSION

The research question asked, What cultural premises do participants describe in association with emotion expression at African American funerals? To formulate a culturally informed response to an identified norm of this speech community, we interpreted the data using Carbaugh's cultural discourse analysis (CuDA). This process began by identifying central "hubs" with radiants of meaning. Through this process of examining these hubs and radiants, discourse about them pointed to cultural premises about the focal activity of crying out. The hubs grounding this study were those of "feeling" and "acting." These hubs associated with displays of grief at a funeral were connected to the radiant of *being* as participants described a deep passion associated with African American identity that finds release through grief expression. The hubs also occurred within a culturally meaningful *dwelling*, the Black Church. A pattern of open emotion expression has already been established in the church setting, so the expression of emotion under emotionally impactful circumstances facilitates and naturalizes the act of "crying out."

The data point to three important cultural premises that promote a deeper understanding of the displays of grief at an African American funeral. First, the bereaved can get the grief "out" by expressing it through actions. Participants described feelings of grief as a burden that they can remove from their body through actions. The second cultural premise is that open expression of emotion comprises an important aspect of African American identity. Participants repeatedly associated a strong sense of passion with an African American sense of personhood. Additionally, the funerals often take place in the Black Church, a site that has long been identified as an important scene for African American identity enactment. The third premise examines the functional accomplishment of the norm, that letting the grief "out" promotes healing and coping. Participants suggest that failing to act upon strong emotions can lead to more dysfunctional coping strategies, such as turning to alcohol. Conversely, releasing these emotions moves the bereaved toward healing.

Participants in all focus groups noted that the actions can be taken too far, and that excessive displays were disapproved. The recognition of disapproval of these extremes may inform the jokes in the Black comedians' comedy routines about funerals. Some funeral attendees may display too much emotion. At this point, the genuineness of the emotion expressed gets called into question. Instead of a healthy release of grief, the person who "overperforms" grief is seen as calling attention to her or himself. Although having someone engage in "antics" and becoming the "center of attention" seemed undesirable to those in the focus groups, it was also expected. Someone taking the emotion expression to an undesired extreme was anticipated, tolerated, and dealt with as needed.

An underlying current throughout this enterprise has been a critical voice. The decision to study African American bereavement responds to the historical academic focus on White bereavement. We viewed the existing focus on the White experience as not only undesirable, but dangerous. Research on Whiteness demonstrates the dangers of creating one standard for understanding, then viewing non-White groups through that standard. The dangers of not understanding differing forms of grief can result in negative stereotyping and other problems. Granek and Peleg-Sagy (2017) noted that "The public expression of grief by wailing, crying, and sobbing could be met with a diagnosis of pathological grief for being too intense or expressive" (p. 392). Rather than judge the act of "crying out" from a White perspective, CuDA helps to give voice to the cultural premises grounding the action. This study offers one step toward addressing a perspective that is not adequately represented in the literature and gives voice to cultural meanings embedded in the practice of crying out.

AFTERWORD FROM GRAHAM

Nearly a year after I conducted this study death came knocking at my door around 2:30 in the morning. On Thursday, June 1, 2017, my husband's mother passed away, and I found myself and the person I love most in this world in the midst of the rituals I had spent nearly a year studying. Following the conclusion of this research I walked away knowing more about my culture and I had gathered a deeper appreciation for the rituals I had been seeing all my life. On June 10, the day of my mother-in-law's funeral, I found myself eternally grateful for these rituals as I saw firsthand how they served as aloe to soothe the family's pain of loss.

Before doing this study I thought that many of the things that I was observing were for spectacle, but as I held my husband's hand and walked down the middle aisle so that he could say goodbye to his mother for the last time, I felt his knees buckle under the weight of his grief. I walked with him as he made his way to the casket, touched his mother's hand, and leaned in to place a gentle kiss on her cheek. I felt the closure that came with closing the casket on the family's own terms. We each took our final look at the body and once everyone had the opportunity to remember how peaceful my mother-in-law looked, my father-in-law gave the ushers the okay to close the casket. I understood once the casket was closed how important it was that all the flowers matched the color of the coffin, because as the casket stood in the middle of the church all the love for my mother-in-law could be seen in the abundance of flowers that were displayed around her. Each flower display expressed people's sentiments of love and attention to detail. Each ritual that I used to see as dramatic and over-the-top began to make sense, as each ritual had a specific purpose. I have this research to thank for perspective, and my rich culture to thank for closure.

REFERENCES

Armstrong, T. D. (2010). African and African-American traditions in America. In L. Bregman (Ed.), *Religion, death, and dying* (pp. 83–110). Santa Barbara, CA: ABC-CLIO.

Battle, M. (2006). *The black church in America: African American Christian spirituality.* Malden, MA: Blackwell Publishing.

Best, W. D. (2005). *Passionately human, no less divine.* Princeton, NJ: Princeton University Press.

Carbaugh, D. (1989/1990). The critical voice in ethnography of communication research. *Research on Language and Social Interaction, 23,* 261–282.

Carbaugh, D. (2005). *Cultures in conversation.* Mahwah, NJ: Erlbaum.

230 *Danielle Graham and Sally O. Hastings*

Carbaugh, D. (2007). Cultural discourse analysis: The investigation of communication practices with special attention to intercultural encounters. *Journal of Intercultural Communication Research, 36,* 167–182.

Carbaugh, D. (2017). Terms for talk, take 2. In D. Carbaugh (Ed.), *The handbook of communication in cross-cultural perspective* (pp. 15–28). New York, NY: Routledge.

Carbaugh, D., & Hastings, S. O. (1992). A role for communication theory in ethnography and cultural analysis. *Communication Theory, 2,* 156–165.

Daniel, J. L., & Smitherman, G. (1990). How I got over: Communication dynamics in the black community. In D. Carbaugh (Ed.), *Cultural communication and intercultural contact* (pp. 27–40). Hillsdale, NJ: Erlbaum.

Granek, L., & Peleg-Sagy, T. (2015). Representations of African Americans in the grief and mourning literature from 1998–2014: A systematic review. *Death Studies, 39,* 605–632. doi: http://dx.doi.org.ezproxy.net.ucf.edu/10.1080/07481187.2015.1047059

Granek, L., & Peleg-Sagy, T. (2017). The use of pathological grief outcomes in bereavement studies of African Americans. *Transcultural Psychiatry, 53*(4), 384–399. doi:http://dx.doi.org/10.1177/1363461517708121

Hymes, D. (1972). Models of the interaction of language in social life. In J. Gumperz & D. Hymes (Eds.), *Directions in sociolinguistics: The ethnography of communication* (pp. 25–71). New York, NY: Holt, Rinehart & Winston.

Kamberelis, G., & Dimitriades, G. (2013). *Focus groups: From structured interviews to collective conversations.* New York, NY: Routledge.

Kochman, T. (1990). Force fields in black and white communication. In D. Carbaugh (Ed.), *Cultural communication and intercultural contact* (pp. 193–217). Hillsdale, NJ: Erlbaum.

Levine-Rasky, C. (2013). *Whiteness fractured.* Dorchester, UK: Dorset Press.

McIlwain, C. (2002). Death in black and white: A study of family differences in the performance of death rituals. *Qualitative Research Reports in Communication, 3,* 1–6.

Ntloedibe, F. (2006). A question of origins: The social and cultural roots of African American cultures. *Journal of African American History, 91*(4), 401–412.

Rosenblatt, P. C., & Wallace, B. R. (2005). *African American grief.* New York, NY: Routledge.

Scollo, M. (2011). Cultural approaches to discourse analysis: A theoretical and methodological conversation with special focus on Donal Carbaugh's cultural discourse theory. *Journal of Multicultural Discourses, 6,* 1–32. Doi: 10.1080/17447143.2010.536550

Ukaegbu, V. (2011). African funeral rites: Sites for performing, participating and witnessing of trauma. *Performance Research, 16,* 131–141. doi: 10.1080/13528165.2011.562037

Part V

Dwelling

Chapter Thirteen

Cultural Discourses in Native American Educational Contexts

James L. Leighter, Eean Grimshaw, and Charles A. Braithwaite

This chapter draws from three empirical studies to illumine the utility of a cultural discourse approach (Carbaugh, 2005, 2007, 2017) for understanding communication practices in Native American contexts. The purpose of juxtaposing these three examples is to demonstrate the utility of cultural discourse approaches in cross-cultural circumstances by briefly illustrating the range of interpretations possible through such an approach. The examples cohere thematically in the investigation of some component or aspect of education in Native American contexts: the first in the examination of a site of education, the second in a practice of language learning, and the third raises questions about teacher identity in instruction. As such, each of the examples illumines discursive hubs of *acting* in Native American education, but in so doing or in order to do so, the examples describe the activation of other discursive hubs, namely *dwelling* in the first and *being* in the third (Carbaugh, 2007).

Common across the three examples is the indication of a critical tension between "white" or Euro-American[1] ways and traditional or tribal ways, tensions that can be found at the crux of a problem or concern in Native communities. Each of these examples, thus, illustrates key moments, means, or methods for coming to terms with cultures (Philipsen, 1981/1987, 2010), albeit in very limited ways, in instances of intercultural contact or cultural reconstruction, through attention to cultural discourses.

It is important to note that each case was developed through separate episodes of fieldwork and thus, juxtaposing them presents a challenge for presentation in this chapter. In the first section, we present Leighter's account of ethnographic fieldwork developed for application in team-based public

234   *James L. Leighter, Eean Grimshaw, and Charles A. Braithwaite*

health research. Leighter writes the account in the first person, occasionally employing "our," "us," and "we," not to reference the present coauthors but to reference other team members on the original public health project including two public health researchers, an architect, and two community members employed as research assistants. In the second section, we present Grimshaw's analysis of a language revitalization and reclamation project. Grimshaw's account evidences how traditional Native American cultural protocols provide a base from which to better understand one tribe's approach to language learning. In the third section, we present Braithwaite's first-person accounts from his experience in intercultural classrooms. The focus of this case is on the tensions in the interaction between Euro-American teachers and American Indian students, which lead some Indian parents to create specific prescriptions and proscriptions for Euro-American communicative behavior.

Finally, we summarize the utility of the cultural discourse approach in these educational contexts, specifically, and Native American contexts more generally by returning to discuss how these examples, taken together, illuminate discursive hubs of *acting* and thus provide poignant cultural understanding of the critical tensions present in Native American education.

"THIS BUILDING HAS HAD MANY LIVES": NOTICING, RECOVERING, AND RECONSTRUCTING A SENSE OF PLACE ON THE WINNEBAGO RESERVATION

This section of the chapter is responsive to Carbaugh's (2017) interpretive assumption that states, "as people reference or talk about their communication, they not only say something explicitly about communication as a practice, they also engage in meta-cultural commentary about personhood or identity and other features of socio-cultural life including their feelings, ways of relating, and dwelling-in-place" (p. 17). Regarding place in particular, communication is "doubly placed," providing both a sense of place (i.e., what is *this* place?) and also, in the social sense, our place within places (i.e., *who* am I and what am I to be *doing* in this place?). Extending this assumption, when people have differing and competing memories of a place, expressed in and through terms and names for places, the significance of the interplay of these memories and the meanings associated with those memories can enrich a cultural understanding of a particular place (Carbaugh & Rudnick, 2006). In many circumstance, these are important questions that often remain hidden under the surface of daily living. Such questions can, however, become critically important for understanding the contemporary practices in a particular place. Basso (1996) characterizes this quality of place when he writes,

as normal experience, sense of place quite simply is, as natural and straightfor-
ward as our fondness for certain colors and culinary tastes, and the thought that
it might be complicated, or even very interesting, seldom crosses our minds.
As sometimes happens, we are deprived of these attachments and find ourselves, literally dislocated, in unfamiliar surroundings we do not comprehend
and care for even less. On these unnerving occasions, sense of place may
assert itself in pressing and powerful ways, and its often subtle components—
as subtle, perhaps as absent smells in the air or not enough visible sky—come
surging into awareness. (p. xiii)

Place asserted itself in the way Basso describes to an interdisciplinary research team brought together to investigate public health concerns on the
Winnebago reservation. Briefly, our reason for frequenting the Wolf's Den
Student Center and cafeteria on the campus of the Little Priest Tribal College
in Winnebago, Nebraska, was to understand how the remodeling of this
cafeteria, built in a community of 700 people squarely situated in the middle
of a USDA-defined food desert, would impact local eating habits and, potentially, obesity and well-being in the Winnebago community. But recruiting
participants for a public health study became difficult, forcing us to wonder if
we were missing important cultural information about this place. As a team
that included two public health researchers, an architect, and a communication scholar, we sought to improve our assessment of the impact of the
Wolf's Den in Winnebago and, more drastically, if what we were hearing
about place would change the way we were thinking about public health
interventions altogether. Our initial inclination to understand public health
concerns by studying changes in the social, spatial, and economic environment was thus radically modified to include an understanding of this physical
structure (a student center and cafeteria), and discourse about this structure,
as a deeply cultural place.

Our approach was developed from the ethnography of communication,
EC (Hymes, 1972), and the related theoretical and methodological approaches developed in speech codes theory, SCT (Philipsen, Coutu, &, Covarrubias, 2006), and cultural discourse analysis, CuDA (Carbaugh, 2007).
Most notably for this chapter, a cultural discourse approach applied to a few
episodes of talk in and about the Wolf's Den adds a layer of analytic resources to our ethnographic inquiry by focusing our attention to discursive
hubs of dwelling and acting heard in the talk about the Wolf's Den.

The first episode occurred at the dedication ceremony of the Wolf's Den
as it was open for business on the LPTC campus. The ceremony included
spoken words by the chairman of the tribe, a prayer to the four corners, the
giving of gifts to distinguished guests, and several drum circle interludes, all
of which are typical for any ceremony (including funerals, namings, powwows, and the like) on the reservation. To begin, I paraphrase the opening

statements of the chairman of the tribe in order to introduce the relevance and relationship of the college to the community. He said,

> Some years ago, we created ICC [an acronym for the original name of the college, now LPTC] and there was a lot of fear. For the sake of the community and children there was debate on the council. Little Priest was our guiding light and leadership in the past. Little Priest understood education was the link to us surviving. Anything else might not have succeeded. . . . This was the campus. It was a good experience for us. We did this all in the name of our creator. The college shall be the place that things happen from. The place for innovation. I want to thank Paul (the president at the time) for insight and what he is doing. We need to be kind, learn how to treat one another.

With these words, the chairman opened the ceremony by describing LPTC generally and the Wolf's Den in particular as significant for the community, the creation of which was *in the name of our creator*. Additionally, he alludes that the decision to build the college, within which the Wolf's Den now sits, was not easy because the original purpose for the buildings, a children's home for the community, was still needed. According to the chairman, the buildings, and their use as a college, were to create a place that things happen from, a place for future innovation.

These words were the first clues to us that the building held deep cultural significance in ways we had not been previously attending to. During the ceremony, other invited speakers reinforced the complex meanings of this place. For instance, later in the ceremony, the president of LPTC opened the floor for anyone in attendance to speak. Ted, a nonemployee of the college, responded to the invitation by standing and facing the audience. A reconstructed account of Ted's words from field notes are as follows.

Ted was from "in town." Ted told of how his grandmother "put us up here" in the children's home because his mother had difficulty with alcohol. While at the home he learned "better hygiene," had a "good diet," and got "new clothes for school." Ted "even had to go to church" (drawing chuckles from the audience) even though he "didn't take it [church] with me." He said, "I was raised with more traditional ways." Ted went on to clarify the distinction between "church" and "traditional ways" by describing church ways as inclusive of being "dependable" and having a "routine." He added, "I never had many bad experiences." "I was not isolated." The children "had to learn social skills because we had to learn to live with one another."

In this account, Ted further elaborates the complex ways in which community members recalled and spoke about dwelling in this place. It was, for him, a home, a place that made salient distinctions between tribal and White ways. It was for him a good place (invoking the discursive hub of *feeling*) with, in his words, limited "bad experiences." For us, the researchers, Ted's remarks at the dedication for "the Wolf's Den" initially seemed curious because they were not remarks that celebrated the dedication of the cafeteria in the way we had expected. Ultimately, however, his remarks, in conjunction with others, forced us to understand the multiple meanings about dwelling that the physical structures, the buildings themselves, called forth for community members.

Mabel, a mother of two daughters, expressed how she felt about the college using these buildings for other purposes, both recalling the difficult transition from children's home to college, as the chairman of the tribe did, and further clarifying why this meaning particular of place is so durable. Mabel said, "Well although it's a good thing right now you know we didn't like it because it was our home. That's all we know this place for is . . . it was our home you know where we grew up for thirteen years." When I asked Mabel about how people have a love and affinity for this place even though boarding schools often stir up difficult memories for Native people, she responded, "well from the time you were five til you were eighteen which we were, yeah it was [a good place]. You know. We got you know we got a warm bed, we got meals. Although there wasn't parental relationship. It still we still had a man and woman that looked over us. So we knew that."

Thus, the dedication ceremony and conversations briefly illuminate critical clues about how those who grew up in Winnebago held memories of this place, not as an eating establishment on a college campus but rather as a powerful physical place for memory of their childhood "home," family relationships, and (at least some) fond memories.

More specifically, the understanding of the collection of campus buildings as a home was narrowed with respect to the newly remodeled cafeteria. Former child residents, both during and after the dedication, recalled all the uses of that building in the prior decades. In speaking about the building, former residents expressed a "long history" with this place and would remind others that the kitchen used to be the "laundry" or the "laundry room."

That the Wolf's Den held different memories for different members of the community was elaborated many times, and the building itself was spoken of in biological terms of life and growth. During the ceremony the chair of the board at LPTC said that "this building has had many lives," including the "laundry," a "cannery," a "print shop," and "programs" for LPTC. During the dedication ceremony the LPTC board chair suggested that at one time, because it was a small building, it was on the "chopping block" and "near death" because some wanted to knock it down and build something new. But instead it was "reincarnated several times" and has had "several lives" and now is "serving our purpose for the students."

The conclusion to draw by comparing our naïve understanding of the Wolf's Den with a more elaborated understanding of place and meaning revealed in the local talk about the place is the way in which physical spaces, place names, and thus cultural understandings for dwelling in place converge. As Carbaugh and Rudnick (2006) suggest, a place can often have multiple meanings, uncovered in one way through place names, "so do all people, in all places, come to know the meanings of at least some places through names, with the stories about them capturing their deeper significance, from the sacred to the mundane" (p. 167). In some circumstances there is a disconnect between stories and names: "it is possible for its names and stories to vary. Names for places change; stories about them get revisited, discarded, or created anew" (p. 167).

One interesting finding from our search of photographic archives was the architectural truth of the notion that the current "Wolf's Den" grew from "the laundry" to its current form was revealed in records collected from the local Reform Church. In figure 13.1, the window nearest to the children on the front face of the building is now the opening on figure 13.2 through which food and dishes are passed by staff and guests.

Catherine, a Native American history teacher at LPTC, understood the convergence of place, place names, and notions of dwelling in her comments to us regarding our elaborated understanding of the Wolf's Den in her use of the biological metaphor for describing place. She said, "place is like a person." Paraphrasing her words, she added, speaking directly to me, there was

Figure 13.1.   Courtesy Lowell TenClay, Pastor, Winnebago Reformed Church.

Figure 13.2.   Courtesy Hooton Images.

probably a period of your life that you struggled with, that you lacked maturity like when we were still boarding kids in these residence halls. We took children and kept them here. Then, there's a transition, a ceremony or a life-changing event. But "people can claim a place and help it grow up. We've claimed this thing [the LPTC buildings] and we're helping it to transition to the entity it's supposed to be."

The physical structure that is now the Wolf's Den has grown up, and the memory of its childhood is durable and vivid. The physical structure holds significance as a place that calls forth memories of different scenes. By listening to how members of the Winnebago community talked in and about the Wolf's Den, newly renovated and designed as both a social and work space for students and to provide healthy food choices for LPTC faculty, staff, students, as well as members of the community, a new way of thinking about public health inquiry and culture was impressed upon us.

From this understanding of place, several key observations can be made. First, physical places referenced by multiple place names such as, in this case, "the Wolf's Den," "the laundry," "the cannery," and "our home," activate distinctive discursive hubs of *dwelling*. Second, the interplay of these discursive hubs of *dwelling* activate additional discursive hubs of *acting* in the present and through stories and memory. The Wolf's Den is both a contemporary place for *acting* through healthy eating, an historical place of *relating* with caretakers, and *emoting* through fond memory of childhood. The interplay of these discursive hubs, for the Winnebago, is the site of critical tension between traditional and White ways, between present needs for the college and memories of the community members who were raised in those same buildings. Finally, this example briefly suggests how explicit recognition of this interplay of discursive hubs of *dwelling* can be a productive means for reconstructing how places become known and modes of action are reconciled.

"WITHOUT LANGUAGE WE ARE NOTHING": AN INDIGENOUS APPROACH TO LANGUAGE REVITALIZATION ON THE BLACKFEET RESERVATION

According to Greymorning (in McDermott, 2014), of the current 139 Native American languages still spoken by Indigenous peoples in North America, more than half of these are at risk of going extinct in the next ten years. As such, contemporary Native Americans face a variety of problems associated with how best to manage language revitalization efforts. Such projects represent the harsh reality facing most contemporary Native American communities, many of whose last remaining fluent speakers are at risk of passing away before new speakers may be cultivated. While various efforts have been made toward producing new fluent speakers, the results are often few and far between (McCarty & Watahomigie, 1999; McCarty, 2008; Greymorning, 2011). Of particular interest across such projects are the various ways in which different Native American groups are trying or have tried to cultivate a new generation of language learners.

Indeed, many Native American peoples are understandably frustrated with recent attempts to record and document their languages (McCarty & Watahomigie, 1999; McCarty, 2008; Greymorning, 2011). The number of proficient new speakers produced is often much lower than desired, resulting in some tribal communities' decision to return to traditional cultural protocols as a means to facilitate the production of new speakers at an accelerated rate. One such approach, from which we may highlight the tension between an Indigenous approach to language revitalization as opposed to the more traditional and Euro-American linguistic one, comes from work taking place on the Blackfeet Reservation in Montana by means of an accelerated second language acquisition program (ASLA).

ASLA was first developed by S. Neyooxet Greymorning (Arapaho) based on an understanding that children learn their first language in a very precise way (2011). Of primary importance in understanding this particular effort for language revitalization is how Greymorning worked to incorporate traditional Arapaho cultural protocols in the development of his methodology, in particular, "how people came together to listen to traditional stories" (Greymorning, 2011, p. 196). Indicative of traditional Indigenous language instruction, ASLA is an immersion-based program taught primarily through the use of observational images and storytelling toward the production of expert language learners.

As of 2011, ASLA has been brought to over 60 Native communities in the United States, Australia, and parts of Canada. Based in part on the explanations provided from one individual, Imiitaisskii (Blackfeet), who is using ASLA as a means to revitalize his own Indigenous language, what follows is a discussion in which the tension between approaches is explored. Furthermore, what this approach provides for better understanding Indigenous language revitalization programs in general is also addressed. In part, because ASLA was developed by an Indigenous language instructor for the purpose of addressing Native American language loss and from a perspective that incorporates the cultural protocols of Native American peoples (Greymorning, 2011), an understanding of ASLA and the tensions surrounding this approach, as constructed through the terms and explanations of those who practice ASLA in their own communities, may be developed (Carbaugh, 2007; Cerulli, 2017).

The understanding developed here is based in part on a continuous dialogue with Imiitaisskii, Blackfoot, who after learning to speak Arapaho, through ASLA and under the tutelage of S. Neyooxet Greymorning, is now instructing Blackfoot language learners at the Blackfeet Community College on the Blackfeet Reservation in Montana. Over the course of several years' worth of conversations surrounding ASLA, an understanding and appreciation of endangered language revitalization efforts, ASLA in particular, has been developed. This understanding relies heavily upon the meaning, values, and beliefs inherent in Imiitaisskii's ways of speaking about the methodology itself as well as his decision to include particular metaphors when doing so (Carbaugh, 2001, 2007). For the better part of eight years, Imiitaisskii and I have collaboratively engaged in understanding the impact of ASLA as a means for producing new Indigenous speakers fluent in their ancestors' language. Highlighted here is but one conversation that took place in the fall of 2016 in which Imiitaisskii offered particularly poignant statements about the tensions inherent in using ASLA as a means for language revitalization.

This particular excerpt[2] selection was made with consideration for how to best highlight the tensions between an Indigenous approach to language revitalization and the more Euro-American linguistic-based approach. Focusing on the radiant of *acting*, Imiitaisskii's decision to use metaphor to describe ASLA as a garden in contrast to linguistics as a storage house offers a particular metacommentary about ASLA, one in turn that illuminates what is being explicitly and implicitly communicated about this practice of language instruction.

1	And a lot of people are using writing down Blackfoot
2	as a means to not remember
3	to learn ASLA you can't do that
4	you can't keep up if you keep writing things
5	and what ASLA did is you're creating a garden of language
6	where you're constantly going to this garden and tending it
7	and getting food that way
8	and then linguistics is causing a storage house
9	a database of language
10	like a museum where you have to get up
11	and go view it and look at it so often
12	but it's not a garden, it's not replenishing itself
13	you don't have a relationship with it as much as it's just there for you
14	at your disposal
15	whereas a garden you need to have a relationship for it
16	you need to constantly go back
17	and love it and care for it
18	and you know, you're a better person

In this excerpt we hear Imiitaisskii relating that ASLA is about "creating" a "garden of language." Moreover, Imiitaisskii speaks to that "creation" as being about developing a "relationship" between you as a learner with the "garden," one in which the learner is "tending" to and "getting food" from the garden, which is "replenished" in turn through the learner's use of the garden (5–7, 12). In return, Imiitaisskii says that the garden takes care of the learner by offering sustenance, in a mutually beneficial way based on "love" and "care," in turn, making the learner a "better person" both physically and mentally for fostering that "relationship" (15–18). Imiitaisskii offers these metaphors in contrast to describing the "linguistic" offering of a "storage house," "museum," or "database" where you "don't have a relationship" as much as it's at your "disposal" (8–14).

From this rich albeit brief excerpt, a set of cultural propositions can be formulated from which our primary concern should be understanding what these competing visions mean for Imiitaisskii in particular and Blackfoot language learners in general. The following cultural propositions are developed from the explicit claims made above by Imiitaisskii:

• ASLA offers "language" as a "replenishing" "garden" of "language," but one that requires "tending"
• This "tending" occurs because of the "need" to "care" and "love" the "relationship" with the "garden"

- ASLA requires you to have a "relationship" with the "language," one that has emotive and physical consequences, as opposed to "linguistics," which treats language as a "database" and "storehouse" for language, devoid of any kind of "relationship" and in which the "language" is there for your "disposal"

These propositions help to develop our understanding of ASLA insofar as it is primarily about creating a "relationship" between the learner and the language. Furthermore, through the particular metacommentary made here by Imiitaisskii we can better understand how this relationship is built upon the deep-seated emotions of love and care through his choice of metaphor (Carbaugh, 2001). The emotive description of the garden of language stands in stark contrast to the static description of the museum, database, and storage house that are for looking and viewing, not interacting. Indeed, the emotionally charged expressions that Imiitaisskii truly develops here highlight how integral this positive relationship with the language is for Indigenous learners practicing ASLA. Of even greater importance for understanding the tension representative in these two approaches is that the love that is expressed here is done so, not in the context of an inanimate database of language, but as very much a part of a living and caring garden, one that will thrive and provide sustenance for being as long as there are learners to care for and love it. Moreover, in relating the tremendous importance of this third proposition for understanding the competing views at stake across these two approaches, is the extent to which the garden metaphor must be understood from the cultural logic employed in Imiitaisskii's choice of metaphor (Carbaugh, 2001, 2007).

Such an understanding allows for the development of cultural premises. These premises, from which considerable consideration can be given, further our understanding of the effort at language revitalization being made here by Imiitaisskii, of which similar efforts are being made by other contemporary Native American peoples and are as follows: understanding why some tribal communities have turned to ASLA as well as why the traditional Euro-American linguistic approach has become increasingly less appealing to Indigenous peoples is clearly related to the capacity for treating the language as a living being, one that has particular emotive and physical consequences. Indeed, we can better understand the link between Imiitaisskii's metacommentary and choice of metaphor once we consider the cultural logic inherent in those choices (Carbaugh, 2001). For Imiitaisskii and other contemporary Native American peoples, part of the tension surrounding and their resulting decision to distance themselves from Euro-American linguistic approaches toward language revitalization is wrapped up in how each treats the language itself. What should be understood is that for these individuals and communities working toward producing new fluent speakers of their Native

American languages, linguistics has always fallen short through its decision to treat the language itself as a static database to be looked at and used. In contrast, the language itself has for many Native American peoples always been treated as an animate being, one that deserves and whose revitalization depends upon that understanding.

Imiitaisskii's choice of metaphor here to describe ASLA as a garden and linguistics as a museum is representative of a greater categorical distinction made in many Native American languages in which words are categorically identified based on their understanding as animate or inanimate in relation to the world in which they live (Boas, 1966). Such a distinction representative here through the choice of metaphor reveals a necessary component for understanding why approaches like ASLA that coincide with cultural proto-cols are being taken up by various Native American communities (see McCarty & Watahomigie, 1999; McCarty, 2008; Greymorning, 2011). Al-though those who practice ASLA rely on a language instructor inside the classroom, they function more so as a guide from which it is equally if not more important to understand that the language itself shares the cultural knowledge and understanding of the world to which those Indigenous peo-ples belong. Furthermore, the language holds answers to all our questions, but there is a correct way to go about listening to what it is the language is telling us (Carbaugh, 1999, 2001). For these contemporary communities treating the language as an animate being, one that deserves to be approached and understood with the emotive and physical consequences of any living being, is tantamount toward understanding such language revitalization ef-forts.

What this cultural discourse analysis hopefully demonstrates then is that for local Blackfoot language learners, and the ASLA method from which they are developing new speakers, learning endangered languages is as much about learning the language itself as it is about language learning you. What I mean by this, as is evidenced in the above excerpt through Imiitaisskki's metacommentary and choice of metaphor, is that ASLA is about teaching language through relationships. Not just the relationship between the basic understanding of words and phrases as you build toward more complicated stories, but the intimate relationship between learner and language in which both have an active and involved role to provide and care for the other. This type of practice is dependent upon a relationship in which learners tend to and receive sustenance from the language. In return, these endangered lan-guages will continue to survive and can begin to flourish and grow, develop-ing relationships with any and all who wish to open up their hearts and minds to listen to what the language has to tell them. In this case, what the language provides the learner, both physically and mentally, must be understood in terms of what both of those rewards mean for Blackfoot and Native American peoples in terms of a cultural foundation from which we know the world as it surrounds and embraces us (Carbaugh, 2005). Furthermore, Imii-taisskii's reflections support and strengthen our understanding of Indigenous languages as being "literally and symbolically, the life giver" (McCarty, 2008) for these communities.

TEACHING THE TEACHERS: AMERICAN INDIAN PARENTS EDUCATE EURO-AMERICAN TEACHERS

By attending to the role of discursive practices in individual and cultural lives, especially those connecting people to place, perhaps we can create a better understanding of communication, especially of each about the other. Perhaps further, we can increase the expressive means available to each of us for our own understandings, and for deeper insights, from personal to global ecologies, if we just listen accordingly (Carbaugh, 2005, p. 116).

The K-12 classroom provides a myriad of examples related to intercultural misunderstandings and miscommunication. This is especially true when it comes to interaction between Euro-American teachers and American Indian[3] students (cf. Brandt, 1992; Braithwaite, 1998; Dehyle, 1992; Dumont, 1972; Peshkin, 1997; Philips, 1983). Narratives abound throughout Indian Country how educational institutions fail to provide adequate learning experiences for students when there are primarily Indian populations. Fortunately, there are resources for Euro-American teachers to help them adapt to Indian students in the classroom (Basso, 1979; Braithwaite, 1997b; Carbaugh & Rudnick, 2006; McCarty, Wallace, Lynch, & Benally, 1991; More, 1989; Salzman, 1992). However, few if any Euro-American teachers understand how the Indian family intersects with the classroom. What occurs in the culture of Indian students outside of school has a significant impact on the learning process, and Euro-American teachers who are not prepared with sufficient cultural knowledge about their charges invariably face criticism and conflict from Indian parents.

My interest is in what American Indian parents have to say about the competing views and tensions that emerge in the interaction between Indian students and Euro-American teachers as they relate to the home culture of the students. This topic became important as I continue to teach a multicultural education course to American Indian college students who are obtaining a B.A. in elementary education. Students taking the course are enrolled members of various Plains Indian tribes, and have all attended Tribal colleges prior to beginning the teacher education program. This latter point is important because Indians who first go to tribal colleges before moving to Anglo four-year institutions are four times more likely to graduate than Indian students beginning a four-year program as freshmen (Boyer, 1989).

From the first day I met the students in the teacher-training program they were vocal in their dissatisfaction with the way Indian children are taught in the schools run by primarily Euro-American teachers. All the students have had children in the K-12 system, which means they all had experience with dealing with the school system and their children's teachers. The issues raised had less to do with the specific lessons or assignments given by the Euro-American teachers. The Indian parents' concerns focused on the lack of understanding and empathy demonstrated by the Anglo teachers toward some important cultural aspects of the children. To address this issue, I gave assignments where the prospective Indian teachers prepared presentations to be delivered to a new group of Euro-American teachers who would be teaching their children. The purpose was to address the question "What do Euro-American teachers need to know about the culture of Indian children to be successful in the classroom?" The assignments allow students to turn their concerns about Anglo teachers into an opportunity to explicitly address how, if at all, their children's teachers were failing to meet the cultural needs of the community.

The Indian student presentations were examined with an eye toward describing the cultural communicative *radiants* as used by the Indian students when they talked about what Euro-American teachers need to know. According to Carbaugh (2005), this type of discourse may reveal "something about our common senses of acting . . . of being . . . of relating . . . of feeling . . . and of dwelling *together*" (p. 1). What I heard were points of potential tensions and specific communicative prescriptions for Euro-Americans when interacting with Indian children. What emerged were three general prescriptions for Anglo teacher behavior. Each of these was prefaced by descriptions of how the speaker had experienced problems with Anglo teachers in the past that did not follow these prescriptions, and the negative consequences that resulted.

Radiant 1—"Who are you?" (Being)

For those people who have never lived on an American Indian reservation, the experience often takes considerable time adjusting to the juxtaposition of dominant culture characteristics, e.g., fast food chains, contemporary clothes and music, with the traditional characteristics of the tribe, i.e., powwows, native languages, terms of address, and subtle nonverbal communicative behaviors (cf. Basso, 1979; Braithwaite, 1997a, 2006; Carbaugh, 1995; Klesert, 1992; Patin, 1991; Walters, 1992). This is also true in the K-12 classroom on reservation schools. All teachers are expected to follow federal and state guidelines for what counts as good teaching, which usually entails strict adherence to codes of conduct required by law, cf. https://www.education.ne.gov/tcert/. What is not spelled out to new teachers who find themselves in

schools with predominantly Indian students is the importance of using introductions and personal background stories to start the process of creating trust
in the classroom. For many American Indian people, interactions should
begin with introductions that let all interactants know where they can be
placed in terms of social and cultural points of reference (cf. Braithwaite,
1997a). Indian people will self-identify in terms of their tribe, tribal location,
position in the tribe, and, when applicable, clan affiliation. Although no one
expects a Euro-American teacher from outside the reservation to do a formal
tribal introduction, Indian parents describe how new teachers fail to give the
most basic information about who they are and why they are at a reservation
school. The parents ask, "How do I know I can trust them (the new teachers)
if I don't know anything about them?" For the parents, and subsequently the
children, it means knowing age, marital status, cultural background, current
living situation, and, most importantly, why they came here instead of "their
own" community. For most Euro-American teachers, this degree of disclosure in a classroom seems out of place and inappropriate. However, Indian
parents prescribe this degree of personal information as a method of communicating the teacher's commitment to being part of the community. Additionally, it serves to distance the new teachers from the mostly faceless Euro-
American bureaucrats that Indian students and parents usually encounter.
When new teachers "jump right in" the classroom and fail to take time to
share personal details, students and parents describe feeling like the teacher
does not care and, more than likely, will not stay very long on the reservation. The degree of turnover by non-Indian teachers in predominantly Indian
schools is higher than any other group in almost every U.S. state. (Final
Report, 2015; Johnston-Goodstar & VeLure Roholt, 2017). The prescription
for communicating self-identity is presented as one of the most critical aspects of becoming a "good teacher" on the reservation.

Radiant 2—"What do you know?" (Acting)

Not surprisingly, little is taught in U.S. American schools about the specific
history and culture of the *562* federally recognized Indian tribes, bands,
nations, pueblos, rancherias, communities, and Native villages in the United
States (Pember, 2008). Therefore, it is understandable that new teachers to
reservation schools come with little knowledge about the people they will
teach. Although Indian parents do not expect Euro-American teachers to
know much about tribal history and customs when they first arrive, they are
continually amazed at the lack of interest demonstrated even after teaching
on the reservation year after year. The specific prescriptions provided explicitly call for new teachers to dedicate themselves to learning important information such as tribal nomenclature, important tribal events (both contemporary and historical), and, most importantly, an understanding of cultural prac-

tices that impact students. For example, many Indian parents who attempt to raise their children in "traditional" fashion talk about the importance of following behavioral prescriptions and proscriptions handed down from generation to generation. Nowhere is this more evident than in the expectations for behavior surrounding the death of a kinsman. All tribes have specific rules for how to talk about the dead, how to prepare the dead, how the family will conduct ceremonies related to the dead, and the length of time all these activities will take. Where Indian children run into trouble is when they attempt to follow these Indian rules even when they violate the Euro-American rules for education. Some tribes have a funeral ritual that runs for four full days. During this time, all the extended family, as well as those affiliated by clan and those persons considered friends of the deceased, are expected to stay close to the body to facilitate the movement of the soul to what lies for the person after death. It is especially important that children attend because of the belief that their "innocence" will provide significant comfort for the deceased and all the relatives. Few if any Euro-American teachers seem able to accept the need for the Indian children to miss school four consecutive days. From the perspective of most Anglo teachers, children who are related to the deceased "only" by a second, third, or fourth cousin relationship do not "qualify" as needing to be at a funeral for four days. Children who have no blood relationship whatsoever are never seen as needing to attend the funeral rites. From the Indian parent's perspective, this unwillingness to acknowledge a different version of what constitutes a "family" is particularly unreasonable. Euro-American teachers unwilling to learn cultural knowledge continue to be a source of frustration for many Indian parents.

Radiant 3—"Do you care?" (Feeling)

As was noted above, Indian parents want to know about the motivation of "outsiders" when the new teachers come to work on the reservation. Most Indian parents want new Euro-American teachers to communicate why they are here, and why they care about their charges. Several presentations by Indian parents prescribed that new teachers must let their students know how they have come to help, not just in the classroom, but in all aspects of life. Indian parents are not afraid to detail how children on the reservation often come from homes where there is drug and alcohol use, physical abuse, domestic violence, and, most of all, crushing poverty. What they ask of new teachers is the willingness to address these issues and communicate how the teachers might make a difference. This means new teachers must learn their job does not end when the school bell rings in the afternoon, and is beyond grading assignments and preparing for the classroom. Indian parents want teachers to answer the question "Do you care?" by demonstrating their involvement with all aspects of student life, especially what happens outside the classroom. All the presentations made it clear that the Euro-American teachers were more than welcome to attend the frequent tribal events and celebrations. All said that the teachers would be welcome to many of the funeral activities, especially those intended for friends and community members. The presentations included detailed prescriptions on what Euro-American teachers should say and do to communicate to their students the willingness to learn more about Indian culture and thereby improve the relationships among teacher, student, and parent.

The three general prescriptions provided by American Indian parents allow us to hear a concern about three radiants of communicative action. First, there is the radiant of "being" as evidenced by the stated importance of using introductions and personal background stories. Second, there is a radiant of cultural "acting" as evidenced by the prescription to learn important information about the local people in order to understand contemporary tribal practices. Finally, there is the radiant of "feeling" as it pertains to the need for Euro-American teachers to explain why they are working with American Indian children and, most importantly, why this is a task they value. Taken together, we can see the fundamental tensions experienced in the education context where parents are questioning the issues of identity, knowledge, and relationships of Euro-American teachers. Having had my own qualifications as a teacher of American Indian students called into question, I can understand how the communication of these concerns would lead some new teachers to be unwilling to continue. However, in all cases, the American Indian parents who generated these prescriptions could give examples of Euro-American teachers that were successful in the classroom, and they generally had hope for the future of American Indian education, especially since they had the goal of becoming K-12 teachers themselves.

CONCLUSION

According to Carbaugh (2007), "cultural analysts benefit from knowing what communication practices are saying about where people are, how they are related to those places, and what should be done when inhabiting them" (p. 11). The three sections in this chapter each attempt to provide the kind of data that Carbaugh has described as necessary for increasing our understanding of communicative life. In the preceding pages, we hear how, even with the best intentions, Euro-Americans create tension in their communication with some American Indians. We hear how some American Indians talk about place in a way that creates a different view of dwelling from that described by Euro-Americans. We hear how the lauded goal of language preservation can result in competing methods between American Indian and

Euro-American educators. In addition, we hear how some American Indian parents appeal to well-meaning Euro-American teachers to learn about culturally appropriate ways of speaking and relating on reservation schools. Taken together, these three glimpses into American Indian communicative life illustrate the vitality of Carbaugh's approach to cultural discourse.

NOTES

1. The term "Euro-American" is used according to recommendations that color-based terms for ethnicity be avoided, cf. R. Sheehy (2015). Let's stop using "white" and "black" to describe European-Americans and African-Americans. Retrieved from https://www.raceinquiry.com

2. Excerpts were transcribed based on and according to Hymes's discussion of ethnopoetics, cf. D. H. Hymes (2003). *Now I know only so far: Essays in ethnopoetics*. University of Nebraska Press.

3. I use the term "American Indian" and "Indian" in accordance to the preferences described by Russel Means, Lakota activist and founder of the American Indian Movement (AIM), cf. R. Means, (1996). *I am an American Indian, Not a Native American.* Treaty Productions.

REFERENCES

Basso, K. H. (1979). *Portraits of "the whiteman": Linguistic play and cultural symbols among the western Apache*. New York, NY: Cambridge University Press.

Basso, K. H. (1996). Wisdom sits in places: Landscape and language among the Western Apache. Albuquerque, NM: University of New Mexico Press.

Becker, H. S. (1995). Visual sociology, documentary photography, and photojournalism: It's almost all a matter of context. *Visual Sociology, 10*, 5–14.

Boas, F. (1966). *Introduction to handbook of American Indian languages* (Vol. 301). Lincoln, NE: University of Nebraska Press.

Bogdan, R. C., & Biklen, S. K. (1982). Qualitative research for education. Boston, MA: Allyn and Bacon.

Boyer, P (1989). *Tribal colleges: Shaping the future of Native America*. Princeton, NJ: Carnegie Foundation for the Advancement of Teaching.

Braithwaite, C. A. (1997a). Sa'ah Naaghi Bik'eh Hozhoon: An ethnography of Navajo educational communication practices. *Communication Education, 46*, 219–233.

Braithwaite, C. A. (1997b). Helping students from Tribal colleges succeed. *About Campus*, November–December, 19–23.

Braithwaite, C. A. (1998). Navajo communication and higher education. *Intercultural Communication Studies, 8*, 33–42.

Braithwaite, C. A. (2006). Roast mutton, fry bread, and Tilt-a-Whirls: Cultural and intercultural contact at the Navajo Nation Fair. In R. Lustig and J. Koester (Eds.), *AmongUS: Essays on intercultural communication* (2nd ed), (pp. 232–238). New York, NY: Addison Wesley Longman.

Brandt, E. (1992). The Navajo area student dropout study: Findings and implications. *Journal of American Indian Education, 31*, 48–63.

Carbaugh, D. (1988). *Talking American: Cultural discourses on Donahue*. Norwood, NJ: Ablex.

Carbaugh, D. (1995). "I can't do that" but "I can actually see around corners": American Indian students and the study of public communication. In J. Lehtonen (Ed.), *Critical perspectives on communication research and pedagogy* (pp. 215–234). St. Ingbert, Germany: Rohrig

Universitatsverlag. [Reprinted in J. Martin, T. Nakayama, & L. Flores (Eds.), *Readings in Cultural Contexts* (pp. 160–172). Mountain View, CA: Mayfield, 1998.]

Carbaugh, D. (1999). "Just listen":"Listening" and landscape among the Blackfeet. *Western Journal of Communication* (includes *Communication Reports*), *63*(3), 250–270.

Carbaugh, D. (2001). The people will come to you. Blackfeet narrative as a resource for contemporary living. In J. Brockmeier & D. Carbaugh (Eds.), *Narrative and identity: Studies in autobiography, self and culture* (pp. 103–127). Philadelphia, PA: John Benjamins.

Carbaugh, D. (2005). *Cultures in conversation.* New York, NY: Routledge.

Carbaugh, D. (2007). Cultural discourse analysis: Communication practices and intercultural encounters. *Journal of Intercultural Communication Research, 36*(3), 167–182.

Carbaugh, D. (2017). Terms for talk, take 2: Theorizing communication through its cultural terms and practices. In D. Carbaugh (Ed.), *The handbook of communication in cross-cultural perspective* (pp. 15–28). New York, NY: Routledge.

Carbaugh, D., & Rudnick, L. (2006). Which place, what story? Cultural discourses at the border of the Blackfeet Reservation and Glacier National Park. *Great Plains Quarterly, 26*(3), 167–184.

Cerulli, T. (2017). "Ma'iingan is our brother": Ojibwe and non-Ojibwe ways of speaking about wolves. In D. Carbaugh (Ed.), *The handbook of communication in cross-cultural perspective* (pp. 247–260). New York, NY: Routledge.

Collier Jr., J., & Collier, M. (1986). Visual anthropology: Photography as a research method, revised and expanded edition. Albuquerque, NM: University of New Mexico Press.

Dehyle, D. (1992). Constructing failure and maintaining cultural identity: Navajo and Ute school leavers. *Journal of American Indian Education, 31,* 24–47.

Dumont, R. V. (1972). Learning English and how to be silent: Studies in Sioux and Cherokee classrooms. In C. B. Cazden, V. P. John, & D. Hymes (Eds.), *Functions of language in the classroom* (pp. 32–65). New York, NY: Teachers College Press.

Final Report: South Dakota Native American Student Achievement Advisory Council (November 1, 2015). Retrieved from https://indianeducation.sd.gov/documents/NASAAC-FR.pdf

Greymorning, N. (2011). A language warrior's eighteen years of running a gauntlet for indigenous languages. *The Canadian Journal of Native Studies, 31*(1), 193.

Hagedorn, M. (1994). Hermeneutic photography: An innovative esthetic technique for generating data in nursing research. *Advances in Nursing Science, 17,* 44–50.

Hale, D. K. (1991). *Researching and writing tribal histories.* Grand Rapids, MI: The Michigan Indian Press.

Holbrook, M. B., & Kuwahara, T. (1998). Collective stereographic photo essays: An integrated approach to probing consumption experiences in depth. *International Journal of Research in Marketing, 15*(3), 201–221.

Hymes, D. (1972). Models of the interaction of language and social setting. *Journal of Social Issues, 23*(2), 8–28.

Hymes, D. H. (2003). *Now I know only so far: Essays in ethnopoetics.* Lincoln, NE: University of Nebraska Press.

Johnston-Goodstar, K., & VeLure Roholt, R. (2017). "Our kids aren't dropping out; They're being pushed out": Native American students and racial microaggressions in schools. *Journal of Ethnic & Cultural Diversity in Social Work, 26*(1–2), 30–47.

Killion, C. (2001) Understanding cultural aspects of health through photography. *Nursing Outlook, 49,* 50–54.

Klesert, A. (1992). A view from Navajoland on the reconciliation of anthropologists and Native Americans. *Human Organizations, 51*(1), 17–22.

McDermott, B. (2014). *Language healers—Native Americans revitalizing native languages.* United States: EmpathyWorks Films.

McCarty, T. L. (2008). Native American languages as heritage mother tongues. *Language, Culture and Curriculum, 21*(3), 201–225. doi:10.1080/07908310802385881

McCarty, T. L., Wallace, S., Lynch, R., & Benally, A. (1991). Classroom inquiry and Navajo learning styles: A call for reassessment. *Anthropology and Education Quarterly, 22,* 42–59.

McCarty, T. L., & Watahomigie, L. J. (1999). Indigenous community-based language education in the USA. In S. May (Ed.), *Indigenous community-based education* (pp. 79–94). Philadelphia, PA: Multilingual Matters.

Meadows, D. H. (2008). *Thinking in systems: A primer.* White River Junction, VT: Chelsea Green Publishing Company.

Means, R. (1996). *I am an American Indian, not a Native American.* Treaty Productions.

More, A. (August 1989). Native American learning styles: A review for researchers and teachers. *Journal of American Indian Education (Special Issue),* 15–28.

Patin, T. (1991). White mischief: Metaphor and desire in a misreading of Navajo culture. *American Indian Cultural Resources Journal, 15*(4), 75–89.

Pember, M. A. (2008). A mandate for native history. *Diverse Issues in Higher Education, 24*(7), 18–19.

Peshkin, A. (1997). *Places of memory: Whiteman's schools and Native American communities.* Mahwah, NJ: Erlbaum.

Philips, S. (1983). *The invisible culture: Communication in classroom and community on the Warm Springs Indian Reservation.* New York, NY: Longman.

Philipsen, G. (1981/1987). The prospect for cultural communication. In D. L. Kincaid (Ed.), *Communication theory from Eastern and Western perspectives* (pp. 245–254). New York, NY: Academic Press.

Philipsen, G., Coutu, L., & Covarrubias, P. (2005). Speech codes theory: Restatement, revisions, and response to criticism (pp. 55–68). In W. B. Gudykunst (Ed.), *Cross-cultural and intercultural communication.* Sage.

Philipsen, G., & National Communication Association. (2010). *Coming to terms with cultures: Carroll C. Arnold Distinguished Lecture.* Boston: Allyn & Bacon.

Riley, R. G., & Manias, E. (2004). The uses of photography in clinical nursing practice and research: A literature review. *Journal of Advanced Nursing, 48*: 397–405.

Salzman, J. (1992). The construction of an intercultural sensitizer training non-Navajo personnel. *Journal of American Indian Education, 30,* 25–33.

Sheehy, R. (2015). Let's stop using "white" and "black" to describe European-Americans and African-Americans. Retrieved fromhttps://www.raceinquiry.com

Szymanski, M., Whitewing, L., & Colletti, J. (1998). The use of participatory rural appraisal methodologies to link indigenous knowledge and land use decisions among the Winnebago Tribe of Nebraska. *Indigenous Knowledge and Development, 6*(2), 3–6.

Teacher Certification/Nebraska Department of Education. (July 13, 2017). Retrieved from https://www.education.ne.gov/tcert/

Walters, A. L. (1992). *Talking Indian: Reflections on survival and writing.* Ithaca, NY: Firebrand Books.

Chapter Fourteen

Engaging Change

*Exploring the Adaptive and Generative Potential of
Cultural Discourse Analysis Findings for Policies and
Social Programs*

Lisa Rudnick, Saskia Witteborn, and Ruth Edmonds

One form of discourse that is especially consequential to the quality of people's lives is policy discourse.[1] We use the term *policy* broadly here to refer
to administratively situated plans to guide institutional action in an effort to
create, or change, some set of conditions. In this sense, some policies can be
seen as agendas for change. This broad definition invites us to consider a
wide range of agendas for action, for example, from those developed to
affect conditions *within* an organization (like a university, or company, or
government ministry) to those developed to change conditions outside of
organizations (such as within or across communities or nation-states). By
their nature, policies identify both a problem to be addressed and what can
and should be done about it. In doing so, they set parameters for action for
communities and institutions alike that have powerful impacts upon people's
well-being and lived experience.

Policy *discourse*, then, in our usage here, refers both to forms of communication *constituting* policy itself (such as treaties, laws, regulations, etc.) and
communication *about* policy (such as discussions integral to the very design
and negotiation of such legal or administrative frameworks, as well as those
that explore approaches to implementation, or that represent, analyze, debate,
or critique policy positions). Just like other discourses, policy discourses
reflect a particular set of assumptions and interpretations, for example about
people, places, and action. But these assumptions are not always active
among the communities toward which policies themselves are targeted. This

disconnect between institutional policy discourses on one hand and community discourses on the other is problematic because, at best, it can lead to agendas that are ineffective in creating the change they seek. At worst, it can lead to unintended harm. Therefore, this asynchrony, and the stakes concerning well-being involved, calls out for both analysis and evidence-based intervention (Miller & Rudnick, 2008).

In this chapter we, therefore, discuss the utility of Carbaugh's approach to cultural discourse analysis (CuDA) for attending to this asynchrony by illuminating instances in which policies appear to be deaf to local discourses (intentionally or unintentionally), and in enabling a grounded critical approach to this dynamic. CuDA's central thesis is that "communication presumes and creates a rich meta-cultural commentary through socially situated, culturally named practices" (Carbaugh, 2017, p. 19). Within these practices, "we can identify a small range of discursive hubs . . . [which] create an ongoing largely implicit and also presumably shared commentary" in relation to who we are (*hub of being* or *identity*), what we are doing (*hub of acting*), how we are related (*hub of relating*), what and how we feel and express such feeling (*hub of feeling*), and about "the nature of things" (*hub of dwelling*) (p. 19). Thus, by mapping this system of hubs and radiants, the analyst is able to construct, describe, and interpret cultural discourses. When employed in the comparative mode, CuDA provides an empirical and interpretive basis upon which to detect differences between such discourses. Hence, turning the CuDA lens upon policy discourses can do two important things: produce useful findings about the cultural premises and meanings active in them, and illuminate key differences, both in terms of form and meaning, between institutionally and communally situated discourses (see Carbaugh, 2007).

Such differences are important to know about and understand, we argue, because of the consequentiality of policy in the lived experiences of people. On this point, CuDA can be usefully employed in the critical mode. Like Hymes (1985), who pointed to the existing hierarchies of communicative repertoires in a given speech community in terms of availability, access, and possibilities of performing those repertoires, Carbaugh pointed to the critical mode of researching and theorizing communication as a cultural practice. He defines the critical voice as "*an evaluation from an ethical juncture*" (1989/ 1990, p. 264). Hence, the critical approach, grounded in the larger theoretical trajectory of the ethnography of communication (Carbaugh, 1989/1990; Hymes, 1972), features evaluation and ethics as key components, with object (what is evaluated), stance (cultural actor, researcher, or third entity), and mode of criticism (direct or indirectly inferred) being three essential elements to identify.

When employed in the critical mode, CuDA creates valuable resources for improving our understanding of the dynamics between different, and differently positioned, communities of actors, such as the authors and subjects of policy initiatives. By analyzing the distinctive meanings about persons, social relations, actions, emotions, and dwelling that shape agendas for change, and by bringing local premises and values into view, CuDA provides grounded empirical evidence on such dynamics between authors and subjects. In this way, CuDA generates grounded insights that have the potential for enabling more positive, ethical, and effective engagement between these communities.

In this chapter, we explore two cases in which policy discourses differ from local discourses in the ways they thematize key hubs of *being, relating, acting*, and *dwelling*. First, Rudnick and Edmonds discuss their work at the United Nations Institute for Disarmament Research (UNIDIR), comparing how the hub of *being* and the related radiants of *acting* and *relating* take shape in different discursive models of *child*: one animating international policy discourse, and one active in some local discourses in the Terai region of Nepal. They consider the implications of their findings for (re)orienting international programming for local children. Next, Witteborn discusses how CuDA can be applied to work with displaced people and can help spur an agenda for change in a place where such persons are positioned as bureaucratic and legal categories. Hence, the hub of *dwelling* and the radiants of *being* and *relating* will be highlighted from the perspective of the displaced, and how those stand in competition with dominating policy discourse. We conclude the chapter by discussing how CuDA findings can be employed in what we refer to as the adaptive and generative modes in relation to agendas for change, while also considering the challenges in the usability of CuDA findings in the design of policies and programs.

MODELS OF *CHILD* IN TWO DISCOURSES[2]

International Policy Discourse

The UN Convention on the Rights of the Child (UNCRC) lays the foundation for all the work that UNICEF does as well as the work of other UN agencies and international actors engaging children (UNICEF, 2017). It is a legally binding international agreement initially ratified in 1989. To date, the United States is the only UN member state to have not ratified the convention (United Nations, 2017). The UNCRC is the "world's most ratified human rights treaty," indicating just how prominent a policy discourse this represents (United Nations, 2017, p. 1).

The UNCRC sets out *what* to attend to—in this case, the rights to be granted and protected for persons identified as *children*—but typically refrains from instruction for *how* this is achieved in practice. Rather it is the job of implementing actors to translate this broad policy into plans and actions;

for example, in creating legislation, developing standards, or developing local programming, all to be carried out in local contexts.

The UNCRC consists of 52 articles (United Nations, 1989). As with all human rights conventions, some of these are procedural, but others pertain to substantive matters of defining persons, expressing values, and delineating rights. In looking across some of the articles with the aid of CuDA we can observe how the hub of *being* is expressed in this text, and the radiants of acting and relating that are activated along with it. In doing so, we trace some common assumptions that are also reflected more broadly in international policy discourse about *children* and *childhood*.

For example, Article 1, "Definition of the Child," sets out the definition of person who is the primary subject of the UNCRC. This very definition reflects a model of person based on certain premises of *being*, which serve as an anchor to the rest of the convention. Article 1 states that "a child means every human being below the age of eighteen years unless, under the law applicable to the child, majority is attained earlier" (United Nations, 1989, p. 2). This definition builds on a perceived natural and universal distinction, delineating and distinguishing the categories of persons *children* and *adults* first and foremost on the basis of biology and age, and draws from an idiom of biology that can be observed in certain cultural discourses of personhood and identity.[3]

Article 12, which is titled "Respect for the Views of the Child" (also sometimes referred to as "The Child's Opinion"), states that "States Parties shall assure to the child who is capable of forming his or her own views the right to express those views freely in all matters affecting the child" (United Nations, 1989, p. 4). Here, as in the Declaration of Human Rights, "free expression" is enshrined as a "right." Of note is what this free expression should be about, that is, the views of the child, in all matters affecting the child.

Furthermore, such persons are depicted throughout the UNCRC as rights-bearing individuals, that is to say, they are first and foremost persons to whom rights are accorded on the basis of their individual selves (i.e., irrespective of, and not through, their relationship to another person). For example, consider the first part of Article 13,[4] which is titled "Freedom of Expression" and states that:

> [t]he child shall have the right to freedom of expression; this right shall include freedom to seek, receive and impart information and ideas of all kinds, regardless of frontiers, either orally, in writing or in print, in the form of art, or through any other media of the child's choice. (p. 4)

Taken together, these three statements begin to sketch a central logic that is reflected throughout the UNCRC. Children are a specific category of human being determined by biological age (17 years and younger). Like all human beings, children are rights-bearing individuals and, as individuals, they have views about themselves and all things affecting them. The expression of these views, as well as ideas and information of all kinds, is a right. The nature of this right includes the freedom to seek, receive, and impart information and to do so in the form of their choosing (written, orally, artistically, etc.).

To our reading, this logic recalls findings from a rich literature exploring the hub of *being* as it is often active in a range of communication practices and instances taking place in, or involving participants from, the United States, especially where the symbol of self is used (Carbaugh, 1989, 1996, 2005; Katriel & Philipsen, 1981; Philipsen, 1992). With it, Carbaugh explains, a model of person is conveyed, in which people are understood as "individuals, with their own thoughts, feelings, and experiences," which are presumed to be "uniquely within each person," and to a great extent, unique *to* each person. "For this reason, it is crucial to hear . . . from every one of us," with such expression to be enjoyed freely, as a "fundamental right, protected by institutions of law, and championed in the folk's morality" (2005, p. 121). Here there is a premise of *being*. People are unique individuals, different and separate from each other, with their own experience, feelings, and opinions. And there is a premise of *action* as communicating these experiences, feelings, and opinions freely is a right and a primary means of connecting with other unique individuals.

These premises can be observed radiating strongly in the public and professional commentary, which interprets the convention as well as in its additional articles. While beyond the scope of this chapter, such an analysis reveals a rich discourse in which people are understood as individuals with selves with their own views and opinions; that the expression of those views and opinions takes shape through a range of communicative practices; that such expression is a right; and finally, importantly, that the exercise of this right by all members of society is the foundation of a societal ideal: a "democratic" society.

Our claim here is not that the UNCRC is built upon a U.S. American model of personhood, but to note the close similarities. This is significant because the models of person and society reflected in the examples above can be contrasted with others in the world, which cast persons less as independent, expressive individuals and more as embedded within an important complex set of family and community relationships. Importantly, the model of child enshrined in the UNCRC reflects a globalized notion of childhood that permeates much policy discourse in both the domestic and international spheres (see Burman, 1996; Niewenhuys, 1998; White, 1996, 1999). Embedded within ideas about Western modernity, this globalized notion of childhood serves as a universal ideal or *standard* of childhood and takes shape as normative values that guide both the goals and purposes of much child-focused programming (White, 1996, 1999). From this perspective, the category of *child* is based on a natural and universal distinction between *children* and *adults*, defined on the basis of biological age. *Childhood* is depicted as a rather passive time of play, education, and protection (by adult others), dependency (upon adult others), and very limited responsibility, as contrasted with *adulthood* as a time of work, independence, decision-making, and responsibility (Robson, 2004). Where childhoods are deemed to be somehow outside of this globalized model, they are often depicted as lost or stolen (Boyden, 1990).

Policies and programming developed on the basis of this discourse reflect an agenda for change that orients toward (re)establishing these conditions of childhood. However, this orientation can prove problematic when applied in local contexts, where there may be a very different version of *childhood* active as a feature of local cultural systems, but also as a result of the experience of protracted violent conflict. This was a key discovery in our fieldwork, which was conducted in several small rural villages in the Terai region of Nepal, including one near the town of Ranjitpur in Saptari District, South Eastern Nepal, which we describe next.

Local Discourse

The analysis presented here is derived from research conducted as part of the Security Needs Assessment Protocol project at UNIDIR (Miller, Rudnick, Payne, & Acharya, 2010) and is based on talk generated both through interviews with community members and through group discussions and interviews with our Nepali team members who played a central role in both collaborative data generation and analysis.[5] A key finding from this research was that when community members spoke to us in Mathili about children and childhood, *child* was not a fixed identity or category of person, nor was it tightly associated with age or age ranges. Instead, community members oriented to phases of *development* associated with particular *capacities, activities, and kinds of relationships*. Therefore, there were many terms of identity to understand when learning about the category of *child*. For example, one term of identity, *baacha*, is used for someone who, among other things, does not earn money to support the family and "plays near the home," while the term *jabaan* is used to refer to someone who, among other things, helps around the house, may work outside the home (though only under specific conditions for girls), and contributes financially to the family. Chronological age, therefore, is a less central feature in many social roles and identities here, in comparison to some in other places. (Consider, for example, the term for identity *teenager*, which is directly associated with biological age.) Hence, the social roles or identities available for children, both in families and communities, are made available to them by family and community members on the basis of an ongoing evaluation of maturity, responsibility, and capability as primarily demonstrated through a range of practices and qualities.

In this village, as well as others we visited in the Terai, ways of demonstrating maturity were explicitly linked to a range of practices that demonstrate an orientation to others, for example, the ability to look after others, to bring honor to parents, community, and village, to support the family financially, and to make *good decisions*—that is, decisions that are focused on the needs of and obligations to others (as opposed to putting yourself first) and being mindful of the impact on others. This was systematically explained to us in terms of "fulfilling *iksha* and *akaanksha*," or the set of *expectations* and *obligations* between parents and children (but also implicating community and caste relationships) that make up what is known as *good sanskar*, or a *good upbringing*.

These terms tap into a set of complex concepts, such as a model of person as both fluid and inherently interconnected (to both other such persons and spiritual entities); a privileging of connections between people (as opposed to individual desires, for example); and an understanding of such connections as being created and maintained in great part through reciprocal relationships that places emphasis on actions and tasks. These concepts, which are also reflected in other studies of culture and models of sociation in the region (see Zharkevich, 2009), seem to crystallize some key beliefs about how people can and should relate to one another, through what kinds of actions, and what meanings (for example, about identity) radiated through such actions (see Lamb, 2000). While too complex to adequately capture here, we can nevertheless attempt a summary through formulating some key premises:

1. A premise of relating: *A person is always inherently connected to others and therefore understood in and through their relationships with others* (specifically between parents and children, and families and communities, but also extending to neighboring communities and castes).

2. A premise of acting: *By doing certain things for you—especially things that contribute to your economic well-being and honor and reputation—I fulfill your expectations (of me, of our relationship). By fulfilling these expectations, this in turn obliges you to do the same for me, in ways that are appropriate to your role/position. Therefore, through such actions, we remain interconnected.*

3. A premise of *being*: *As a growing person, I progress through this system of reciprocal relationships by demonstrating increasing maturity. This involves an awareness of the expectations others have of me*

and showing an increasingly other-orientation (as opposed to self-orientation) in my decisions and actions.

These premises provided us with a crucial interpretive frame that enabled us to more appropriately understand some of the tensions we were observing in this postconflict context. Set against a backdrop of a decade of civil war, notions of *childhood* and transitions to *adulthood* in Nepal are now strongly associated with gaining experience of violent activities and becoming politicized. Such experiences provide a pathway for transitioning from childhood to adulthood, which certainly differs from those valued from the point of view of Western policy discourse. However, they also vary from many locally held notions of acceptable and valued transition as well. This is especially the case when it comes to girls, who, by leaving home under unsanctioned conditions, traveling to unknown locations, and engaging in unknown practices with strangers, have violated countless tenets of good *sanskar*. In joining the Maoists to fight in distant places, they have broken the reciprocal *iksha* and *akaanksha* with their parents, casting dishonor on their family. For some parents and daughters alike, the pain of this rupture was too difficult to even recount.

Young people returning to civilian life in the villages we visited faced a challenging and complicated process of reestablishing a place for themselves within their families and communities. On the one hand, familiar pathways to practice-based identities have been disrupted or broken, presenting real challenges from local points of view. On the other, their own perceptions and lived experiences, in which they perceive themselves to be *warriors* and *fighters*, no longer occupying the social position of *child* despite their biological age but rather having earned a different role in their communities, can clash with the globalized notions of childhood of international assistance and programming.

Implications

Our assertion is that these insights have implications for programming to be conducted in this place and others like it. Namely, these findings indicate that in order to be locally effective, agendas for change, and the approaches to programming used to implement them, must consider how they identify what is problematic, determine what kinds of steps can be taken to remedy that, and decide who can go about doing that and *how*, from the vantage point of local discourses (see Miller & Rudnick, 2008, 2010, 2011; Edmonds, 2016).

At the time of this research (2009 and 2010), the change being contemplated by our implementing partner (UNICEF) was the reintegration of several thousand children associated with armed forces or armed groups (CAA-FAG), with ex-combatants among them. Equipped now with an understanding of the two discourses discussed above, the difference between them, and some of the tensions emerging around local discourse itself, we are able to reconsider some standard elements of international programming. For example, the contrasting findings here invite program designers and policy makers to reflect on the following:

1. *Beneficiary targeting:* Policy guidelines direct who can and should be targeted for assistance. However, community members reported to us, with a sense of unfairness, benefits for "children" being given to people who were considered to have passed out of that phase of their lives. In fragile contexts, where needs are vast and tensions are high, approaches that do not take cultural discourses and models of person into consideration can contribute to social tensions and vulnerabilities of individuals.

2. *Programming "packages" or options:* Programming that focuses on restoring "lost and stolen childhoods" according to the standards enshrined in the policy discourse of the UNCRC is potentially problematic for several reasons. First, approaches that remove children from their productive roles in families and communities because this is seen to contradict globalized ideals about how children should spend their time can inadvertently interrupt a child's forward progression in their community. For example, the system of *iksha* and *akaankasha* observed in the Terai, and the powerful meanings associated with it, suggests the importance of household tasks and income-generating activities (among others) for participating in the central networks of care for these communities. Removing children and young people from such participation could block off a primary local route to reintegration itself, by inhibiting the very forms of participation through which one can both cultivate and demonstrate their belonging. Second, such approaches can fail to acknowledge children's own perceptions (which is meant to be a cornerstone of approaches grounded in the UNCRC), but rather can place them between two competing discourses with little recourse or power.

3. *Indicators of success:* Programming that fails to adequately consider children and young people in the context of their family and community relationships while instead focusing on individual achievement can miss locally meaningful indicators of successful reintegration in Ranjitpur and places like it. This can inadvertently encourage the very things that undermine rather than help strengthen social cohesion.

These few examples demonstrate how CuDA can highlight the ways in which policy discourses, which may be presumed as neutral tools, are in fact also built upon notions of *being*, *relating*, and *acting* that reflect cultural, rather than universal, premises and meanings. Further, we have shown that CuDA can generate findings that have profound implications for (re)orienting, or adapting, agendas for change to local contexts. This is a powerful contribution, especially when combined with other work in the sociology of childhood and children's rights, which increasingly draws attention to children's differentiated lived experiences (for example, Hansen, 2008; Honwana & De Boeck, 2005; Payne, 2009, 2012; Punch, 2002; Robson, 2004) and the fact that guidance and direction for realizing the rights of children should be consistent with their evolving capacities rather than age dependent (Lansdown, 2005). While the discussed case has explored an asynchrony between policy and local discourse through the discursive hub of *being* and the radiants of *acting* and *relating*, Witteborn's focus will now turn to the asynchrony between policy and local discourse through the lens of the hub of *dwelling* and the radiants of *being* and *relating*.

COMPETING DISCOURSES ON DWELLING

The Example of Refugees and Asylum Seekers in Hong Kong

Like other hubs and radiants of meaning in CuDA, dwelling, understood as physical and symbolic place-making and being-in-place, is central for humans as it grounds them in material and social textures and relations (Carbaugh, 2007; Milstein, Anguiano, Sandoval, Chen, & Dickinson, 2011; Philipsen, 1992; Witteborn & Sprain, 2009). Dwelling not only shapes how people live their lives (e.g., physical environment or social positioning), but is also setting the structures within which such life is lived (e.g., policies). Hence, it is important to understand how policy makers create discourses about place and thus set the physical, social, and positional place structure within which people live. The question is what happens when people are deemed placeless and become deprived of their need to engage in place-making through policy discourse and practice as in the case of refugees and asylum seekers.[6] Hong Kong SAR, the geopolitical and cultural context for this study, has a comparatively small asylum seeker and refugee population (around 10,000) from African, South, and Southeast Asian countries (Justice Centre Hong Kong, 2017). The problems the displaced in Hong Kong encounter are similar to those in other countries such as long asylum processes, uncertainty, and limited finances (Witteborn, 2011, 2015). In addition, Hong Kong SAR has not signed the Geneva Refugee Convention from 1951, and recognized refugees need to be resettled to third countries, which makes it difficult for refugees to create a sense of place for themselves during the months and years spent in the city.

This section discusses the meanings of being a *refugee* and *asylum seeker* in Hong Kong SAR through the hub of dwelling and the radiants of *being* and *relating*. It does so by illustrating two competing discourses: refugee and asylum seeker as a bureaucratic and legal category (policy discourse) and refugee and asylum seeker as a person-being-in-place (discourse by the displaced). As the focus on dwelling will illustrate, refugees and asylum seekers articulate their own meanings about the importance of place during transit in Hong Kong, including the importance of digital place to enact themselves as a person. This articulation of the importance of dwelling, understood here as embodied, digital, and positional, does not alleviate the hardships imposed by the local legal and political asylum system but eventually allows people to shift models of imposed personhood and ways of being and relating.

Refugee and Asylum Seeker as Bureaucratic and Legal Category

UNHCR processed asylum claims in Hong Kong until 2014. Since then, the immigration department of the Hong Kong government has taken over through the unified screening mechanism (USM), with UNHCR being responsible for recognizing refugee status and resettlement. The implementation of the USM sets up a policy tension among institutional actors that directly impacts the lives of the displaced. This is evidenced in the following excerpt:

> The commencement of the USM does not affect the Government's position that the Refugee Convention and its 1967 Protocol have never been applied to Hong Kong and our firm policy of not determining the refugee status of or granting asylum to anyone. . . . The UNHCR will continue to provide international protection to refugees in accordance with its mandate. In this connection, persons whose non-refoulement claim is substantiated under the USM on grounds of persecution risk will be referred to the UNHCR for recognition as refugees under its mandate and, if so recognised, arrangement of resettlement of them to a third country. (Hong Kong Information Services Department, 2014)

This excerpt from governmental sources pertaining to the treatment of people seeking asylum in Hong Kong summarizes key policy premises related to the physical, symbolic, and legal place of *refugee*. The main premise related to dwelling can be summarized in the following way: *As Hong Kong has not signed the Geneva Refugee Convention, refugees have the right to have their claim processed and access to related services in Hong Kong but no right to stay.* Through the lens of this premise, asylum seekers and refugees become legal and bureaucratic categories (Zetter, 1991, 2007), dwelling in bureaucratic and legal places. Asylum seekers in Hong Kong are not allowed to work. They receive housing assistance, food stamps, and some transport money, which amounts to around USD 385 per month. As the monthly housing allowance is approximately USD 230 in one of the most expensive real estate markets in the world, people have to share the already small apartments in Hong Kong with strangers, often for years. There are NGOs, which cater to the legal needs of the displaced, their social needs, and the need for political representation. And yet asylum seekers and refugees live on the physical and positional fringes of society as they have no right to work and there is limited access to education for adults, restricting participation in the life of Hong Kong and making material and social life dependable on the category of being an asylum seeker or refugee.[7] The premise of refugee as only being allowed to dwell in legal and bureaucratic places is supported by the low recognition rate in Hong Kong. The recognition rate is below one percent (Ming, 2016), which is another indicator by the government to deter refugees with the message that Hong Kong is neither a place for settlement nor a place to gain refugee status.

This premise of bureaucratic dwelling relates to the premise of what it means to be a person, relating in place: *A person seeking protection under existing international treaties is bound by the parameters of these treaties and the parameters set by the government of Hong Kong. Under these conditions, the person has to oblige the rules set within these parameters and relate with others only insofar as not to violate those rules (e.g., not working while the asylum claim is pending)*. Hence, a substantive number of asylum seekers and refugees live in precarious physical and social places (Witteborn, 2012a/b), with the knowledge of having few opportunities to create relations with social groups in Hong Kong beyond other asylum seekers or marginalized communities (e.g., domestic helpers). In sum, there is a Hong Kong policy premise of the asylum seeker and refugee as a bureaucratic and legal category with the consequence of allowing people referred to as such only to dwell, relate, and be within the limits of a predefined judicial and bureaucratic place. This leaves asylum seekers and refugees in a precarious physical, social, and emotional position. From the perspective of asylum seekers and refugees, this precarious situation is not desirable and requires change (Witteborn, 2012b).

Refugees and Asylum Seekers as Persons-in-Place: The Role of Digital Technologies

Discourses of dwelling are operative as key symbolic resources for refugees and asylum seekers in Hong Kong, with digital dwelling playing a major role. Digital platforms and mobile technologies have become spaces of place-making and sociality for asylum seekers and refugees for more than a decade (e.g., Khorshed & Imran, 2015; Leung, 2007). Research in Germany has illustrated, for example, that refugees are using digital platforms and social media for resource allocation like news, learning German, finding educational and work opportunities if the status allows, for creating social networks, and for entertainment to beat the daily boredom and uncertainty (Witteborn, 2012a, 2014). In Hong Kong, the platforms might differ (e.g., using WeChat instead of WhatsApp) but the importance of the digital as a space and place of dwelling is equally important. In the following, I will provide one example to illustrate the claim. The analysis will show that dwelling cannot be looked at in isolation but is intimately intertwined with the radiants of *being* and *relating*.

The people my research assistants and I interviewed from 2014 to 2017 in Hong Kong[8] and accompanied in their journeys through urban and digital spaces have talked about digital platforms as a place of dwelling. In the interviews, participants pointed repeatedly to the digital as a place of dwelling and even a home, as in "Facebook is my home," "Facebook is the place to meet people," "Social media is great as I can control who comes in and who stays out," or "We use WhatsApp and email to share information." Those phrases point to a pattern that imagines the digital as a place of dwelling. This place of dwelling is private and public as it is a "*space-to-be* and a *space-to-share*" (Cotter & Wilson, 2014). People talked about Facebook or WhatsApp as a space to share information and contacts, as a space to meet people, and as a safe space that can create a sense of ownership. Social media in particular were described as sanctuaries whose boundaries and thresholds could be controlled by allowing or denying access. In their daily digital conduct, participants marked digital place by employing algorithms to create profiles, post pictures and texts. They established a digital home as a place of sociality and interactivity by decorating it through profile pictures, visuals of their daily life, by inviting people on Facebook, or using the platform as a place of entertaining, sharing, or discussing, thereby enhancing social capital (compare Ellison, Vitak, Gray, & Lampe, 2014). Like a physical home, the digital one was essential for the newcomers to socialize and present themselves as a living person with shared interests, skills, and aspirations beyond a bureaucratic category.

Joe (name changed), an asylum seeker from an African country, is a case in point. Joe is an artist and musician and has been in Hong Kong for many years as his asylum claim is still pending. He has made Hong Kong friends and had regular visits from other local friends from the African country he had fled from. Joe performed in the city for free as he was not allowed to work, but he was very interested in creating cultural encounters through music and art. He went to church regularly and had close relationships with the congregation. Although he was worried, he tried to remain hopeful regarding his asylum claim, counting on the relationships and social support he had developed with the church community, NGOs, and Hong Kong friends.

Joe was also an avid social media user and promoted his band performances and art exhibitions through Facebook. Facebook became one of the homes in which Joe welcomed new friends, shared insights on his music and art, and networked with other people seeking asylum and Hong Kongers through the passion for the arts. This digital home became a place of cultural encounter. This encounter was characterized by meaning-making in the commonly shared language of performative art, of sounds, sights, and affective relating that did not require the terminology of forced migrancy, bureaucratic categorization, and being out of place. Joe connected people by inviting them to be-with-each-other in the digital setting of the Facebook page and by engaging in shared communicative practices, such as commenting on the performances of the band, replying to each other and sharing pictures, by scheduling meetings in physical spaces, and having snippets of conversations. Joe thus built a digital home not only for himself but also for others who were supportive of encounters through art. For him, being a displaced person was a personal, social, and political mode of being. But even more, being a displaced person did not mean being a victim defined by legal and bureaucratic typologies and related support. Being displaced, for Joe, meant being a person with talents and skills, hopes and aspirations that pushed back against the category of *refugee* or *asylum seeker* as a person only defined by international treaties and local jurisdiction. Based on this case study and data from interviews, participant observations, and social media analysis, a formulation of the following premises for *dwelling, relating,* and *being* from the perspective of asylum seekers and refugees in Hong Kong can be made:

1. *Dwelling is an integrative part of life and participation in a social group. As asylum seekers and refugees in Hong Kong are limited in their participation, digital space becomes an alternative for dwelling.*
2. *Digital space allows for expanding identities and what it means to be a person beyond the category "refugee" or "asylum seeker."*
3. *Digital space allows for expanding ways of relating, although relating in digital space does not replace relating in physical space.*

The digital home became a place to create a model of personhood, which was grounded in notions of connection and social interaction (see Diminescu, 2008). This model of connected personhood was in contrast to the placeless model of personhood promoted by the government.

Implications

There are at least two competing discourses about *refugee* and *asylum seeker* in Hong Kong. There is the policy discourse on the category of the *asylum seeker* or *refugee*, creating a model of personhood, which is out of place until normalized through legal and bureaucratic procedure. Refugees and asylum seekers generated their own discourses about *dwelling, relating,* and *being* through migration to digital places (e.g., social media like Facebook, WhatsApp, or Instagram). As such, the people enacted themselves as being-in-place through personal skills, aspirations, and the desire for sociality and social participation.

The insights into how displaced people create a digital home and local social networks through digital technology and how they envision themselves as *persons in place* is key to changing the conditions for asylum seekers and refugees in Hong Kong. Part of this change is acknowledging the desire of refugees for social participation and interaction and changing public opinion in Hong Kong, influenced by negative media discourses about the displaced as social parasites taking resources from society (Read, March 31, 2016). A change in public opinion, in turn, can increase public mobilization and support for refugees, including additional government services and material resources, less bureaucracy for schools and universities to accept asylum seekers, and social perspective change, including acknowledging Hong Kong as a migrant society and city of refuge. Even more, understanding how people build place through digital technologies is key to fulfilling the vision of Hong Kong as a connecting space *between East and West* (see Hong Kong Tourism Board, 2017). Asylum seekers like Joe worked on this goal by creating cultural encounters in the city, efforts that should be acknowledged by local policy discourse. Although Hong Kong has decided to remain a transit city for refugees, it still has the moral and ethical responsibility as a wealthy global node of finance to provide the displaced with the infrastructure to prepare themselves for their lives elsewhere. Access to education, work, and technology, integrating intercultural expertise like the one by Joe into local education and providing monetary rewards for this expertise, support of nongovernmental initiatives, and fast asylum processes are some ways to put this vision into practice. In sum, the comparison of two discourses on dwelling, relating, and personhood is one of the examples of the theoretical and social impact of CuDA and its critical and comparative potential.

CONCLUSION

In the two cases explored here, the value of CuDA lies in part in generating findings that are both empirical and cultural in nature, applied in the comparative mode. In both, the use of a key discursive hub revealed particular meanings and assumptions radiating through two instances of policy discourse. These hubs and their radiants of meaning were then shown to stand in stark contrast to the systems of premises and meanings active in the very communities to whom these policies were addressed. By demonstrating such contrasts, we believe we can improve the ways different actors think about agendas for change—the problems they address, the people who define them, the solutions they indicate, and the conditions they envision.

The further value of CuDA, as we see it, is in fostering a grounded critical approach. A grounded approach means that the basis for criticism derives from the system of practice and meaning itself. Agendas for change are inherently critical as they are products derived from evaluations that find that some *thing* is not as it should be, with such evaluation expressed from the ethical juncture presented by the obligation of governance or administration. However, as analysts and practitioners working at the intersection of policy and learning, we find we too face an ethical juncture. For us, this juncture is presented by the very kinds of knowledge CuDA produces about the variation in the world, and our awareness of the harm that can occur when this knowledge is absent from policy discourses, especially in their most powerful iterations.

This brings us, as any discussion of the critical mode must, to the question of use. In other words, to what use can or should CuDA findings be put in relation to agendas for change? The two cases here represent two options. The first case uses insights about contrasting cultural discourses for the purpose of (re)orienting program and policy design so that it might be better aligned with, and be reflective of, local ways and meanings. This is an example of using CuDA findings in the *adaptive mode*.[9] The second case shows how people under duress can make use of cultural discourses themselves to challenge policy discourse, raise awareness of present conditions and future potential, and in so doing create their own agendas for change. This is an example of using CuDA findings in the *generative mode*. In this mode, cultural actors themselves critique communicative practices and premises by policy actors through their mode of engagement with those practices and premises.[10] The mode presented here was a shift into a way of dwelling, being, and relating enabled by the digital. In both instances, CuDA findings are employed as potential resources for informing locally intelligible, relevant, and meaningful agendas for change on diverse issues by highlighting contrasts that count for people on the receiving end of policy. Because of this potential, we hope to see more scholars applying CuDA and other approaches within the ethnography of communication tradition to the study of policy and communal discourses, so this dynamic might be more widely followed, illustrated, and more deeply understood.

It bears noting, perhaps, that while understanding an issue is indeed important, it involves neither the same activities nor creates the same outcomes as creating a solution to a problem. In our (Rudnick and Edmonds) more than 30 years of collective experience working in applied contexts of security, peacebuilding, development, and public policy, we have systematically encountered significant issues with the usability and application of rigorous communication and/or cultural research findings in the various policy and programming design processes we have encountered at the UN, with governmental units, NGOs, and other organizations working at the intersection of policy and practice. These challenges stem, in our view, not from a flaw or shortcoming in CuDA, communication research, or cultural research more broadly, but instead from a range of practical issues including alignment of purpose, strategic relevance, conditions of use (including time frame and available expertise), and techniques for application (see Rudnick & Boromisza-Habashi, 2017). CuDA may not be fit for purpose as a research approach to be carried out by UN research staff, or field teams or policy units within governments themselves. Nevertheless we believe there is a genuine need for an agenda of research applying CuDA to policy discourses within universities, and that the understandings this will produce can help fuel meaningful social change by making communities of actors audible to each other. In this way, CuDA findings show potential to play a vital role in guiding culturally informed and locally situated change, for decision-makers and community members alike.

NOTES

1. The authors would like to thank Prof. Eric Morgan, New Mexico State University, for his thoughtful and stimulating contributions to early discussions of this chapter.
2. The authors wish to thank UNIDIR for permission to present some of the unpublished work from that project here. Research in Nepal was carried out by a team of UNIDIR staff including the authors, Derek Miller, and Nikhil Acharya, and with the invaluable support of our Nepali colleagues and consulting researchers, including Rajesh Jha, Anita Ghimeri, Suman Poudal, Shrijana Dao, Saubughya Shah, Elizabeth Fullon, David Boromisza-Habashi, and several others who assisted us as social interpreters.
3. See Carbaugh (1996, pp. 3–24).
4. For the full text of Article 13 and further discussion see https://www.crin.org/en/home/rights/convention/articles/article-13-freedom-expression.
5. Data used in this case were produced during two field missions to Nepal, in 2009 and in 2010. Each mission was 4 weeks in length. Overall, 6 locations were visited in both Eastern and Western Nepal. Data was generated through a series of in situ interviews, focus groups, and community visits conducted by SNAP staff together with Nepali researchers, as well as through collaborative data generation and analysis activities conducted within the integrated team as part of the SNAP approach.
6. *Asylum seeker* refers to people who apply for asylum based on grounds of social, political, environmental, and cultural persecution according to the 1951 Refugee Convention, eventually hoping to be recognized as *refugee* (see Forced Migration Online, n.d.). The terms are used interchangeably in some places of this chapter.
7. The policy discourse is paradoxical as Hong Kong is a city of migrants and refugees (Wong, Moore, & Chin, 2008), with people who fled Mainland China beginning in 1945 due to famine, persecution, and the lure of a free market economy. During the arrival of thousands of refugees from Vietnam in the 1970s, social fears increased of how to accommodate the increasing population within the restricted physical space of Hong Kong. These fears are mirrored in a noncommittal attitude toward international treaties like the Geneva Refugee Convention from 1951.
8. The data collection for this study included personal interviews, participant observations, and analysis of social media profiles in Hong Kong. I would like to thank Mr. Lee and Dr. Khan for their invaluable help with conducting the field research. The work described here was

fully funded by a grant from the Research Grants Council of HK SAR, China (RGC ref. no. 14610915).

9. See Miller and Rudnick (2012) for a discussion of implementation, adaptation, and innovation in approaches to policy and program design. Similarly, we use the term *adaptive mode* here to refer to the use of CuDA findings for the purpose of adapting existing frameworks, approaches, or agendas to local contexts; we use the term *generative mode* to refer to the ways in which CuDA findings can be used to create new frameworks, approaches, or agendas, from the ground up.

10. See also Sprain and Boromisza-Habashi (2013) for a discussion of how, when working in the applied mode, "scholars draw on the EC tradition to address social and communication problems. The applied mode has two key characteristics: (1) a coorientation to a social problem with others at the table (fellow scholars, practitioners, and, especially, community members) and (2) a commitment to seek a workable solution with them for that problem. The commitment to impact problems transforms the practical potential of EC envisioned by Hymes (1974) into resources for addressing social problems" (p. 185).

REFERENCES

Boyden, J. (1990). A comparative perspective on the globalisation of childhood. In A. James & A. Prout (Eds.), *Constructing and reconstructing childhood: Contemporary issues in the sociological study of childhood* (pp. 190–225). London: Falmer Press.

Burman, E. (1996). Local, global or globalised? Child development and international child rights legislation. *Childhood, 3*(19), 45–66.

Carbaugh, D. (1989). Fifty terms for talk: A cross-cultural study. *International and Intercultural Communication Annual, 13*(93), 93–120.

Carbaugh, D. (1989/1990). The critical voice in ethnography of communication research. *Research on Language and Social Interaction, 23*, 261–282.

Carbaugh, D. (1996). *Situating selves: The communication of social identities in American scenes.* Albany, NY: SUNY Press.

Carbaugh, D. (2005). *Cultures in conversation.* Mahwah, NJ: Erlbaum.

Carbaugh, D. (2007). Cultural discourse analysis: Communication practices and intercultural encounters. *Journal of Intercultural Communication Research, 36*(3), 167–182.

Carbaugh, D. (2017). Terms for talk, take 2: Theorizing communication through its cultural terms and practices. In D. Carbaugh (Ed.), *Handbook of cross-cultural communication* (pp. 15–28). New York, NY: Routledge.

Cotter, S., & Wilson, K. (2014). How the meaning of home influences residential architecture. Archi*Ninja. Retrieved from http://www.archi-ninja.com/how-the-meaning-of-home-influences-residential-architecture/

Diminescu, D. (2008). The connected migrant: An epistemological manifesto. *Social Science Information, 47*(4), 565–579.

Edmonds, R. (2016). Generating local knowledge: A role for ethnography in evidence-based programme design for social development. In S. Bell & P. Aggleton (Eds.), *Monitoring and evaluation in health and social development* (pp. 81–94). London: Routledge.

Ellison, N., Vitak, J., Gray, R., & Lampe, C. (2014). Cultivating social resources on social network sites: Facebook relational maintenance behaviors and their role in social capital. *Journal of Computer-Mediated Communication, 19*(4), 855–870.

Forced Migration Online. (n.d.). *What is forced migration?* Retrieved fromhttp://www.forcedmigration.org/about/whatisfm

Hansen, K. T. (Ed.). (2008). *Youth and the city in the global south.* Bloomington, IN: Indiana University Press.

Hong Kong Information Services Department. (2014). *Press release.* Retrieved fromhttp://www.info.gov.hk/gia/general/201402/07/P201402070307.htm

Hong Kong Tourism Board. (2017). East meets west. *Discover Hong Kong.* Retrieved fromhttp://www.discoverhongkong.com/eng/see-do/insiders-guide/east-meets-west/index.jsp

Honwana, A., and De Boeck, F. (2005). *Makers and breakers: Children and youth in postcolonial Africa.* Oxford, UK: James Currey.

Hymes, D. (1985). Toward linguistic competence. *Aila Review, 2,* 9–23.

Hymes, D. (1972). Models of the interaction of language and social life. In J. Gumperz & D. Hymes (Eds.), *Directions in sociolinguistics: The ethnography of communication* (pp. 35–71). New York, NY: Holt, Rinehart and Winston.

Justice Centre Hong Kong. (2017). *Facts.* Retrieved from http://www.justicecentre.org.hk/facts/

Katriel, T., & Philipsen G. (1981). "What we need is communication": "Communication" as a cultural category in some American speech. *Communication Monographs, 48*(4), 301–317.

Khorshed, A., & Imran, S. (2015). The digital divide and social inclusion among refugee migrants: A case in regional Australia. *Information Technology & People, 28*(2), 344–365.

Lamb, S. (2000). *White saris and green mangoes: Aging, gender, and body in North India.* Berkeley, CA: University of California Press.

Lansdown, G. (2005). *The evolving capacities of the child.* Innocenti Research Centre, UNICEF & Save the Children. Retrieved from https://www.unicef-irc.org/publications/pdf/evolving-eng.pdf

Leung, L. (2007). Mobility and displacement: Refugees' mobile media practices in immigration detention. *M/C—A Journal of Media and Culture, 10*(1), 1–5.

Miller, D., & Rudnick, L. (2008). *The Security Needs Assessment Protocol: Improving operational effectiveness through community security.* Geneva: UNIDIR.

Miller, D., & Rudnick, L. (2010). The case for situated theory in modern peacebuilding practice. *Journal of Peacebuilding and Development, 5*(2), 62–74.

Miller, D., & Rudnick, L. (2011). Trying it on for size: Design and international public policy. *Design Issues, 27*(2), 6–16.

Miller, D., & Rudnick, L. (2012). *A framework for evidence-based programme design on reintegration.* Geneva: UNIDIR.

Miller, D., & Rudnick, L. (2014). *A prototype for evidence-based programme design on reintegration.* Geneva: UNIDIR.

Miller, D., Rudnick, L., Payne, R., & Acharya, N. (2010). *Using local knowledge for effective programming in Nepal's Terai: Special focus on children and community security.* UNIDIR. Unpublished document.

Milstein, T., Anguiano, C., Sandoval, J., Chen, Y.-W., & Dickinson, E. (2011). Communicating a "new" environmental vernacular: A sense of relations-in-place. *Communication Monographs, 78*(4), 486–510.

Ming, Y. S. (March 15, 2016). Rethinking asylum-seeker detention in Hong Kong. Oxford Human Rights Hub. Retrieved from http://ohrh.law.ox.ac.uk/rethinking-asylum-seeker-detention-in-hong-kong/

Nieuwenhuys, O. (1998). Global childhood and the politics of contempt. *Alternatives: Global, Local, Political, 23*(3), 124–145.

Payne, R. (2009). *Child-headed households in Zambia: From concepts to realities* (Unpublished doctoral thesis). Royal Holloway, University of London, UK.

Payne, R. (2012). "Extraordinary survivors" or "ordinary lives"? Embracing "everyday agency" in social interventions with child-headed households in Zambia. *Children's Geographies, 10*(4), 399–411.

Philipsen, G. (1992). *Speaking culturally: Explorations in social communication.* Albany, NY: SUNY.

Punch, S. (2002). Youth transitions and interdependent adult-child relations in rural Bolivia. *Journal of Rural Studies, 18,* 123–133.

Read, T. (March 31, 2016). Hong Kong has no refugee crisis, only a crisis of response. *South China Morning Post.* Retrieved from http://www.scmp.com/comment/insight-opinion/article/1932216/hong-kong-has-no-refugee-crisis-only-crisis-response

Robson, E. (2004). Children at work in rural northern Nigeria: Patterns of age, space and gender. *Journal of Rural Studies, 20,* 193–210.

Rudnick, L., & Boromisza-Habashi, D. (2017). The emergence of a local strategies approach to human security. *Journal of Multicultural Discourses, 12*(4), 382–398. Special Issue: Multicultural discourses of "security" (B. C. Taylor & H. Bean, guest editors).

Sprain, L., & Boromisza-Habashi, D. (2013). The ethnographer of communication at the table: Building cultural competence, designing strategic action. *Journal of Applied Communication Research, 41,* 181–187.

UNICEF. (2017). The convention. Retrieved fromhttps://www.unicef-irc.org/portfolios/crc. html

United Nations. (1989). *Convention on the Rights of the Child.* Treaty Series 1577: 3. Print.

United Nations. (2017). *United Nations Treaty Collection.* Retrieved fromhttps://treaties.un. org/pages/ViewDetails.aspx?src=IND&mtdsg_no=IV-11&chapter=4&lang=en

White, B. (1996). Globalisation and the child labour problem. *Journal of International Development, 8*(6), 829–839.

White, B. (1999). Defining the intolerable: Child work, global standards and cultural relativism. *Childhood, 6*(1), 133–144.

Witteborn, S. (2011). Constructing the forced migrant and the politics of space and place making. *Journal of Communication, 61*(6), 1142–1160.

Witteborn, S. (2012a). Forced migrants, new media practices, and the creation of locality. In I. Volkmer (Ed.), *The Handbook of global media research* (pp. 312–330). Malden, MA: Blackwell.

Witteborn, S. (2012b). Testimonio and spaces of risk: A forced migrant perspective. *Cultural Studies, 26*(4), 421–441.

Witteborn, S. (2014). Forced migrants, emotive practice and digital heterotopia. *Crossings: Journal of Migration and Culture, 5*(1), 73–85. Special Issue: Digital Crossings in Europe (S. Ponzanesi & K. Leurs, guest editors).

Witteborn, S. (2015). Becoming (im)perceptible: Forced migrants and virtual practice. *Journal of Refugee Studies, 28*(3), 350–367.

Witteborn, S., & Sprain, L. (2009). Grouping processes in a public meeting from an ethnography of communication and cultural discourse analysis perspective. *The International Journal of Public Participation, 3*(2), 14–35.

Wong, S., Moore, M., & Chin, J. K. (2008). *Hong Kong: Demographic change and international labor mobility.* PECC-ABAC Conference on Demographic Change and International Labor Mobility in the Asia Pacific Region, Seoul, March 25–26.

Zetter, R. (1991). Labelling refugees: Forming and transforming a bureaucratic identity. *Journal of Refugee Studies, 4*(1), 39–62.

Zetter, R. (2007). More labels, fewer refugees: Remaking the refugee label in an era of globalization. *Journal of Refugee Studies, 20*(2), 172–192.

Zharkevich, I. (2009). *Becoming a Maoist in a time of insurgency: Youth in Nepal's "People's War"* (Unpublished master's thesis). University of Oxford, UK.

Chapter Fifteen

"The Things I Leave Behind"

Negotiating Bulgarian and Latvian Identities in Relation to Dwelling and "Proper Action" in Public Discourses on Remigration

Liene Locmele and Nadezhda Sotirova

This study compares public media discourses on economically driven emigration within Bulgaria and Latvia, with special focus on discourses of returning. Particularly, we examine and compare the communicative role and functions of "blaming the state" that economic emigrants direct toward respective governments and other responsible units when attempting to make sense of their (potential) return to their home countries. By examining public media discourses on re-emigration within radio, television, and online content we explore: What discourses on returning are available in both countries? How are such discourses similar and different for both countries? What communicative resources and forms are utilized when engaging in this discourse on emigration? What do these communicative forms and their enactment say about local cultural notions of action/agency literally as well as metaphorically? How are these cultural notions linked to the larger historical context?

When exploring discourses on returning, in many cases the logical link between participant-identified problems (that make return impossible) and the state (seen as responsible for these problems) is either nonexistent or not correspondent with what one would typically associate with the responsibilities of the state in a democratic society. Our observations indicate that when engaging in a conversation about return options, the participants, instead of focusing on content and problem-solution discussions, attempt to engage in a different discussion of the ongoing struggle of brokering what the role of the state in general and in everyday life is: a cultural milieu many postsocialist countries struggle with as a result of the economic and social paternalistic redistribution developed during socialism (Verdery, 1996).

Our data highlights such negotiations of the role of the state not merely as a topic that surfaces in the discourse, but as the enactment of a ritualized form in which the main cultural purpose is not to define such state role, but to reinforce and renegotiate the larger cultural values and notions of who emigrants are, proper action, and how to relate to each other. Our study not only builds upon other research seeking to illuminate this common postsocialist state struggle, but also to identify the cultural functions and possibilities "blaming of the state" offers as a ritualized communicative resource. Thus, our study highlights "blaming of the state" as a communicative move a participant has when their emigration choices are being confronted by others. Such a ritualized practice provides a useful cultural communication tool when engaging in the sensitive topic of why one leaves their homeland and, as such, is a very useful hub of meaning-making, with radiants of meaning not only for identity (what being a Latvian and a Bulgarian means when one leaves the country) but also action (providing a metacommentary of the context, when no proper other action is possible).

THEORETICAL FRAMEWORK

Hymes's (1962) push toward the ethnography of communication addresses the need for the investigation of language in contexts and the role of the community in which it exists as an historically positioned communal resource. A similar call for more nuanced, and particularly ethnographic, studies comes from the field of anthropology, and specifically the postsocialist context, where examining living discourses within countries with a Communist past becomes crucial for understanding the variety of local social arrangements (Verdery, 1996). Examining present-day discourses and local cultural negotiations of self and social relations in Latvia and Bulgaria offers an opportunity for a deeper understanding of the larger political systems as they are navigated and made sense of on an everyday basis. As Verdery points out, no socialist country is "typical" (ibid.). We use an ethnography of communication (EC) and cultural discourse analytic approach when examining the communicative ways of the specificities within each country, offering unique insight as to the ways in which the "transition" has been managed in everyday lives.

Cultural discourse analysis (Carbaugh, 2007) is a development within EC and interactional sociolinguistics (Hymes, 1972; Gumperz, 1982), which explores culturally distinct uses of communication practices and vocabulary within everyday contexts. Studies within cultural discourse analysis build on the notion of speech codes as the cultural structuring of deep meanings through communication practices (Carbaugh & Cerulli, in press). The method builds on the communication theory of culture (Carbaugh, 1991; Philipsen, 1992) and examines the ways communication helps constitute culture and society. According to this theory, symbols and their meanings are not just suspended out there but are "culturally accessible, historically grounded, socially occasioned, and individually applied" (Carbaugh, 1995, p. 284). Carbaugh discusses the way these symbols, forms, and meanings function (or are "justifiable" to the participants) through a normative rule system, which establishes certain positions and relations for the participants that are "robust" and "stable" (Carbaugh, 1995, p. 285).

Three cultural structures become prominent in the way communication is conducted and interpreted, or namely, models of personhood, models of society, and models of strategic action. The theoretical principles, in summary, are that when there is a culture, these three cultural structures are important in communication and provide "material vehicles" (Carbaugh, 1995, p. 287) as well as general principles for the carrying out and interpretation of communication. These three structures are the symbols, symbolic forms, and meanings that identify ways of being a person, being organized socially, and conducting action. The main assumptions within this theoretical development relevant to our use of cultural discourse analysis is the focus on communication as distinct and culturally situated, as cross-culturally variable, and constitutive of social life (Carbaugh, 2007), or communication and discursive resources as bringing social institutions into life (Carbaugh & Cerulli, 2017).

Such an understanding of communication as the main site for meaning-making then highlights the multiple levels on which cultural discourse operates, organizing social life through explicit and implicit messages about identity, social relations, actions, feelings, and the nature of things (Carbaugh, 2007). Through cultural discourse analysis, Carbaugh (2007) draws attention to the existence of discursive hubs of meaning, rich sites of cultural expression with potent meaning, which bring insight into the cultural world active underneath. Each hub can be investigated at length, providing access to meanings about who we are and symbols of personhood (identity); what we are/should be doing (action); what we do/should feel (feeling); where and how we are positioned in the world around us (dwelling); and how we are connected (social relations). Cultural discourse analysis offers just the tools for understanding how a communicative practice can be approached not only in order to be described in detail but also to offer insight and be interpreted for its norms and premises, significant terms and vocabulary, radiants of meanings about personhood, identity, and sociality, social relations, emotion and affect, dwelling, environment, and action that are presumed in it. Such an analysis gives the researcher tools and components to examine it and be able to compare it to similar practices elsewhere, thus enriching the understanding of how people "do" reality in and through communication, how they gossip, understand emotion, social action, silence, themselves, their relations to everything else, even what "everything else" is for them.

Our study highlights local cultural meanings, which inform and prompt enactments of "blaming the state" in discourses on returning in Latvia and Bulgaria as the only meaningful action (communication through a ritualized form in this case). By fixing the discursive hub of meaning on action (in this case the speech acts of "blaming the state") in our data, we examine the larger sociohistoric context that this practice is embedded in and highlight the way participants use the enactments to skillfully navigate problematic and sensitive discussions on their emigration choices. Such communication maneuvering not only allows for navigating complex discussion in which there is no "proper way out" and their national identity and alignment is questioned, but also provides a useful tool in reexamining the larger contextual relations between the participants and the state, while attempting to make sense of current migration changes. Per the cultural discourse analysis framework, we provide a descriptive analysis of the discourses on returning within Latvia and Bulgaria, then interpret them from the participants' point of view identifying explicit meanings as well as implicit ones about the relevant hub via formulating relevant cultural propositions of belief and value and then larger cultural premises linked to the cultural communication form of ritual.

One communicative form very often used to bridge the individual and the communal in social interactions, to link the larger cultural understandings and values with everyday practices, is *ritual*. Through enacting various rituals as well as other communicative forms (social drama, myth), communities engage in an ongoing negotiation of the larger cultural values and notions they hold about being and identity, action and social relations, their surrounding and proper emotions. Philipsen (1992) suggests that ritual is a communication form that is frequently utilized in order to engage and reinforce the larger cultural milieu through the replaying of symbolic acts; homage is paid to what is deemed valuable in the community. Philipsen uses Turner's definition of ritual as a "structured sequence of actions the correct performance of which pays explicit homage to a sacred group or culture" (Turner, 1988, cited in Philipsen, 1997, p. 144). The function of the ritual lies upon maintaining the societal order, especially the nonrational consensus (Philipsen, 1987, p. 251), namely, upon "maximizing the certainty in interaction" (Knuf, 1993, cited by Philipsen, 1993, p. 107). Communication involves patterns, which show the ordering of this social life, where verbal means and modes carry various meanings and interactions involve and are structured by the work between such means and meanings and their weight within the social order (Carbaugh, 1995). This highlights that something larger is happening through the enactment of communicative practices, where practices reaffirm and reconstitute particular social relationships and places of the individuals involved. Such cultural structuring sometimes occurs in the form of a communicative ritual as bonding between the individuals.

This is not to say that all communication Latvians and Bulgarians utilize is "blaming of the state," but only that it is a well-known, widely accessible, and deeply meaningful interactional ritual, with a particular structure and function. Such "blaming of the state" as an interactional ritual can be employed by the participants to fulfill cultural functions or to connect to others in a particularly cultural way. How can we make sense of the media discourse within Latvia and Bulgaria through this cultural communicative lens and what rules of conduct and existence within the particular speech community become visible? It is important to note that ritual is seen as a part of mundane interactions. Hall describes the sacred object that it celebrates to be anything—an ideal or cultural good—that is of a high value for the group for which the said ritual is a part of everyday life (Hall, 2002, p. 86). Even if a person would privately try to avoid her/his participation in the ritual, "the real desire to build and maintain certain images and relationships makes their enactment anything but hypocritical" (Hall, 2002, p. 87). It can be rather difficult to notice the ritualized forms of one's everyday communicative performance. Hall points out some of the popular notions that mistakenly treat rituals as something redundantly repeated, hypocritical, located and performed only in specialized settings such as religious contexts, or performed by less sophisticated others. To overcome the difficulty, he suggests turning to important social events where some kind of relationships undergo change; examine what is it that we do because we have some sort of social role; and finally, what happens during those moments when we make negative attributions about our counterparts. Namely, he challenges us to examine everyday interactions where rituals inevitably compose our ordinary lives and might manifest their presence only when violated (Hall, 2002).

We focus on the context of emigration and the discourses surrounding it as both countries have experienced numerous waves of emigration yet are currently at different stages in these migratory processes. In both countries, the larger sociohistorical and economic context has created a ground of long-lasting economic change or instability, deeply rooted nationalistic trends, and larger local cultural connectedness to the land that makes any mobility questionable and in need of justification. Also, both countries were strongly affected by the recession of 2007 and have struggled in negotiating their economic and national identities as comparatively new members of the European Union. The topic of emigration and remigration has been consistently resurfacing in Latvia. In the absence of reliable statistics, the first attempts to estimate the accurate numbers of emigrants in Latvia (e.g., Krasnopjorovs,

2011; Hazans, 2011; Central Statistics Bureau of Latvia, 2011) ensured emigration its permanent place in scholarly, political, and media agendas.

As such, the two countries offer a unique point of comparison on several levels: similar historical context of agriculture, socialist rule, geopolitical position in relation to "Western Europe," membership in the European Union, and connections to Russia; economically prompted emigration waves, which are widely discussed by the public; and both countries seem to incorporate their particular relationship with the government/state in said discourse on emigration. These two countries offer not only a unique view of postsocialist social worlds as negotiated in everyday interaction, but also very similar backgrounds for public discourse. Such a comparison proves very useful as it offers insights into both the development of such postsocialist countries and the continuous struggle to redefine self and fellow countrypeople in a constantly changing nationalist context.

EMIGRATION CONTEXTS IN BULGARIA AND LATVIA

While Bulgaria and Latvia generally have a long history of politically, economically, and religiously motivated emigration, mainstream emigration research explores the emigration after the collapse of Soviet Union in its own right, focusing primarily on its potentially damaging socioeconomic consequences associated with the shortages of workforce and extensive "brain drain."[1] Both are also seen as currently experiencing a continuous stream of mobility, which, if compared with other EU countries in similar positions, have somewhat exceptionally devastating consequences. Bulgaria is predicted to be one of the first countries among others in terms of the loss of most of its population by 2050 (World Population Prospects, 2015). However, Latvia stands out from the rest of the Baltic States as having the most pronounced demographic risk, threatening the reproduction of population, sustainability of the social security system, and economic development (Hazans, 2014). In both countries, the economic recession was generally seen as the source of a major increase in economically motivated emigration but also foregrounded the challenge to estimate the number of people who actually left.

As a response to the problematization of a rapid increase of the flow of primarily economically motivated emigration, the Latvian Ministry of Economics in cooperation with other ministries and partner institutions developed the Re-emigration Plan 2013–2016, which at the time received criticism from a variety of stakeholders for prioritizing the return of highly skilled educated emigrants. The emigration waves leaving Bulgaria since 1989 have been addressed in a few national strategies, the latest of which is "National Strategy in the sphere of Migration, Asylum and Integration 2015–2020."[2]

The country's attempts to address the emigration concerns can be summarized as (Ivanova, 2015) no dynamic actions in the first decade, where the state was mostly just observing at first; the impact of a potential membership in the EU and preparations for such membership spurred the government around the year 2000; the decade after saw intensified attempts to address emigration via several similar national strategies visible up to 2012. These national strategies, however, focused on outlining plans that target highly skilled and educated emigrants and were underlined by strongly nationalistic and ethnic concerns, rather than economic, and were not well adapted to address the actual reality of emigrant populations abroad.

These plans focused on nationalism and more permanent residency, and as such encouraged the theoretical desire of only some (highly skilled, ethnically Bulgarian) to return and stay, disregarding the changing economic needs and global mobility. In the years following 2012, no continuous or bottom-up activities, plans, or policies have been attempted (Ivanova, 2015). The institutions associated with such activity are the State Agency for the Bulgarians Abroad (SABA), the Presidency, and the Ministry of Labor and Social Policy with its Labor and Social Affairs Offices in several European capitals (Ivanova, 2015). In other words, both countries have experienced large waves of emigration, such outward migration has been framed as problematic in the popular and political discourses, and both countries have implemented various policy articulations aimed at attracting back certain selected (high educated/skilled) populations as opposed to others, which makes comparing migration (and particularly about returning to the home country) discourses within these two countries particularly productive.

METHOD

We examine broadcast programming from Latvian and Bulgarian media, which includes excerpts from Latvian public radio (LR1) and NOVA TV in Bulgaria, both devoted to investigating emigrant stories, remigration policies, and the opinions of those affected by it. The Latvian broadcast is part of the weekly broadcast called *Twenty First Century Latvian* (*21.gadsimta latvietis*), aired since 2012. The particular radio broadcast used in the analysis was first aired on September 8, 2013. The Bulgarian broadcast includes segments from the television series *Miroluba Benatova predstavya* (Miroluba Benatova presents) aired in 2015–2016. The segments examined are two of her programs on emigration: "Bulgari ot America" ("Bulgarians from America") in 2015 and "Bulgarska ulica v London" ("Bulgarian street in London") in 2016. Per cultural discourse analysis (Carbaugh, 2007), we first provide a descriptive overview of the data, then we extrapolate cultural propositions and premises of belief and value active in the discourses, and finally explore the ways the communication form of a ritual is then utilized by the participants to navigate said notions of proper action and being.

ANALYSES

Bulgaria

Within segments from *Miroluba Benatova presents*, the broadcasts focusing on Bulgarians living in both the United States and the United Kingdom, as well as the broadcasts addressing emigrants living in Germany (2015–2016), a few details stand out consistently throughout the various interactions. One of the examples illustrating the phenomenon comes in the closing minutes of the last episode of "Bulgarians from America," where the two presenters chat with Miroluba Benatova before and after the video of the series. The author of the series, journalist Miroluba Benatova (MB), begins the segment expressing the opinion that she hopes a lot of people will return to Bulgaria, but she does not see it happening. Then, closing the episode, when asked by the hosts of the program what awaits her next (professionally and personally), MB states, quoting an emigrant from the episode:

> all Bulgarian politicians should hear [this] and remember [it]: "The lack of order and corruption is what keeps our fellow country people far from Bulgaria." Not only the money. The feeling of absolute nonsense and lack of rules in our country has actually chased away half of the Bulgarians.

In an episode focusing on another successful Bulgarian emigrant living in the United States, he addresses his struggles with disability and demonstrates the various accommodations he has on his car and wheelchair that facilitate his life in the United States. At this demonstration, MB asks how difficult it would be to do the same (accommodations) in Bulgaria, to which he responds with a grunt and a curt "we have no sidewalks, what for accommodations!" A Bulgarian emigrant in Chicago, when asked if he would return to Bulgaria, responds, "nepotism is so bad in Bulgaria, it's like we produce unemployment. Obviously no new smart people are born in Bulgaria, we'll have to look for new people elsewhere." In a similar fashion, numerous emigrants living in London highlight that originally, they moved to Spain, but soon it became the same as Bulgaria: "they give you little money, there's no work, and they lie." Another Bulgarian worker who has been quite successful in the United Kingdom (a fruit farm that employs mostly Bulgarians) emphasizes that yes, English people do employ and like Bulgarians as they are "quick, efficient, and handy," to which MB asks, "Why aren't Bulgarians quick, efficient, and handy in Bulgaria, too?" The quick response that follows is a shrug and "no one appreciates us there." These threads from the emigrants' side are frequently elaborated on by the interviewer (MB) and program hosts framing the broadcast, who highlight that "people in Bulgaria rarely succeed, and when they do it is despite the country," further emphasized by the description MB gives to all episodes from the series: "we cover the stories of Bulgarian emigrants who have (a) succeeded (contrary to what politicians have us believe) and (b) are not a product of the previous political system."

Several cultural propositions (explicit statements by the participants) become visible in these examples, echoed throughout the discourse within the rest of the Bulgarian media programming, which can be formulated as:

1. The current situation in Bulgaria is problematic: the situation in the country is described as "lack of order," lack of accommodations, smart/quick people are not appreciated, and when other problem areas are described, they are referred to as "becoming like Bulgaria" with a strong negative connotation.
2. The current "Bulgarians" (occupants of the country) are problematic: "new people" need to be imported, the current "nepotism," "no new smart people" being born in the country, people rarely succeeding and only "despite the country," no one appreciating hard work, etc.
3. Such behaviors/treatment is chasing people away: politicians should know that it is not money that "seduces people away" but the problems at home that make them leave.
4. This problematic situation is because of the previous political system (communism), and thus the "state" as a whole is to blame: people are products of the previous political system (deemed negatively), nepotism, etc.

Within these media discourses, beyond the literal meanings made explicit by the participants, several larger premises of belief and value can be extrapolated more abstractly. Or, when people engage in these interactions, they evoke larger local cultural understandings about the self, social relations, acting, and the reality they inhabit. In this case, within the data from the Bulgarian media programming, cultural premises of being, acting, and dwelling become particularly relevant within discussions on emigration:

1. Dwelling: A larger notion of the "Bulgarian situation" is consistently constructed in the discourse. Very often this notion is referred to as "the situation," "it," *dargavata* ("the state"), or "things in Bulgaria."
2. Being: This problematic "Bulgarian situation" has become such due to behaviors/individuals/structures that are in some way associated with *dargavata*, "the state," and allude to political structures and behaviors linked to communism/socialism.

3. Acting: one has no choice but to leave Bulgaria. Or at least the "smart people" do. People who are free from such "old-system" behaviors cannot stand staying within the "Bulgarian situation" and leave. If you stay, you have either lost your mind or are a part of the problem (somehow benefiting from the current problems).

Here, this explicit statement of "one should leave the country" is once again reinforced as the "proper" action. And a person aware of the cultural logic, through enacting this exchange, reinforces their alignment: are they on the side of the "smart" (not corrupted by the system) or on the side of the old system (communism). In this way, by engaging in such an interchange, it is not about discussing emigration and the reasons for leaving, but alignment within the realm of what is "Bulgarian" and reconstituting what the proper action is: leave or talk about having to leave. The use of such common communicative resources, where the main interactional achievement is not necessarily focused on what is literally said, alludes to the use of a communicative ritual where its enactment performs a task that is more phatic and indirect than just the sharing of information.

Within the Bulgarian media data corpus, a certain sequence of acts is visible: (a) general commentary on the "Bulgarian situation" (vague and broad evaluative statement as to how "bad" things in Bulgaria are); (b) particular instances from the country or the life of Bulgarians that illustrate said "bad" situation (stand-alone or in comparison to how the same things are in other countries); (c) general commentary as to the negative future of Bulgaria as a result of this "Bulgarian situation" (or the futility of doing anything about it). Within the media data corpus in particular, mostly instances and concluding evaluative statements were offered, as the journalist was not taking up the ritual in an attempt to ask probing questions instead. However, in the commentary offered by the show broadcasting the episodes, often full enactments of the sequence were offered. The sacred object in these instances can be understood as the proper enactment of "Bulgarians," commemorating a shared fate of doom due to the sociopolitical situation that has bound all in a problematic situation—one that, unless "new smart people (from elsewhere) are imported"—will not change anytime soon, thus legitimizing leaving or wanting to leave the country and not returning.

Latvia

The following data excerpt comes from the Latvian public radio (LR1) broadcast called *Twenty First Century Latvian* (*21.gadsimta latvietis*) that was devoted to investigating the content of one of the policy initiatives aimed at facilitating the remigration of Latvian people—the re-emigration plan and the opinions of those affected by it. The journalist of the radio program (J) is interviewing a middle-aged couple (W and H) from a small town in Latvia who moved to Ireland more than 10 years ago where they work as a cook at the guesthouse (wife) and an unspecified job for some business owner (husband). The episode was first aired on September 8, 2013. The analyzed excerpt of the interview is the couple's response to the content of the re-emigration plan, but that quickly turned out to be an exchange on the reasons why returning to Latvia is impossible:

1	J	What is the re-emigration plan for you?
2	W	It [the plan] is not ridiculous but to my opinion in reality it is not possible to return.
3		[Suppose] we will go to Latvia, what kind of help we will have? Will the work be given? Help? Could
4		we start to live?
5	J	[notes that in IR support was not available and expresses respect for their success]
6	W	Of course, we went, looked in all city, gave our CVs. We went again, and again, and again
7		asked at the same place. Because here [in Ireland] it is like this if you will not go and do,
8		there will be nothing. Will there be work in Latvia? I think it will be very difficult to find it.
9	J	[notes that LV owes its citizens, the plan is the invitation to return, asks why they hesitate]
10	W	I think there are dreadfully small salaries [elaborates on minimum wage]
11	J	[notes their courage and language skills] why do you think about the minimum [wage]?
12	H	[explains that their hometown is lacking better job opportunities]
13	J	But what are you afraid of, if you already proved that you can achieve a lot with your own
14		hands and no one helped you?
15	W	First, we will go to Latvia. Where will we go, to relatives? Who will help us? It is totally
16		impossible to go to live in Latvia . . .
17	J	If that [accommodation] would be solved, which are the next points that worry you? . . .
18	H	As far as I listened news from Latvia, it is told that people with higher education only
19		that type of people and that type of jobs are offered. I do not know about these jobs mainly
20		[I am] terribly afraid that there will not be such job offers. If only the job market in Latvia
21		would be bigger, wider, then one would think, if only that salary would be [higher] . . .
22	J	[note the lengths of their absence] Could it be that your fear was born then when you left?
23	H	There have been some changes in Latvia, developments. Private business develops rapidly.
24		Something also closed. These taxes in Latvia are very big, high. Too high for everything.
25		All that system is not somehow in order a little. If only these taxes could be a little [better]

26		in Latvia, it would be different.
27	J	[points at their courage, experience and suggests starting small business in Latvia]
28	H	It would be difficult to start it at Latvia, I do not know, it is terribly difficult.
29	J	Is not it so that you hear it from the press?
30	W	No, it is not like that, it is difficult without resources and if you borrow . . .
31	H	Need support, some support is needed from Latvia . . .
32	W	I do not believe that someone will lend something. You must calculate how to repay . . .
33	J	[notes that they already think as entrepreneurs when calculating expenses]
34	W	I think if I will go to Latvia—I do not have anything. Maybe I will arrange someone who
35		will move [things]—where will I put them? I do not have place where to live. Ok, I have
36		some relative. I definitely will not go [to ask him]. Only, to stay overnight . . .

When asked how they feel about the plan's activities interviewees express disagreement with a popular criticism of the plan (that it does not serve the real needs of emigrants) by responding that for them it is not "ridiculous" but rather that returning itself is "not possible" [2]. The whole segment contains a variety of meanings associated with reasoning about such an impossibility to return that, except through the journalist's questions and comments, for the interviewees are not linked with the support the re-emigration plan offers. The interviewees echo this way of speaking by "blaming the state" for the lack of "help" [3–4, 15], "support" [31], and work that should be "given" [3] to them as well as difficulties to find "work" [3–4, 8, 15], "dreadfully small salaries" [10], "small job market" [20–21], and being afraid of the lack of such "job offers" [20] that would not demand "higher education" [18]. Finally, "too high taxes" [24] and the tax system that is "not in order" [25] is something that would make starting their own business in Latvia a "terribly difficult" [28] enterprise. For the Latvian ear said reasoning sounds familiar because of its wider use for expressing general dissatisfaction with the order of things. If only the state took care about these failures, the situation would be "different" [26] and one could "think" [21] about returning. When the journalist points out that the couple was able to start a new life without anyone's support in Ireland rather successfully [5], something happens— Ireland and Latvia are symbolically constructed as two different localities. While Latvia for them is the place where living is possible only when the described failures are fixed, Ireland is a place where none of these are relevant to expect. There [in Ireland] people persistently "go and do" [7], otherwise they will have "nothing" [8]. This speaks to a difference in cultural logics that is applied to one's acting in a hosting country as opposed to experience and expectations from the home country.

Several cultural propositions (explicit statements by the participants) are illuminated by the description above:

1. Returning to Latvia "is not possible" without "help" and "support" from the state.
2. "Dreadfully small salaries," "small job market," lack of "job offers," "too high taxes," and lacking "a place to live" make the new starting of life/business upon returning to Latvia a "terribly difficult" enterprise.
3. Only a type of people with "higher education" and types of work requiring it are available in Latvia for returnees.
4. If these failures could be fixed by the state, the situation would be "different" and one could, at least, start "to think" about returning.
5. Ireland is a place where a person "goes and does" as many times as necessary, otherwise "nothing" will be achieved.

As observed, the reasons associated with the impossibility of remigration are either related to the support that the state is failing to provide or economic failures that the state fails to fix. On a more general level this reasoning can be summarized under the following cultural premises:

1. Dwelling: Latvia is the place that lacks proper salaries, low-skilled job offers, and a tax system.
2. Being: Highly educated people are in a better position in Latvia.
3. Acting: Return to Latvia is impossible unless said failures are fixed by the State.
4. Acting: Ireland is a place where one must be persistent in order to achieve better circumstances.

We now turn to the description of the act sequence of the same interaction.

First of all, the context of the broadcast invites discussion on the re-emigration plan that is aimed at facilitating the return of Latvians who emigrated for a variety of reasons, but the economic aspect is foregrounded since the recession provoked the intensity of the phenomenon. Thus, providing reasoning related to the impossibility of such a decision [2–3] as opposed to scrutinizing the validity of the re-emigration plan that the journalist seems to propose [1] is a response to the context of conversation. After the wife directs the interview toward the impossibility of their return, the interaction starts to follow a particular rhythm—the act sequence is composed of (a) interviewee naming directly or indirectly the state-related obstacles of an economic nature and (b) journalist offering person-based evidence from interviewees' background proving that they have individual capabilities to overcome the said obstacles. To each fact-based evidence that the journalist offers, the response is the enumeration of yet another set of similar obstacles. There is also a certain cycle in terms of specificity of obstacles that are offered. The interaction starts out with the call to rather abstract "help" upon imagined arrival to Latvia [2–3] then moves to more particular job- and salary-related aspects [3, 10, 12] as well as lack of accommodation [15], which then cycles back to more abstract "support" that is "needed from Latvia" [31]. Seemingly, the interaction is one of those where the solution to named problems is not expected or even appropriate to provide. The journalist's evidence in this interaction serves as a catalyst for offering elaborations on why his suggestions will not work. In fact, the interaction seems to merge two kinds of genres—interview and blaming. What was initially started as the journalistic interview with the question on the meaning of the re-emigration plan [1] that demands an answer somehow related to the actual content of the plan, then with the second part of the response on impossibility to return and immediate call for nonexistent help from Latvia [2–4], became the enactment of the blaming of the state. No matter how the journalist then attempts to bring the interview back to its terms by indirectly introducing the content and purpose of the re-emigration plan and related supporting activities that were discussed publicly at the time of the broadcast [e.g., 9 on invitation to return, 17 on accommodation as solved], interviewees respond with an elaboration on the impossibility of returning given the state's failures to support or to fix economy-related aspects as evidence.

Kļaviņa (2014), who studied how economic emigrants perceived the content and communication of the re-emigration plan, illuminated a certain paradox—while the economic situation is mentioned as the most essential when it comes to the emigrants' decision to return, the areas of the re-emigration plan that speak to economic support informants evaluate rather negatively. However, the economically unrelated activities such as support for maintaining Latvian language while abroad is approved more. The main themes in Kļaviņa's informants' talk about the re-emigration plan overall seems to stand at odds with each other since discrepancy can be observed between what is said to be bad in the country (criticism toward the state's economy); what is criticized in the re-emigration plan (exactly attempts to fix at least partly the said economic failures); what is prized about the plan (maintaining Latvian language, recognition process of foreign education diplomas in Latvia); what the perceived function of the plan is (shows that the state cares but will not facilitate return); and what is said to be a significant role in returning (family, personal matters, and individual situations) (ibid.).

This is not to say that there are no objective reasons for an economic emigrant to be critical toward one's state. It is also not to say that the state can symbolically police people who do not comply with the preferred performance of national belonging. However, the aforementioned paradoxes show the presence of a specific communicative function when one chooses to talk about countries' economic failures when her/his choice to stay abroad or to return is under scrutiny.

More recent studies confirm that in practice remigration takes place due to rather personal and often emotional reasons (Šūpule, 2015). The dominant motivation to remigrate is related to the fact that remigrants miss family, friends, and country as well as other family-related or personal reasons (Hazans, 2016), such as the sense of belonging to one's place of birth or willingness to interact in one's native tongue (Šūpule, 2015, p. 4). Once returned, they experience difficulties in adapting that are related to the difficulty of finding a job, adjusting to a different working culture, an unclear tax system, health care, or difficulties related to educating children (Hazans, 2016b). However, these are not Latvia-specific obstacles and can be expected in a variety of other contexts given that a person has been away for a longer period (most of them more than five years) and, upon return, naturally finds her/himself in somewhat unknown territory. Research shows that the majority of re-emigrants, in fact, return without clear job prospects (ibid.) but admit that their absence from the country of origin has helped to reorient their value system, namely, the possibility to be in close proximity to relatives while living "at home" has gained new meaning and importance (Šūpule, 2015, p. 26).

Considering the repetitive nature of the studied interaction along with the fact that interviewees did not uptake the arguments offered by the journalist and vice versa, and evidence from other ethnographic data, we argue that this fragment might belong to a wider ritualistic performance that completes culturally symbolic work of reaffirming the common faith with similarly suffering people be they abroad or in Latvia.

THE BLAMING RITUAL: SIMILARITIES AND DIFFERENCES

While being critical toward policies of one's country generally is not a new phenomenon (for instance, in democratic societies that value the freedom of speech, besides attempting to be heard and facilitate societal change) the communicative functions it serves and the resources it creates across cultural groups can vary. The above-mentioned phenomenon of how economic emigrants make sense, through a variety of contradictions of their reasons for leaving and returning, speaks to the criticism of economic-related issues and specific kinds of "blaming the state" as having a special function in the communication. What our study highlights is the use of such blaming from a communication perspective, where such ritualized forms play a strong role in navigating the relationship among the people and their relationship to the land/country, and conceptualizes the role of the state. In both countries, mobility out of the country long-term is questioned publicly, and one is expected to explicitly rationalize their reasons for leaving or not returning.

The ritualized form of blaming then serves to legitimize one's choices of mobility within countries still not comfortable with such open mobility.

In the Bulgarian example, when one is asked about his/her prospects to return, several outcomes are available:

1. One can highlight the fact that there is nothing to return to, indicating the socioeconomic situation still has not changed enough for it to be a feasible option.
2. One can highlight that returning will only be because you miss people/culture (emotional reasons).
3. One can express that they will return immediately as things are wonderful in Bulgaria (and highlight all the problems at the current location they are occupying).

The larger outcomes of such responses, however, are more in the form of alignment with the larger context and a Bulgarian identity as inextricably linked to postsocialist and slave (Ottoman Empire) ways of being and acting. If one chooses option 1, they are culturally understood as one of the lucky "smart" ones who knows "better," can adapt to other "functioning" countries, can follow rules, is hardworking, has skills, and can overcome the old way of being and thinking created during the Ottoman slavery and communism (often this amalgam of thinking and behaviors is called the "Bulgarian mentality," explicitly fusing psychological and national elements). If one chooses options 2 or 3, they are culturally understood to be part of the problem: one of those still carrying the old ways of being and acting, still used to the socialist and slave problematic behaviors that landed us in the present "Bulgarian situation," "lack of order," "not normal country." They are perceived to have the "Bulgarian mentality," benefit because of it, and be invested in maintaining such economic disarray.

In this way, the ritual "blaming of the state" in Bulgarian media discourse serves the function of distancing oneself from all that is deemed still problematic in the country struggling to transition out of a socialist past: corruption, lack of stability, lack of a functioning judiciary system, nepotism, lack of work ethic, lack of appreciation and reward of work ethic, a state system that functions only in short bursts of self-service and disregards the common well-being, short-sightedness and desire to out-trick/out-cheat everyone around. By enacting the blaming of the state, one shows that they are aware of the "Bulgarian mentality," are struggling to overcome it, and find it problematic. However, as the "mentality" is constructed communicatively as "nationally psychological," a cultural notion of ways of being and acting as both physiological and national, by enacting the ritual, another cultural notion, or the understanding of the national identity as biological (and thus unable to change and allow for agency) is reconstituted and affirmed. Thus, by enacting the "blaming of the state," the only available action—to blame—is once more reaffirmed. As one cannot go against biology and Bulgarians are who they are, and if one cannot leave the country for a place where they can "stop being Bulgarian," then all that is left is to enact the ritual.

By blaming the state, a person highlights their awareness of the problem, awareness of the context that has created it, and the futility of fighting it, thus rendering leaving or not returning the only viable option. This ritualized enactment also reinforces aspects of a national identity that is conceptualized as deeply psychological and thus difficult to change. It renders agency and action as beyond "Bulgarian" and legitimizes the lack of individual acts promoting change from the bottom up. In this way, blaming the state actually perfectly coalesces the need to act and change the status quo without actually acting. Thus, the blaming of the state serves as the only available action that still allows the participants to feel like they have "done their" part, while not actually having agency. The ritualized blaming also reinforces the schism of "us" versus "them" (regardless of who *them* is in the case), which can be traced back to socialist production practices: the exact workplace rules and strategies meant to politicize and strengthen the positive image of the Party and the ideology acted as the opposite, and thus socialism managed to create a rift between "us" and "them," between the workers and the Party leaders and representatives, because it highlighted the notion that "they" exploit "us" (Verdery, 1996, p. 23).

In the Latvian example, when one is asked about her/his prospects to return, the common expectation is to somehow give a positive answer or at least to state intentions to stay connected. If one publicly confirms unwillingness to return, he/she risks criticism from one's counterparts. Dzenovska (2013) illustrates how contemporary ethical concerns directed toward those with the desire to leave the country can be traced back to emigration of freed serfs during the second half of the nineteenth century to obtain cheap land in Russia after German lords freed them from service and land. This movement corresponded to the time of "national awakening" inspired by intellectual elites who consolidated the Latvian cultural nation within the borders of the Russian Empire. Such an emigration was considered a threat to the newly formed nation (Dzenovska, 2013, p. 208), and desire for departure as a product of an unenlightened worldview and ignorance of the concerns of the nation (Šķilters, 1928, p. 5, cited by Dzenovska, 2013, p. 208), as an act that was not reflecting "a particular Latvian manner in their search for their own piece of land" (Dzenovska, 2013, p. 208).

This morality was used to struggle against occupation (most returned from Siberia once they could) and Russification (popular criticism toward mainly Russian people from other Soviet republics who arrived to live and work in Latvia as people who lack morals due to their disconnectedness with their own land, as Bunkše [1999] describes) employed by the Soviet regime;

today one finds her/himself stuck between national values associated with the particular place and land and personal economic struggles brought by the "new situation." We argue that in this juxtaposition, out of all other reasons, blaming the state's economic failures for inability to return functions as the "lesser of all evils" as far as one at least vaguely mentions a possibility to return. A correct performance of ritual sense-making of the new situation is enacted by directly or indirectly stating: I could return if only the state will be fixed and able to provide me with missing goods. The fact that individual responsibility is present, performed but not in association with Latvia, shows how the studied ritualized practices are part and product of postsocial ways of being in a special kind of relations with one's state that are absent in the "new system."

Those who hear the ritual blaming of the state might not necessarily agree with what is criticized since their financial position is better or they align more with the ideas of individual responsibility that democracy and liberal economy values entail. However, the struggle of those less fortunate is recognizable and, in the context of a rather poor social support system, acceptable as a valid reason. However, the blaming also can provide one with a proper resource to participate correctly in these ritualistic exchanges instead of providing alternate albeit culturally unacceptable reasons for leaving and staying away. Additionally, it can potentially function to:

1. Protect one from criticism since there is no culturally acceptable way of saying that one truly does not care where s/he lives or sees her/himself as not tied to a particular place;
2. Avoid giving out the reasons that cast the speaker in an unfavorable light in the new context of liberal economy, individual responsibility, personal success, or emotional assumptions (e.g., lack of education or future plans, bad loan-taking decisions, establishing family before gaining financial stability, failing to achieve personal goals, being angry/offended by the impossibility of fulfilling certain expectations, etc.);
3. Align with other emigrants and claim a legitimate identity in the situation where their position is questioned by the state.

The limiting side of this ritualized performance potentially can trap those who want to return, if they do not adjust ways of relating with the state. If the state is really as bad as public discourse claims, how can one justify his/her return even when cultural morals or personal emotional attachments prescribe precisely that?

IMPLICATIONS AND SIGNIFICANCE

In this way, for both countries, we see the importance of enacting "blaming the state" as a communication tool in a crucial moment when the countries are experiencing and struggling with new migration patterns. Social relationships previously deeply rooted in relationship to the land and location need to be reexamined and renegotiated. For both countries, social roles and the way people make attributions about each other need to be reexamined. The social role of being a proper "Latvian" or "Bulgarian" needs to be renegotiated based on attributes other than location and land. And just responding that you "do not care/do not want to" return to your "own" country simply will not do.

As we can see, the two countries are similar in resorting to the use of a communication form, such as ritual, when participating in conversations about migration. Both countries utilize a ritualized blaming of the state in order to communicatively make sense of their national identity in a changing context, their relationship to the state, and the rationale involved in the decision to stay or leave their home country. When enacting this ritualized blaming, the focus is drawn away from what is literally said (reasons for staying or leaving, personal choices, and economic and/or social needs) toward a larger metaphorical negotiation of who one is (personhood), how they are supposed to relate to each other and the state (social relations), and what role choice plays in emigration (agency). In this way, the ritualized blaming serves as a communicative resource that functions both on a practical everyday level to explain (to self as well as others) why one makes the decision to stay or leave the country, and on a larger cultural level, where national conceptualizations and past are reevaluated, contested, or reinforced.

In the Bulgarian case we see, on the first level, emigrants attempting to highlight the economic needs and lack of stability (political, social, judicial) in the home country that led them to leave, highlighting the notion of *dargavata*, or state, as a cruel, uncaring, and evil stepmother that "chased" them away, and on the second level, a negotiation of what it means to be a "Bulgarian" and the cultural expectations behind the state's role in people's everyday lives. One has to be well versed in the larger local mythology about the "Bulgarian situation" (political context, economic instability, and behaviors carried over from socialism) in order to fully grasp the creative cultural work involved in enacting the blaming ritual as interlocutors pull from the local widely accessible communicative forms to cocreate the intricate relationship between *dargavata* and Bulgarian-ness.

In the Latvian case, we see, on the first level, emigrants missing a certain kind of economically motivated support that led them to leave, yet, if provided, would determine their return. On the second level, it then becomes a negotiation about one's relationship with the state and longing for the role the state used to have under the previous political system when ensuring a specific kind of stability and security. Moreover, the blaming ritual provides participants with communicative resources for dealing with cultural morals that are in contradiction with their decision to leave or perspectives on returning as well as how to overcome personal insufficiencies associated with the transition to democracy and liberal market values. It has potential to create new meanings to emigrants' relationship with the state, to reinforce nationalist-inspired meanings about the one and only right way of being connected with one's land. It can also serve as a symbolic trap for those who would like to return.

This is not to say that we ignore or devalue the very real struggle people from both countries face. Obviously, economic inequalities do exist among "old" and "new" EU member countries as well as among different social groups within respective countries. However, we argue that when one engages in the public or private criticism or "the ritual blaming of the state," something more should be asked besides how the illuminated failures of the state could be fixed; how to ensure that emigrants maintain diasporic identity and connections with their homeland while abroad; or what kind of policies would eventually be most successful for bringing them back. We hope our comparative case highlights the need for exploration of the variety and use of such contextual communication resources available across similar, yet different, postsocialist locations: their embeddedness, and the cultural differences constituted in communication that prompt the differences.

Examining the underlying cultural premises for action, being, and dwelling discursively then would also help shape current and future discussions on re-emigration. Latvia has engaged with ways to accommodate the return of its people through activities, policies, and other support initiatives, while Bulgaria does not seem to be heading in an active direction when it comes to its emigrants. Larger areas and villages within Bulgaria, which have lost all their population to emigration, have even prompted the term "a people for rent." Context, history, cultural notions of self and relationship to others and the land certainly play a large role in how the choice of leaving or staying is culturally constructed as a moral imperative. You are a "good Latvian" if you return to Latvia. You are a "good Bulgarian" if you leave Bulgaria.

NOTES

1. For instance, Topalova, 2000; Deneva, 2007; Toshkov, 2009; Hazans, 2011; Eughersen et al., 2013; Hazans, 2014; Aleksandrova, 2014; Hazans, 2015a; Hazans, 2015b; Mieriņa, 2015.

2. The Re-emigration Plan 2013–2016 by Latvian Ministry of Economics aimed to develop supporting activities for Latvians abroad who considered or had already decided to return to work in Latvia or were willing to establish enterprises or business relations with the country. The plan covered eight areas: (1) establishing a single supporting institution for those who seek out the possibilities to return (e.g., for receiving support online); (2) ensuring the accessibility of information related to the job market; (3) motivating the return of highly skilled profession-

als; (4) ensuring Latvian language teaching to remigrants; (5) developing relationships with the diaspora, especially for business networking; (6) supporting remigrant children and parents upon entering the Latvian secondary education system; (7) reevaluating the demands posed by public sector institutions to prospective employees; (8) enlarging the scope of persons eligible for repatriant status.

REFERENCES

Akule, D. (2007). The effect of fears of immigrants on the decision making in Latvia: A boost or an obstacle to development? Effect of migration on European political thought and decision-making process (pp. 77–85). Conference proceedings, conference organized by Vidzeme University College in cooperation with European Commission in Latvia on December 8, 2006.

Aleksandrova, B. (2014). On a pathway to a global society? The role of states in times of global migration—implications for Bulgaria's handling of Syrian refugees (2013–2014). *Turkish Journal of International Relations, 13*(4): 29–40.

Apsīte-Beriņa, E. (2013). *Starpvalstu migrācija Eiropas Savienībā: Latvijas iedzīvotāju migrācija uz Lielbritāniju*. Dissertation defended at University of Latvia, Faculty of Geography and Earth Science. Available from www.lu.lv/fileadmin/user_upload/lu_portal/zinas/Prom-kops-Apsite.pdf

Benatova, M. (2015). *Miroluba Benatova presents* [online content]. Available at https://nova.bg/news/subcategory/42/миролюба-бенатова-представя/

Bogustovs, A., Gulbinska, P., & Rozītis, T. L. (2013). *Vērtējam reemigrācijas plānu* [online content]. Available from http://replay.lsm.lv/lv/ieraksts/lr/28307/vertejam-reemigracijas-planu/

Bunkše, E. (1999). God, thine earth is burning: Nature attitudes and the Latvian drive for independence. In A. Buttimer & L. Wallin (Eds.), *Nature and identity in cross-cultural perspective* (pp. 175–188). The Netherlands: Kluwer Academic Publishers.

Carbaugh, D. (1991). Communication and cultural interpretation. *Quarterly Journal of Speech, 77*(3), 336–342.

Carbaugh, D. (1995). The ethnographic communication theory of Philipsen and associates (pp. 269–297). In D. Cushman & B. Kovacic (Eds.), *Watershed research traditions in human communication theory*. Albany, NY: SUNY Press.

Carbaugh, D. (2007). Cultural discourse analysis: Communication practices and intercultural encounters. *Journal of Intercultural Communication Research, 36M*(3), 167–182.

Carbaugh, D., & Cerulli, T. (2017). Cultural discourse analysis. In Y. Y. Kim (Gen. Ed.) & K. L. McKay-Semmler (Assoc. Ed.), *The international encyclopedia of intercultural communication* (pp. 1–9). Hoboken, NJ: John Wiley & Sons. doi: 10.1002/9781118783665.ieicc0117

Central Statistics Bureau of Latvia. (2011). *Population census 2011*. Available from http://www.csb.gov.lv/en/statistikas-temas/population-census-30761.html

Council of Europe. (1999). *Recent demographic developments in Europe*. Strasbourg: Author.

Deneva, N. (2007). "The role of ethnicity in the re-construction of the community: Internal and international migration in a Bulgarian Muslim village." In A. Szczepanikova, M. Canek, & J. Grill (Eds.), *Migration processes in Central and Eastern Europe: Unpacking the diversity*. Prague: Multicultural Center Prague.

Dzenovska, D. (2013). The great departure: Rethinking national(ist) common sense. *Journal of Ethnic and Migration Studies, 39*(2), 201–218.

Elchinova, M. (2009). Migration studies in Bulgaria: Scope, experiences and developments. *Anthropological Journal of European Cultures, 18*(2): 69–86.

Engbersen, G., Leekers, A., Grabowska-Lusinska, I., Snel, E., & Burgers, J. (2013). On the different attachments of migrants from Central and Eastern Europe: A typology of labor migration. *Journal of Ethnic and Migration Studies, 39*(6): 959–981.

Gumperz, J. J. (1982). *Discourse Strategies*. Cambridge University Press.

Hall, B. (2002). How can we learn about our own and others' cultures? In B. Hall (Ed.), *Among cultures* (pp. 61–96). Fort Worth, TX: Harcourt College Publishers.

Hazans, M. (2011). The changing face of Latvian emigration 2000–2010. In B. Zepa & E. Kļave (Eds.), *Latvia. Human Development Report 2010/2011* (pp. 77–101). Riga: Advanced Social and Political Research Institute.

Hazans, M. (2014). Migration experience of the Baltic countries during and after the economic crisis. Presentation at the conference "Coping with Emigration in the Baltic and East European Countries," Riga, Latvia, April 2, 2014.

Hazans, M. (2015a). Emigrācija no Latvijas 21. gadsimtā reģionu, pilsētu un novadu griezumā. In I. Mieriņa (Ed.), *Latvijas Emigrantu Kopienas: Cerību Diaspora* (pp. 11–25). Rīga: SIA "Aģentūra Radars."

Hazans, M. (2015b). Smadzeņu aizplūde no Latvijas 21. gadsimtā. In I. Mieriņa (Ed.) *Latvijas Emigrantu Kopienas: Cerību Diaspora* (pp. 84–92). Rīga: SIA "Aģentūra Radars."

Hazans, M. (2016a). Migration experience of the Baltic countries in the context of economic crisis. In M. Kahanec & K. F. Zimmermann (Eds.), *Labor migration, EU enlargement, and the Great Recession*. Berlin–Heidelberg: Springer.

Hazans, M. (2016b). Atgriešanās Latvijā: remigrantu aptaujas rezultāti. Rīga: LU Disaporas un migrācijas pētījumu centrs.

Hazans, M., & Philips, K. (2010). The post-enlargement migration experience in the Baltic labor markets. In M. Kahanec & K. F. Zimmermann (Eds.), *EU labor market after post-enlargement migration* (pp. 255–304). Berlin Heidelberg: Springer-Verlag.

Hymes, D. (1962). The ethnography of speaking. In T. Gladwin & W. Sturtevant (Eds.), Anthropology and human behavior (pp. 13–53). Washington, DC: Anthropological Society of Washington.

Hymes, D. (1972). Models of the interaction of language and social life. In J. J. Gumperz & D. Hymes (Eds.), Directions in Sociolinguistics: The Ethnography of Communication (pp. 35–71). New York, NY: Holt, Rinehart & Winston.

Hymes, D. (1974). *Foundations in sociolinguistics. An ethnographic approach*. Philadelphia, PA: The University of Pennsylvania Press.

Ivanova, V. (2008). Return migration: Existing policies and practices in Bulgaria. In Zwania-Rößler, I., & V. Ivanova (Eds.), Welcome home? Challenges and chances of return migration, Transatlantic Forum on Migration and Integration.

Ivanova, V. (2015). Return policies and (r)emigration of Bulgarians in the pre- and post-accession period. University of National and World Economy Sofia. Available from http://problemypolitykispolecznej.pl/images/czasopisma/31/PPS-31-119-136.pdf

Ijabs, I. (2014). Starp etnisko un pilsonisko: daži apsvērumi par nacionālās identitātes problēmu. In J. Rozenvalds & A. Zobena (Eds.), Daudzveidīgās un mainīgās Latvijas identitātes (pp. 23–31). Rīga: Latvijas Universitāte.

Kaprāns, M. (2015). Latviešu emigranti Lielbritānijā: transnacionālā identitāte un attālinātā nacionālisma konteksti. In I. Mieriņa (Ed.), *Latvijas Emigrantu Kopienas: Cerību Diaspora* (pp. 108–127). Rīga: SIA "Aģentūra Radars."

Karamihova, M. (2014). *Amerikanski mechti: Patevoditel sred parvata generatsiya imigranti*. Sofia, Bulgaria: Krotal.

Kļaviņa, S. (2014). Latvijas Reemigrācijas atbalsta pasākumu plāns: Ekonomisko emigrantu viedoklis. Unpublished bachelor thesis. Faculty of Society and Science, Vidzeme University of Applied Science.

Ķešāne, I. (2011). Emigration and identity. In B. Zepa & E. Kļave (Eds.), *Latvia. Human Development Report 2010/2011* (pp. 70–76). Riga: Advanced Social and Political Research Institute.

Krasnopjorovs, O. (2011). Is public capital more productive than private capital? Evidence from Latvia 1995–2009. *Economic Studies* (Bulgarian Academy of Sciences, Economics Institute, Sofia, Bulgaria), *3*, 168–180.

Latvijas Republikas Ekonomikas ministrija. (2013). *Reemigrācijas atbalsta pasākumu plāns 2013.-2016.gadam.* Available from http://polsis.mk.gov.lv/documents/4428

Lulle, A. (2012). Vietas un telpas problemātika mobilitātes pētījumos. In A. Cimdiņa & I. Raubiško (Eds.), Dzīve-attīstība-labbūtība Latvijas laukos (pp. 135–152). Rīga: Zinātne.

Mancheva, M. (2008). Trudova migratsiya na B'lgarskite turtsi v Germaniya. S'etnichni migrantski mrezhi i kulturi. *Kritika i Humaniz'm*, *25*(1): 25–44.

Mieriņa, I. (2015). Introduction. In I. Mieriņa (Ed.), *Latvijas Emigrantu Kopienas: Cerību Diaspora* (pp. 5–10). Rīga: SIA "Aģentūra Radars."

Mihaylova, D. (2005). Reopened and renegotiated borders: Pomak identities at the frontier between Bulgaria and Greece. In T. M. Wilson & H. Donnan (Eds.), *Culture and Power at the Edges of the State*. Berlin: Lit.

Nagle, J. D. (1994). Political generation theory and post-communist youth in East-Central Europe. *Research in Social Movement, Conflicts and Change 17*, 25–52.

Penchev, V. (2001). *Paradox v ogledaloto, ili za migrantskite obshnosti v chuzdoethnichna sreda (Chehi i Slovatsi v B'lgaria, B'lgari v Chehiya)*. Sofia: Heron Press.

Philipsen, G. (1987). The prospect for cultural communication. In *Communication Theory: Eastern and Western Perspectives* (pp. 245–254). Cambridge, MA: Academic Press.

Philipsen, G. (1992). *Speaking culturally*. Albany, NY: State University of New York Press.

Philipsen, G. (1993). Ritual as a heuristic device in studies of organizational discourse. *Annals of the International Communication Association, 16*, 104–111.

Philipsen, G. (1997). A theory of speech codes. In G. Philipsen & T. Albrecht (Eds.), *Developing communication theories*. Albany, NY: SUNY Press.

Šūpule, I. (2015). *Reemigrācijas prakses analīze: atgriešanās modeļi, iemesli un process*. Insitute of Phylosophy and Sociology, University of Latvia. Unpublished manuscript. Available from http://fsi.lu.lv/userfiles/file/ESF_Latvijas_emigrantu_kopienas/Ex-ante/FSI_Supule_Reemigracijas_prakses_analize.pdf

Topalova, V. (2000). Europe and European identity concepts of young Bulgarians. In P. E. Mitev (Ed.), *Balkan youth and perception of the other*. Sofia: International Center for Minority Studies and Intercultural Relations.

Toshkov, A. (2009). On the inadequacy of the ethnic/civic antinomy: The language of politics of Bulgarian nationalism. *Nationalities Papers, 37*(3): 277–298.

Turner, V. (1980). Social dramas and stories about them. *Critical Inquiry, 7*(1), 141–168.

Verdery, K. (1996). *What was socialism, and what comes next?* Princeton, NJ: Princeton University Press.

World Population Prospects. (2015). United Nations. Available from https://esa.un.org/unpd/wpp/

Chapter Sixteen

Cultural Discourse Analysis within an Ecosystem of Discourse Analytic Approaches

Connections and Boundaries

David Boromisza-Habashi, Leah Sprain, Natasha Shrikant, Lydia Reinig, and Katherine R. Peters

CULTURAL DISCOURSE ANALYSIS AND TWO OTHER HYBRID APPROACHES TO DISCOURSE

Everyday communicative practice occurs at the point of convergence among available discursive resources (or discursive forms), meanings (or ideologies), and communicative activity (context-bound interaction). As a discourse analytic approach, cultural discourse analysis (CuDA) directs the analyst's attention to culturally distinctive communication practices—how different groups of people cultivate discursive resources with particular meanings activated by the context-bound use of those resources that, through their use, constitute social life (Carbaugh & Cerulli, 2017). In this chapter, we highlight CuDA's unique features and contributions to language and social interaction (LSI) research by bringing it into conversation with two other discourse analysis (DA) hybrids: action-implicative discourse analysis (AIDA) and socioculturally oriented discourse analysis (SODA). By discussing CuDA as a hybrid, we honor how it weaves together insights from multiple DA traditions to propel communication inquiry; by situating CuDA in relation to other DA hybrids, we honor Donal Carbaugh's career by enabling future scholars to similarly work with and combine different DA traditions to advance our understanding and appreciation of communication, culture, and social problems.

Discourse can mean anything from a historical monument, a policy, text, talk, a speech, topic-related conversations, or language per se—it can be a genre, a register, or style just as it can be a political program (Wodak, 2008). Given this range of possibilities, it is not surprising that DA can take multiple forms that do not always resemble each other (see Gordon, 2015, and Wodak, 2008, for extended discussions of different discourse analytic approaches). In this chapter, we use DA as a big-tent label for the study of particular segments of talk or text, where researchers use excerpts to make scholarly arguments (Tracy, 2005). That is, we focus on DA as it is situated within LSI research, wherein discourse refers to "language in use," "talk," "text," or "social interaction." DA is strongly empirical, predominantly qualitative, theoretically grounded, detail-oriented, and focused on illuminating how language and communication construct our social and cultural worlds (Gordon, 2015).

CuDA and the other two approaches we focus on here—AIDA and SODA—fall into the category Gordon (2015) calls DA hybrids, which are approaches developed from and informed by more than one of the central LSI approaches to DA: conversation analysis, ethnography of communication, interactional sociolinguistics, and critical discourse analysis. The first three coauthors (Boromisza-Habashi, Sprain, and Shrikant) are members of a group of researchers and educators at the University of Colorado Boulder who work regularly with graduate students (such as the fourth and fifth coauthors, Reinig and Peters) in a program committed to training LSI scholars in multiple LSI traditions and approaches. This training frequently prompts students to develop an interest in the individual approaches and the possibility of combining them as they pursue research questions. In our experience, it can be challenging, at least initially, to track distinctions among approaches and to determine which might be best used in a particular project.

In our experience, one particularly productive way of helping newcomers and LSI scholars appreciate CuDA is juxtaposing it with other DA approaches, such as SODA and AIDA. In doing so, we hope that, besides bringing into relief CuDA's contributions to the study of discourse and LSI, our chapter upholds the value of putting multiple kinds of DA into dialogue with each other (Gordon, 2015) while also enabling scholars to forge new hybrids or work across scholarly tracks. Whereas this chapter is an insufficient resource for *doing* CuDA, AIDA, or SODA analysis, it should help readers navigate between these approaches and develop a better understanding of the kinds of insight CuDA can generate.

Our discussion will not focus on how each approach defines discourse. Relying on that term to trace intellectual boundaries tends to result in confusion. Instead, we attend to the three approaches' hybrid influences, methodology, analytical claims, and orientation to normativity. After sketching the contours of each approach, we provide a sample analysis that illustrates each approach. In the conclusion, we draw on this illustration to situate CuDA with reference to the other two approaches and to highlight the promise of all three to serve as resources for scholars interested in developing hybrid projects.

HYBRID INFLUENCES

CuDA derives from the ethnography of communication and interactional sociolinguistics (Carbaugh & Cerulli, in press). It draws on interactional sociolinguistics' attention to culturally distinctive uses of vocabulary and linguistic styles, linking linguistic and stylistic differences to local meanings made relevant in social interactions. As the editors discuss in the introduction to this volume, the intellectual and historical source of CuDA's impulse to study discourse culturally is the ethnography of communication tradition. Many of the theoretical commitments and methodological moves come from Hymes, Philipsen, and their associates. Indeed, scholars need a deeper understanding of the ethnography of communication's commitments in order to fully utilize CuDA since this hybrid draws so heavily from that tradition.

AIDA is a method for analyzing the talk and texts that comprise social scenes to develop grounded practical theories of communication (Tracy, 1995; Tracy, 2005; Tracy & Craig, 2010). As such, AIDA draws on the practical theory tradition as well as several approaches to discourse analysis (see Tracy & Craig, 2010, for AIDA compared to conversation analysis and interactional sociolinguistics). Practical theory provides the goal of cultivating practice through the reconstruction of communication practices. From conversation analysis, AIDA takes a commitment to study the particulars of everyday interaction, intonation, abrupt cut-offs, and so on. From interactional sociolinguistics (Blum-Kulka, House, & Kasper, 1989; Gumperz, 1982), AIDA adopts the view of assessments about conversational actions as culturally inflected judgments (Tracy & Craig, 2010). Discursive psychology informs AIDA's rhetorical stance toward discourse and provides its notion of dilemma. AIDA shares the critical discourse analytic desire to link micro practices with macro discourses.

SODA embodies the generative interplay between DA traditions as a hybrid approach that has been grounding published work for over a decade (e.g., Bailey, 2000; Shrikant, 2014, 2015); yet naming this approach—calling it SODA—is new. Interactional sociolinguistics (Gumperz, 1982) provides SODA's foundational focus on how linguistic features like word choice, tone, and pauses act as contextualization cues that make racial, ethnic, or cultural differences relevant in implicit ways often not recognized by the participants. As the result of this focus, SODA encourages the use of specific concepts from other DA traditions as appropriate. Conversation analysis (e.g., Heritage & Clayman, 2010) provides a means to study how, on an interactional level, participants construct identity as emergent, relational, and display shared knowledge about normative kinds of identities through the sequence of their interactions. To make connections between micro and macro, SODA draws on the linguistic anthropological concept of indexicality (Ochs, 1992; Silverstein, 2003), as indexicality holds that, in addition to indexing identities on an interactional (micro) level, participants' linguistic features also index identities through making ideologies (macro) about iden-tity categories relevant to participants' interactions. Critical discourse analy-sis (Weiss & Wodak, 2003) informs the move to link the micro and macro, particularly with regard to relations of power.

METHODOLOGY

We caution that the easy tendency to rely on specific methodological choices (e.g., ethnographic fieldwork, transcripts of naturally occurring talk) pro-vides incomplete guidance regarding the fundamental concerns of each ap-proach. All three hybrids draw on ethnographic methods and naturally occur-ring interaction that researchers collect, transcribe, and systematically ana-lyze, albeit in different ways. Like SODA and AIDA, CuDA often favors naturally occurring talk (see Fitch, 2006, about this turn in ethnography of speaking), providing instances of transcribed talk to make scholarly argu-ments (although exceptions to this trend remain; as recent examples see Nuciforo, 2016, and Poutiainen, 2017). Additionally, participant observation, interviews with members, and the study of organizationally important docu-ments frequently inform AIDA interpretation (Tracy, 2005).

Nonetheless, the extent to which an ethnographic epistemology is central to analysis varies significantly among the three approaches. AIDA and SODA usually do not commit to an ethnographic epistemology that treats the embodied researcher as the primary instrument of the investigation of cultu-ral meanings. Conversely, CuDA analysts are situated ethnographically as they focus on culturally distinctive communication practices (Carbaugh & Cerulli, 2017). Often, this means that an analyst is conducting fieldwork, engaging in participant observation of social interaction, and collecting a range of related data (e.g., documents, interviews, etc.) to fully understand a communication practice. As an example, the status of a particular lexical item as a key term—the "salient word which is identified as standing alone, but around which recurrent or new conceptual allusions may be invoked or created during the very use of the term" (Parkin, 2015, p. 7)—cannot be apparent to the cultural analyst unless she spends an extended amount of time observing and participating in the life of a target social group. When a CuDA study claims, for example, that "hate speech" is a key term in Hungarian public discourse (Boromisza-Habashi, 2013), that claim is grounded in months or years of the embodied experience of fieldwork. Conversely, a CuDA study may use similar evidence to claim that what many would expect to be a cultural key term (e.g., "dialogue") in fact does not function like one in some contexts (Sprain, van Over, & Morgan, 2016). Such studies sometimes start with fieldwork to discover cultural terms for talk or cultural practices; at other times they start with a cultural term for talk or cultural practice in order to develop its form, function, and meanings. It is possible to complete a CuDA study without extensive ethnographic fieldwork, instead using CuDA as a type of close reading. However, even if ethnographic fieldwork is not the primary form of data collection, CuDA is an ethnographic approach because it privileges participants' meanings.

ANALYTICAL CLAIMS

Following descriptive analysis, CuDA is used to generate interpretative claims about the cultural meanings immanent in a particular communication practice. In other words, it allows the analyst to answer the question, what do participants have to take for granted to use discursive resources in this context in these ways? CuDA attends to the implicit and explicit meanings that people assume about being (personhood, identity), acting (communication), relating (social relations), feeling (affect), and dwelling (connections to places and nature). These claims can be used to provide specific insights into both communication practices and social organization in the groups in which they occur. AIDA is "centrally interested in describing the problems, interactional strategies, and ideals-in-use within existing communicative practices" and aims to develop an understanding of communication that will be action-implicative for practical life (Tracy & Craig, 2010, p. 146). As it pursues that interest, AIDA highlights the frequent discrepancy between how members believe they interact with others and how those interactions actually unfold. SODA focuses on making claims about how the micro (communication features such as word choice, tone, and sequence) reflects, reproduces, negotiates, or challenges the macro (communication ideologies or structural hierarchies). Studies taking this approach illustrate how participants index racial, ethnic, gender, or sexual identities and their intersections in everyday conversations, and how these interactions shape and are shaped by structural relationships among social groups. In sum, the difference among the three approaches' typical analytical claims becomes apparent when we contrast the types of ideology they center as analytic foci. While CuDA brings into relief taken-for-granted cultural meanings that inform indigenous standards for competent communicative action and social participation, AIDA is concerned with members' taken-for-granted notions about their own practices in contrast to the actual practices they perform, and SODA interrogates taken-for-granted hierarchical distinctions between linguistic varieties and social groups that shape everyday interactions.

ORIENTATION TO NORMATIVITY

Typically, when CuDA moves to critical analysis it does so following an extensive, iterative process of description, interpretation, and comparison. Critical analysis explicitly asks normative questions about what is better and worse within a communication practice, either from the participants' perspective (natural criticism) or from the perspective of the analyst's moral commitments in order to express a normative stance toward the cultural practices under consideration. Through interpretive analysis, CuDA studies can also provide an understanding of why particular ways of speaking are valued (or not) for accomplishing particular social goals within a given speech community.

AIDA is centrally committed to addressing normative problems that arise within particular, situated social practices (Tracy & Craig, 2010). This is accomplished through a positive reconstruction that considers how particular communicative practices should be conducted. The starting point for this reconstruction is the situated ideals pertaining to the focal practice—participants' beliefs about good conduct apparent in moments where they praise and criticize. The scholars' reconstruction of the practice can, of course, move beyond the participants' situated ideals to offer new discourse moves or normative ideals.

By starting with research questions about how micro discourse moves reflect, reproduce, negotiate, or challenge dominant ideologies and hierarchies, SODA begins with an interest in hegemonic norms—the taken-for-granted norms that structure power relations. People may unwittingly reproduce these hegemonic norms through their everyday talk or explicitly challenge them (e.g., via identity politics). By linking micro discourse with these hegemonic norms, SODA provides an account of how hegemonic norms are implicated and upheld in talk while also providing a way of recognizing these relationships in cases where people aim to resist or dismantle hegemonic identities.

ANALYSIS

To illustrate the kinds of distinctions discussed above, we analyze audio-recorded data gathered during Shrikant's eight months of ethnographic fieldwork with a Texas chamber of commerce (Shrikant, 2016). The data come from an extreme networking workshop held by the "North City" Chamber of Commerce (NCC). The two participants who appear in the data include Dan, the leader of the workshop, and Sarah, a workshop participant. Overall, there are about 50 participants in this speech event. In the below excerpt, Dan and Sarah define networking and discuss reasons that networking is important. For purposes of confidentiality, names used for people and organizations are pseudonyms. Data transcription is adapted from conversation analytic conventions (Jefferson, 2004). In the analysis below, we juxtapose CuDA, AIDA, and SODA by grounding our analysis in the transcript itself and in observations and documents gathered during ethnographic fieldwork. None of the DA hybrids would rely on this data alone for a full analysis, but we aim to provide an efficient illustration of these approaches. The analysis below (Excerpt 1) highlights the cultural propositions and premises about networking practices that underlie, explain, and are reflected in the interactions (CuDA), a dilemma inherent within networking and situated premises used for resolving it (AIDA), and how participants orient to masculinity as a hegemonic professional identity through their interactions (SODA):

1	Dan	Um (.) other reasons to network?
2		(5.0)
3	Sarah	If you let people know you care about them and you listen to
4		where they are and what they need=
5	Dan	=Bingo=
6	Sarah	=then they'll come back to you=
7		=That's great. Bob's right. Ultimately (.) at the end of the da:: ↓y is
8		(.) a lot of this is about (.) building business. But what I'm thrilled
9		(.) nobody raised their hand and said it's about selling stuff. (1.0)
10		Cuz there's there's definitely two schools of thought about
11		networking, if you've been to an event where there's a guy
12		working the room passing out business cards, you know hey I
13		wanna come sell ya, I wanna come sell ya, wh-who loves to be
14		sold anym↓ore

First, CuDA and AIDA share an interest in this example as a form of meta-communication, where participants talk about networking as a practice. CuDA highlights that this is an important practice within the community. Making this claim, of course, would not stem only from an analysis of this one example, but rather from spending extended time with the community and/or through interviewing community members and gathering documents. In the case of these data, during Shrikant's ethnographic fieldwork with the NCC she noted the prominence of networking (both as being practiced and being talked about) across a variety of NCC events. For example, Shrikant attended and audio-recorded an NCC small business committee that met monthly. The purpose of the small business committee was to discuss the needs of chamber members who owned or worked for small businesses and to plan events that help small businesses build their networks. Shrikant kept a copy of the agenda for this meeting, and after the meeting, a staff member used the agenda to explain to Shrikant the importance of this particular meeting. The staff member, George, explained that this committee was one of the most important in the chamber because it taught people how to net- work—which he defined as "how to interact"—and gave people opportu- nities to practice networking. He then identified four of the five upcoming chamber events listed on the agenda, including the networking skills work- shop where the data from this paper is drawn, as networking events. The fifth event, called the "Leads Group," was not discussed by George in this in- stance but was identified by other chamber staff members as a networking event primarily targeted toward businesspeople who wanted to gain "leads," that is, people they can connect with to grow their business.

Like CuDA, AIDA begins by developing an extended knowledge of net- working as a common institutional practice through multiple forms of data that include both how participants talk with each other in the practice (the focal discourse) and how they talk about their practice (metadiscourse). Us- ing AIDA involves teasing out how participants experience communication problems surrounding networking, the communicative means that partici- pants use to address those problems, and the situated ideals (what counts as good and bad) about networking practices in this community. From this excerpt of metadiscourse, an analyst can reconstruct situated ideals about participants' beliefs about good conduct from the moments where Dan and Sara criticize and praise particular forms of networking.

Let us take a closer look at some of the particular discourse moves in the data that inform all the approaches. Sarah uses pronouns to create two groups: "you" and "they." Sarah constructs "you" as a business professional who "cares" and "listens," and "they" as a client or customer who tells a businessperson "where they are or what they need." The interactional goal of "you" (the businessperson) is to get "they" (the potential client) to "come back to you." Sarah proposes that these particular enactments of professional identities—someone who listens and cares—are valued ones in this commu- nity because they reach a particular interactional goal of "building business" (said earlier by another member and repeated later in this excerpt by Dan, line 8). Dan's repeated affirmation of Sarah's response illustrates his agree- ment.

Dan then contrasts Sarah's relational definition of how networking can build business with the notion of "selling stuff" (line 9). Dan provides a concrete example of what "selling stuff" looks like by discursively constructing a hypothetical situation that is familiar to his participants ("if you've been to an event where," line 11) and a hypothetical "guy working the room passing out business cards" (lines 11–12) that participants might have met at this event. Dan voices this "guy" as repeatedly saying "I wanna come <u>sell</u> ya" (lines 12–13) and then negatively evaluates the "guy's" communication actions through the utterance "who loves to be sold to anymore" (lines 13–14). Although he phrases his evaluation as a question, Dan ends the question with a falling intonation, which indicates it is more of a declarative statement negatively evaluating the "selling stuff" form of networking.

Taking a CuDA perspective we notice how "networking" functions as a cultural term for talk (Carbaugh, 1989, 2017) and how participants' interactions reflect and construct cultural discourses of networking that are prominent in this community. More specifically, a cultural discourse analyst is interested in making broader claims about who the person doing it can and should be, how they are related to other people, what they should feel, and how they should live in place (Scollo, 2011; Carbaugh, 2007).

Dan's question (line 1) explicitly invokes the cultural term for talk "networking," and through asking about "reasons to network" he is inviting participants to construct meanings about networking for these community members. Sarah's answer, in addition to constructing a valued professional identity, also reflects culturally valued notions of personhood and relationships. One cultural proposition of personhood is that a good businessperson is someone who "lets people know you care about them" and "listens to where they are and what they need" and achieves the goal of getting people to "come back to you." Another, related, proposition of personhood is that a typical client is someone who has particular needs ("what they need") given their particular position in the business community ("where they are"). A cultural premise about relating, therefore, is that businesspeople and clients should develop relationships where they care for one another, take interest in one another's business needs, and attempt to maintain long-term relationships to facilitate a potential future business relationship. Through the sequence of their interactions, Dan and Sarah display their agreement about these cultural propositions and premises.

Dan's extended turn, where he contrasts Sarah's relational definition of networking with "selling stuff," also reflects several cultural propositions of personhood and relating. First, the act of networking is about "building business" and building business is *not* about "selling stuff." Through using voicing, Dan's utterances reflect a cultural proposition negatively evaluating a businessperson who simply wants to "sell ya." He contrasts the "selling" relationship with the relationship Sarah described earlier, where a businessperson cares about and listens to someone's needs and then waits for them to come back. Thus, these utterances point to a cultural premise of relating according to which networking involves building long-term relationships between businesses and clients that are based on care and not on the ability to immediately sell something. Dan also casts clients as persons who do not like to be "sold to anymore." In doing so, Dan points to a shift in the culture of the business community, where previously good business was more directly about selling, but now good business is defined by building relationships that may eventually result in a financial benefit. In addition to propositions and premises, Dan's utterances invoke cultural norms and preferences about what one ought (not) to do during networking. Among good businesspeople, if one wants to build business, it is preferred to listen to clients and create a long-term relationship defined by caring about one another's needs; it is *not* preferable to try to sell your products and services immediately to clients. A CuDA perspective would not make these claims from simply one excerpt, but rather would make claims after seeing patterns of cultural propositions and premises related to networking interactions across ethnographic observations. This excerpt could then be one example of a larger pattern found by the cultural discourse analyst.

By contrast, AIDA can be used to foreground interactional dilemmas within the practice of networking. Overall, an AIDA analysis of this excerpt can highlight a common dilemma business professionals face when networking: how to sell products and grow business without seeming like someone whose primary interest is in selling products. A full analysis would include further instances of metadiscourse about networking (including interviews and documents about the practice) and actual networking practices where participants use particular communicative actions to both establish relationships and market their products and services, constructing participants' situated ideals of how they should network in different scenarios given their goals and institutional structures. Based on an understanding of actual practices, the AIDA analyst would reconstruct networking to show how participants might better approach networking, which might include new ideals and/or different use of discursive resources within the practice itself.

Last, from a SODA perspective, one interesting question about this set of data is how participants index a male identity as a normative professional identity. Drawing from both discourse analytic theory and social theory, a SODA analyst would illustrate how the relationships between everyday conversational practices and gender ideologies reproduce structural inequalities. In analysis of this excerpt, in particular, the analyst would focus on lines 11–12, where Dan constructs a hypothetical situation about "a guy," and in doing so, Dan constructs a man as a typical businessperson. To start, SODA would note how Dan indexes gender in this interaction through using the person reference term "a guy" (line 11) and constructs explicit meanings about "a guy" through describing and evaluating activities in which this "guy" participates ("working the room," "passing out business cards," "who loves to be sold to anymore"). Through using these descriptors, Dan is constructing a "guy" as a typical businessperson who many in the room might have met, and he is negatively evaluating this person's behaviors. Furthermore, Dan's use of "a guy" contrasts with Sarah's use of nongendered references ("people" and "they") for business clients, thus indicating that there are multiple ways participants index a businessperson identity, and Dan's use of *guy* does foreground gender as relevant in this interaction. Thus, Dan's utterances reflect and reproduce gender ideologies that position men as natural professionals (Lakoff, 1973) and, therefore, maintains their cultural hegemony (Woolard, 1985) as authorities in business communities.

This example on its own is not enough to make general claims about how people index men as normative professional identities through communication or about whether the male identity is indeed a normative professional identity in this organization. "Gender ideologies are socialized, sustained and transformed through talk, particularly through verbal practices *that recur innumerable times in the lives and members of social groups* (Ochs, 1992, p. 336, emphasis added). Thus, the next step for SODA would be to examine audio-and-video-recorded data across multiple speech events to see if participants regularly position men as normative professionals and identify the ways they do so. A SODA analyst would *not* claim that Dan (or other participants) are necessarily aware of this activity or are sexist people. Instead, a SODA analyst would simply highlight how the everyday, mundane practices in this business community reflect and reproduce gender ideologies and thus contribute to maintaining gender hierarchies.

CONCLUSION

Through the parallel use of CuDA, AIDA, and SODA, we hope to have demonstrated how they might together strengthen analytic insight a researcher can gain from data. CuDA can establish that *networking* is a locally recognized and culturally meaningful term for talk. It can also show that members interpret *networking* as a particular way of acting that stands in sharp contrast with other, culturally dispreferred (Carbaugh, 2005) ways of acting such as *selling*. *Networking* points the analyst to other radiants of meaning, particularly personhood (who is a good businessperson? who is a client?) and social relations (what ought to be the relationship between businesspersons and clients?). This type of insight nicely complements AIDA's interest in developing a grounded account of networking as communication practice to improve how people engage in that practice. AIDA's reconstruction of the ideals and discourse moves within networking can be further nuanced with the cultural knowledge CuDA provides. Insight from CuDA also resonates with the SODA finding that, in the business community under consideration, the businessman has hegemonic, normative status. Taking this type of finding into consideration can serve as a reminder that the model of personhood immanent in talk about *networking* can become subject to contestation by those members of the business community who find the gendered interpretation of "doing business" objectionable. CuDA, on the other hand, reminds the SODA analyst that the model of acting immanent in *networking* may resist, or may be used to resist, such contestation ("We all just want to do good business here.").

Placing insights from these three approaches side-by-side helps us understand CuDA's unique strengths within the ecosystem of discourse analytic approaches. CuDA is particularly useful for analysis that aims to demonstrate people "doing culture" (Otten & Geppert, 2009)—or what Carbaugh (2005) calls "cultures in conversation"—that is, seeing how culture is both revealed and cultivated in practical action. Such insight can deepen AIDA analyses of situated ideals by demonstrating the ways in which such ideals may be deeply rooted in cultural discourses, which can explain their powerful presence in a social group's communicative habitus. The analysis of "doing culture" can also contribute to SODA's understanding of the cultural discursive terrain on which communicative contestation of hegemonic norms can unfold and is resisted.

It is worth pointing out that we are not the first to suggest that CuDA can usefully complement other discourse analytic approaches. As Bingjuan Xiong (2017) demonstrated in her work on categories of citizenship in Chinese public discourse, membership categorization analysis can be used to describe the available meanings of identity categories, and then the radiants of meaning (CuDA) can be used to interpret the implicit meanings (metacultural commentary) about being, acting, relating, feeling, and dwelling. CuDA may also provide a way to bridge the relationship between micro and macro discourses. For example, Fox and Robles's (2010) close examination of "it's like" enactments used DA to demonstrate this phrase as a resource for introducing affect-laden responses to prior events, action, or hypothetical utterances. Drawing on Carbaugh's work, they situated this discursive resource within a broader American practice of the lionization of self-revelation as a preferred mode of speaking.

We hope that the promise of combining CuDA and other DA approaches is compelling to established scholars and newcomers alike who are interested in the analysis of situated interaction. Yet we recognize the specific need for this chapter to demarcate some boundaries around CuDA so that newcomers can more ably navigate this intellectual terrain and select the path that best allows them to answer their research questions.

Our comparison of DA hybrids demonstrates that the choice, collection, and representation of data are not CuDA's primary distinguishing features. What are they, then? First, CuDA focuses on a communication practice or event in order to make claims about its cultural meanings. CuDA brings into view cultural forms of communication, historically transmitted systems of expression, key cultural terms, cultural forms or sequences, practical norms or rules for conduct, and the conventionally codified meanings participants activate and cultivate as they use this expressive system (Carbaugh, 2008). This cultural orientation attends to ideologies about the conduct of social life, the "unspoken coherence participants take-for-granted in order to understand their communication" (Carbaugh, 2017, p. 19). Second, to support these descriptive and interpretive claims, CuDA presents interpretations of cultural patterns. A CuDA study might present a single instance in a research report, but making a cultural claim requires a broader pattern that stretches across and connects various orders of data including interactions, documents, field notes, and so on. Third, as the sample analysis illustrates, CuDA must establish the relationship between a practice and the ideological foundations of its competent use (i.e., its local "taken-for-grantedness")—this is an essential methodological move even if it does not constitute the primary intellectual contribution of the analysis. This operation involves interpreting explicit and implicit cultural meanings of one or more of the radiants of meaning: being, acting, relating, feeling, and dwelling.

As students of language use work at the nexus of CuDA, AIDA, and/or SODA—as they combine these hybrid approaches into further hybrids that serve them best as they pursue answers to their research question—their research would benefit from explicit reflection on how they mobilize the three approaches. With regard to CuDA, Carbaugh (2007) lays out five basic modes of inquiry: theoretical, descriptive, interpretive, comparative, and critical. Explicitly referencing the mode(s) in which CuDA is being used lends additional force to the analysis, findings, and claims of researchers who decide to use this approach. Following Xiong (2017), scholars can note that they are only using CuDA for interpretation, as an example. The language of modes provides a way of tracking when an analyst is using CuDA in the interpretative mode but not the theoretical mode (or vice versa), such that the analyst is better accountable to the grammar and logic of each mode of inquiry within the corresponding approach. As more scholarship combines AIDA, SODA, and/or CuDA we imagine that additional differences may require accounting for. We call for more of this type of accounting as it helps newcomers and LSI scholars alike better understand the relationship among DA hybrids such that all our work can be enriched.

CuDA is the intellectual fruit of cross-pollination, experimentation, and deep thinking between DA traditions. This book demonstrates the rich insight generated through this approach. We hope scholars embrace Carbaugh's legacy by deftly developing their own hybrids that capture his rigor, generosity, and patience to figure out how to really listen.

REFERENCES

Bailey, B. (2000). Communicative behavior and conflict between African-American customers and Korean immigrant retailers in Los Angeles. *Discourse & Society, 11*(1), 86–108.

Blum-Kulka, S., House, J., & Kasper, G. (1989). *Cross-cultural pragmatics: Requests and apologies*. Norwood, NJ: Ablex.

Boromisza-Habashi, D. (2013). *Speaking hatefully: Culture, communication, and political action in Hungary*. University Park, PA: Pennsylvania State University Press.

Carbaugh, D. (1989). Fifty terms for talk: A cross-cultural study. In S. Ting-Toomey & F. Korzenny (Eds.), *Language, communication and culture: Current directions* (pp. 93–120). Newbury Park, CA: Sage.

Carbaugh, D. (2005). *Cultures in conversation*. Mahwah, NJ: Erlbaum.

Carbaugh, D. (2007). Cultural discourse analysis: Communication practices and intercultural encounters. *Journal of Intercultural Communication Research, 36*(3), 167–182.

Carbaugh, D. (2008). Putting policy in its place through cultural discourse analysis. In E. E. Peterson (Ed.), *Communication and public policy: Proceedings of the 2008 International Colloquium on Communication* (pp. 54–65). Blacksburg, VA: Virginia Tech.

Carbaugh, D. (2017). Terms for talk, take 2: Theorizing communication through its cultural terms and practices. In D. Carbaugh (Ed.), *The handbook of communication in cultural perspective* (pp. 15–28). New York, NY: Routledge.

Carbaugh, D., & Cerulli, T. (2017). Cultural discourse analysis. In Y. Y. Kim (Gen. Ed.) & K. L. McKay-Semmler (Assoc. Ed.), *The international encyclopedia of intercultural communication* (pp. 1–9). Hoboken, NJ: John Wiley & Sons. doi: 10.1002/9781118783665.ieicc0117

Fitch, K. L. (2006). Cognitive aspects of ethnographic inquiry. *Discourse Studies, 8*(1), 51–57.

Fox, B. A., & Robles, J. (2010). It's like mmm: Enactments with it's like. *Discourse Studies, 12*(6), 715–738.

Gordon, C. (2015). Discourse analysis. In K. Tracy, C. Ilie, & T. Sandel (Eds.), *The international encyclopedia of language and social interaction* (pp. 382–397). Hoboken, NJ: Wiley-Blackwell.

Gumperz, J. J. (1982). *Discourse strategies*. Cambridge, UK: Cambridge University Press.

Heritage, J., & Clayman, S. (2010). *Talk in action: Interactions, identities, and institutions*. Malden, MA: Blackwell.

Jefferson, G. (2004). Glossary of transcript symbols with an introduction. In G. H. Lerner (Ed.), *Conversation analysis: Studies from the first generation* (pp. 13–31). Philadelphia, PA: John Benjamins.

Lakoff, R. (1973). Language and woman's place. *Language in Society, 2*(1), 45–79.

Nuciforo, E. V. (2016). Russian folk discourse on problem drinking. *Russian Journal of Communication, 8*(1), 80–93.

Ochs, E. (1992). Indexing gender. In A. Duranti & C. Goodwin (Eds.), *Rethinking Context: Language as an Interactive Phenomenon* (pp. 335–358). Cambridge, UK: Cambridge University Press.

Otten, M., & Geppert, J. (2009). Mapping the landscape of qualitative research on intercultural communication: A hitchhiker's guide to the methodological galaxy. *Forum Qualitative Sozialforschung/Forum: Qualitative Social Research, 10*, Art. 52. Retrieved fromhttp://nbnresolving.de/urn:nbn:de:0114-fqs0901520

Parkin, D. (2015). *Revisiting: Keywords, transforming phrases, and cultural concepts. Working papers in urban language & literacies, No. 164*. London, UK: King's College London.

Poutiainen, S. (2017). Finnish terms for talk about communication on a mobile phone. In D. Carbaugh (Ed.), *The handbook of cross-cultural communication* (pp. 168–181). New York, NY: Taylor & Francis.

Scollo, M. (2011). Cultural approaches to discourse analysis: A theoretical and methodological conversation with special focus on Donal Carbaugh's cultural discourse analysis. *Journal of Multicultural Discourses, 6*(1), 1–32.

Shrikant, N. (2014). "It's like, 'I've never met a lesbian before!'": Personal narratives and the construction of diverse female identities in a lesbian counterpublic. *IPrA Pragmatics, 24*(4), 799–818.

Shrikant, N. (2015). "Yo, it's IST yo": The discursive construction of an Indian American youth identity in a South Asian student club. *Discourse & Society, 26*(4), 480–501.

Shrikant, N. (2016). "Race talk" in organizational discourse: A comparative study of two Texas Chambers of commerce (Doctoral dissertation). Retrieved fromhttp://scholarworks.umass.edu/dissertations_2/668 (668)

Silverstein, M. (2003). Indexical order and the dialectics of sociolinguistic life. *Language & communication, 23*(3), 193–229.

Sinclair, J. M., & Coulthard, M. (1975). *Towards an analysis of discourse: The English used by teachers and pupils.* London, UK: Oxford University Press.

Sprain, L., van Over, B., & Morgan, E. L. (2016). Divergent meanings of community: Ethnographies of communication in water governance. In T. R. Peterson, H. L. Bergea, A. M. Feldpausch-Parker, & K. Raitio (Eds.), *Communication and community: Constructive and destructive dynamics of social transformation* (pp. 249–265). New York, NY: Routledge.

Tracy, K. (1995). Action-implicative discourse analysis. *Journal of Language and Social Psychology, 14*(1–2), 195–215.

Tracy, K. (2005). Reconstructing communicative practices: Action-implicative discourse analysis. In K. L. Fitch & R. E. Sanders (Eds.), *Handbook of language and social interaction* (pp. 301–319). Mahwah, NJ: Erlbaum.

Tracy, K., & Craig, R. T. (2010). Studying interaction in order to cultivate practice: Action-implicative discourse analysis. In J. Streeck (Ed.), *New adventures in language and interaction* (pp. 145–166). Amsterdam: John Benjamins.

Weiss, G., & Wodak, R. (2003). Introduction: Theory, interdisciplinarity and critical discourse analysis. In G. Weiss & R. Wodak (Eds.), *Critical discourse analysis: Theory and interdisciplinarity* (pp. 1–34). New York, NY: Palgrave McMillan.

Wodak, R. (2008). Introduction: Discourse studies—Important concepts and terms. In R. Wodak and M. Kryzanowski (Eds.), *Qualitative discourse analysis in the social sciences*, pp. 1–29. New York, NY: Palgrave MacMillan.

Woolard, K. A. (1985). Language variation and cultural hegemony: Toward an integration of sociolinguistic and social theory. *American Ethnologist, 12*(4), 738–748.

Xiong, B. (2017). *Understanding internet-mediated social change in China: Analyzing categories of citizenship in Chinese public discourse* (Unpublished doctoral dissertation). University of Colorado Boulder.

Epilogue

Donal Carbaugh

With Deep Gratitude

Like other readers of this volume, I am grateful for the many works included herein. Each in its own way raises important questions about the nature of communication or discourse, how it is uniquely designed in situated ways, what it does for its users, and the range of meanings it holds for participants who are being situated by it. Reading through the volume we discover, as the analysts of the works have, what participants have made of their communication, how it is socially managed, and how it works (or doesn't work). The variety in the ways this is done is apparent and unveiled in the chapters. As a result of these analyses, and the stance the authors have taken to them, we come to a better understanding of just how discourse both constructs and reveals models for being/identity, relating, acting, feeling, and dwelling; we learn how these discursive hubs of activity are situated around the world in Singapore, Latvia, Bulgaria, variously in the United States, Israel, Finland, Britain, Mexico, Japan, Germany, and more. We find how discourse, when studied as so situated and so structured, shapes peoples' lives, human institutions, relations with animals; we see how it addresses a staggering array of social issues concerning health, immigration, online communities, in-car technology, political actions, suicide, education, rhetoric, politics, romance, hunting, and funerals. This is certainly not an exhaustive list of the matters treated in this volume. For example, the chapter by Nadezhda Sotirova and Liene Locmele demonstrates furthermore how discourses of immigration activate concerns of nationalism, family, economy, education, as well as international relations. I hope such a list alone somehow captures the excitement, the depth and breadth introduced in such studies, the productive feel when reading each, as well as the tremendous promise such works together hold for our future.[1]

Each contribution to the volume makes explicit the approach it assumes when responding to the question it raises, that is, cultural discourse theory (among other approaches). I am especially pleased that the authors have found this approach so useful. One of the major strengths of the volume in my view is this crucial thread of theoretical consistency. Not only do the contributions raise important questions about the particulars of discourse, its local structure, functions, and meanings, but taken together, the studies use and advance—albeit in different ways—this general conceptual approach. As a result the works cohere strongly in theory and method, by addressing discursive practice in local scenes, all the while setting the scholarly stage for subsequent comparative works. I emphasize, the approach is being used in variously productive ways to address different types of questions. This is also a major strength—as the general theory is shown to have deep heuristic value. By the end, the reader is treated to various creations of knowledge about discourse, its situated structure and functions, on a variety of fronts. This is highly impressive in its breadth at the level of local substance, as in its depth via this investigative stance; that is, the cultural approach to discourse being used and developed here.

The cultural discourse studies gathered here use a methodology that is systematic and rigorous; it is also complex and nuanced. The methodology brings into view various types of data. No matter the type, each is recorded and inscribed in an exacting way, fixing on the page some actual discursive accomplishment for the analyst's and the reader's detailed considerations. This is a creative part of the research enterprise as these sorts of *descriptive analyses* provide a product that not only researchers can analyze but also readers can consult in a considered and deliberative way. There is no particular dogma for creating such descriptive analyses in cultural discourse studies, only the unrelenting requirement that it be done systematically, fixing for analytic scrutiny actual bits of discourse for consideration, in a way that is defensible to "a" or "our" scholarly community. As a result, forms of descriptive analyses vary; some appearing in the form of Hymesian ethno-poetics; some in Jeffersonian conversation analytic form; some as quotes from archival data; some through visual images, photos, diagrams; some as also linked to audio and/or visual files, and so on. Each datum thus presents the claim: this bit of discourse did indeed actually occur as an actual moment of social life; this descriptive rendering of it situates the discourse as it was used in this way on that occasion. The descriptive claim provides a necessary toehold of our studies on actual bits of sociocultural reality—at least as these are immanent or evident in a discursive form and context.

I will add a quick question that is raised by the studies and warrants a more detailed discussion than can be offered here. What indeed is an adequate descriptive datum in cultural discourse research? The responses vary, and with good results. Some studies show the discourse itself as enough, typically as bits of language use—but what, in these cases, is "the discourse itself"? Some find bits of vocabulary or larger strips of language itself as sufficient. Others like Charles Braithwaite, Jay Leighter, and Eean Grimshaw find the discourse so intimately tied to physical, social, and cultural contexts that its sociocultural life is murdered if this—matters of place and health—is not explicated as an intimate part of the "discourse itself." Given the interests of some, physical structures must be included in the descriptive analyses, or accompanying gestures, images, verbal emphases, symbolic aspects, and so on. As the studies gradually reveal the meanings in the discourse, they find in social situations of discursive practice, culture(s) at work. Yes, the question of what is an adequate descriptive record is not responded to simply in these chapters. It is in each case responded to adequately, but across the cases variously, with this inviting further discussion and reflection. The matters run deep.

The depth is cultivated by moving from descriptive to interpretive analyses. What in these descriptive accounts is the focus of detailed interpretive analyses? When responding to this question, we find in the descriptive accounts various discursive devices at play, with analysts drawing our attention to many. The authors may conceptualize these as terms, symbols, forms, rules, agons, and each may play a role in informal events such as dining events, medical scenes, more formal administrative meetings, or generic types of discourse such as statements of policy. Interpretive analyses draw our attention to the meanings participants understand to be active as people use such devices, formulating these meanings as cultural propositions, cultural premises, semantic dimensions, an ideology, a code. In the end, we find participants to be actively utilizing a set of propositions, premises, dimensions, ideologies, codes, or, in short, in their discourse, a *cultural logic*. The point is demonstrated repeatedly, in discourse itself a cultural logic is—or in multicultural scenes various cultural logics are—at work! The studies help us understand exactly what is involved in this work that is, the meanings people presume, as it is being structured, implemented, and/or challenged, in this way.

Each contribution has in turn, then, by raising and addressing an important question, assuming a robust theoretical stance to it, and by investigating data in systematic and vigorous ways, provided readers with an account of that discourse, describing how it is socially situated, and the ways in which it is culturally meaningful to participants. The volume is a veritable feast for readers interested not only in understanding the varieties in discourse practices, but also in developing ways for its rigorous study. The editors are to be congratulated for assembling such an impressive range of studies. When reading through them myself, and when hearing many such works presented earlier at a highly stimulating conference (sponsored in part by the National Communication Association) at the College of Mount Saint Vincent in New

York, I recalled Hymes's statement about ethnography being cooperative, cumulative, and comparative. He discussed that ethnography of communication is cooperative among people in its use of a similar approach, cumulative across time in that the studies come together to offer insights each alone cannot, and comparative across places as studies—put side-by-side—help contribute knowledge about both what is locally unique in communication and more general as insights are gleaned across such studies (Hymes, 2003a, p. 17). These features of ethnography generally and cultural discourse studies particularly are not only evident in the volume's works but promising for future works as well.

WHAT IS A CULTURAL DISCOURSE?

A cultural discourse is a *system* of expression, an ordering of communication in its ways of "saying" and conceiving of something; it does so through various means of communication, including the meanings of whatever means of communication is being used. The system of expression is understood to be composed of parts, the organization of which can be understood by using various concepts. One set draws attention to the detailed ways discourse is being structured for example through terms, words, symbolic agons, or non-linguistic symbols; another set draws attention to sequences of social interaction such as symbolic forms for example of ritual, social drama, and other act sequences (see Philipsen, 1987, below); a third set draws attention to norms that guide conduct from morality-laced enactments and motivational themes to participants' statements of rules. These various means can be understood as creating a system of expression, respectively, as a system of symbols, symbolic forms, norms, and their meanings. The concept, *discursive device*, is used to discuss any one of these parts of this system of expression. And further, any expressive system is understood to have, in its own terms, limits, that is, it structures itself in ways that limit what is indeed communicable. But these limits vary and this point is the central thesis of the chapter by Brion van Over, Gonen Dori-Hacohen, and Michaela Winchatz on the limits of the communicable.

A cultural discourse includes the meanings of each device; the analysis of each reveals the means of expressing those meanings. The working model focuses, in other words, on *means AND meanings*. This is a conjunctive concept, both elements being required for consideration together; a discursive means includes its meanings just as meanings include at least one discursive means of expression. Meanings in this sense include the taken-for-granted knowledge that is active when a discursive device is being used. This includes participants' beliefs and/or values that radiate from a device and that may more generally hold the discursive parts together—if sometimes tightly, sometimes loosely. These meanings involve the knowledge—the audible intelligence—participants presume when using discourse in this way, the basic concepts at play, the definitions, principles, ethical stances, and so on that participants "hear" as significant and important to them when that cultural discursive device is in use. These, each discursive device and its meanings, must be interpreted and explicated, as is shown throughout the volume. The interpretations of the devices reveal, then, a cultural logic, this being formulated by analysts as a system of cultural propositions, cultural premises, semantic dimensions, norms or rules, and largely, as codes.

When the analysts of the volume's chapters examine a cultural discourse, they are examining a part of a system of expression, a symbol, symbolic form, norm, and its meanings. Analyses as these are always of "a part" of a discursive system since, inevitably, each part is connected to others, which are connected to others and on and on. Readers may be reminded of Clifford Geertz's comment that all ethnography is to some degree incomplete or partial (Geertz, 1973). But each part is examined within a "useful fiction" that there is indeed a whole system of expression within which any discursive device plays a formative role. This assumption of a part-whole relationship provides both theoretical and empirical utility to such studies, providing a limiting range of scope conditions in which one is thinking, generating data, recording, and analyzing a cultural discourse, so conceived. This investigative utility is important analytically as any bit of discourse, such as a word, or a sequence, can play differently in multiple cultural discourses such as the symbol "democracy" plays one way within an American discursive system yet another within a Chinese discursive system. The studies in this volume among others make this point amply.[2]

The construct of cultural discourse links easily to others like "expressive order" as used by Erving Goffman (1967) or "discursive formation" as used by Michel Foucault (1972) or "habitus" as used by Pierre Bourdieu (1990). Each draws attention to social interaction, discursive practices, and fields of action, including the morals and the architecture of meanings that presumably holds the discursive parts together. The concept of cultural discourse has proven as valuable to the authors in this volume as in others' works that demonstrate the construct variably, richly, and amply.

A NOTE ON SOME FOUNDATIONS

Cultural discourse studies derive from research traditions that they activate in their design and implementation. Principal among these is interactional sociolinguistics and the ethnography of communication (e.g., Gumperz, 1982; Hymes, 1972). The commitment to a descriptive mode of analysis involves some sort of Hymesian situating of discourse; this appears explicitly at times in our studies by using the components of the SPEAKING mnemonic. Hymes's insistence on studying discourse in situ and in depth provides not only a motivating impulse but also a conceptual apparatus used in cultural discourse studies (e.g., Hymes, 1986). As much is made explicit in the focus of this volume, in the situating of discourse studies. One additional means of doing so occurs through an ethno-poetic style of transcription and analysis (mentioned above). This helps analysts and readers understand qualities in spoken lines, verses, and stanzas as well as discursive devices of repetition, speakers' propositional statements, and the use of a discernible cultural logic. Hymes's (2003b) exposition of oral poetry in the form of ethno-poetics is evident in several recent publications, including some chapters in this volume.

The theory of cultural communication earlier explicated by Gerry Philipsen (1987, 2002) provides a similar foundation for the chapters included here. Particularly notable are the sequential and symbolic forms of ritual and social drama that Philipsen explicated as key generic forms of cultural communication; each, along with the mythic form, has proven highly heuristic as cultural discursive practices are explored. Additionally, the discursive devices under study explore formative aspects of conversation, community, and code, as these are explicated by Philipsen (1987). The latter, code, is the central construct in the theory of speech codes (Philipsen, Coutu, & Covarrubias, 2005). I have reviewed and discussed the links to these foundations in detail elsewhere.[3] Here, I simply restate that cultural discourse analysis embraces and complements but does not supplant the foundations laid in these studies of Dell Hymes, Gerry Philipsen, Tamar Katriel, Charles Braithwaite, Lisa Coutu, Patricia Covarrubias, among many others. Our studies are conceived at the nexus of these and other works (see below), not somehow outside of them. In fact, cultural studies of this sort can help discover, describe, interpret, and comparatively analyze communication codes, as has been shown in many earlier works (e.g., Carbaugh, 2005; Coutu, 2008; Katriel, 2004) including discourse and dialogue generally (Berry, 2009; Carbaugh, Gibson, & Milburn, 1997; Scollo, 2011; Sleap & Sener, 2013).

One rich focal discursive device is evident in the cultural discourse studies of *metapragmatic terms* as is evident in many chapters of this (see Richard Wilkins, Fran Gulinello, and Karen Wolf) as well as a recent volume (Carbaugh, 2017). This discursive device was explicated earlier as a central part of speech codes theory. Another is the basic assumption, in cultural discourse studies, that discursive devices involve meanings where, in effect, "culture is talking about itself." In other words, discourse can be understood as involving a *metacultural commentary*; as people use discourse so we are saying something about who we are (identity, being), how we are related (relating), what we are doing together (acting), what emotions are relevant to this (feeling), and what indeed is the nature of things (dwelling). Any device can activate this commentary in one or more, multiple directions. It is in the explication of this metacultural, semantic field, activated through discursive devices, that we capture the meanings in the message, the culture of the discourse.

DISCURSIVE HUB *AND* RADIANTS OF MEANING

In earlier works, we have discussed the value of the *five discursive hubs* with each being studied in some detail. The chapters in this volume are productively organized around each hub, of being, acting, relating, feeling, and dwelling, respectively.

The concept, discursive hub, draws attention to a device that is being used by participants to cue cultural meanings. By focusing on membership categories or terms of nationality or being online (see Tabitha Hart and Trudy Milburn) one can make explicit a hub of identity; by focusing on terms about communication or metapragmatic terms for conduct more generally, one can make explicit a hub for acting; by focusing on terms of address or human-animal links, one can make explicit a hub for relating; by focusing on terms of emotion or its expression, one can make explicit a hub of feeling (see Danielle Graham and Sally Hastings); by focusing on place-names or stories about places, one can make explicit a hub of dwelling. Each hub, so conceived, can be explored by examining discursive devices that make it explicitly a part of the discourse or expressive system.

A discursive hub can also radiate implicitly more meanings; one expression, such as a shift in pronouns, can activate a range of meanings concerning identity, relations, emotions (for an example see the chapter by Patricia Covarrubias, Dani Kvam, and Makoto [aka Max] Saito). A hub in this sense is the socially understood discursive "object" from which semantic light or heat radiates. The radiants or beams or rays of meanings activated by a hub can be difficult for some to trace, and nearly impossible for those nonsocialized in the discourse to understand. A well-chosen cultural discursive hub, then, like being "heaty" in Singapore, as explored by Evelyn Ho, Sunny Lie, Pauline Luk, and Mohan Dutta, can provide a bright source of light for such analyses. Conceived in CuDA as possibly expressing a metacultural commentary, as shedding some light on issues of identity, acting, relating, feeling, and/or dwelling. By using the framework in an open and investigative way, we may understand some of the richness in the meanings that are activated by a discursive hub.

Note that a hub need not necessarily be explicitly affiliated with one and only one radiant of meaning. The chapters in the volume show how discursive hubs of being activate meanings of relating, or feeling, and vice versa, as by Michelle Scollo and Saila Poutiainen, who find the hub of relating implies messages also of romantic feelings and identities. We find how a hub of relating is largely contained within a discourse of dwelling examined by Tovar Cerulli and Tema Milstein as it implies rich meanings about identities and involves details of action. The discourses spin webs of meanings with the goals of our conceptual apparatus being to discover, describe, interpret, comparatively analyze, and critically assess each web; with a discursive device in view, an expressive system at a time. (With regard to the latter mode of analysis, a grounded participant-based critique of discourse, the chapters by Jolane Flanigan and Michael Alvarez, and by Danielle Graham and Sally Hastings, are particularly instructive.) The conceptual apparatus of discursive devices, hubs, radiants of meanings, metacultural commentary, cultural logic, modes of analysis, and so on up to cultural discourse itself helps us in doing so.

CONTINUING ADVANCES

I am delighted that the discursive hubs explored embrace and extend into issues not only of dwelling space but also in movement across time. Discourses can and must conceive of time in some way, including at times changing or transforming, although how they resist change is crucial also to understand. Tamar Katriel and Oren Livio's contribution is notable here and came to me as I was wrestling myself with Blackfeet data that included an equi-temporal discursive device that goes at once deep into the past of ancestral time while also anchoring several contemporary practices. The importance of these "timely" discursive devices is essential to consider in these matters, and for others where social change is considered in matters of policy as by Lisa Rudnick, Saskia Witteborn, and Ruth Edmonds. These studies demonstrate the need for theoretical developments, adding devices or a hub of "time" to our systematic considerations. Such development is most welcome; this is exciting.

Similarly, the chapters accumulated here at times examine and/or implement distinct yet complementary theoretical concerns. CuDA is considered alongside action implicative discourse analyses and other sociocultural approaches to discourse by David Boromisza-Habashi, Leah Sprain, Natasha Shrikant, Lydia Reinig, and Katherine Peters. Similarly, prior works have used CuDA to examine various health practices as in the "heaty" research in Singapore integrated with a well-established culture centered approach to health communication.

The focus on agonistic devices is nicely revitalized by Patricia Covarrubias, Dani Kvam, and Makoto Saito. Through careful empirical and conceptual work, their chapter advances our knowledge about agonistic forms as active parts of cultural discourses (see also Philipsen, 1986). One deep agonistic play involves discourses of life and death; these are active in different ways in two chapters, one by Sally Hastings and Danielle Graham, the other by Lauren Mackenzie and Kelly Tenzek. Both offer depth of insight into discourses surrounding life and death. The latter chapter also brings into view matters of education, and efforts to design discourse as preparation for a final stage of life. These are deeply touching, human moments.

How cultural discourse studies are related to matters of discourse design are also addressed relative to policy by Rudnick, Witteborn, and Edmonds (following Miller & Rudnick, 2008, 2010; see also Rudnick & Boromisza-Habashi, 2017), and relative to the fascinating developments we are making in the human-machine interface, especially in automobiles, by Laura Rosenbaun, Ute Winter, and Brion van Over.

There is much work to do in the study of cultural discourses. The chapters assembled here will repay reading and rereading. They will provide ways of moving forward as well as perspective on where we have been. Creative, theoretical advances are being made, as are significant conceptual developments. But we must never lose care of the grounds upon which we find our feet! The ways discourse structures social and cultural lives here and there is essential to keep in view. And so we move onward, on the bases of our discoveries, our descriptive, interpretive, comparative, and critical studies. In the process, we advance our field(s) of research with the grand variety of discourses, of peoples and places in view; onward, down our paths to social, cultural, and intellectual betterment!

NOTES

1. A comprehensive treatment of these summary points here is warranted but not possible given limitations of space. Nonetheless, I will essay a few thoughts in a general way with apologies to each author for not being able to give the attention each chapter deserves.

2. I will resist illustrating the points here with many important details of the specific chapters of this volume as this would run too long. I will briefly mention a few as the epilogue moves onward.

3. I note here my deep debt to Gerry Philipsen for his mentoring, collegiality, and friendship. I have written of this debt earlier (Carbaugh, 1995, 2010).

REFERENCES

Berry, M. (2009). The social and cultural realization of diversity: An interview with Donal Carbaugh. *Language and Intercultural Communication, 9,* 230–241.

Bourdieu, P. (1990). *The logic of practice.* Cambridge, UK: Polity Press.

Carbaugh, D. (1995). The ethnographic theory of Philipsen and associates. In D. Cushman and B. Kovacic (Eds.), *Watershed research traditions in human communication theory* (pp. 269–297). Albany, NY: State University of New York Press.

Carbaugh, D. (2005). *Cultures in conversations.* London and Malwah, NJ: Lawrence Erlbaum Associates.

Carbaugh, D. (2010). Language and social interaction at the University of Washington (pp. 369–384). In W. Leeds-Hurwitz (Ed.), *The social history of language and social interaction research: People, places, ideas*. Cresskill, NJ: Hampton Press.

Carbaugh, D. (Ed.). (2015). *The handbook of communication in cross-cultural perspective*. Abingdon, UK: Routledge.

Carbaugh, D. (Ed.). (2017). *The handbook of communication in cross-cultural perspective*. New York and London: Routledge.

Carbaugh, D., Gibson, T. A., & Milburn, T. (1997). A view of communication and culture: Scenes in an ethnic cultural center and a private college. In B. Kovacic (Ed.), *Emerging theories of human communication* (pp. 1–24). Albany, NY: State University of New York Press.

Coutu, L. (2008). Contested social identity in communication in text and talk about the Vietnam war. *Research on Language and Social Interaction, 41*(4), 387–407.

Foucault, M. (1972). *The archaeology of knowledge*. Translated by A. M. Sheridan Smith. New York, NY: Pantheon Books.

Geertz, C. (1973). *The interpretation of cultures*. New York, NY: Basic Books.

Goffman, E. (1967). On face-work. an analysis of ritual elements in social interaction. In *Interaction Ritual* (pp. 5–45). New York, NY: Doubleday.

Gumperz, J. (1982). *Discourse strategies*. New York, NY: Cambridge University Press.

Hymes, D. (1972). Models of the interaction of language and social life. In J. Gumperz & D. Hymes (Eds.), *Directions in sociolinguistics: The ethnography of communication* (pp. 35–71). New York, NY: Holt, Rinehart, and Winston.

Hymes, D. (1986). Discourse: Scope without depth. *International Journal of the Sociology of Language, 57*, 49–89.

Hymes, D. (2003a). *Ethnography, linguistics, narrative inequality: Toward an understanding of voice*. Bristol, PA: Taylor and Francis.

Hymes, D. (2003b). *Now I know only so far: Essays in ethnopoetics*. Lincoln, NE: University of Nebraska Press.

Katriel, T. (2004). *Dialogic moments*. Detroit, MI: Wayne State University Press.

Miller, D., & Rudnick, L. (2008). *The security needs assessment protocol: Improving operational effectiveness through community security*. New York and Geneva: United Nations Publications.

Miller, D., & Rudnick, L. (2010). A case for situated theory in modern peacebuilding practice. *Journal of Peacebuilding & Development, 5*, 62–74.

Philipsen, G. (1986). Mayor Daley's council speech: A cultural analysis. *Quarterly Journal of Speech , 72*, 247–260.

Philipsen, G. (1987). The prospect for cultural communication. In L. Kincaid (Ed.), *Communication theory: Eastern and Western perspectives* (pp. 245–254). New York, NY: Academic Press.

Philipsen, G. (2002). Cultural communication. In W. Gudykunst and B. Mody (Eds.), *Handbook of international and intercultural communication* (pp. 51–67). Thousand Oaks, CA: Sage.

Philipsen, G., Coutu, L., & Covarrubias, P. (2005). Speech codes theory: Restatement, revisions, responses to criticism. In W. Gudykunst (Ed.), *Theorizing about intercultural communication* (pp. 55–68). Thousand Oaks, CA: Sage.

Rudnick, L., & Boromisza-Habashi, D. (2017). The emergence of a local strategies approach to human security. *Journal of Multicultural Discourses*, http://www.tandfonline.com/action/showCitFormats?doi=10.1080/17447143.2017.1365079.

Scollo, M. (2011). Cultural approaches to discourse analysis: A theoretical and methodological conversation with special focus on Donal Carbaugh's cultural discourse theory. *Journal of Multicultural Discourses, 6*(1), 1–32.

Sleap, F., & Sener, O. (2013). Donal Carbaugh. In F. Sleap & O. Sener (Eds.), *Dialogue theories* (pp. 67–82). London: The Dialogue Society.

Index

About the Editors

Michelle Scollo (Ph.D., University of Massachusetts Amherst) is associate professor of communication and faculty member of the International Development and Service Graduate Program at the College of Mount Saint Vincent. Her research and teaching are part of the ethnography of communication research program in which she examines the nexus of communication and community, interpersonal communication and culture, and environmental communication and culture, with a focus on cultural discourse analysis and qualitative research methodologies. She is the recipient of the National Communication Association's Outstanding Publication Award for Language and Social Interaction Scholarship for a 2011 article on cultural discourse analysis and has published in multiple academic journals.

Trudy Milburn (Ph.D., University of Massachusetts Amherst) is assistant dean for the School of Liberal Arts and Sciences at Purchase College, SUNY. Her previous books include *Communicating User Experience: Applying Local Strategies Research to Digital Media Design*; *Citizen Discourse on Contaminated Water, Superfund Cleanups, and Landscape Restoration: (Re)making Milltown, Montana*; and *Nonprofit Organizations: Creating Membership through Communication*.

About the Contributors

Mike Alvarez (M.F.A., M.A., Goddard College) is a doctoral candidate at the University of Massachusetts Amherst. His dissertation explores how suicidal individuals use the Internet to create meaning and community and how their experiences online are represented in film and other moving image media. He is also the author of two forthcoming books: *The Paradox of Suicide and Creativity* (under contract with Rowman & Littlefield's Lexington imprint) and a memoir of his past struggle with so-called mental illness and psychiatric hospitalization.

David Boromisza-Habashi (Ph.D., University of Massachusetts Amherst) is associate professor in the Department of Communication at the University of Colorado Boulder. He studies the cultural foundations and global circulation of particular forms of public discourse such as public speaking and hate speech. His first book, *Speaking Hatefully: Culture, Communication, and Political Action in Hungary*, is an ethnographic study of public debates surrounding hate speech in Hungary.

Charles A. Braithwaite (Ph.D., University of Washington) is the editor of *Great Plains Quarterly* for the Center for Great Plains Studies and senior lecturer in the Department of Communication Studies at the University of Nebraska-Lincoln. He received his B.A. in communication studies at the University of California-Santa Barbara and his M.A. and Ph.D. from the University of Washington. He has a special interest in American Indian higher education and tribal colleges in the United States and Canada.

Donal Carbaugh (Ph.D., University of Washington) is professor of communication at the University of Massachusetts Amherst. His recent works include *The Handbook of Communication in Cross-Cultural Perspective* (editor, in the International Communication Association's series) and *Reporting Cultures on 60 Minutes: Missing the Finnish Line in an American Broadcast* (with Michael Berry), both in 2017. He is deeply grateful for conversations with colleagues, especially those in this volume.

Tovar Cerulli (Ph.D., University of Massachusetts Amherst) is a consultant, writer, and speaker whose work focuses on cultivating insight into—and common ground among—diverse understandings of human relations with nature and wildlife. He is the author of *The Mindful Carnivore* (2012).

Patricia O. Covarrubias (Ph.D., University of Washington) is associate professor in the Department of Chicana and Chicano Studies and the Department of Journalism and Communication at the University of New Mexico, where she teaches cultural and intercultural communication, Chican@ ways of speaking, cultural discourse analysis, global metaphors, qualitative research methods, and the ethnography of communication. Her research has been dedicated to understanding the linkages among culture, communication, and peoples' unique ways of life.

Gonen Dori-Hacohen (Ph.D., University of Haifa) is associate professor in the Department of Communication at the University of Massachusetts Amherst. He is a discourse analyst, studying interactions in the media and in mundane situations, focusing on the intersection of interaction, culture, politics, and the media. Currently he studies civic participation in Israeli radio phone-ins, American political radio talk, and other arenas of public participation, such as online comments.

Mohan J. Dutta (Ph.D., University of Minnesota) is Provost's Chair Professor and head of the Department of Communications and New Media at the National University of Singapore (NUS), adjunct professor at the Interactive Digital Media Institute (IDMI) at NUS, and courtesy professor of communication at Purdue University. At NUS, he is the founding director of the Center for Culture-Centered Approach to Research and Evaluation (CARE), directing research on culturally centered, community-based projects of social change.

Ruth Edmonds (Ph.D., University of London) is ethnographer and social development consultant at Keep Your Shoes Dirty and honorary associate at the Centre for Research on Families and Relationships at the University of Edinburgh. She works at the nexus of generating "local knowledge" to inform program design with organizations across the globe, including the United Nations, governments, international charities, trusts, and foundations. She has fifteen years' experience in applied ethnographic research, especially in relation to vulnerable children and families in wide-ranging research contexts in Africa, Asia, and the United Kingdom, and her research has appeared in online client reports, academic journals, and edited books.

Jolane Flanigan (Ph.D., University of Massachusetts Amherst) is associate professor of communication studies at Rocky Mountain College, where her research focuses on interpersonal and cultural communication. She is currently completing her master of science degree in clinical and rehabilitation counseling—a degree she began when her experiences with people with autism and personality disorders helped her to realize the limits of a communication focus on managing interpersonal and cultural barriers to satisfying relationships.

Danielle Graham (M.A., University of Central Florida) studied interpersonal communication at the undergraduate and graduate levels. Her work was highly influenced by the philosophical teachings of Sally O. Hastings. She currently works at Full Sail University, where she teaches foundational communication skills.

Eean Grimshaw (M.A., University of Montana) is a doctoral student in communication studies at the University of Massachusetts Amherst. He is interested in Native American and Indigenous ways of speaking and what a focus on these ways of speaking reveals about Native American and Indigenous identity and meaning-making practices. He has a special focus on concerns surrounding language revitalization efforts and the meaning-making inherent to those Indigenous communities as well as their approaches.

Fran Gulinello (Ph.D., Graduate Center, CUNY) is professor in the Department of Communications at Nassau Community College, SUNY. She holds a Ph.D. in linguistics and an M.A. in rhetorical studies. Her research interests include adult and computer-assisted language learning, sociolinguistics, and ethnography of communication.

Tabitha Hart (Ph.D., University of Washington) is assistant professor of communication studies at San Jose State University. Her research areas include speech codes and the ethnography of communication, inter/cultural and organizational communication, technology-mediated communication, and applied communication. As a teacher/practitioner she is interested in civic engagement and high-impact practices such as service learning, study abroad, and internships.

Sally O. Hastings (Ph.D., University of Massachusetts Amherst) was among Donal Carbaugh's first doctoral students. She currently works at the University of Central Florida, where her research addresses issues of communication and marginalization.

Evelyn Y. Ho (Ph.D., University of Iowa) is professor of communication studies, Asian Pacific American studies, and critical diversity studies at the University of San Francisco. Her teaching and research focus broadly on the intersections of health, culture, and communication, specifically examining the discursive construction of holistic, complementary, and integrative medicine and Chinese medicine.

Tamar Katriel (Ph.D., University of Washington) is professor emerita in the Department of Communication at the University of Haifa and conducts research in the ethnography of communication and discourse studies.

Dani S. Kvam (Ph.D., University of New Mexico) is assistant professor of communication studies at the University of Wisconsin-Oshkosh. She uses the ethnography of communication to explore Latino/a communication in U.S. immigration contexts.

James (Jay) L. Leighter (Ph.D., University of Washington) is associate professor in the Department of Communication Studies at Creighton University. He investigates how moments for speaking are culturally influenced and, in instances of planned intervention, what needs to be known, culturally and communicatively, about the community who will be affected by the intervention.

Sunny Lie (Ph.D., University of Massachusetts Amherst) is assistant professor of communication at California State Polytechnic University Pomona (Calpoly Pomona). Her research interests include culture and communication and the relationship between religious communication and ethnic identity.

Oren Livio (Ph.D., University of Pennsylvania) is lecturer in the Department of Communication at the University of Haifa. His work focuses on discourses of nationalism, militarism, and protest.

Liene Ločmele (M.A., University of Jyväskylä) is a Ph.D. candidate at the University of Massachusetts Amherst and a lecturer at Vidzeme University of Applied Sciences, Latvia, where she teaches courses in interpersonal, intercultural, and mass communication. In 2009 she received a Fulbright student fellowship and started her doctoral studies in communication at the University of Massachusetts Amherst. Her research interests include the interpersonal and intercultural aspects of human communication with a special focus on the communication of Latvian identity in a variety of contexts, particularly the context of migration.

Pauline Luk (Ph.D., National University of Singapore) has research interests in health communication, especially in alternative medicines, health information seeking, and health policy. She has also worked as a research assistant at the Center for Culture-Centered Approach to Research and Evaluation (CARE) at NUS on a variety of social justice–oriented health communication campaigns.

Lauren Mackenzie (Ph.D., University of Massachusetts Amherst) is professor of military cross-cultural competence at the Center for Advanced Operational Culture Learning, Marine Corps University. She conducts research relating to cross-cultural competence, oversees culture-related curriculum development and outcomes assessment, and teaches communication and culture courses across the professional military education spectrum. She received her M.A. and Ph.D. in communication from the University of Massachusetts and lives with her husband and two sons in Fredericksburg, Virginia.

Tema Milstein (Ph.D., University of Washington) is associate professor at the University of New Mexico specializing in the intersections of culture, discourse, and ecological relations. Her research includes examinations of ecocultural meaning systems, ecotourism and endangered wildlife, ecological activism, culture jamming, and ecopedagogy. She is her university's Presidential Teaching Fellow, coeditor of *Environmental Communication Pedagogy and Practice* (2017), and author of many studies examining ways communication as a cultural force closes and opens doors to the re/articulation of human relations with/in/as nature.

Katherine R. Peters (Ph.D., University of Colorado Boulder) uses ethnography to investigate organizational meetings as emergent events that produce the effects of organization and culture. She is also interested in how technologies participate in communication events, like meetings, and the appearances of order and disorder in organizing.

Gerry Philipsen (Ph.D., Northwestern University) is professor emeritus of communication at the University of Washington. He is an ethnographer of communication and the originator of speech codes theory.

Saila Poutiainen (Ph.D., University of Massachusetts Amherst) is university lecturer in speech communication and the director of the intercultural encounters master's program at the University of Helsinki, Finland. Her research interests are interpersonal communication, Finnish communication culture, and intercultural communication.

Lydia Reinig (M.A., Colorado State University) is a doctoral candidate in the Department of Communication at the University of Colorado Boulder. She researches cultural forms of public engagement, focusing on how local communities use shared linguistic resources for democratic action. Her dissertation uses cultural discourses analysis and action-implicative discourse analysis to explore cultural understandings and practical dilemmas of public participation in energy democracy.

Laura Rosenbaun (Ph.D., University of Haifa) is speech interaction designer in the User Experience Group at General Motors. Her research areas and work focus on linguistics, human-machine interaction, and computer-mediated communication.

Lisa Rudnick (M.A., University of Massachusetts) is principal at The Policy Lab (Boston/Oslo) and specializes in the design of strategy, policy, programming, and applied ethnographic research in both fragile contexts and organizational settings. As a senior researcher at the United Nations Institute for Disarmament Research, she pioneered new approaches to local strategies research and evidence-based policy and program design for challenges of security and peacebuilding in UN interventions. She has worked in Europe, the Middle East, Asia, and widely in sub-Saharan Africa, with recent work focusing on collaborative humanitarian response and resilience to violent conflict; localizing humanitarian innovation and protection; and addressing challenges for private and public sector actors around the intersection of innovation and cybersecurity in humanitarian contexts.

Max Saito (Ph.D., University of Massachusetts Amherst) explores how various issues dialectically intersect with each other, such as sexuality, gender, race, class, consumer culture, human rights, food, global warming, justice, and peace. His recent research projects probe ways in and through which lifestyle and daily conversations can contribute to promotion of peace both locally and globally.

Natasha Shrikant (Ph.D., University of Massachusetts Amherst) is assistant professor in the Department of Communication at the University of Colorado Boulder. She uses ethnography and discourse analysis to examine how people collaboratively create meanings about culture and identity through their everyday conversations. She has published several articles focusing on how people interactionally accomplish ethnic, racial, gender, and sexuality identities in interpersonal and institutional contexts.

Nadezhda Sotirova (Ph.D., University of Massachusetts Amherst) is assistant professor at University of Minnesota Morris, where she teaches courses in intercultural, health, nature and belonging, as well as communication theory. In 2016 she received the Language and Social Interaction Dissertation of the Year Award from the National Communication Association. Her research interests include sociolinguistic and ethnographic examinations of social interaction, with particular interest in Bulgarian identity and ways of speaking in various public discourses.

Leah Sprain (Ph.D., University of Washington) is assistant professor in the Department of Communication at the University of Colorado Boulder. Her research focuses on democratic engagement, studying how specific communication practices facilitate and inhibit public action. She coedited *Social Movement to Address Climate Change: Local Steps for Global Action*, and her work appears in the *Journal of Applied Communication Research*, *Communication Monographs*, and *Communication Theory*.

Kelly E. Tenzek (Ph.D., University of Wisconsin-Milwaukee) is clinical assistant professor of communication at University at Buffalo, SUNY. Her scholarly interests include interpersonal and health contexts, especially end-of-life communication. Her work has been published in *Behavioral Sciences* (Special Issue of Family Communication at the end of life), *Journal of Health Care Chaplaincy,* and *Western Journal of Communication.*

Brion van Over (Ph.D., University of Massachusetts Amherst) is associate professor of communication at Manchester Community College. His work focuses on issues of identity, culture, technology, and the environment and is primarily concerned with the range of culturally distinctive forms and means for communicating. He has published in a variety of journals such as *Text & Talk*, *Communication Quarterly*, *Journal of Pragmatics*, and *Journal of Applied Communication Research*, among others.

Richard Wilkins (Ph.D., University of Massachusetts Amherst) is associate professor of communication studies at Baruch College, CUNY. He is lead editor of the book *Speech Culture in Finland* and coauthor of the book *Culture in Rhetoric*. He has also published widely in domestic and international journals of communication and his interests include methods of cultural discourse analysis, the rhetorical means toward identification, and cultural models for both the experience and expression of emotion.

Michaela R. Winchatz (Ph.D., University of Washington) is associate professor and associate dean of academic affairs in the College of Communication at DePaul University in Chicago. Her work focuses on discovering and formulating culturally distinctive ways of speaking in both English and German, as well as the underlying speech codes that inform them. She has published in a variety of journals such as *Research on Language and Social Interaction (ROLSI), Communication Monographs, Discourse Studies*, and *Field Methods.*

Ute Winter (Ph.D., RWTH Aachen University) is staff researcher in the User Experience Technologies Group at General Motors Advanced Technical Center in Israel. She has almost 20 years of experience in computational linguistics and human machine interface technologies.

Saskia Witteborn (Ph.D., University of Washington) is associate professor in the School of Journalism and Communication at The Chinese University of Hong Kong, associate director of the Research Centre on Migration and Mobility, and has held visiting fellowships with Humboldt University and Free University of Berlin as well as Télécom ParisTech. Her research focuses on (forced) migration and digital technologies, spanning Asia, North America, and Europe. Her work has appeared in leading journals and edited collections.

Karen Wolf (Ph.D., University of Massachusetts Amherst) is professor of communication at Suffolk County Community College, SUNY. She is coauthor of the book *Culture in Rhetoric* and her work has been published in various communication journals. Her research investigates the ways situated communication practices and rhetoric shape identity in various cultural groups.